Delayed Impact

Delayed Impact

The Holocaust and the
Canadian Jewish Community

FRANKLIN BIALYSTOK

McGill-Queen's University Press
Montreal & Kingston · London · Ithaca

© McGill-Queen's University Press 2000
ISBN 0-7735-2065-1

Legal deposit third quarter 2000
Bibliothèque nationale du Québec

Printed in Canada on acid-free paper

This book has been published with the help of a grant
from the Humanities and Social Sciences Federation of
Canada, using funds provided by the Social Sciences
and Humanities Research Council of Canada.

McGill-Queen's University Press acknowledges the
financial support of the Government of Canada
through the Book Publishing Industry Development
Program (BPIDP) for its activities. We also acknowledge
the support of the Canada Council for the Arts for our
publishing program.

Canadian Cataloguing in Publication Data

Bialystok, Franklin
   Delayed impact: the Holocaust and the Canadian Jew-
ish community
   Includes bibliographical references and index.
   ISBN 0-7735-2065-1
   1. Holocaust, Jewish (1939–1945)—Influence.   2. Jews—
   Canada—Attitudes.   3. Jews—Canada—History.
   I. Title.

   FC106.J5Z84 2000   971'.004924   C00-900191-3
   F1035.J5B54 2000

Typeset in 10/12 Palatino by True to Type

To my mother, Rebeka Bialystok-Zloto, and my father,
Sioma Bialystok, of blessed memory, my daughters,
Sandra and Lauren, and my wife, Ellen

Contents

Acknowledgments

This book has had a gestation period of twenty years. In that time, friends, family, and academic colleagues have provided encouragement. My first debt of gratitude is to the staff at McGill-Queen's University Press for having faith in this project. Donald Akenson and Roger Martin have been supportive from the outset and have guided me through the shoals of academic publishing, and Joan McGilvray and Elizabeth Hulse have been patient and helpful editors.

This study is an outgrowth of a dissertation of the same name that was submitted to the Department of History at York University in partial fulfillment of the PhD program. The research was supervised by Irving Abella, who was my colleague, adviser, and co-author on an early part of this research.

The bulk of the research was done in archives. My task was eased by the help of Lawrence Tapper at the National Archives in Ottawa, Miriam Warner at the Archives of the Jewish Historical Society of British Columbia, Esther Slater and Harry Gutkin at the Archives of the Jewish Historical Society of Western Canada, and Ronnie Finegold and Carol Katz at the Jewish Public Library in Montreal. Janice Rosen at the Canadian Jewish Congress National Archives in Montreal and Dr Stephen Speisman at the Ontario Jewish Archives in Toronto were patient, knowledgeable, flexible with time restrictions, and indefatigable in finding sources related to this work. I owe them a debt of gratitude.

Some of the research was gleaned from documents in private papers and restricted office files. Thanks to Manuel Prutschi, Lou

Zablow, Abraham Arnold, and Adam Fuerstenberg for providing me with important information from their private store, and to Kalmen Kaplansky, of blessed memory, Frank Diamant, and Rabbi Gunther Plaut for allowing me access to the papers of the Jewish Labour Committee, B'nai Brith Canada, and the Plaut papers. Bill Surkis of the Montreal Holocaust Memorial Centre and Erwin Nest of the Canadian Jewish Congress, Pacific Region, allowed me free reign in their office files. Harold Troper, Janine Stingel, and Charles Novogrodsky provided me with unpublished drafts of their papers. Professor Troper was an early and enthusiastic supporter of my work.

I could not have learned about the post-war Jewish community without the memories and reflections of those Canadians who lived through these decades. The interviews and informal conversations I had provide the human element of this story. Two individuals must be singled out. Louis Lenkinski, of blessed memory, was a friend, mentor, and sounding board. Unfortunately, I never captured his words on tape, not thinking that his love of life would be betrayed by a weak heart. My error in not recording him is compounded by the absence of his words in these pages. Ben Kayfetz is, in some respects, the subject of this work. I could not have understood the complexity of the Jewish community nor the minefield of issues and disagreements within the community without Ben's guidance.

Many people graciously read drafts of this work and offered their comments and criticisms. I thank Dr Paula Draper, Professors Louis Greenspan, Irving Abella, Michael Brown, Michiel Horn, John Saywell, Howard Adelman, Kathy Bischoping, Jacques Kornberg, Gerald Tulchinsky and Harold Troper, Bernie Farber, Manuel Prutschi, Sharon Weintraub, Judge Sydney Harris, Ben Kayfetz, Nathan Leipciger, Dr Carole Ann Reed, Michael Herman, and Dr Mark Nusbaum for their interest and encouragement.

I dedicate this book to my immediate family. My mother, Rebeka Bialystok-Zloto, and my father, Sioma Bialystok, of blessed memory, stimulated me with the love of learning, especially the life and times of European Jewry in the modern era. Part of their story is part of this story. My daughters, Sandra and Lauren, have inspired me with their myriad accomplishments, maturity, and unfailing support. My wife, Ellen, has been my intellectual alter ego, teacher of the most elemental computer skills, and best friend. Without her support, this book, and most of what I have done in the last thirty years, would not have been possible.

My final gratitude is to thousands of people, most of whose names I do not know. Without the gift provided by donor X, the medical wisdom, skills, and compassion of Laurie Zeilig, Jenny Heathcote,

Gary Levy, Les Lilly, Paul Craig, Kirsten Lewis, the staff at the Transplant Clinic at the Toronto General Hospital, and the unknown others who have created the medical miracle that allows organs to be successfully transplanted, I would not be writing these words.

Abbreviations

ADL	Anti-Defamation League of B'nai Brith Canada
AJCS	Allied Jewish Community Services of Montreal
BB	B'nai Brith Canada
BJE	Board of Jewish Education of Metropolitan Toronto
COIN	Canadian Organization For The Indictment Of Nazism
CANC	Community Anti-Nazi Committee
CCLA	Canadian Civil Liberties Association
CJC or Congress	Canadian Jewish Congress
CJN	*The Canadian Jewish News*
CNCR	Canadian National Committee on Refugees
FWD	Family Welfare Department of Montreal
HIAS	Hebrew Immigrant Aid Society
HRA	Holocaust Remembrance Association
HRC	Holocaust Remembrance Committee
IRO	International Refugee Organization
JCRC	Joint Community Relations Committee
JDC or Joint	American Joint Distribution Committee
JIAS	Jewish Immigrant Aid Society
JLC	Canadian Jewish Labour Committee
JPL	Jewish Public Library of Montreal
JPRC	Joint Public Relations Committee
JVS	Jewish Vocational Services of Toronto
LHR or the League	League for Human Rights of B'nai Brith Canada

NHRC	National Holocaust Remembrance Committee
NJPRC	National Joint Public Relations Committee
NPD	Nationale Partie Deutschlands
ORT	Organization for Educational Research and Technical Training
TJC	Toronto Jewish Congress
UJWF	United Jewish Welfare Fund of Toronto
UNRRA	United Nations Relief and Rehabilitation Administration
URO	United Restitution Organization

Delayed Impact

Introduction:
"A community of memory"

> Communities ... have a history – in an important sense they are
> constituted by their past – and for that reason we can speak of
> a real community as a "community of memory," one that does
> not forget its past.
>
> Robert N. Bellah; with special thanks to L.B.

> Memory ... has become the discourse that replaces history.
>
> Charles S. Maier

On 19 April 1993, the lead story on *The World at Six*, the national radio news broadcast of the Canadian Broadcasting Corporation, was the commemoration of the fiftieth anniversary of the Warsaw Ghetto Uprising. On the surface, this was an unexpected choice for the most important news story of the day. After all, Canada had not played any role in the event, and the uprising itself was only a footnote to World War II. The commemoration was significant for the Canadian Jewish community, but there were only 350,000 Jews in Canada, of whom fewer than 10 per cent were survivors of the war. At a deeper level, however, the decision to begin the news with this item was not surprising. For more than a decade, the Holocaust had been part of the national discourse. Canadians had become aware of the destruction of European Jewry through movies, books, public education, and extensive media coverage of an inquiry into suspected Nazi war criminals resident in Canada and the trials of hate-mongers. More than two hundred Canadians were part of a global contingent visiting Poland that week to mark the event. Their trip was covered by the Canadian Press and the *Toronto Daily Star*, and was the subject of a documentary by TV Ontario.

For Canadian Jews, the attention lavished on the commemoration created a sense of pride. It underscored the perception that one aspect of their ethnic identity was appreciated by other Canadians. But what constitutes identity for an ethnic community in a multicultural society? Several components can contribute to an ethnic community's self-definition. One is the experience of the first immigrants. Oral and written testimonies of their travails in crossing oceans and frontiers, the discrimination that they may have faced, and the hardships they endured in creating a new life are passed down to successive generations. A second component is the creed unique to the ethnic group. Not all groups have a religion that is not shared by other groups in their host society, but certain practices and rituals may be distinctive to that group. A third component is the contributions made by members of the ethnic community to their new country. These are often portrayed as advances made by successive generations that help to shape the community's integration into the wider society. Finally, there is the history of the community prior to its arrival. This is generally a source of pride as military triumphs, cultural, religious, and intellectual achievements, and other past glories are recounted. I submit that these and other components create a mythos about the ethnic community, which, as with all myths, is a combination of events that have been faithfully recorded and memories of events that have become skewed or even imagined in order to provide a positive, if not glowing, picture of the ethnic community from its origins in the homeland to its present status in the host country. In creating such a mythos, the community assumes a distinctiveness within the multicultural society by adopting a collective memory of its history.

I see two inherent problems in this process. The first is how the unsavoury aspects of that past are dealt with. Does the community confront its past honestly? Does it exculpate or relativize this past? Or does it evade it altogether? The second problem is the way in which the community adjusts its self-definition to accomodate changing circumstances in the adopted society. Its collective historical memory is constantly subject to revision. In this sense, ethnic communities recreate their history according to the dictates of the time. Both these problems are evident in the Canadian Jewish community's collective memory of the Holocaust.

I define the Jewish community as those individuals who were members of organizations with an interest in domestic and international affairs which they felt affected their position as an ethnic minority in Canada. This definition would include a majority of Canadian Jews, who have had a long tradition of organizational involvement. In the post-war era, this was manifested in their membership in religious institutions, charitable foundations, service clubs, ideologically based organizations, Zionist organizations, local federations, and *landsmanschaften* (societies of people from the same town or region in eastern Europe). Their views were expressed in meetings, conferences, public and private correspondence, and the ethnic press. In most cases, these views were articulated and acted upon by the community's leaders. When I speak of community leaders in the context of Holocaust memory, I refer to the officers and staff of the Canadian Jewish Congress (CJC, or Congress). One of the themes developed in this study is the change in the composition of Congress and its leaders. Until the mid-1960s the members of Congress committees were usually prominent individuals in the community, reflecting a narrow group of professionals and businessmen born or raised in Canada and part of the religious or secular and ideological mainstream of the community. Few women (aside from the leaders of women's organizations), radicals, immigrants, or Orthodox Jews were found in these bodies. These barriers were gradually eroded over the next twenty years. By 1985 the leadership was much more diverse, and this change partly explains the appropriation of the Holocaust in the collective memory of the community.

For this study I have relied mainly on the archives of the two major organizations in the community, the Canadian Jewish Congress and B'nai Brith Canada. Congress, however, was not a monolithic body. In fact, it was, and remains, an umbrella organization of many groups, especially local federations, reflecting the ideological and religious spectrum of Canadian Jewish society. Congress's policies emanate from resolutions passed at national and regional plenaries by delegates from these groups and from recommendations made by standing committees. The most important of these with respect to antisemitism – and by default, Holocaust remembrance (until the early 1970s) – was the Joint Community Relations Committee (JCRC). Its minutes, correspondence, and clippings are virtually intact in its archives, and Ben Kayfetz, its director from 1947 to 1984, has been of invaluable aid in helping me to understand the concerns of the community. The JCRC consisted of representatives from groups under the Congress aegis and, until 1981, representatives of the fifteen thousand members of B'nai Brith Canada, hence the term "Joint." Nevertheless, to emphasize the above, its composition was restricted in the first two decades after the war.

To further clarify the meaning of "community" as it related to Holocaust memory, it should be stated that several segments of the Canadian Jewish community had little input or interest in the issue during the period under discussion. These included elements among the Orthodox Jews, Sephardic Jews, and Soviet Jews. Some Orthodox Jews believe that the Holocaust was retribution for the failure by some European Jews to adhere to the tenets of the faith. Most Sephardic Jews have come to Canada in the last twenty years, when Holocaust consciousness has already been established in the community. Of greater import, it was a calamity that befell European

Jews. Those in the Middle East and North Africa, while under the same edict as all other Jews, were largely spared the fate of their coreligionists because of German military setbacks in those areas. Therefore there are few Sephardic survivors in Canada, and the destruction of a civilization of which they were not members has not had as great an impact as it had for the vast majority of Canadian Jews. Like the Sephardim, most Russian Jews have arrived in Canada during the last two decades. Under Communist rule they were indoctrinated with the legacy of the great war against fascism, in which all Soviet citizens suffered, and the millions of civlians murdered by the Germans and their collaborators were not distinguished according to their religion or race. Only in the past few years has the term "Holocaust" entered the Russian lexicon.

Interest in the Holocaust was late in coming. For the first twenty years after the war, Canadians knew little about the event. This amnesia was not restricted to the gentile world. It was also pervasive within the Canadian Jewish community, as it was in other Jewish communities outside continental Europe. Certainly, many Canadian Jews had lost family members and now lived with the reality that a civilization had been destroyed, but the community, as represented by its leaders, did little to instill knowledge of the catastrophe, and there was no grassroots desire for this situation to change. During the next two decades, however, there was a gradual reversal as the Holocaust entered the collective historical memory of the community. By 1985 most Canadian Jews felt that the destruction of European Jewry was *their* loss as well, even though most were both too young to have remembered the war and not descendants of those who had survived.

I address two questions in this book. What was the impact of the Holocaust on the Canadian Jewish community? And why was this impact delayed for a generation? Historical memory of the Holocaust evolved between 1945 and 1985 as a by-product of the changing circumstances of the Jewish community. This evolution can be measured in three periods – from the end of the war to 1960, from 1960 to 1973, and from 1973 to 1985. In the first period the legacy of the Holocaust was a low-priority item on the community agenda. The community's response was limited to providing relief for the surviving fragment in Europe, lobbying the government to admit refugees, facilitating the arrival of survivors, and absorbing them into the community. Its leaders had an exaggerated sense of their influence in these endeavours and masked some of the difficulties in integrating the newcomers. This self-delusion shielded the community from comprehending the magnitude of the Holocaust and confronting its own relative powerlessness and passivity. As these developments took place in the first years after the war, the remainder of the period, the decade of the 1950s, was virtually devoid of a communal consciousness of the Holocaust.

It was recognized that the event was a tragedy of unparalleled proportions in modern times, but Canadian Jews were removed from the calamity. Simply put, the Holocaust was not part of their world. The community needed to distance itself from the loss because to have confronted the enormity of the catastrophe, it was felt, might have produced a collective trauma. Moreover, there was a sense of shame in commemorating an event that, according to the presumed knowledge in the first decades after the war, had occurred without resistance by the victims. In putting aside the memory of the loss, the community also set aside the human remnants of the Holocaust who arrived in Canada. By the mid-1950s almost 15 per cent of Canadian Jews were survivors and their children born in post-war Europe. Their presence was a challenge to the community: to establish a dialogue that recognized the experience of the survivors while sympathizing with their pain. The challenge was daunting. Most Canadian Jews did not want to know what happened, and few survivors had the courage to tell them. For both groups the main obstacle to dialogue, apart from experience, was an inability to comprehend the event.

After the war, Canadian Jews sought to distance themselves from their European background. They were emerging from their position as undesirable immigrants and becoming accepted as part of the Canadian social mosaic. Their domestic priority was to free themselves of the constraints of the traditional immigrant community by moving to the suburbs, speaking English instead of Yiddish, rising from the proletarian ranks to the professions through education and acculturation, and abandoning their traditional secular and religious bonds. They could embark on these paths because of post-war prosperity and greater tolerance by the mainstream. Although antisemitism was still a feature of Canadian life, legislation was passed that barred discrimination on the basis of race and creed. Secure in their belief that the systemic antisemitism which had plagued the community had ebbed, Canadian Jews had achieved a measure of ethnic comfort. The divisions that had been a feature of community life in Canada, as well as in most other Jewish communities, were disappearing. Thus community leaders were able to close rifts by including disparate voices under the aegis of Congress and by professionalizing the social service agencies. In foreign affairs the priority moved from Europe to the Middle East. Canadian Jews clamoured for the independence of Palestine, and once the state of Israel was created, they provided material support and lobbied for its security.

For survivors the first decade or so after their arrival was devoted to starting a new life. The most pressing demands were finding work, learning the language and customs, and establishing their own networks via *landsmanschaften*, but these exigencies were soon met. More difficult was dealing with their recent tragedy. Most survivors would not speak about their experiences outside their families or *landsmanschaften*, and some could not summon the courage to do so even in those circles. Those who did speak to Canadian Jews were met with a range of responses, from extreme sympathy to incomprehension or derision. In short, most survivors were not prepared to talk and most Canadian Jews were not willing to listen.

Between 1960 and 1973 a change took place, so that a collective memory of the Holocaust gradually emerged by the end of the period. The central factor was the perception that antisemitism had not ebbed; rather, it had been dormant in the immediate post-war era. A series of disturbing events shook the community from its comfortable perch and alarmed Holocaust survivors. Neo-Nazi groups erupted in Canada and brazenly proclaimed their existence through publications and rallies. They were copying more militant and pernicious organizations in the United States, Europe, and Latin America. Canadian neo-Nazis relied upon these foreign contacts for their inspiration and their hate propaganda. Most appalling was the upsurge of neo-Nazism in West Germany. The country was also proposing to invoke a Statute of Limitations for Nazi war criminals. At the same time, the revelations of Nazi atrocities resulting from the trial of Adolf Eichmann and the knowledge that many other Nazi war criminals were walking free, made Canadian Jews aware of the scope of the tragedy and contributed to their disquiet. Further, the security of Israel had become a major concern. The wars that broke out between 1967 and 1973 and international condemnation of the Jewish state increased the community's sense of vulnerability. Canadian Jews felt that an embattled Israel might lead to its destruction. Not only would this be a tremendous calamity, but it would mark a return to Jewish powerlessness – the precondition that had allowed centuries of oppression which ultimately and inexorably led, in the minds of many, to the Holocaust. The security of Israel and the memory of the destruction of European Jewry thus became intertwined by the early 1970s.

Congress initially responded to Canadian hate-mongers by monitoring their activities, but it privately dismissed their significance. As the concerns of the community increased, Congress leaders relied on their traditional tactics by backroom lobbying for legal restrictions. Meanwhile, the status of many survivors had changed since the first years after their arrival. Some had achieved economic stability, fluency in English, and an ability to arouse public sympathy. A nucleus of survivors and Canadian Jews outside the mainstream of the community leadership were not satisfied with Congress's tepid response. They denounced the behind-the-scenes approach in Yiddish as *sha shtil* (don't rock the boat). They demanded a more concerted and public response, and even though Congress adopted a public posture in 1964 which included an exposé of hate-mongers in Toronto and an open campaign for legislation to limit hate propaganda, some survivors were not satisfied. They created their own groups to pressure politicians and actively confront the neo-Nazis. In fact, the leaders and the survivors were both subject to misperceptions. The leaders did not gauge the intensity of feeling among the survivors, who saw swastikas on television, in public parks, and on hate sheets as a visceral reminder of their experience. Rather, they perceived the survivor groups as self-appointed watchdogs of the community who could only alienate Canadian society and set back the decades of progress that had been achieved. The survivors – and here we are speaking of a handful of individuals who had the support of many newcomers – did not understand that an immediate threat from local neo-Nazis was non-existent and that Congress, given its limited options, had a handle on the situation.

The politicization of survivors widened the gulf between them and the established community. In order to close the rift, Congress grudgingly brought some of the survivors into the organization and in 1973 created a national body, the Holocaust Remembrance Committee, to deal with commemoration and education about the Holocaust. Concurrent with these developments, the community was successful in lobbying the government to pass legislation to criminalize hate propaganda. Consequently, by 1973 a cognizance of the Holocaust had materialized.

During the third period, from 1973 to 1985, the legacy of the Holocaust surfaced as a marker of ethnic identification for most Canadian Jews. Four factors accounted for this phenomenon. First, survivors who had become active in the community in the previous decade were joined by others in creating projects that elevated the knowledge of the Holocaust within the Jewish community and among Canadians in general. Survivors were in the forefront in raising consciousness in several ways. They created local Holocaust remembrance committees which included their grown children, Canadian

Jews, and in some cases, gentiles. These committees had a twofold purpose: commemoration and education. By the mid-1980s almost every urban centre had a Holocaust memorial service and at least one monument to the victims in local cemeteries. Thousands of students were learning about the event in their school curricula and/or in seminars, as a result of the efforts of these committtees. Survivors played a key role in public education by offering their services as speakers and resource people. On another level, they pressed Congress and the government to ferret out suspected Nazi war criminals and bring Holocaust deniers to justice. The stridency of some survivors in these endeavours created tensions within the community, which was less willing to embark on radical measures. The most tangible aspect of the survivors' presence could be found in memorials, museums, and education centres. Most notable were those in the Jewish federation buildings in Montreal (1979) and Toronto (1985) and the plans for one in Vancouver (completed in 1995). In 1985 the culmination of the survivors' efforts was reached when they and their children held their first gathering in Ottawa, on the fortieth anniversary of Liberation, to commemorate the victims, meet one another, and educate themselves.

A second factor was the appropriation of the Holocaust in the popular media. It had been the subject of memoirs and of a handful of movies in the 1960s, and the dramatization of Anne Frank's story had been performed in a score of countries, but the event was still a part of recent history that was unknown to most Canadians in the early 1970s. That changed in the ensuing decade. The memoirs of Elie Wiesel and others were widely read, but most striking was the impact of the miniseries *Holocaust* in 1978. It elicited widespread publicity and a thirst for more information. In addition, the Holocaust was increasingly a field for scholarly study. As in the popular media, research on the topic had been ongoing since the 1950s but was largely unknown aside from specialists. In 1975 historian Lucy Dawidowicz's *The War against the Jews* reached the non-academic audience. It was one catalyst in the scholarly exploration of the event. By the late 1970s, courses and conferences on the Holocaust were becoming commonplace on Canadian campuses. Less than a decade later, it can be argued, a Holocaust industry had become a feature of North American popular culture.

A third factor was distinctively Canadian. In 1982, the publication of *None Is Too Many*, which documented the refusal by the Mackenzie King government to admit Jewish refugees from Europe, created shock waves. Concurrent with this event was a growing realization that the government had knowingly allowed suspected Nazi war criminals to enter the country after the war. Moreover, it became known that Canada was a major centre for the distribution of antisemitic literature in the guise of Holocaust denial. In response to these developments, Congress increased its pressure on the government to prosecute the war criminals and enact legislation against antisemites. In 1985 the provincial governments of Ontario and Alberta were pressured into bringing charges against Ernst Zundel for publishing hate literature and James Keegstra for promoting hatred in the public education system. At the federal level, the Progressive Conservative government established the Deschenes Commission to investigate the presence of suspected war criminals.

The fourth factor takes us into the dangerous territory of psychohistory. By the 1970s Canadian Jews, especially those too young to have a mature memory of the war, found themselves disconnected from their past. They had become part of the mainstream of Canadian society, but they had lost their connection to the roots of the ethnic community. In interviewing some of these individuals and in working with them in voluntary positions in the community, I came to understand their dilemma. They felt themselves to be Jewish and they were passionately Canadian, but they were hard put to define what it meant to be a Canadian Jew. Consequently, they searched for cohesive elements within the community. These included stricter religious observance, affiliation with the state of Israel, and resurrecting the historical memory of the Holocaust. Appropriating the Holocaust as a pillar of self-definition was not out of character in the context of Jewish history. Rather, it was in keeping with the Jewish proclivity to focus on incidents of victimization. This trend has also been prevalent among some other North American ethnic minorities as well.

This study is broad in scope, in both time and space. Two sets of resources have been utilized. The first consist of documents found in public archives and private holdings in Montreal, Toronto, Ottawa, Winnipeg, and Vancouver. Research has been restricted to these cities because almost all the activity related to Holocaust commemoration and education originated there. Also, information about other cities is available from these documents. They include the minutes of meetings held by national, regional, and local Jewish organizations; the correspondence of lay leaders and the staff of these organizations; government papers regarding immigration policy and legislation relative to the topic; the findings of inquiries and delegations, reports, and briefs to governments emanating from the community; newspapers; notes on Holocaust programs; and the testimony of survivors from archival video and audio tapes. The major part of this study is dependent upon these sources.

The second set of resources consists of interviews with selected individuals who have played a key role in the formation of policy in the Jewish community and in the government's response to that policy. Those who were selected and who acceded to the request to be interviewed were, first, survivors who have been prominent in pushing the community to adopt the memory of the Holocaust as an important component of the community's agenda; second, leaders and staff of the Canadian Jewish Congress, community federations, and other Jewish organizations; and third, other Canadians who have made an important contribution to the issue. It is worth noting that the survivors who were interviewed were asked to discuss primarily their role in community affairs and only secondarily their adaptation to Canada. Unlike other works based on a wide sample, this study does not provide a sociological analysis of the situation of survivors, dwell on their mental state, or celebrate their contributions. Rather, it seeks to uncover their motivations in pursuing the memorialization of the world and the family that they had lost. There are two limitations to using oral history in this study. The first is that some key players in the story died before or during the time that the research was undertaken, while others were too infirm to be interviewed. The second limitation is that an individual's recollection is subjective. Where possible, I have supported the oral narrative with documentary evidence and/or other interviews.

History and memory are often conflated, so that it becomes difficult to separate the two. This development has become more problematic in the past few decades. Pierre Nora maintains that memory is no longer a servant of history but on a par with it. He writes: "Memory is life ... It remains in permanent evolution ... History, on the other hand, is the reconstruction, always problematic and incomplete, of what is no longer. Memory is a perpetually actual phenomenon ... history is a representation of the past ... Memory is absolute, while history can only conceive the relative."[1] How, then, do current thinkers define "collective memory"? Nora Gedi and Yigal Elam contend that it is a "new name for the familiar 'myth.'"[2] Saul Friedländer argues that collective memory of the Holocaust attempts to restore coherence, closure, and even redemption, but fails to do so. He goes on to state that there is nothing redemptive about the Holocaust,[3] including the fallacious claims that Jews died as a moral lesson for humanity so that no other similar tragedies would occur or as the necessary precursor to the establishment of the state of Israel. As Yehuda Bauer, the eminent historian of the Holocaust, stated to my class at Yad Vashem, the national Holocaust memorial in Israel, if the price for the state was six million lives, then it was not worth it.

Friedländer and Bauer are among a number of observers who rightly point to the difficulty of demythologizing the Holocaust, and no less so for Canadian Jews, for whom the issue is less the Holocaust itself than their remembrance of the event. Since the end of the war, three myths have been created in the community's collective memory of the Holocaust. (Again, I am using the term "myth" to describe the embellishment of documented events in order to create a particular historical memory. The term does not posit a falsification of history but, rather, a skewed interpretation of it.) In the immediate post-war years, Canadian Jews wanted to believe that they had done their utmost to provide relief to the surviving remnant in Europe and that they had created a welcoming environment for those who were allowed to enter Canada. In so doing, however, they pushed the event into the margins of historical memory. Twenty years later a new myth emerged. The community came to believe that it was under the threat of escalating antisemitism, which led to a greater awareness of the destruction of Euopean Jewry. By the mid-1980s this myth had been altered. The Holocaust had now become an important marker of ethnic awareness in a multicultural society. Thus the community was able to reinforce its claim to uniqueness in such a society.

Historical memory is dependent on both a representation of a past and a reconstruction of that past. The former is subject to documentation and verification; the latter to selected interpretation. This study analyzes the response to one of the central events of the century, and in so doing, it explains how the memory of the Holocaust in the Canadian Jewish community moved from indifference to self-identification in the post-war era.

1 "The warm safety of North America": The Holocaust and Canadian Jews in the 1930s and 1940s

Maurice Victor was born in Winnipeg, the son of one of the few Jewish doctors in the city in the interwar period. Following in his father's footsteps, he graduated from the Manitoba Medical College in 1943. After a year's internship he was commissioned in the Canadian Army and sent overseas. He recalls:

I had a ringside seat for that event (the invasion of France) with part of the army that made its way through France, Belgium, Holland, and into Germany. And as we penetrated deeper into occupied territories, we saw at first hand what Naziism was all about. It was an experience we could not possibly be prepared for ... We were attached to a British division when we drove our jeep into Bergen-Belsen .... a camp built for three thousand now housed 69,000. There were no ovens at Bergen-Belsen, only places where people lived. Except that you couldn't tell the barracks from the outhouses. The stench of the dead and dying was just overwhelming; cadaverous people were literally stacked up like cords of wood in rows, some of them still squirming. It had to be seen, it had to be smelled, for anyone to grasp what the camps meant. My driver knew now, for the first time, what the war was really all about ... For both of us, what we were doing here, far from home, had finally crystallized.[1]

Sam Lipshitz was a newspaper editor in Toronto during the war. Born in Radom, Poland, he had emigrated to Canada in 1927 at the age of seventeen. Lipshitz was one of two Canadians delegated by the Canadian Jewish Congress to visit Poland and report on the state of Polish Jewry at the end of the war. He arrived in Warsaw on 2 December 1945. Lipshitz remembers:

After eight days in Warsaw we never saw a Jewish child. The first time we saw a Jewish child was in an orphanage near Warsaw .... On December 23rd we were told that the next day they [the Polish authorities] were going to execute the guy who was in charge of the crematorium in Majdanek .... We went to Majdanek the next morning. We saw a group of Jews in their concentration camp uniforms, who said, "This is the happiest day of our lives." There were about 10,000 people there and we were in the front row. They brought him on a horse-driven wagon, the rope was too high, so four young Mapamniks [socialist Zionists] lifted him. That bastard was white when they brought him out with a clergyman, but before they affixed a noose he cried out, "Long live my fatherland."[2]

Two Canadian Jews, one native-born, the other an immigrant, were swept up in the maelstrom of the greatest human-designed calamity in history. Both were post hoc witnesses, yet they could not fathom what they were witnessing. Each had read about the systematic destruction of European Jewry since the first reports leaked out in 1942 and was aware of the persecution of German Jews from the first days of the Nazi seizure of power in 1933. Yet neither was prepared for the spectacle that awaited him. For Dr Victor it was the last victims of the Holocaust, some dead, some waiting to die, in a concentration camp built nine years before the gas chambers were installed in Auschwitz. For Sam Lipshitz it was a Poland without Jews, without Jewish civilization. He returned to Lublin, not far his hometown of Radom, a city that housed the Majdanek camp, in which 400,000 people were murdered in two years, including 18,000 Jews in one day.

In many ways, Maurice Victor and Sam Lipshitz were representative of Canadian Jews in both their background and their experiences as young adults. They knew about the Holocaust (although the term was not yet used), but they could not comprehend what they knew, even after witnessing its impact. For them, as for most Canadian Jews, the Holocaust was an overwhelming tragedy, but it had happened in a world that some had never known and that others remembered as a vibrant entity, rich in tradition and culture. Canadian Jews during the war were, as Dr Victor put it, "in the warm safety of North America."[3] In fact, except for the several thousand Jews in the Canadian forces who, like Victor, stumbled upon the camps and for the few, like Lipshitz, who went to Europe after VE day, the Canadian Jewish community was isolated, far from the horror, cognizant of the calamity, but removed by space, time, and experience from the event.

Separation from their kin in Europe is the most significant factor in explaining the muted response by the Canadian Jewish community to the Holocaust. Most Canadian Jews looked to their community leaders in the Canadian Jewish Congress and their elected representatives, notably the three Jewish members of Parliament at the time, to carry the torch. They had expected that these men would help to pry open the gates of entry to Canada for the German Jewish refugees before the war, to pressure the government to allow refugees who had somehow escaped the snare of Nazi-occupied Europe during the war to be allowed sanctuary in Canada, and to protest the destruction of Jewish lives and civilization. Their expectations were not met.[4]

Other factors were also important in understanding the limited response. The Jewish community was weak, fragmented, and outside the power structure of Canadian decision-makers. Native anti-semitism was pervasive, as reflected both in proto-fascist movements and in entrenched attitudes and policies. The reaction of Canadians and Canadian leaders generally to the Holocaust during the war was similar to that of Canadian Jews – incomprehension tinged with a small dose of guilt. Concern about the murder of European Jewry was submerged by the war effort itself. Indeed, these factors were mirrored in the attitudes and actions of the other non-Continental Allies and their respective Jewish constituencies.[5]

While little more could have been done by Canadian Jews to rescue European Jewry between 1941 and 1945, more could have been accomplished in the first two years after the war, from the spring of 1945 to the spring of 1947. Jewish community leaders had become resigned to the fact that immigration policies were not going to be changed sufficiently to allow more than a token number of the surviving refugees seeking admission. In addition, there was a general feeling that emigration from Europe to British-controlled Palestine was a more desirable option than coming to Canada. Thus the bulk of the post-war effort was to be devoted to sending money, food, and supplies to the displaced Jews in refugee camps.[6] Refugee relief, however, was not the primary foreign policy agenda for the community at this time. Rather, it was to lobby federal authorities to support a withdrawal by Britain from Palestine and to provide input into the refugee policies of the nascent United Nations. Also, there remained the central domestic mandate of the community leadership – to unite the community in the face of antisemitism and to proceed with the transition from a period of economic depression and war-time rationing to a flourishing post-war society.[7] Yet in the immediate aftermath of the Holocaust, the popular view propagated was that the community had rallied to support European Jews, worked effectively with political and civic leaders, and mounted an earnest and effective campaign of relief. This perception created a collective memory within the community that stated that, while a tragic and unprecedented calamity had befallen the Jews of Europe, Canadian Jews had done everything possible under the circumstances.

THE CANADIAN JEWISH COMMUNITY
BETWEEN THE WARS

Jews, disguised as Catholics because of religious restrictions, first came to Canada prior to the British conquest of 1760. Meanwhile, Jewish merchants in France had established economic relations with the authorities in New France. Between the Conquest and Confederation, Jewish immigration was minuscule, as revealed in the census of 1871. The 1,200 Jews in Canada at that time doubled in the next decade and multiplied thirtyfold again, to 75,000, by 1911, as a result of the declining economic and social conditions in eastern Europe and the open immigration policies of the Canadian government. By 1921 there were 126,000 Jews, representing 1.44 per cent of the total population. With increasing immigration restrictions in the 1920s and a further tightening of laws in the 1930s, the population grew marginally, to 156,000 in 1931 and approximately 167,000 in 1939. At the outbreak of World War II, Jews represented 1.5 per cent of the total population, a proportion that has remained relatively constant until the present.[8]

The Jewish community in 1939 was concentrated in three provinces – Ontario (66,000), Quebec (64,000), and Manitoba (20,000) – and specifically in the three main cities, Toronto (49,000), Montreal (60,000), and Winnipeg (18,000). Three-quarters of the community lived in these three cities, and in each case, Jews were the largest non-Anglo-Celtic ethnic community, comprising 6 per cent of each city's population. In all, they were the most urban-based ethnic community in the country, with 83 per cent of the population living in cities of more than 30,000, as compared with the 30 per cent for all Canadians.[9] Half the community was "foreign-born," that is, not born in Canada, the British empire, or the United States, a proportion that was typical for non-Anglo-Celtic communities. Of those foreign-born Jews, half came from Russia, one-quarter from Poland, and one-tenth from Romania.[10] Despite the fact that the other half of the community was "native-born," 96 per cent of the community over the age of ten years listed Yiddish as their first language, but the vast majority had adapted linguistically to the Canadian environment, since only 3 per cent were unable to speak English.[11] As a result of immigration controls and the hardship of the Depression, the net increase (immigration less emigration) from 1931 to 1938 added only eighty-three Jews to the national population.[12]

At the outbreak of the war the Jewish community was urban, proletarian, static in its growth, and outside the mainstream of economic power, social prestige, or political influence. Despite the proliferation of Jewish merchants, their representation in big business was virtually non-existent. As victims of discriminatory hiring practices, Jewish professionals were under-represented as "salary earners," such as engineers and educators, and over-represented as "fee earners," such as doctors and lawyers.[13] Jews were vastly over-represented in the categories of retail merchants (18 per cent of the national total versus 3 per cent for the national average), salesmen (30 versus 14 per cent), and semi-skilled manufacturers (20 versus 5 per cent). They were under-represented in the categories of farmers (1 versus 16 per cent) and unskilled workers (6 versus 33 per cent), and close to the national average as professionals (5 versus 6 per cent) and skilled workers (14 versus 11 per cent).[14] In specific occupations, Jews were most dominant in textile goods and clothing (20 versus 1.7 per cent)[15] and commercial merchandising (36 versus 8 per cent).[16] Despite restrictions on their entry into certain university faculties, Jews represented 4.4 per cent of all university undergraduates in 1935–36.[17]

At first glance, the Jewish community in 1939 appeared to be monochromatic. Seven out of ten Canadian Jews lived in the immigrant neighbourhoods of Boulevard Saint-Laurent in Montreal, Spadina Street in Toronto, and Selkirk Avenue in Winnipeg's North End. These enclaves were almost entirely of eastern European origin and Yiddish-speaking, and their residents confined most of their commercial interests to the neighbourhood. Yet the community's most significant characteristic was its diversity. In Montreal, typesetter Kalmen Kaplansky remembers that the "Jewish community was badly divided. There were two separate worlds, the world around St Laurence Boulevard and the world of Westmount and NDG [Notre Dame du Grâce]. They didn't even speak to each other. I never met those people [the Westmount-NDG sector]. Ours was a vibrant community with all the groups and grouplets fighting each other. There was a blossoming Yiddish cultural life, two *geselschaft* [literally, societies], two schools, storm and stress, *sturm und drang*."[18] Kaplansky was describing one dimension of the community, the secular Jews, who were then split into varieties of Zionists (socialists, leftists, centrists, revisionists, and religious), anti-Zionist socialists (the Bund), communists (orthodox Marxists, pro-Soviets, Trotskyites, anarchists), and unionists, who were allied with some of these political ideologies. Another dimension was the religious one, where there existed divisions between competing Orthodox views, the moderate Conservative movement, and the Reform movement. Toronto tended to be more Zionist and religious than Montreal, while Winnipeg was more influenced by left-wing ideologies than any other Canadian city.[19]

Despite the plurality of political ideologies, religious observance, and nationalist attachments, one issue united Canada's Jews: the struggle against antisemitism.[20] In the interwar period and increasingly in the 1930s, antisemitism had become a constant in Canadian society. It was not confined to any one region, nor was it promoted by one dominant movement. Antisemitism was found in every region and manifested itself in several forms. Its most public face was in the proliferation of nativist and fascist movements.[21] While organizations such as the Ku Klux Klan, the National Social Christian Party (NSCP), and the Nationalist Party of Canada grabbed the public spotlight, a more insidious form of antisemitism lay within the mainstream. Jews were discriminated against in education, employment, and housing,[22] and were prevented from sponsoring their families and townspeople in Europe because of stringent immigration restrictions.[23]

Nativist and fascist movements were the most aggressive and visible form of antisemitism and the most alarming to the Jewish community. In Quebec there were three strands of this phenomenon. The most pernicious was the proto-Nazi activities of Adrien Arcand, a newspaper editor and publisher of antisemitic tracts, notably *Le Goglu*, a weekly similar to the Nazi organ *Der Stürmer*. Until his death in 1967, Arcand was an articulate rabble-rouser, an energetic promoter of his cause, the self-styled führer of the NSCP, and the most notorious Nazi in the country.[24] More significant than Arcand's brand of hate was the nationalist fervour exhibited by Abbé Lionel Groulx. In his world the Jew was the embodiment of the anti-French, anti-Catholic conspiracy that blocked the aspirations of French Canadians. Groulx's influence was widespread in the church and among members of the young nationalist circle that expressed its views in the authoritative newspaper *Le Devoir*. His status as an icon of the nationalist cause continues unabated.[25] The third strand was the nationalism of the Union Nationale party, which came to power in 1936. While its leader, Maurice Duplessis, disavowed Arcand's brand of extremism, some of the party espoused the notorious antisemitic fabrication "The Protocols of the Elders of Zion." Despite distancing himself from Arcand and his cronies, Duplessis was much more eager to curb incipient left-wing activities by means of the discriminatory Padlock Law than to sanction Arcand, against whom no action was taken.[26] Pierre Anctil maintains that these strands were less injurious than the largely Protestant brand of closet discrimination whereby Jews where subjected to a *numerus clausus* at McGill University, refused housing in the tonier neighbourhoods of Montreal, and threatened with expulsion of their children from the Protestant board of education.[27] But his critics have accused him of minimizing the French-Canadian component of antisemitism.

In Ontario, antisemitism was not as widespread in nativist and fascist circles as in Quebec, but it was a feature of this period. Swastika clubs were created in the early 1930s. Their most blatant exposure occurred during a baseball game where the swastika was unfurled in the predominantly Jewish neighbourhood of Harbord and Grace streets in Toronto in 1933. It created the greatest riot in the city's history.[28] These clubs formed bonds with Arcand in the late 1930s. John Ross Taylor, the éminence grise of Ontario Nazis for the next half-century, emerged from this association.[29] Mainstream antisemitism, however, played a greater role in the province. Signs reading "Gentiles Only," "No Jews Wanted," and "Christians Only Need Apply" were hung both in public parks and in private establishments. Jews were prevented from joining certain clubs and organizations, and attempts at introducing legislation banning racial discrimination had no effect until 1943, when the Racial Discrimination Act, passed a year later, came into effect.[30]

In western Canada, where there were only ten thousand Jews outside the Winnipeg community, antisemitism was also pervasive. In Winnipeg, anti-Jewish activity was evident in different forms: an anti-loafing law aimed at Jews was passed in 1918; a commissioner of the Manitoba Provincial Police claimed that "ninety-five percent of the major bootleggers in Manitoba were Jews"; William Whittaker formed the extremist Nationalist Party in 1933.[31] Elsewhere in the region, nativist movements had become part of the landscape prior to World War I and were increasingly militant in the 1920s.[32] While antisemitism was not the most distinctive hallmark of these organizations,[33] it played a role in the regional political movements that led to the United Farmers of Alberta (UFA) and the Social Credit Party. The extent of antisemitism in these parties is open to question. Though not explicit in denouncing the Jews, the writings of Henry Wise Wood of the UFA and the ideology of the Social Credit movement pointed to an international conspiracy to deprive westerners of their Christian heritage and to their exploitation by banks, eastern monopolies, and capitalist enterprise.[34] The leader of Social Credit in Alberta, William Aberhart, disavowed antisemitism, but his mentor and founder of the movement, Major C.H. Douglas, blamed international Jewish financiers for the Depression. Aberhart maintained his belief in Douglas's economic theories and met with arch American antisemites during his tenure as premier from 1935 to his death in 1944. Nor was the federal wing of the party immune from antisemitism. Norman Jaques, a Social Credit MP, "spent much of his political career expounding his views on the international Jewish financial conspiracy and in trying to get segments of the *Protocols* [of the Elders of Zion] read into Hansard."[35]

Another outlet for fascism came from the Italian and German consulates. The former had great success in promoting Mussolini within the Italian-Canadian community.[36] Although they were not vocal in their disapproval of Jews, the German consuls were more reticent than the Italians in expressing their views. The tiny Nazi Party in Canada was formed with consular assistance after the accession of the parent party in Germany, and it succeeded in planting its ideology in sectors of the German-Canadian community and in some parts of the ethnic press, including the popular *Deutsche Zeitung*. Nevertheless, the German Nazis had little regard for their nativist counterparts, such as Arcand and Whittaker, who were viewed as upstarts.[37]

Irving Abella has pointed out that "the Canada of the 1920s and 1930s was permeated with anti-semitism."[38] What did that mean in the context of the period? In the first place, antisemitism was one aspect of an anti-immigrant attitude toward Europeans, notably those from eastern and southern Europe, and toward all Asians. Jews may have been vilified by right-wing groups for being capitalist or cosmopolitan or communist or anti-Christian, and discriminated against by the mainstream, but so were other groups, for other, equally illogical reasons. That fact did not lessen the insecurity and the powerlessness of Canadian Jews, but it put them in good company with most other non-Anglo-Celtic immigrants.

Second, the fascist groups had little impact on the mainstream. Martin Robin maintains that in Quebec, perhaps the hotbed of antisemitism, "the nationalist organizations, although tinged and tainted with anti-Semitism did not, separately or together, comprise an anti-Semitic movement whose primary purpose was to combat and eradicate an alleged Jewish menace."[39] This view is echoed by Pierre Anctil, who writes, "Quebec Jews ... were not endangered by French antisemitic agitation ... This is not to imply that the Jewish community did not feel the sting of prejudice, or that antisemitism was not a force to be reckoned with."[40] Fascist-inspired antisemitism was a manifestation of attitudes that had been in existence in Canada for several decades.

It appears clear that antisemitism was simply one aspect of nativist attitudes and discriminatory behaviour in the 1930s, rather than an obsession for most Canadians. Its appearance was due to several factors: the Depression, the fear that the country was being overrun by foreigners, the importation of European and American brands of the disease, and the desire for the maintenance of power by the Anglo-Canadian elite.[41]

But although antisemitism may have posed little physical danger to Canadian Jews, it had a profound impact psychologically. Suffering from the Depression, restricted by discriminatory immigration laws, hiring practices, employment, and education opportunities, and vilified by right-wing groups without countervailing legislation, the Jewish community in the early 1930s felt vulnerable. It had no national body to speak on its behalf and few allies in the gentile world. The Canadian Jewish Congress had convened its first plenary in 1919, but the original impetus for a national organization had dissipated by the 1920s, and the CJC was not reconvened. Following a protest against the policies of Nazi Germany in Montreal in April 1933, at which former president of the League of Nations, Senator Raoul Dandurand, was principal speaker, Le Jeune Canada, an organization of nationalist French Canadians connected to Abbé Groulx, held an anti-Jewish rally. This public display of Judeo-phobia alarmed the Jewish community. It was one factor that led to the reconvening of the CJC in 1934. Congress's president was Samuel Jacobs, who served until his death in 1938. His successor, Samuel Bronfman, was to remain the head of Congress until 1962.

In its reincarnation, the CJC's primary aim was to provide a unified voice for the community. This was not a feasible goal, considering the ideological, religious, and class fragmentations and the wide dispersal of the community, yet Congress persevered. In the 1930s the most pressing concerns were the restrictions both against Jewish refugees from Nazi Germany and other Jews wishing to immigrate and native antisemitism. The CJC lobbied federal authorities and created two bodies to deal with the situation. One was the United Jewish Refugee Agencies (UJRA), which became the United Jewish Refugee and War Relief Agencies and joined forces with the American Joint Distribution Committee (the JDC, or Joint).[42] The other was the Joint Public Relations Committee, which comprised representatives from Congress and the Anti-Defamation League of B'nai Brith Canada.[43]

However, as a national voice in the 1930s the CJC was almost mute. Congress representatives had no influence with a recalcitrant immigration branch headed by the notorious antisemite F.C. Blair and little luck in persuading Mackenzie King to take a strong stand at the Evian Conference on Refugees in 1938. At the time, the Jewish community did not know that Evian had been organized by the United States to give the illusion that something was being done about the refugee problem. The American State Department knew full well that no country would make a major commitment. A year later Congress's pleas to allow the fated refugee boat the *St Louis* to dock at a Canadian port went unheard. Yet it was unwilling to take a more militant attitude for fear of an antisemitic backlash. Moreover, the three Jewish members of Parliament, Liberals Samuel Jacobs and Sam Factor and the CCF's A.A. Heaps, also found themselves isolated from the halls of power.[44]

Whereas the CJC as a national body had little impact, local organizations made strides within their respective communities. Zionists, communists, socialists, labour groups, and the *landsmanschaften* built schools, created mutual aid societies and credit unions, and involved themselves in cultural activities. They also pressured Congress and some tried to lobby federal officials, with negligible consequences. Other groups active at the local level included women's organizations and religious congregations. The various activities were reported in a plethora of Yiddish and English-language Jewish newspapers and periodicals.[45] Despite these efforts, at the outbreak of the war the Canadian Jewish community was fragmented and ineffectual. According to Abella and Troper,

In the final analysis, Canadian Jewry, weak and divided, had neither the influence to effect any positive change in government policy nor any idea of the low esteem in which they and their cause were held by cabinet members and civil servants. Their sense of being outsiders in their own home, of being *in* Canada but not *of* it, left them uneasy in dealings with government, deferring to *shtadlonim* [Jewish representatives to gentile power structures] in the form of members of Parliament, who themselves turned out to be powerless. Thus, the general timidity of Jewish leaders, even under pressure from their own rank-and-file, and the obsequiousness in the face of government authority led in the end only to friction within the Jewish community.[46]

THE RESPONSE TO THE HOLOCAUST DURING THE WAR

There has been much written about the response by the Jewish communities in the West to the Holocaust. Scholars have demonstrated that, while community leaders had knowledge of the horror, their efforts at rescue and relief were met with obduracy by Allied governments. Nonetheless, criticism has been levelled at communities for not taking a more vigorous approach. These perceptions are no different with respect to Canadian Jewry during the war than with their Allied counterparts. Three questions are central in evaluating this response: What was known about the destruction of European Jewry and when was it known? What was done? What could have been done?

At the CJC plenary in January 1942, Nahum Goldmann, president of the World Jewish Congress, stated, "European Jewry, is for all practical purposes no longer existent."[47] What did that mean at the time? To that point, some twenty-seven months after the war had begun, approximately one million European Jews had been murdered, about 10 per cent of the total Jewish population under Nazi domination. Gassing had begun at Chelmno, near Lodz, but the gas chambers at Auschwitz and other death camps had yet to be built. In that same month, Nazi functionaries met at a villa in Wannsee, a Berlin suburb, to plan the "final solution." Already the mobile death squads (*Einsatzgruppen*) had murdered several hundred thousand Jews during the invasion of the Soviet Union, and thousands were dying each week in the ghettoes of central and eastern Europe.[48] Yet these specific facts were not known to the Jews of Canada at that time. According to Saul Hayes, the executive director of Congress, "the reports were so unbelievable that the responsible Jewish authorities which received them hardly dared make them public and the allied governments were slow to accept them."[49]

By the spring of 1942, however, they were no longer secret. News of deportations to the death camps were reported in the back pages of newspapers.[50] At Passover "the CJC told the Jewish community: 'Every cruelty that a madman could invent against us, the insane fury of the Reich has invented. In the torture-houses of the concentration camps, our brothers fall in their hundreds; before the common graves of the mass-execution, they perish in their thousands; in their tens of thousands they fall victim to the enforced famine and introduced pestilence of the ghetto. The gas-chamber, the air-bubble injector, the firing squad – it is with these that Hitler is taking a grim census of our people.'" [51] Momentum was building for protest against Nazi policies. On 15 September, Hayes wrote that most of the populace of the Warsaw ghetto had been liquidated. On 11 October a mass meeting was held in the Montreal Forum; another protest followed at Massey Hall in Toronto. In December there was a nationwide "Day of Mourning," with some Jews fasting.[52] By the end of the year, Goldmann's statement had become fact, and those Canadians who wanted to know did know.

In the next eighteen months the specifics of the "final solution" were unveiled to the Allies. Authenticated accounts of the program were made known to the Canadian Department of External Affairs in the summer of 1943. In May the following year the department received a detailed report from the British Foreign Office about the murder of most of the Jews in Poland.[53] Shortly thereafter, first-hand accounts of the liberation of Majdanek were in the hands of Jewish community leaders. Raymond Arthur Davies, an independent journalist based in Moscow and on the Congress payroll, described the scene at the camp in a telegram to Hayes and the Yiddish paper the *Jewish Eagle* on 29 August 1944:

[An] unexampled destruction opened before my eyes as I walked about Majdanek at Lublin [the] day before yesterday ... There is no doubt that Majdanek will go down into history as one [of the] most horrible experiences in mankind ... I do wish [to] stress that Majdanek where one million Jews and half a million others [were] killed calls for justice [and] for revenge and [the] world can't ever be satisfied until it is revenge obtained ... Things left by victims fill huge warehouses in Lublin and I saw with my own eyes pile[s] [of] shoes numbering at least eight [or] nine hundred thousand, whole boxes [of] eyeglasses, whole shelves [of] tortoras [sic], tsitsim [phallacteries], prayer books. I saw mountains [of] childrens [sic] toys ... I saw [a] bank of five electric ovens [which] had [the] production capacity per day equalling [the] population [of] a small Canadian town. I saw partly burned bodies their arms and legs chopped off to make [it] easier pushing into ovens and I saw great mountain grey urns Germans used to collect ashes ... You can tell America that at least three million [Polish] Jews [were] killed of whom at least a third were killed in Majdanek ... Five millions [sic] Jews [in] Europe among them three million Polish were annihilated with terrible moral and physical suffering in German Death Camps in Poland. Majdanek, Treblinka, Oswiencin [sic], Sobibor, Powiatowa [sic], Betrec Borek [?] and other places ... On only one day [in] November three forty three in Majdanek under sounds of gay music more than eighteen thousand Jews were shot.[54]

Davies, an enigmatic character, was the author of several books on the Soviet Union, a lecturer, and a promoter of improved relations between Canada and the USSR. On 14 November he spoke to a reported audience of 1,400 at the Monument National Theatre in Montreal after the destruction.[55]

In April 1944, two inmates of Auschwitz-Birkenau, Rudolf Vrba (Rosenberg) and Alfred Wetzler, had escaped and returned to their native Slovakia. They had gathered extensive and detailed information about each transport that had arrived in Birkenau during their twenty-month incarceration. The Jewish-Slovak underground published their findings in a thirty-page report and smuggled it to Switzerland. The information did not reach the West until the summer, when it came to the attention of President Franklin Roosevelt's War Refugee Board. A summary of the report was released by the board to the Jewish Labour Committee in New York. This organization was concerned that "public opinion should not think the various news stories about the Nazi extermination camps to be exaggerations." A branch of the organization, the Canadian Jewish Labour Committee (JLC), had been formed in 1939. It published the report in its paper, *Underground and on the Ground*, on 31 December. The JLC also passed on the information to the Canadian Research and Editorial Institute, an group of independent journalists. The institute's chief wrote a series of three articles on the report for the Canadian public.[56] The Vrba-Wetzler report is the most detailed and authentic eyewitness testimony on record of the operations of Birkenau from the vantage point of the victims.

After the war, Vrba immigrated to Canada. He settled in Vancouver, where he became a professor of pharmacology at the University of British Columbia. His astonishing memory of the transports and his dedication to detail were displayed at the 1985 trial of Ernst Zundel for publishing "false news" in Toronto. As a chief witness for the Crown, together with the testimony of the acclaimed Holocaust scholar Raul Hilberg, he helped destroy the canard that Jews were not gassed at Birkenau. Vrba also related his experiences in Claude Lanzmann's epic movie, *Shoah* released in 1985.

For three years the Jewish community had been receiving information, at first general and unconfirmed but soon after specific and verifiable, about the Holocaust. There can be no doubt that the leaders of the community were well aware of the mass murder of European Jewry shortly after it began. The shocking revelations about atrocities in the camps in Germany that were liberated by the Allies, virtually by accident in the final weeks of the war, confirmed what had been known for three years. Given that the community knew what was occurring, the next question focuses on what action it took.

At the sixth plenary session of the CJC in January 1945, a summary of Congress's response to the Holocaust was presented, titled "Efforts to Rescue the Surviving Jews of Europe." Five initiatives taken by Congress were reported. The first was communication between Samuel Bronfman and the government over the deportation of Jews from Vichy France to Poland. The report stated that "the

Prime Minister formally protested against the cruelty of the deportations and made this protest public." The second was a submission made by Congress to the government in preparation for the Bermuda Conference on Refugees in 1943. The report stated that "our attitude at the time was quite realistic and we did not lay any undue hopes on the results of these discussions and we so informed the leaders of the community. Nevertheless, we left no stone unturned in the hope that effective rescue measures may be initiated as a result of these deliberations." The third initiative was to request that the government admit a "number of refugees" and allow shipments of food to the Polish ghettoes. Neither request was granted. Fourth, Congress had made a formal representation that "a number of Jewish refugees" in neutral Spain and Portugal be allowed entry; four hundred and fifty refugees arrived in 1944. Fifth, Congress had worked with the Canadian National Committee on Refugees and Victims of Political Persecution (CNCR) in sponsoring a mass petition for the admission of refugees.[57]

There were also Jewish refugees outside Europe. The CJC was more successful in dealing with their plight than with those trapped under German occupation. In 1940 some 2,200 Jewish refugees, mostly of German origin, who had sought refuge in Britain, were interned there and then shipped to concentration camps in Canada. Through the efforts of the UJRA of the CJC and the CNCR, some 960 were released in Canada and the rest returned to Britain in 1944. In another footnote to the Holocaust, the UJRA, with the assistance of the Polish government in exile, secured permits of entry for eighty Jews who had escaped to Japan. Twenty-seven came to Canada before the invasion of Pearl Harbor, and the remainder were transported to Shanghai, where they survived through the efforts of the JDC. They were eventually allowed to enter Canada in the summer of 1946.[58]

Despite the gloss put on these efforts in Congress reports, they had a negligible impact on government policy either to relax immigration strictures during the war or to mount an international protest over the "final solution." As Paula Draper has noted, the permission for the former internees of the camps in Canada to apply for Canadian citizenship, which was granted by the government on 25 October 1945, was the "only major wartime success of the CJC." She says that this minor triumph was largely due to the efforts of Saul Hayes, the executive director of Congress. Draper writes: "Hayes himself walked a fine line – never able to completely satisfy the refugees, Blair (the Director of Immigration), or the Canadian Jewish community which he served. Yet in the constant guessing game Blair forced Hayes to play, Hayes was reasonably successful. This success ... was in itself a great achievement. Canadian Jews were experiencing their most insecure period in a country where discrimination against Jews was still commonplace."[59]

Efforts were made by other organizations as well. The Jewish Labour Committee raised $100,000 in three years in cash and supplies for the underground movement in Europe. Its report noted that this aid reached the French and Soviet undergrounds.[60] The United Romanian Jews of Canada protested the persecution of Jews in the 22 December 1942 edition of the *Toronto Jewish News*. The Federation of Polish Jews of Canada, in collaboration with the Jewish Immigrant Aid Society of Canada (JIAS) and the World Federation of Polish Jews, forwarded clothing to refugees and helped in the campaign of the UJRA for refugee admission. Several *landsmanschaften* joined the federation in these efforts. Some societies attempted to distribute funds and supplies to their kin in their hometowns and districts.[61]

Considering what was known at the time, the response by the leadership of the Jewish community was lukewarm. Its attempt at quiet diplomacy with the King administration and federal bureaucrats was a failure. The funds raised for relief were minimal, and the attempts to provide a haven for the refugees futile. Within the ethnic press there was criticism of the leadership. The *Hebrew Journal* lamented: "It is becoming apparent that the secret negotiations [between Congress and Ottawa] accomplished nothing." David Rome, the *Journal*'s editor, excoriated the "business as usual" attitude. In the *Canadian Jewish Chronicle*, the editor asked: "Where is the thunderbolt of invective which these events should call forth? Where are the keepers of the world's consciousness, its intellectual leaders?" The *Jewish Post* wrote, "Too long have we stood in abject fear of our own shadow." At the end of the war, the editor of the *Post* lamented, "The people of Canada were too indifferent to the agony of helpless victims of the Nazis, and in closing their hearts, they allowed thousands to perish outside their doors."[62]

In an assessment of the leadership's reaction to the plight of Europe's Jews during the war, the key consideration is what was possible for the community to achieve. In essence, there were three main obstacles preventing it from doing more. The first was the nature of the war and its relation to the Holocaust. The Holocaust took place throughout Europe, but the "final stage" occurred in the death camps of Poland and the mass shootings in the Soviet Union, far from the watchful eye of the Western allies. Given that Germany controlled transalpine Europe to the Soviet frontier without any Allied penetration until D-Day, it was extremely difficult to supply the trapped Jews with money or materials, let alone find them refuge in North

America. The few possibilities for rescue lay within pockets of eastern and central Europe, but as Yehuda Bauer has pointed out, even the hopes for these areas were dashed.[63] At most, supplies could only be fed through underground networks into some ghettoes and forest locations. Perhaps the Jewish leadership in Canada did not realize the extent of the total isolation of Jews in Europe since it did not actively seek contact with the underground. Nevertheless, a mass rescue initiated by Jewish communities in North America was impossible after the Casablanca Conference in 1943, which demanded Germany's unconditional surrender.

The second obstacle was the intransigence of the Canadian government in refusing to aid captured Jews, either through an ongoing campaign of diplomatic pressure or by modifying the restrictions against refugees. As Abella and Troper have pointed out, there was no political capital for King's administration in saving the Jewish remnant. The Bermuda Conference of 1943 on refugee adoption was a mirror of the Evian Conference. It was also designed to fail. Even when the camps were liberated, the publicity surrounding the atrocities there did not shake the government's determination to keep out Jewish survivors.[64]

Finally, the community's leaders, despite knowing what was occurring from mid-1942 to the end of the war, could not comprehend the scope of the event or its catastrophic consequences on Jewish civilization in Europe. In this respect, they were on similar ground to their counterparts in the other Allied countries.[65] The Holocaust was unprecedented in either Jewish or human history. Even the victims did not appreciate its enormity until their fate was sealed. Most of them viewed it as simply another tragic chapter in the history of Jewish suffering. As Elie Wiesel has written, in the spring of 1944, Hungarian Jews refused to believe the stories of the camps that were filtering back to them, even though by that time almost five million Jews had been killed.[66] Emmanuel Ringelblum, the historian and archivist of the Warsaw ghetto, saw the ghetto as a recreation of the concentration and isolation that Jews had faced in the late Middle Ages. It was not until reports of the death camps at Treblinka and elsewhere were confirmed that he realized that this tragedy was different in scope, intent, and efficiency.[67] If the victims could not comprehend the event that they were witnessing, how could Jews in the "warm safety of North America" grasp the enormity of the catastrophe? The obstacles in their path, both political and psychological, ensured that efforts at rescue and relief would not succeed. Nonetheless, these obstacles did not completely absolve the community. Its leaders were unduly timorous in their efforts with the government.

Protests and demonstrations on Parliament were not contemplated. There was no concerted, organized plan for fundraising for relief programs, and there was no barrage of information dispensed to the community by its leaders.

THE IMMEDIATE POST-WAR YEARS

Shortly after VE day, a delegation representing the Central Committee of Jews in Poland came to North America to report on the condition of the surviving community. Its secretary was Emil Sommerstein, minister of war and munitions.[68] The committee had been created in November 1944 as a temporary body; it then became a fixed organ with support from the fledgling Polish government established immediately after the German retreat in the winter of 1944–5.[69] Later that summer Sam Lipshitz was informed that officials of the Polish ministry would be in New York and would welcome the idea of inviting a delegation of Canadian Jewry to Poland. Lipshitz was a member of the CJC executive, and he proposed the idea to Congress.[70] Having already been exposed to the dire circumstances of the survivors in Poland through the meetings with Sommerstein's delegation, Congress approved the plan. Saul Hayes approached the Department of External Affairs for the necessary documents to proceed with the mission.[71]

For Congress, the mission to Poland would fulfill four objectives: make the Poles aware of Canadian Jewry's interest in their fate; trace the names and whereabouts of relatives; bring back first-hand information so that funds collected by *landsmanschaften* could be turned over to the Canadian Jewish Committee for Refugees (CJR) of Congress; and indicate to Canadians that the CJC was a "participator" (*sic*) and was not working "through remote channels."[72] The hidden agenda, however, was that the project would both defuse Congress's critics, who argued that much more should have been done, and serve to centralize relief projects The main obstacle, which was never acknowledged by community leaders, was the huge gap between their perception of Jewish existence in Poland at the war's end and the reality of the situation facing both Jews in Poland and the Polish nation. In its effort to come to the rescue of Polish Jews, the Canadian Jewish community would do little but apply some band-aids. Having satisfied themselves and their constituency that it had discharged this responsibility, its leaders quickly turned to matters of greater importance.

To counteract its critics and restore confidence in the community that Canadian Jews were in the forefront of the post-war relief effort,

Hayes chose two formidable leaders of the community to travel to Poland. Congress's delegate was H.M. Caiserman. The other was Lipshitz, who was endorsed by Congress and twenty-five Jewish organizations in Toronto.[73] Hannaniah Meir Caiserman was a Romanian Jew who at the age of twenty-six had emigrated to Montreal in 1910. He quickly established himself as a successful businessman,[74] but his lasting contribution was in service to the Jewish community. He helped convene the first plenary of the Canadian Jewish Congress in 1919 and was the driving force in its reconstitution in 1934. As secretary general of the CJC, he was an outspoken and energetic defender of Jewish causes. Lacking organizational abilities, Caiserman reported to Saul Hayes, the executive director. His strength was his tireless devotion to the unity of Canadian Jewry. As one writer put it, "for a considerable time the impression was that Caiserman is the Jewish Congress and that the Congress is Caiserman. His name is connected with the organization of the entire Jewish community. He is one of those who have made history in the Jewish life of Canada."[75]

Sam Lipshitz, who had been born in 1910, was editor of the left-wing *Canadian Jewish Weekly*. As a young immigrant from Poland to Montreal, he had worked as a Linotype operator before venturing into journalism. He was arrested and jailed briefly when the Communist Party of Canada was declared illegal and released when the Soviet Union joined the Allies. As a member of the United Jewish People's Order (UJPO), Lipshitz became its representative on the CJC National Executive in 1943. He was also a founder of the Labour-Progressive Party in 1943. Lipshitz renounced communism after visiting the Soviet Union in the wake of Stalin's death, and broke with UJPO in 1959 when it refused to follow suit.[76] Caiserman and Lipshitz represented two of the numerous strands of Canadian Jewry in the 1940s. One was an establishment immigrant who had not abandoned his roots, while the other had emerged as a radical within the established community who also retained a passionate devotion to his homeland. They were the first official Jewish delegates from North America to Poland after the war, and their reports were the first on-site descriptions of the situation facing Jewish survivors there. Their findings help to illuminate our understanding of the community's response to the survivors and to clarify the collective memory of the Holocaust that was shaped in the immediate post-war period.

The condition of the survivors in Poland at the end of 1945 was both alarming and hopeful. Of the pre-war population of 3.3 million Jews, some 300,000 had survived the war, of whom approximately 200,000 had escaped to the Soviet Union. Most of the Soviet refugees had yet to be repatriated to Poland. Estimates of the number of Jews in Poland in 1945 vary. According to one survey, there were 74,000 in May; another report put the figure at 130,000 in July; a third listed 86,000 in December. The last estimate is the most reliable one.[77] The survivors found themselves in a land devastated by war, without family, friends, communal services, funds, or infrastructure. As the historian Lucjan Dobroszycki put it, "Shortly after liberation, Jewish survivors returned to their native villages, towns, and cities, but no one awaited them; no relatives, friends, or neighbours were there to greet them. The houses and dwellings, businesses and workshops they had left behind years ago were occupied by others and no longer belonged to them. Each one had to begin anew, alone and without means, in a country that had been more extensively devastated than any other under Nazi rule."[78] The most pressing needs were housing, workshops and factories, and orphanages and asylums. Of the main cities, only Lodz and Cracow had not been razed to the ground. Without massive aid the survivors would have had to flee the country to Germany, where concentration camps were being converted into settlements for displaced persons. In addition, the survivors were awaiting the release of the Polish refugees in the Soviet Union, whose influx would exacerbate the survivors' already desperate condition.

The situation, however, was not entirely without hope. The Central Committee of Jews in Poland had been established in the eastern city of Lublin in November 1944. During its first year of operation, it created a miracle. It had branches in every county in which more than five hundred Jews were resident. It had established twenty-seven cooperative workers' unions, communal kitchens, schools, hospitals, and youth clubs. Under the committee's aegis, the Central Jewish Historical Commission was created to gather documentation on the Holocaust, while the Jewish Historical Institute became the repository for the archives of Jewish life before and during the Holocaust, including the Ringelblum archives of the Warsaw ghetto.[79] The committee encompassed the various political ideologies and religious groups of pre-war Polish Jewry. It was supported and protected by the Government of National Unity, the precursor to the Soviet puppet regime that came into being in the next three years. The government had responded vigorously to antisemitic incidents by some Polish citizens, especially an accusation of "ritual murder" in Rzeszów and attacks in Cracow. In addition, Cardinal Hlond of the Polish Roman Catholic Church denounced the attacks.[80]

Caiserman and Lipshitz were unprepared for the scene that awaited them on their entry into Warsaw on 2 December. Caiserman described the devastation of the city, the rubble that had been the ghetto, the *Umschlagplatz* (the deportation point to Treblinka), the notorious Pawiak prison, and the site of the destroyed Tlomackie synagogue. He wrote, "The impression was shattering." Upon visiting Auschwitz, he mourned, "Oschwienchin [*sic*] is the greatest inhumanity in the imagination of human beings. There are no words to describe it." Stunned by the absence of Jewish children, Caiserman and Lipshitz were told that the Central Committee had placed 1,600 in communes to prepare them for life in Palestine, and another 2,400 were in orphanages. When Caiserman stated that Canadian Jewry was "ready to take care of five hundred children," the committee was outraged. It responded that it had no intention of "permitting even one child to leave the country." Caiserman was surprised to find that there was a scintilla of Jewish communal life in the ruins. "To my great amazement I found, first, that the remnant of Polish Jewry had the courage, the initiative and the determination to organize and to unite. Secondly, to reconstruct their religious, their economic, their political, their cultural and educational life on the basis of the ideals of the groupings of the past, who have survived in present time Poland."[81]

Meetings took place in sixteen cities and towns with branches of the Central Committee. The delegation was informed of local and national conditions, but the discussions were also marked by acrimony. The delegates were told in no uncertain terms that the North American community had abandoned the survivors in Poland. The committee's report stated: "We have several times applied for help to Jewish organizations abroad asking them for financial support. We regret to state that during the years 1944/45 we did not receive a single *cent* from foreign Jewish organizations" (emphasis in original).[82] It was not that funds were not distributed, but that the currency was in Polish zlotys not American dollars, which had a far greater value. Not recognizing the discrepancy in the meaning of the word "cent," Lipshitz stated that large amounts of money had been collected. A representative of the Organization for Educational Research and Technical Training (ORT), an international Jewish Organization, criticized the relief effort. He stated that it was "insulting", and added that in Poland lay the best chance for a "small good Jewish community." Another member of the committee criticized the "green uniforms" sent by Canadian Jews and the supplies of food. He said that the greatest need was money to buy food and clothing and to publish books for schools.[83]

The criticism voiced in Warsaw was echoed elsewhere. In Lodz, which had the largest number of Jews at that time, the chairman of the local committee told the delegation that the Joint "has established a good apparatus but not for constructive purposes ... Its activity does not strengthen Polish Jewish Unity." Another member said that the Canadian Jewish community should not think of Polish Jews as *schnorrers* (freeloaders) and that Polish Jewry was most concerned about developing professional (training) schools for young adults in order for them to live in Poland or emigrate to Palestine, a cause that necessitated strong support from North America. In Bialystok the delegates were told that the committee needed funds to record the destruction of Polish Jewry, to reclaim children hidden in Polish homes, institutions, and churches, and to repair cemeteries.[84] Caiserman despaired at the future of the survivors in Poland. Despite being told in Warsaw that the committee was trying to rebuild life for Jews in a new Poland, and despite seeing the attempt to construct a semi-autonomous Jewish republic in Lower Silesia, he wrote, "I am *not* [Caiserman's emphasis] a Zionist, but the only solution is the building of a peoples [*sic*] Republic in Palestine, progressive in every way."[85]

Upon his return to Warsaw, Caiserman began a summary of the trip in a handwritten letter to Hayes. The letter was finished several days later in London. He described the desperate situation of the community and stated that "the Joint was attacked at mass meetings by the leaders of the Central Committee as being responsible for the situation on political grounds (negotiations for dollar exchange) and the argument was that the 'Joint dollar exchange is more important than the life of Polish Jews.'" Again, the reference was to the discrepancy in exchange rates. The Joint, it appears, was changing dollars into zlotys at the official rate and passing that currency to the committee. Instead, the committee wanted the money in dollars, which could be exchanged at a much higher rate on the black market. This distinction was lost on the Canadian delegates. Caiserman disagreed with Lipshitz, who wanted to "immediately" relieve the "critical situation." Caiserman wanted first to investigate all the facts and submit the findings to Congress. He indicated that he was bringing "a few hundred letters from [i.e., for] Canadian relatives." His thoughts regarding the Joint, the Polish government, and the Central Committee are noteworthy. "One thing I can tell you in advance and that is that the Joint has done and is doing a very good job inspite [*sic*] of the abuses in the Communist papers in Canada and by the Central Committee leaders ... The Government is decent as far as its atitude [*sic*] to the Jewish question is concerned and deserves praise... The Polish Government and the Jewish Central Committee are controled [*sic*] by the PPR [the Polish Communist Party] and Lifshitz [*sic*] takes the facts from the Party point of view. I am happy of our understanding that I first report to Mr. Bronfman, you and Mr. [Michael] Garber [of the CJC National Executive]. I am sure that I will get the guidance I need."[86]

Upon his return to Canada, Caiserman gave a public address on the Trans-Canada Network of the CBC. In contrast to his experience at meetings and the comments in his letter to Hayes, he told the nation:

Canada is very popular in Poland ... Everywhere I went I saw people wearing clothing sent from Canada by the Canadian Jewish Congress ... The Canadian Jewish Congress was very anxious to help Canadians locate the surviving members of their families in Poland, so that they could send them help, food, money and advice ... I've brought back some 1,500 letters and messages for Canadians in various parts of the country. The supply condition in Poland is improving through the help of organizations as the UNRRA [United Nations Relief and Rehabilitation Administration], the American Joint Distribution Committee and the Canadian United Jewish Relief Agencies ... Statistics never tell a story, but perhaps this will mean something to you: out of every hundred Jews who lived in Poland in 1939 only three are left. Those who have survived are broken, childless, in many cases still bearing on their bodies the brands of life in German concentration and labour camps. Everyone of them is alive only through a miracle.[87]

The Joint was quick to pick up the credit. In a press release, it quoted Caiserman: "The Jews of Poland could not have existed in recent months without the help of the Joint Distribution Committee, and not a single group in Jewish life in present-day Poland has failed to receive such help."[88] Caiserman's address was based on inaccuracies and half-truths. The "few hundred letters" he had mentioned in his report to Hayes had multiplied to fifteen hundred. This figure was further magnified in his biography to "thousands." He confused the proportion of Polish Jews who had survived the war (10 per cent) with the number of Jews in Poland at the time of his visit. Of greater significance, he whitewashed the reception of Canadian and Joint aid. Rather than honestly reporting the complaints of the Polish committee, he told the community what he thought it wanted to hear.

For the rest of March, Caiserman was sent on a countrywide speaking tour by Congress. Addressing audiences in cities and such small communities as Prince Albert and Vegreville, he spoke of the destruction of Polish Jewry and described the current situation. In a draft of his speech, he reinforced the misperceptions created by his national address. "I would only say that in so far as there was any effort, it was done by the J.D.C." He stated that the Joint had sent 91 million zlotys' worth of relief over the previous seven months, and he explained the protest of Polish Jews as an "irrational outcry [that] is in reality the folks' instinct which has given them the strength to live with self-respect." Caiserman praised the "many" Poles who had saved thousands of Jews and the government, the army, and the press for denouncing race hatred. He said that the "greatest wonder was the finding of a Polish Jewry... fully organized ... composed of existing Jewish political parties," which he then enumerated, including the PPR. Addressing the immediate future of the community, he intoned, "90% of Polish Jews are activistically [sic] Zionist and desirous to go to Erez-Israel [sic] if the doors are open." As with much of his report, he declared what he believed to be the case, rather than acknowledging the reality. A major survey of Jews in Poland conducted between 1947 and 1950 recorded that 38 per cent of the respondents regarded Israel as their homeland and 47 per cent preferred Poland.[89] Considering that this study was taken *after* the spate of antisemitic attacks and the imposition of communism, one would assume that the attachment to Poland would have been even greater at the end of 1945. Caiserman concluded: "Our entire conception of Relief must be adjusted so that the difference between ourselves and our brethren in Poland, and for that matter, everywhere, balance a little better than at present. On one side, on this continent, we have a high standard of living, on the other side, we have need – simply need. This after liberation, after having lost everything, all their families and have returned not families but single individuals, with sadness imprinted on their faces and greater sadness in their looks. I am sure my message is a message that Polish Jewry itself would like to present to you."[90]

To address the need, Congress set a goal of $1.5 million for European (not only Polish) relief for 1946. This figure amounted to about $10 per capita.[91] It was lauded as an impressive achievement by Caiserman, but his view was not shared by A.B. Bennett of the *Canadian Jewish Chronicle*. Regarding the Jewish situation in eastern Europe and the community's response to the condition of Jews there he wrote: "They scramble for a foothold, and they cry out from the depth of frustration in the awesome pitch of universal tragedy. We putter around here; try this device and that scheme to raise a bit of money; a campaign, a raffle, a chicken dinner for charity; a concert with proceeds. And we intone the inane syllable *'bis, bis, bis'* [a little]. By the time the sense of catastrophe reaches us, it is bereft of poignancy and our responsive chant is quite adequate: *'bis, bis, bis.'*" Bennett's rebuttal to the goal of $1.5 million was a sarcastic "very penetrating, very profound, very noble."[92]

Congress's response to the plea for massive aid in Poland was minimal. It is not clear how much of the aid for European relief was in fact targeted for Poland, but if even half of the funds had gone there, it would have amounted to only $5 per Jewish survivor in Poland in mid-1946 and a fraction of that figure to survivors elsewhere. Caiserman returned to Canada with reams of reports from the Central Committee typed in their original Polish, replete with statistics on production, occupations, and aid, which had been prepared for him and Lipshitz. They still sit in Congress files in their original form, untranslated and ignored. Caiserman had no notes on these reports. He was flabbergasted that some of the Jews he had met did not speak Yiddish, and that he had had to communicate in his broken German and their broken English. After he finished his cross-Canada tour, he was shunted off to South America to speak about relief operations and raise funds there. Lipshitz and Caiserman argued publicly over the extent of antisemitism in Poland and whether there was a future for Jews there. Lipshitz downplayed the anti-Jewish attacks, while Caiserman repeated his belief that Jewish life had to be rebuilt in Palestine.[93] At the next plenary in 1947, the delegation merited only two lines in the presidential address.[94] This tepid reaction is not surprising given the original motives for the delegation. They had less to do with securing an accurate appraisal of the conditions in Poland than with concocting a mirage that Congress was taking a leading role in the relief efforts.

Caiserman, in fact, was not a central figure in the policy-making decisions of Congress, despite his public persona. He had been enlisted as a fact-finder and speaker to keep him occupied. His public pronouncements were written by David Rome, the Congress archivist and historian.[95] Lipshitz, without Congress's imprimatur, had a smaller audience, although he also viewed the situation through his ideological filter. Nonetheless, they were genuinely overwhelmed by their experience. They were inundated with requests for contacts with Canadian relatives, spending much time following up these requests upon their return to Canada and arranging for sponsorship of immigrants where possible.[96] While in Poland, Caiserman also arranged for the formal adoption of a young Jewish woman, who finally arrived in 1948.

The delegation's reports helped to frame the perceptions of the Canadian Jewish community at the time. It did not understand the situation in Poland, from the needs of the community to the nuances of black-market profiteering to the illusion of some that a viable Jewish existence could be resurrected. Caiserman could not comprehend why any Jew would want to remain in Europe, so he overcame his squeamishness about Zionism and proclaimed that the survivors wanted to emigrate to Palestine, while Lipshitz was over-apologetic about antisemitism in the post-war conditions because communists were supposedly not antisemitic. Caiserman praised the Joint because of the strong links between that organization and Congress. Two years later, few remembered the delegation, but the image of the surviving remnant in Europe and the community's response to it had become ingrained. The picture was that Canadian Jews were in the forefront in providing relief and restitution and that their European kindred were thankful for these sacrifices. This image was one basis for the community's collective memory, a memory largely built on misperception.

THE REFUGEE CAMPS

On 6 July 1945 the Soviet and Polish governments had signed an agreement whereby pre-war Polish citizens who had escaped to the Soviet Union during the war could be repatriated. Between February and August 1946 some 140,000 Polish Jews returned to Poland, joining the 100,000 who were already living there. Two-thirds of the Jewish population, however, left Poland the next year. The overriding reason for their departure was the numerous attacks by local antisemites, in which approximately 1,000 Jews were killed. The single greatest pogrom took place in the city of Kielce on 4 July 1946, when 42 Jews were murdered.[97] The vast majority of those who fled Poland went to Germany and other European countries. There they joined other Jewish refugees. By the middle of 1946 there were approximately 300,000 Jewish refugees in central and eastern Europe. Of these, 170,000 were under the protection of UNRRA, 138,000 in the British, French, and American zones in Germany. Consigned to displaced persons' camps, they could not and would not be repatriated to their former homes. They longed to leave Europe, preferably for Palestine, the first choice of 85 per cent of those in the Allied zones.[98]

A DP camp had been established at Bergen-Belsen. In April 1946 it housed 7,000 Jewish refugees. Paul Trepman, who eventually emigrated to Montreal, edited *Unzer Sztyme* (*Our Voice*), the organ of the Central Jewish Committee in the camp. Using the analogy of Jews as "footballs" because rugby was played by the British soldiers, he wrote: "We Jews have long been the 'sport' of nations and peoples, we have been kicked, murdered and gassed, pursued and buffeted ... but the game is being played in a bigger arena, and the reward in the game is life or death to us, the remnants of six million massacred European Jews ... We demand the right to leave for ever this land of searing memories and plead with the spectators of our miseries to leave us our remaining years to live in peace, away from close proximity of Europeans. The ball has had enough. We have only one goal, our land – Eretz Israel."[99] Ben Kayfetz, too, observed the misery. He had been sent to Germany as a member of the Canadian Control Commission in the British sector. He first met survivors in a DP camp near Hanover in October 1945, and he remembers: "There I was in the middle of it. They were aged seventeen, eighteen, nineteen. I was impressed by the upness of their spirit. They were not disillusioned. The stories they told me were hair-raising."

While on leave in Basel, Switzerland, in December 1946, Kayfetz attended some sessions of the World Zionist Congress, held in that city on the fiftieth anniversary of the first meeting of Zionists. He observed the Canadian contingent led by Eddie Gelber and Sam Zacks, two luminaries of the Jewish community.[100] As well as sending its leaders to Europe to attend such meetings and to gather information about the refugees, the community was continuing to work behind the scenes with politicians and bureaucrats in Canada. As the months wore on, the frustration of refugees in the camps over the British restrictions on immigration to Palestine was escalating, and many joined the underground that smuggled survivors into the country.[101] In increasing numbers, refugees besieged Canadian immigration authorities, while in Canada, Jews with surviving relatives applied to the government to allow them to sponsor their families. These efforts produced few results. Hayes pleaded with Mackenzie King[102] and Congress petitioned immigration officials for a relaxation in the restrictions, but wartime attitudes persisted.[103] Ever the politician, King saw no political gain in changing immigration policy. Public opinion toward Jews remained unfavourable. In a public opinion poll taken in October 1946, in response to the question "If Canada allows more immigration, are there any of these nationalities which you would like to keep out? the least-favoured group was the Japanese at 60 per cent, followed by Jews at 49 per cent and Germans at 34 per cent.[104] The total number of Jewish immigrants admitted to Canada via ocean ports and via the United States between 1 April 1945 and 31 March 1947 was 2,918. This figure represented 3 per cent of the total number of 98,011 immigrants admitted to Canada in the period.[105]

At the seventh plenary of the CJC, held in Toronto from 31 May to 2 June 1947, Sam Bronfman reviewed the organization's work in the two previous years. He said that since VE day the "plight of the refugees is only technically improved ... The general outlines of the situation still remain grim and tragic. In the final analysis, the refugee problem is one which can be solved only by international action." He spoke of the need to continue the relief effort. "We speak of 'we' and 'they.' We are over here and they are there, and we give it to them. It is not really a matter of 'we' and 'they'... It is one whole, and we must face that responsibility." The plenary adopted a resolution calling for a drive to raise two million dollars for the UJRA in 1947. Monroe Abbey, the president of the Eastern Region of Congress, outlined the specifics of the relief effort. He noted the work of the Joint "and to a lesser extent the ORT and a number of individual committees overseas with which we deal from time to time." He singled out the Federation of Polish Jews for their campaign, at the request of Congress, to purchase sewing machines and for arrangements made with the Canadian Meat Board to purchase one million pounds of kosher meat. Congress announced that it had negotiated the entry of one thousand Jewish orphans into Canada and had submitted a request to allow Jewish skilled workers to be admitted as well, schemes that were to be the main thrust of communal activity in response to the refugee problem over the next two years. A resolution was adopted in which "the Canadian Jewish Congress records its profound appreciation of the steps already taken by the Government of Canada to modify the restrictions upon the admission of immigrants into this country."[106] This resolution was pusillanimous since the government, until its agreement to accept the orphans, had been deaf to the pleas of the community.

While Congress's initiatives in the two years following Liberation were not the only attempts at relief and rehabilitation in the Jewish community, they represented the bulk of what was accomplished.[107] The two main thrusts of communal response – the campaign for funds and supplies and the lobbying of federal officials to loosen immigration restrictions – had a marginal effect on the plight of the survivors. The funds raised in this period amounted to approximately $20 per Canadian Jew, a rather insignificant sum given the magnitude of the tragedy. The telegrams to King and the representations to Ottawa were dismissed by the mandarins and politicians. The community's clout was only slightly less negligible after the war than it had been during the conflict. Moreover, delegations to Europe such as the Caiserman-Lipshitz mission and the representation at the Zionist plenary did little to sway public opinion or inspire communal response, partially because they were forgotten within weeks after they took place. Another instance was a fact-finding mission by Joe Salsberg, an Ontario MPP, who reported to Congress on the antisemitic bias shown in the selection process in DP camps by Canadian authorities.[108] These deputations were window dressing, for Canadian Jews were told what they wanted to hear: that European Jews sought to flee the camps for Palestine; that there was widespread antisemitism and constant physical danger; and that relief supplies were coming in in adequate amounts as a result of the herculean efforts of local and international relief agencies. They were also assured that, while immigrants were not being admitted in large numbers, no stone was being left unturned by community leaders in their attempts to effect an easing of the restrictions.

Despite Bronfman's refrain that the community's responsibility necessitated an erasure of the 'we' and 'they' mentality, the lukewarm efforts by Canada's Jews during and immediately after the war to the plight of the survivors belied the belief that the gulf had closed. Given the "warm safety of North America," it is understandable but not excusable that Canadian Jews did not respond with more vigour and generosity.

2 *Greener* and *Gayle*: The Arrival of Survivors in the Late 1940s

On 1 May 1947 Prime Minister Mackenzie King rose in the House of Commons to present the government's long-awaited post-war immigration policy. In what historian Freda Hawkins characterized as a "sober and cautious" tone, he described the course that would dictate immigration policy for the next fifteen years. "The policy of the government is to foster the growth of the population of Canada by the encouragement of immigration. The government will seek by legislation, regulation and vigorous adminstration, to ensure the careful selection and permanent settlement of such numbers of immigrants as can be advantageously absorbed in our national economy."[1]

A month later, at its biennial plenary session, the CJC sought to capitalize on the new policy by unveiling two initiatives. The first was a resolution to sponsor the admission of 1,000 Jewish orphans into Canada. This was not a resolution designed to lobby the government for the approval of this project but, rather, a cautious response to an order-in-council that had already been approved by the governor general on 29 April 1947. The motion read as follows:

The Canadian Jewish Congress records its profound appreciation of the steps already taken by the Government of Canada to modify the restrictions upon the admission of immigrants into this country and it calls upon the authorities to give effect at the earliest possible opportunity to the representations of the Canadian Jewish Congress, looking towards the progressive extension of the categories of admissible immigrants. The Canadian Jewish Congress urges the Government of Canada to offer its hospitality to as many as possible of the Jewish victims of the war who are tragically in need of a haven.

We express our gratification to the Government of Canada for the issuance of the Order-in-Council which provides for the admission of 1,000 Jewish orphans into Canada. We approve of the guarantee given by the officers of Congress in this respect and in other immigration matters and we further approve of the plans for the handling of the movement of these immigrants. We authorize the national executive to continue its work in this field.[2]

The second initiative was more modest. In his address to the plenary, Monroe Abbey, president of the Eastern Division of the CJC, in speaking about the rehabilitation of European refugees, mentioned that Congress had made a submission to the government to allow carpenters, needle-trade workers, "and other workers [sic] in which Jews specialize" to enter the country.[3] These two endeavours, the orphans' project and the workers' project, were to be the prime efforts made by the Canadian Jewish community in response to the plight of the survivors in the displaced person's camps between 1947 and 1949. The two schemes allowed more than 3,000 survivors and their children to immigrate to Canada. With further immigration restrictions removed, from 1 April 1947 to 31 March 1950 between 15,000 and 16,000 Jews immigrated to Canada and remained here. This influx was the largest three-year migration of Jews to the country since the period from 1911 to 1914.[4] The most prominent factor in the new policy was the need for labour in the booming post-war economy, Congress hyperbole notwithstanding. David Rome, the distinguished historian and archivist at Congress headquarters in Montreal, wrote forty years after the fact that "the Canadian government's reversal of its federal immigration policy after Hitler's destruction was a major act of liberation. Domestically, Canada opened its hermetic doors to the survivors of the Holocaust ... This governmental response to the appeals of the Jewish Congress opened a vast chapter in the cooperation of all classes and institutions."[5]

The arrival of Jewish refugees presented the established Jewish community with two challenges. The first was creating an infrastructure for those immigrants for whom it was directly responsible, most notably the more than 1,100 orphans. Their immediate needs included housing, education, social welfare, emergency cash, and employment. The second challenge was dealing with the psychological and emotional dislocations of the new arrivals. Unlike earlier immigrants, who had not experienced the Holocaust and who were part of a three-decade stream of migrants with friends and family from their home regions in Europe already in Canada, most survivors arrived as true refugees, without national status, their families having been killed, and without a support network in their adopted country.

A measure of the established community's response was its ability to meet these challenges. Jewish organizations were ill-equipped to deal adequately with the needs of most survivors. With regard to the second challenge, the response by the community was also disappointing. Dealing with the psychological needs of the refugees meant first comprehending their experience and understanding interwar European Jewish society. This was difficult for most Canadian Jews. For them the Holocaust was a disastrous calamity, but its enormity, aside from the often-stated figure of six million, remained outside their experience and comprehension. This attitude would endure for another generation. Perhaps it was too much to ask of the established community in the late 1940s to realize that these refugees were unlike the immigrants who had come in the first three decades of the century. Of greater import, issues relating to immigration policy and refugee rehabilitation and absorption were not foremost among community concerns. Rather, attention was focused upon creating a Jewish homeland in Palestine and elevating the status of Canadian Jewry in the post-war climate.

IMMIGRATION POLICY

The new policy introduced on 1 May 1947 was based on six considerations: it was required for population growth; it was required for economic development; it was to be selective; it had to be related to "absorptive capacity"; it was a national prerogative; and it was not intended to distort the present character of the Canadian population, meaning that the restrictions on Asian immigration would remain.[6] These considerations had emerged from the recommendations of the Senate Committee on Immigration and Labour, which began to hold meetings in May 1946 and continued as a standing committee until 1953. Briefs were submitted by government officials and independent bodies. One such group was the Canadian National Committee on Refugees, a pro-refugee pressure group founded in 1938. Another was Congress. Saul Hayes and Louis Rosenberg presented Congress's brief on 3 July 1946. Referring to recent history, they pointed out that the main barrier to Jewish immigration was that Jews were classed as a "race" rather than as citizens of specific countries. In effect, they were stating that immigration officials were wilfully discriminating against Jewish immigration and appealing for a non-discriminatory act.[7]

The Senate committee, in its reports of 1946 and 1947, concluded that immigration was important for the national good, that Canada should follow the lead of other countries, that its population needed a substantial increase, and that the country should do its share in helping refugees and displaced persons, but that immigration should be geared to "absorptive capacity," a term that was not defined. While the committee may have been influenced by the CNCR and Congress briefs, of greater significance were the deputations from the Canadian Chamber of Commerce, the Department of Reconstruction and Supply, which was responsible for establishing the post-war economic framework for the country, and public corporations such as the Canadian National Railways. These agencies were optimistic in their assessment of Canada's economic potential. Their arguments for the economic need for massive immigration struck a chord with the committee and ultimately with King and his cabinet. Seizing the opportunity to facilitate the coming change in immigration policy, J.A. Glen, the minister of mines and resources, whose department included immigration, appointed Hugh Keenleyside to the vacant post of deputy minister. In effect, the appointment was dictated by King and C.D. Howe, the minister of reconstruction and supply, rather than the inconsequential Glen. King and Howe by early 1947 had realized that the anti-immigrant policy of Keenleyside's predecessors, F.C. Blair and A.L. Jolliffe, was no longer viable. The postwar recovery was dependent upon an expanded workforce that could only be filled by immigration.[8] Under Keenleyside's direction, a thorough reform of policy and procedure was inaugurated.

What did the Senate committee recommendations and King's speech portend for the Jewish refugees? To what degree did Saul Hayes's efforts influence government policy on behalf of the surviving remnant? Indeed, how favourable was public opinion to increased immigration in the immediate post-war era? Three indicators show that it tended to be marginally in favour of massive immigration, but not particularly receptive to the admission of Jewish refugees. The first was a survey of press opinion on immigration conducted by Congress and released by Saul Hayes in a confidential memo on 3 October 1946. The memo summarized the comments of approximately fifty publications, but did not contain an analysis or commentary. Two generalizations can be drawn from the survey. The first is that a majority of English-language publications favoured immigration from the British Isles. Among the most vociferous proponents of Jewish immigration was *Saturday Night*, which "commented on the deterioration of morale in the camps for displaced persons (that) Canada has a great deal to answer for in this matter, having kept her door shut during the years when Jews were being threatened and murdered in Germany." Nevertheless, most of the papers echoed the Brockville, Ontario *Recorder and Times* in stating that "in formulating a selection policy for immigrants only those be admitted who stand a good chance of assimilation and becoming good citizens ... There has been foreign, or at least, a non-Anglo-Saxon flavour to a large percentage of the names associated with black marketing and similar illegal operations in this country during recent years." The *Windsor Star* said, "Canada can well use farm labourers and lumber workers. These can be obtained from Britain and Northern Ireland." A dissenting voice on increased immigration came from the *Montreal Star*, which charged that "pressure groups have sought a reckless flinging wide of our doors to all and sundry .... [that] customary regulations and restrictions regarding any immigrant be entirely waived in the case of European refugees and that they will be admitted en masse, regardless."

The second generalization that can be made is that the French-language press surveyed opposed increased immigration. *Le Devoir* summed up the general fear of most French Canadians that "powerful groups in Canada are conducting an intensive pro-immigration campaign, assisted by minority groups whom assimilation can make partners of the Anglo-Saxons in Canada, with the purpose of perpetuating the majority of British origin within the dominion." *Le Guide* of Sainte Marie de Beauce stated, "If Canada thinks in terms of immigration as intense and as poorly prepared as we had in the past, the hidden purpose of some imperialists might be balanced by French immigration."[9]

A second indication of the public mood, in this instance specifically regarding the Jewish refugees, can be found in the comments and correspondence of government representatives. In a national radio address on 2 May 1945, Georges Vanier, Canada's ambassador to France, spoke at length about the horrors of Buchenwald without once mentioning the Jewish victims.[10] A memorandum from Minister of National Health Brooke Claxton to King on 20 April 1946, which described the horrible conditions in the camps and asked for permission to allow the entry of foster children, went unheeded until the order-in-council one year later.[11] A directive to the Immigration Branch on 6 February 1946 stated that there were at present no concrete proposals for refugee resettlement, but that when there were, they would be based on national status (since Jews were not a 'nation,' they were without status). A memo in August stated that the cabinet "commits nothing" regarding displaced persons.[12] A directive to the Immigration Branch on 6 February 1946 placed Jews at the bottom of the list of prefered groups for admission since "they demonstrated less charity to others not members of their own group than do the remaining nationals."[13] In the House of Commons a MP stated on 9 July 1946 that "the government is breeding a monster which sooner or later will devour it. Let it beware of the hammer and sickle. The Jewish-Masonic gang can effect the worst interventions in Canada."[14]

Public opinion polls regarding immigration constitute a third indication of the national mood. A Gallup poll of October 1946 showed the persistance of an anti-Jewish bias despite the Holocaust.[15] Another Gallup poll taken in the late summer of 1947 showed that 51 per cent of Canadians agreed that the country needed more immigrants, 11 per cent supported admitting the "right type" of immigrant, and 30 per cent opposed immigration.[16] While attitudes toward immigration were softening, there was little evidence that the general public felt the same pressing concerns for an expanded labour force and consumer market as business interests did. From these surveys it is apparent that support for increased immigration had risen marginally between 1946 and 1948, but that nativist attitudes were still predominant. Despite the efforts of the Jewish community, the easing of restrictions on displaced persons was not motivated by an overriding concern with the plight of the survivors. This fact was reflected both in public attitudes and in government policy in the three years following King's speech.

While in previous years the low public support for immigration might have dissuaded King from changing the policy, he recognized that the pragmatic course was to increase the population in order to stimulate the economy. He may have been moved by pleas from the CNCR, or he may have been sympathetic to Hayes's mild pressure. In the end, however, he was motivated less by a concern about the plight of the refugees than by consideration for Canada's economic goals. The new policy was not revolutionary. It still reeked of the racist elements of previous directives: prohibiting "Oriental" immigrants; only slightly easing the "first degree" policy; slating eastern Europeans for menial work on farms and in the forests; giving priority to British, French, and western Europeans. And Jewish immigrants were still deemed less desirable than all other Europeans.

For the survivors languishing in the camps, the change in policy was too slow in coming and too slow in being implemented. Prevented from reaching Palestine by British restrictions and shut out of the United States by the restrictions of American immigration bureaucrats, the survivors implored their contacts in North America for help. Two years after the war they had less need for material provisions than earlier, but they were becoming increasingly desperate in their desire to escape the DP camps. A letter from the Bialystoker organization in the camp in Bamberg, Germany, to the Bialystoker

Relief Committee in New York dated 10 June 1947 summed up the situation:

The sending of parcels ... we consider, unnecessary, and in spite of big expenses it gives no positive results, since nearly all living in Germany are earning enough for dry bread, and considering the difficult times and what we have gone through, this ought to satisfy us. We were not, and do not want to be beggars, stretching out our hands for alms, we would only want you to render us assistance in the turning point of our lives ... We would want to draw your attention to the fact, that only the australian [sic] Relief Committee has kept to that line and sent for a certain number of Bialystoker Permits to Australia. We realise fully, that the way to the U.S.A. is not open to us, but there are many other countries and first of all Canada, which receive D.Ps.[17]

Word of King's speech reached the camps quickly, but the optimism of the Bialystoker organization was premature. It would be another year until restrictions would be loosened and even longer for the full-scale implementation of the new directives that would allow entry to the refugees. Meanwhile, the Jewish community continued to lobby for a more open door.

THE ORPHANS' PROJECT

At the plenary session of the CJC in 1942 it had been determined that the community should ask the government to permit the admission of 1,000 Jewish orphans. The government had agreed with the request, but did not fulfill its promise for another five years. In response to the Allied assault on North Africa, Germany occupied Vichy France, from where the children were to have been shipped. The rescue was aborted, and the children were seized and deported to the death camps by the Germans and their French collaborators.[18] On 21 April 1947, order-in-council 1647 authorized the admission of 500 orphans from France and stated that another 500 "might later be authorized upon it being ascertained that the second group could be properly placed and cared for." The orphans were to be less than eighteen years old, Congress was to assume responsibility for their maintenance, and their care was to be entrusted to casework agencies.[19] With King's announcement of the new immigration policy ten days later, the CJC rightly felt that it had scored a coup. Saul Hayes praised the government in a confidential memo to the executive. He referred to two government directives: the orphans' project and another order-in-council, which widened the "first degree" sponsorship provision to include orphaned nieces and nephews under the age of twenty-one (previously the age had been eighteen), and married brothers and sisters.[20] Samuel Bronfman echoed Hayes's enthusiasm. He wrote to King: "The government's announcement of Canada's revised immigration policy has surely brought satisfaction to the Canadian public. May I take the opportunity of expressing our appreciation for the relief which will be accorded those for whom we appealed when you and members of your Cabinet were good enough to receive our submissions. The Order-in-Council for one thousand children under our auspices is gratefully acknowledged as well as the extension of the categories of relatives who may now qualify. May we express the hope that it presages further extensions so that a wider range of kith and kin of Canadian residents will be able to find refuge here."[21]

Congress quickly sprang into action. Within a month, arrangements were made with the Joint in Paris to assemble 150 children for emigration.[22] In the meantime, Congress had convened a meeting on 12 May with representatives from the Jewish Welfare Fund of Winnipeg, the Federation of Jewish Philanthropies in Montreal, and the United Jewish Welfare Fund of Toronto to raise the needed funds for the reception of the children.[23] That this meeting was called indicates that Congress did not have the infrastructure required to handle the children but was dependent upon community organizations for the task. The CJC was to create a national coordinating committee using child-welfare agencies for the supervision of the children. The ultimate goal was adoption. Congress was the sole organization making the arrangements with government departments at all levels, and it assumed responsibility for all financial guarantees. It was to appoint one or two professional workers to implement the project overseas (Ethel Ostry was hired for this position), and international Jewish agencies in the field were to act as the agents for the CJC. Foster parents could refund the costs of transportation if they so desired.[24] Given the organizational structure of the Jewish community in those years, it was understood that Congess had the authority to plan policy but not the means to implement it at the local level. Therefore the welfare agencies assumed the role of creating the infrastructure to handle the immigrants.

To a degree, Congress's deal with the government was disingenuous. A total of 1,116 "children" arrived through the project, 764 boys and 352 girls. Of these, only 647 were under the age of eighteen, and only 23 were under the age of ten. Most of the children over fifteen were not adopted but remained in group or foster homes until they were able to gain employment and self-sufficiency. Given the harsh realities of the Holocaust, this outcome is hardly surprising. Only a handful of children survived the catastrophe without their families, and of these a tiny minority found their way to French orphanages. No Jewish child under the age of eighteen in 1947 had experienced a normal adolescence, and no child under ten had had a normal child- hood. Of the total, 783 of the orphans were liberated from concentra- tion camps, while the remaining 229 had been hidden.

The first contingent landed in Halifax on 18 September 1947; the 1,000th orphan arrived on 24 January 1949, and the final four on 10 March 1952.[25] According to Ben Lappin, the executive director of the Central Region, the total cost of the project was $1,188,000, or $1,065 per child. In addition to the other funds raised for relief, rehabilita- tion, and absorption, "the financing of services to such a large clien- tele produced a continuous state of crisis."[26] The orphans' scheme was the high point of the community's effort to provide a haven for the refugees. As Lappin commented, "in fulfilling this historic com- mitment, Canadian Jewry was redeemed no less in its own eyes than in those of the 1,116 children it had rescued and rehabilitated."[27]

THE WORKERS' PROJECT

News of the pogrom in Kielce, Poland, on 4 July 1946 was a cause of great concern in the Jewish diaspora. Incensed at this outrage, Bernard Shane, president of the Jewish Labour Committee, wrote to Congress a week later, calling for a nationwide campaign to petition for the admission of displaced Jews into Canada, to be followed by a delegation of Jews and "leading non-Jews" to Ottawa. In his reply to Shane, Saul Hayes wrote that, after consulting with the CNCR and the United Jewish Refugee Agency, he concluded that the petition would be difficult to organize. Instead, he suggested that a non-Jewish com- mittee to lobby for change in government policy would have to be created by Congress. He stated that "this can't be done in a day or a week but would require months of effort."[28] The committee was not established. Instead, organized labour teamed up with manufactur- ers to lobby the government for the entry of skilled labour from the DP Camps.

Bernard Shane was the driving force behind this initiative. He had been born in Russia in 1890 and had immigrated to the United States at age sixteen. He became involved with the International Ladies' Garment Workers' Union (ILGWU), coming to Toronto in 1934 as an organizer. After the war he was the general organizer of the Montre- al General Council of the Cloak and Suit Makers' Union. In addition to his position in the JLC, in later years he became involved with the Human Rights Advisory Committee of Congress and was elected to the Canadian Labour Congress executive.[29] In 1947 Shane orchestrated a joint brief on behalf of the ILGWU and the Ladies' Cloak and Suit Industry of the Dominion of Canada to the Immigration Branch. The brief read, in part:

This industry requires employees of the highest skill in the needle industry ... the majority of these workers, originally immigrants from Europe into Canada, have continuously worked in the industry which constitutes their life's vocation ... Since approximately 1930, there have been few, if any, immigrants who have entered the country. Consequently as the key employees so essential to the operation of this industry pass from the scene, it has become more difficult to replace them. The industry today is in a precarious position ... This industry has been informed that there are presently in Displaced Persons Camps in Europe, persons of the necessary skills who have been born into this industry and who are urgently required to replace outgoing employees who are irreplaceable in the Dominion of Canada.[30]

The JLC was instrumental in moving the government to take action. Until July 1946 the Canadian branch of the committee had been staffed by volunteers. Then Kalmen Kaplansky was hired as director, and Moshe Lewis, father of David Lewis (the national secretary of the Co-operative Commonwealth Federation, Canada's democratic socialist party, and later leader of its successor, the New Democratic Party), was appointed secretary without pay. The JLC, in preparation for its appeal to the government, concluded an agreement with manufacturers' associations for the sponsorship of skilled workers from the camps. One such agreement, signed with the Montreal Hat and Cap Manufacturers' Association, read, "Employers shall assume one and only one obligation, namely, to employ the said workers when they arrive in Canada in the numbers stipulated by each said Employer."[31]

In October 1947, approval was granted for the admission of 2,136 tailors and 500 furriers under Order-in-Council 2180. The order was given after a year of intensive lobbying by the CJC, unions, and manufacturers. Unlike the orphans' scheme, the workers' project was not solely a Congress initiative. Two other Jewish organizations, the Jewish Labour Committee and the Jewish Immigrant Aid Society, also played central roles. Although the order did not specify that the workers would be Jewish refugees, in its deliberations with the government, Congress had assumed that this would be the case. The government, however, stipulated that only half the workers would be Jewish and that their wives and children would count against this quota.[32]

The JLC set up a tripartite committee of labour, manufacturers, and government to select immigrants for the scheme. Several missions were sent to Europe. The first one was to choose tailors. It consisted of Shane, Sam Herbst, a labour leader from Winnipeg, and David Solomon, a manufacturer from Ottawa. They were joined by manufacturers Max Enkin and Samuel Posluns of Toronto.[33] It is interesting to note that this delegation was sent to select workers before the order-in-council was approved, indicating that the cabinet had already sanctioned the initiative.

Initial meetings were held between the industrial team, representatives of the Hebrew Immigrant Aid Society (HIAS), the American counterpart of the Jewish Immigrant Aid Society, and the Joint, beginning on 21 September 1947. Meetings were also held with V.G. Phelan of the Canadian Military Mission. One team worked in the British zone and the other in the American zone. Writing the final report on behalf of the committee to A. MacNamara, deputy minister of labour, Max Enkin made the following points: 5,048 individuals had been screened, and 3,103 chosen; selections were made from the British and American zones in Germany and Austria and the French zone in Austria; applicants were given a "job test" using either sewing machines or a demonstration of their skill in hand tailoring. Enkin observed, "In the D.P. camps the world had one of the greatest reservoirs of skilled craftsmen in all fields of industry as well as the sciences." He commended the Canadian government for its "practical and humanitarian attitude" and paid tribute to the International Refugee Organization (IRO) for "doing a herculean job in coping with the very serious and tragic problem of resettling hundreds of thousands of men and women who find themselves in a helpless and dispossessed position waiting for countries to open their doors." And he continued: "After seeing how a million uprooted people live in a war torn area and listening to the experiences of hundreds of these people, we are all moved to stress the humanitarian aspect of this project ... To each and every displaced person we bring to Canada you are offering the opportunity of re-building a new life – now blighted by years of war and frustration after liberation. Canada is one of their havens and anything we can do to facilitate their rehabilitation and re-settlement will ever redound to our credit as a nation."[34]

Bernard Shane documented the mission in a ten-part series in the *Jewish Chronicle*. The series was titled "In Search of Tailors – Impressions Gained during a Recent Two Month Journey through the Continent." The articles are a valuable account of the conditions in the camps and the obstacles faced in selecting Jews and non-Jews when there were so many of the former who were qualified and so few of the latter who were capable. Of the DP camp in Bucholtz, Shane wrote: "Before us appeared helpless, dispirited human beings who saw in our mission a spark of hope for their liberation from their present misery. They looked upon their present situation as a death sentence, and at us as saviours in whose power it was to liberate them and give them a new lease on life." Of the 4,000 inmates of the camp, 500 were selected.

Shane commented on the obstacles to interviewing the 1,100 DPS whose names had been given to the committee in Canada. The IRO opposed the delegation's efforts, stating that since the refugees were scattered, arranging meetings would be difficult. But the persistence of the committee forced the IRO to find the individuals. Shane wrote of the difference between Jewish DPS, who had hope, and non-Jewish refugees, who had been uprooted because of post-war politics rather than annihilation, but who were without hope. In Emberg a rabbi pleaded with the delegation to free all Jews willing to leave Germany. "We don't dare consider the possibility of staying here even a while longer. We have nothing here," he said. All the Jews in Emberg came to the synagogue claiming to be tailors. At the end, 3,100 people (including families) were selected for the project, but Canadian immigration officials gave approval for only 2,100. In his last article, Shane wrote: "We felt depressed at the thought that hundreds of thousands of others to be left in these camps without any immediate hope of salvation ... We left Europe convinced that a great responsibility rests with American and Canadian Jews. The fate of hundreds of thousands of lives is in their hands."[35]

Shortly after, the first Jewish garment workers sailed from Europe bound for Halifax. A telegram from Phelan to MacNamara, sent on 11 March 1948, informed the deputy minister, "461 DPS due Halifax nineteenth / 287 close relatives and Jewish orphans / also 90 garment workers plus 84 dependents of garment / analysis garment with dependents follows / with wife only Jewish 2 nonJewish 5, with wife and children Jewish 5, nonJewish 18." Phelan added that "garment workers have protested most vigorously to IRO and will continue protests."[36] Presumably the protests were made by Jewish workers who felt that they had been discriminated against in the initial decision regarding who was allowed to sail. Frustration with immigration authorities had been brewing for several months. J.B. Salsberg, an Ontario MPP, who went to Germany to observe the selection process, wrote to Hayes from Hanover on 12 December 1947 that "the first 80 tailors who left on a boat recently were all non-Jews. That is no accident. To make things worse, the Canadian vice-consul who came to [the] Munich area to examine the group of tailors awaiting examination immediately after the first ship had left, baldly stated that he had instructions to examine the non-Jews first."[37]

Disheartened by the selection process, the JLC mounted a campaign to apply pressure on Keenleyside. One of its allies was the CCF. David Lewis met with Keenleyside on 8 July 1948 to present the case for several specific individuals whose names had been submitted to the department by MP Stanley Knowles. He also presented the request for admission of other groups, including three refugees still captive in Shanghai, and asked for an explanation of the discrimination against Jewish DPs, especially domestics. In a letter to his father, Moshe, the secretary of the JLC, summarizing the meeting, David Lewis wrote:

He [Keenleyside] agreed (again this must be treated confidentially) that from the information, the Labour Department officials in Germany are very definitely discriminating against the admission of Jewish domestics ... With this information I shall feel a little stronger about putting the matter very frankly before Mr. MacNamara ... Whether he will be able to get any results or not is a different question. Between you and me, one of the difficulties is that while every word from Dr. Keenleyside can be relied on 100%, the same is not the case for other people ... There is no doubt that there is discrimination. However, there is equally no doubt that the situation in the past year or more has been very much better than it had been for the previous twenty-five years. The fact is that between 15 and 20% of all immigrants coming to Canada today are Jewish. In view of the special hardships to which the Jewish D.P.'s were subject for fifteen years, it certainly is not fair that so small a proportion of all immigrants should be Jews. On the other hand justice is never [a] complete monarch in the present immoral world.[38]

Discrimination against Jewish refugees in 1947–48 was even more widespread than Lewis suspected. In that year, 5.6 per cent of all immigrants were Jewish, in 1948–49, only 7.2 per cent were Jewish.[39] It has been estimated that over one-quarter of the DP's were Jews,[40] yet less than 12 per cent of those admitted to Canada were Jewish. While Enkin and Congress were playing the traditional *shtadlonist* (compliant) role in lauding the government initiative, barriers toward Jewish immigration were still being thrown up by Canadian bureaucrats in Ottawa and Europe. It is somewhat ironic that the delegation to select the workers was Jewish, but that its mandate was to find as many non-Jewish skilled tradespeople as Jewish ones.

As the workers arrived and were absorbed into the community, Congress, JIAS, and the JLC all took a measure of credit for the scheme. In his address to the CJC plenary in 1949, Monroe Abbey stated: "The Canadian Jewish Congress financed the further transportation costs for the immigrants and their families to the point of settlement (from the point of landing). There hostels had been set up to receive them until permanent housing was found. They were provided with the essentials for setting up their households. They were advised on the rudiments of housekeeping in Canada. The children were placed in schools and the tailors were given employment at prevailing rates of pay ... The housing problem was so severe that in Toronto Congress was forced to the expedient of purchasing houses for these immigrant workers." Abbey, however, did go on to state that Congress "enjoyed the co-operation" of JIAS and the JLC.[41]

The role of JIAS was crucial to the success of the project. At its National Executive Committee meeting in Toronto on 15 March 1947, the society urged the government "to implement its repeated declaration about assuming its rightful share of the solution of the D.P. problem."[42] At the JIAS conference in Toronto in January 1948, M.J. Coldwell, leader of the CCF, praised the organization's work on behalf of the needle workers. JIAS was asked by the JLC to take responsibility for the needs of workers sponsored by the committee. In a letter to M.A. Solkin, executive director for JIAS, Moshe Lewis wrote: "The Jewish Labour Committee is sponsoring a number of Jewish refugees for admission to Canada and we expect a limited number of immigrants to arrive during the year. As we are in no position (and our funds do not provide for this) to assist the new arrivals with housing, furnishing, etc., we are asking the Jewish Immigrant Aid Society to take care of them."[43]

The Jewish Labour Committee operated in the shadow of Congress. While the JLC saw itself as a grassroots organization representing the worker, with ties to the progressive forces in the labour movement and the CCF, the CJC commanded the spotlight in the Jewish community. With respect to the workers' project, however, the two organizations relied on each other, although the record in the community has given little recognition to the contribution of the JLC. Kalmen Kaplansky, the director of the committee had been born in Poland in 1912 and had worked as a typographer after immigrating to Canada in 1929.[44]

In presenting his own perspective, he redressed the slighting of the JLC in the workers' project.

The CJC of course claims 100 per cent credit for that [the project]. Well, I who lived through that period and the people with me don't think so ... The JLC said saving lives is the first priority ... Who were the spokespeople in Canada, the official policy was *shtadlonist* .... We had the support of the trade unions [but first] we had to turn around the anti-immigrant attitude of the trade unions .... When I started to work in 1946, the TLC [Trades and Labor Congress] had an anti-immigrant attitude ... So we decided to adopt a resolution at the TLC convention that said as follows: "Immigrants should be admitted on the economic absorptive capacity of the country, not on the basis of their race, colour, religion" ... We set up the tripartite committee of labour, manufacturers, and government. The TLC couldn't oppose the scheme when their own representatives were selecting immigrants. We joined in the presentations made to C.D. Howe. The big effort was to overcome the reluctance of the government to a Jewish project, so it was solved by making it a non-Jewish project as well as a Jewish project ... CJC gave 50 per cent of the funds and we gave 50 per cent. JIAS arranged for the workers' arrival here and we arranged their jobs and homes ... I met them in Montreal; in Halifax they were met by Lloyd Shaw – the father of Alexa McDonough, the current leader of the NDP – at our request .... David Lewis ... helped us establish contacts. We got a number of individual visas. In 1949 I got a list and received sixty-five or seventy visas by getting a letter, and the refugees showed it to immigration officials. Lenkinski and his family was one.[45]

The Lenkinski family came from Lodz, Poland. Louis, Helen, and their infant son, Berek, were sponsored by the JLC because Louis had been an active trade unionist in Poland. They had already spent almost two years in the Aschau bei Mueldorf camp in Bavaria when their application was processed on 20 December, 1948. It would take another year, however, until their admission was approved by the Immigration Branch. They finally left Europe in 1950.[46]

The workers' project would not have taken place without the efforts of the wider Jewish community. Congress was instrumental because of its lobbying efforts and its standing as the umbrella organization in the community. It could raise the funds and delegate its authority while continuing its gentle behind-the-scenes prodding of politicians and bureaucrats. JIAS was needed to help the refugees in their first weeks in Canada. But most important was the work of the JLC. It undertook the selection process, established the guarantees with the manufacturers, orchestrated the joint brief from the manufacturers and the unions, and helped to change anti-immigrant attitudes in the TLC. The project was also dependent upon the aid provided in Europe by the Joint, HIAS, and the IRO. While Keenleyside was instrumental in restructuring the immigration bureaucracy, the Jewish community still had to contend with entrenched discrimination. The workers' project was a central part of the community's initiative. It required incessant lobbying, fundraising, and coordination. But while two thousand or more Jewish refugees to found a new home in Canada, tens of thousands remained in Europe.

INTEGRATING THE POST-WAR REFUGEES

Between King's announcement of the new immigration policy and the spring of 1949, approximately 12,000 Jews entered and remained in Canada.[47] Their arrival presented a daunting challenge to the established community, which had to create an infrastructure that could absorb the newcomers. Although the Jewish organizations apportioned a large amount of money and received help from volunteers, these could not satisfactorily meet the task at hand. The community was overburdened, organizations replicated each other's work but were reluctant to divest themselves of their power, and they had to deal with the needs of the immigrants, which differed from those of previous waves.

Integration of the post-war refugees was unlike any previous effort at immigration absorption in the history of the Jewish community. The fundamental difference was that the survivors of the Holocaust came to Canada without the traditional support networks of earlier immigrants. Three factors accounted for this unique situation. First, few survivors had families in Canada, and those that did had been separated from them for at least two decades. Many of these "first degree" relatives were nieces and nephews who had never met their aunts and uncles. Unlike the huge wave of Jewish immigrants who arrived prior to and immediately after World War I, these people were bona fide refugees. Second, the traditional community organizations and support systems that had made integration into the community somewhat smoother thirty years earlier were in decline. The earlier immigrants had lived and worked with friends and family or had connections to individuals from the same towns and regions. Free-loan associations, small synagogues, *landsmanschaften*, ideologically based groups such as communists and the revisionist Zionists, and small local businesses were among the markers of Jewish urban life in North America until World War II. In the late 1940s that world was starting to change. Traditional neighbourhoods were being fractured as the suburbs, sometimes only a short distance away from the old areas, tempted young Jewish adults. The old neighbourhoods of the Main in Montreal and Spadina Avenue in Toronto were no longer the central preserve of Jewish life by 1950. With their decline, the immigrant culture was being eroded. Members of this generation, born and raised in the interwar period and having served God and King for Canada in the war, wanted to create new lives for themselves. They tended to be more educated than the average Canadian, English-speaking (although Yiddish was their first language), and less likely to enter the trades and small commerce that had sustained their parents.[48] Thus the immigrant community of the previous two generations was disintegrating just as the survivors were arriving.

The third factor was that the refugees were unlike their predecessors. In Jewish communities, newcomers had been referred to as *greeners* ("greenhorns"), while those who had "made it" were described as *gayle* (pronounced "gay-le," literally the yellow ones). In the late 1940s these terms took on a new meaning. The survivors resented the *greener* sobriquet. They considered it insulting, both personally and to their murdered families. Many felt that they were the last witnesses of a cultured, cosmopolitan Jewish civilization that had been destroyed during the war. Further, they believed that it was a civilization alien to their Canadian kindred, who had emigrated from a more primitive society. If anything, some felt that Canadian Jews were "green," at least those who lived and worked in the immigrant neighbourhoods. Canadian Jews were also hurt. Most of them had not "made it" and had recent memories of being called *greener* themselves. They had not been the recipients of community largesse when they arrived, and some were resentful of the services provided to the newcomers, many of whom, they believed, arrived with ill-gotten wealth. As Harris Silver remarked to the JLC upon his return from the DP camps, "some of these people are rich – they have made money in the Black market."[49]

Irrespective of the attitude of either the newcomers or Canadian Jews, the community had to deal with immediate needs of the former. The pressure upon Congress, its affiliates, and Jewish welfare organizations to absorb this influx was unprecedented, especially in Toronto and Montreal. Saul Hayes recognized that the community structures in their current form were unable to deal with this challenge. He also felt that the service segment of the community was too inexperienced to handle what was rapidly becoming a crisis. Consequently, in January 1949 he wrote to the Council of Jewish Federations and Welfare Funds (CJFWF) in New York City to ask for assistance. The council appointed Mary Palevsky, a member of its Social Planning Department, to undertake a survey of Congress and Jewish federations in Toronto and Montreal that were dealing with refugees.[50] To gain a clearer understanding of her report, it is necessary first to describe the organizational structure of the Jewish communities in Toronto and Montreal.

Organized community life in the two cities was a maze of interlocking funds, societies, and campaigns. Understanding the relationships between these groups requires an unravelling of a complex fabric that had evolved without an apparent plan in the interwar period. In general, the following picture emerges. The Canadian Jewish Congress acted as the national body , and as such, it established the United Jewish Relief Agency in 1938. The UJRA was the Canadian counterpart of the American Joint Distribution Committee (the Joint), which was responsible for the relief of European Jewry. The UJRA provided funds to the Joint, and the Joint operatives in Europe acted on behalf of the UJRA. Congress received its funds from annual campaigns in communities across the Canada. These were conducted by local federations.

The Toronto federation, the United Jewish Welfare Fund (UJWF), created in 1937, raised money for local and overseas relief. Some of these funds were directed to Congress, which then siphoned off a portion of its allocation to its three regional offices in Montreal (Eastern Region), Toronto (Central Region), and Winnipeg (Western Region). The remainder of the UJWF collection went to a number of social welfare agencies. These included the Jewish Family and Child Service (JFCS), the Jewish Vocational Service (JVS), and the Young Men's and Young Women's Hebrew Associations (YM and YWHA). These organizations worked with Jewish and non-Jewish residents and received most of their funds from the community chest, called the Red Feather Campaign and later the United Appeal. The contributions from the UJWF augmented these funds. In addition, a plethora of other organizations, from camps to schools to loan associations, received monies from the UJWF. Later the UJWF changed its name to the Toronto Jewish Congress, and it is now called the UJA/Federation. Until 1948 there was a second, separate, annual campaign in Toronto to raise money for Palestine called the Combined Palestine Appeal. Those funds went to the Zionist Organization of Canada. Since 1948 there has been one campaign, the United Jewish Appeal.[51]

In Montreal a slightly different scenario emerged. There were also two fundraising campaigns, one for local needs and another for overseas, until the early 1950s. These were the Combined Jewish Appeal and the War Victims Emergency Relief Appeal.[52] Unlike in Toronto, however, there was no local community chest. One of the recipients of the Combined Jewish Appeal was the Federation of Jewish Philanthropies. It became the Montreal Allied Jewish Community Services (AJCS) and now called the Federation CJA. One of its constituent agencies was the Baron de Hirsch Institute, which included the Family Welfare Department (FWD). Other agencies of the federation dealt with camps, geriatric care, health, vocational services, and a sanatarium. Outside the federation, the CJC, the Jewish General Hospital, and JIAS received funds from the Appeal. The YMHA and the Hospital of Hope did their own fundraising.[53]

The case of JIAS was somewhat anomalous. It had been created as a result of a Congress initiative during the first plenary in 1919. As already noted, it was the Canadian counterpart to the Hebrew Immigrant Aid Society established in the United States. An autonomous body independent of Congress, it co-operated with Congress in undertakings such as the workers' project. JIAS was based in Montreal, and in the late 1940s, filled a void in the social welfare area that could not be met by the federation. In Toronto, JIAS was superseded by the local federation, mainly because of poor leadership. Between 1947 and 1950 there were five directors of the local JIAS office.[54]

Three sets of organizations dealt with refugee absorption and integration: Congress, the local federations, and JIAS. In the late 1940s they were working both together and separately, at times duplicating functions. These problems were particularly acute in Toronto. There the Central Region of Congress had a direct hand in seven areas of immigration absorption, under the aegis of the UJRA/Central Region, chaired by Arthur Gelber. These were a housing division chaired by Jacob Shindman, who personally signed the note for the purchase of twenty-five houses for refugees; a loan division, which helped to fund the Hebrew Free Loan Association; a committee of European Youth (Orphans); funds diverted to the JFCS to deal with the emotional problems of the refugees; funds diverted to the JVS to provide counselling and job placement; funds to the YM and YWHA for recreation; and a scholarship committee to provide funds for promising orphans for secondary and post-secondary education.[55] Thus Congress had its own committees, which overlapped with similar structures in the federation and JIAS.

Mary Palevsky must have been astonished at this Byzantine bureaucracy when she began her research in the winter of 1949. The immediate problem, she surmised, was that the agencies were unable to cope with the ever-increasing caseload. At a meeting in Montreal in April, she stated, "The FWD machinery and standards are totally inadequate to meet either its normal load or the present expanded situation, let alone the additional load which is yet to come." With regard to the orphans, she pointed out that the FWD "did not handle the scheme as well as its counterpart in Toronto" since the children were "rushed into employment thus leading them to dead-end jobs," instead of being placed in educational training facilities. David Weiss, the chairman of the FWD, and Saul Hayes took opposing views on the role of their respective organizations. Hayes said that Congress could not "wash its hands" of the programs for which it had ultimate responsibility, and that the Baron de Hirsch Institute had refused to take part in the orphans' scheme. Weiss agreed with Palevsky inasmuch as she recommended that Congress should withdraw from any administrative role in local activities. Palevsky noted that this discussion confirmed her conviction that the communities in both Montreal and Toronto were "very complex, confused and difficult."[56]

Two months later, a national conference of professional social welfare agencies was held in Toronto. Its roster was a who's who of the bureaucrats in the Jewish community at the time. That such a conference was held, and that the leading lights were there, underscores the problems in the community regarding refugee absorption. Palevsky provided an interim report to the conference. In summary, she made three recommendations: first, that Congress had to act both as a local agency and as a national one since there was not enough time for the local agencies to get ready; second, that in Montreal the immediate needs were being well met by JIAS, and co-operation between Congress and the agencies was satisfactory, but that the referral service, housing, and recreational facilities were poor; there the family agency needed to be strengthened "immediately" and an immigration section should be established; and third, that in Toronto, temporary shelter and community co-operation were poor, and that overall responsibility should be transferred to the JFCS. The ensuing discussion dealt with the need for professional social workers and the dearth of individuals with this training. The conference urged that Palevsky's report be written without delay.[57]

The report was an elaboration of her preliminary findings, revealed in the spring. Its summary of findings and recommendations began as follows:

> The settlement of thousands of immigrants is essentially a large scale welfare operation. The resources for an operation of such scope were lacking in Canada. Canadian communities are not well organized to serve the normal demands of even the native population. Confronted by the need to extend its limited resources to meet the urgent and almost unlimited needs of the immigrants, the program collapsed at pressure points and emergency measures had to be improvised from day to day.
>
> On the whole, therefore, the services for the immigrants were not well administered because there was a lack of (1) clarity ... (2) advanced planning .... (3) sufficient numbers of professional qualified workers (4) professional direction.
>
> Despite these shortcomings the services for the orphans achieved reasonably well the objectives of care and protection ... The other immigrants fared less well.[58]

The report's recommendations provided the details and specifics for those made in the interim findings. On the national level, Congress was to retain its role as the national coordinator for the refugee program. In Montreal, coordination and planning was to be done by the federation, while in Toronto the Jewish Family and Child Service would inherit the responsibility from the UJRA, and housing functions, now divided between Congress and JIAS, would be combined into one department. Palevsky continued that, "in spite of Congress' venture into real estate the present situation is far from satisfactory."[59] Among the noteworthy comments in the report was her finding that "there has been a certain amount of rivalry, duplication, and overlapping of activities between Congress and JIAS."[60] She chided Congress for pressing the claims of the Jewish groups "without stopping to consider all the implications or to count the cost. Congress never knew from one project to another, whether its advocacy with Government would succeed, or, if successful, how much time would be available for implementation ... At no time, had Congress intended to supply a full-scale social welfare operation for the care of the immigrants."[61]

After the report was presented, there was a flurry of activity for three months. Gurston Allen, a member of the survey committee, wrote to Hayes with his own responses to Palevsky's specific recommendations. Aside from agreeing with the first point, that Congress retain its role a national coordinator, he questioned some points and rejected others. He felt that services had been transferred to the JFCS already inasmuch as Congress had allocated funds to the various welfare agencies in Toronto. Hayes responded by stating that in both Montreal and Toronto, consultation and co-operation between the local federations and Congress was ongoing anyway, and that many of Palevsky's recommendations were either being carried out or were not applicable.[62] Nevertheless, Congress was still reluctant to abdicate its supervisory position. Arthur Gelber, representing a dissenting view, wrote to Hayes: "I don't think there is a great deal to be gained by any lengthy discussion of the report, which if anything, is fairly well dated as far as Toronto is concerned. The only point of real interest to me is her recommendation that Congress get out of the social welfare business. With this, I am heartily in agreement, but seem to be having a great deal of difficulty convincing my colleagues of the Central Region executive to agree, even on principle."[63]

Ben Lappin, the executive director of the Central Region, represented the predominant view. He wrote to Hayes that "there is ... a unanimity of feeling regarding the coordinative function, and all members of the Regional Executive committee feel that if Congress is to pay the shot, it must control and supervise the projects being carried out by the direct functioning agencies."[64] Nevertheless, the UJRA (i.e., Congress) did transfer the casework to the local agencies, with JIAS responsible for reception services for the first month and the JFCS thereafter.[65]

After that, the Palevsky report disappeared from the minutes of Congress committees or the correspondence of Congress officials and lay people. Its recommendations and its critique of the delivery of services to the new immigrants were not made public. Even Ben Kayfetz, who as director of the JCRC was involved in community affairs, but whose office did not have a direct hand in immigrant aid, says that the report's recommendations were unknown to him. This comment would indicate that the report was available only to the professionals and lay people who were directly involved in immigration absorption. Kayfetz read the report for the first time during our discussions in the mid-1990s. He felt that Palevsky could not have conceived that a national organization had the resources and ability to deliver local services. Since she was American, he surmised that she assumed that, since such a project would not be possible in the United States, the same would be true of Canada.[66] Ben Lappin, who *was* directly involved in immigrant aid as the director of the Central Region, viewed the report as political "gainsmanship" on the part of the local federations to wrest control away from Congress and also move social welfare from the hands of volunteers to professional social workers, a process that was flourishing in the United States. Lappin, who became a professor of social work at the University of Toronto after leaving Congress, saw the report as a "stone in the slide" leading to the diminution of Congress.[67]

Five conclusions can be drawn in evaluating the absorption of the survivors. First, in the context of the late 1940s, the community had little choice but to deal with the influx of immigrants in an ad hoc manner. Government policies, bureaucratic decisions, and ship schedules were outside the purview of the community. It had little warning when a change in policy or the whim of an immigration or labour authority would signal the release of applicants from the camps. After lobbying for years for the freeing of refugees, the community could not then complain to the authorities that they were allowing too many to enter the country. On the contrary, too few Jews were being allowed in. Until 1949, discrimination against Jewish refugees was rife, and as the correspondence reveals, Congress, the JLC, and the *landsmanschaften* regularly complained about roadblocks in the process. Thus to condemn the community for not being prepared is to deny the underlying premise of its initiative and to question its humanitarian impulse, which played a minor role in the immigrants' ability to finally leave Europe.

A second observation is that the plethora of bodies within the established Jewish community was both a product of its relative weakness in Canadian society and of the divisions within the community. Congress, despite the vision and fortitude of Hayes and many lay people, had not succeeded in uniting Canadian Jewry in the 1940s. The task was extremely difficult because of fractures, ideological, religious, regional, or class-based, and it was complicated by the transition from an immigrant culture to the Canadianization of the second and third generations. That there were scores of social welfare agencies is not surprising, given the history of Jewish communal self-help organizations, and it is understandable that no group was willing to divest itself of its position in the community. Congress had undertaken the financing of the orphans' project as part of its agreement with the government; Congress, JIAS, and the JLC had to lobby, fund, and administer the workers' project; the local federations had to provide the services for these immigrants and the thousands of others who came via different schemes. At no time did any level of government commit itself to provide monies or services. The Jewish community, still without political clout and still divided, was left to fend for itself.

Third, given the rapidly evolving situation between 1947 and 1949, the community did nevertheless mobilize itself to provide services, albeit without a central direction and without performing a satisfactory job in all areas. Within weeks of King's announcement, arrangements had been made for fundraising efforts and for the reception of the first expected immigrants, the orphans. When it was apparent a year later that the community was ill-equipped to deal with the influx, Congress called for an assessment of the situation, which resulted in the Palevsky report. Thus there was a continued effort to meet the challenge of absorption, and while most of the initiatives fell short of expectations, the spirit and intent of the enterprise cannot be underrated.

A fourth conclusion is that the leaders glossed over the mismanagement of some aspects of the absorption process in order to provide a positive perspective to their constituents, upon whom the organizations depended for funding and volunteers. The Palevsky report, released on 13 October 1949, revealed more than Hayes and Congress wanted to know. It was critical of the community's attempt to integrate the newcomers. According to Palevsky, the central problem was the relationship between Congress and the local federations. The report was shelved, most of its recommendations were not followed, it was never mentioned in Congress publications, and until now, it has been unknown to all but the survey committee. The community at large was left with the impression that immigration absorption was progressing smoothly, a perception that remained for decades.[68] The report, however, vindicates the view of many survivors that the established community was ill-equipped to deal with their needs, yet put up a public front that it was successful in helping them to acclimatize themselves to their new home.

Fifth, the crisis in immigration absorption was short-lived. With the transferral of services to the federations, and with the professionalization of social work, the structures for integration had become more solidly based by the early 1950s. Further, the projects which the community had to fund, the orphans and the workers, were coming to a close by 1950. While immigration remained high until 1954, many of the newcomers who arrived after 1950 were sponsored or, more likely, were allowed entry because of further relaxation in the regulation. When they did arrive, both the organized community and the first group of survivors were able to meet many of their needs. By 1954 the survivors had established their own network of self-help groups, and newcomers were less dependent upon the established community.[69]

That the Jewish community fell short in its integration of the survivors in the late 1940s is not an astonishing revelation. It did not have a single vision regarding the newcomers. Community leaders were still powerless and somewhat obsequious in their relations with government officials. In 1948 approximately 10,000 Holocaust survivors emigrated to Canada. More Jews arrived in that year than in any year since the 1920s. Their entry could not have gone unnoticed, especially in Toronto and Montreal. In the traditional interwar immigrant neighbourhoods in those cities, the 1948 immigrants would have constituted between 15 and 20 per cent of the Jewish population. Given their knowledge of the ghettoes and German-run camps, and of efforts to free the survivors from the displaced persons' camps made by the organized community, Canadian Jews could not have been unenlightened about who these people were and what they had gone through. Yet there is little indication that the established community in the late 1940s was interested in their experience. An analysis of the *Jewish Chronicle*, the most important English-language newspaper in the Jewish community at that time, is instructive as to what is not found there. Not a single article on the survivors' experiences, as expressed by them themselves, appeared in 1948. While there were pieces on the orphans' and workers' projects and the odd snippet on conditions in the DP camps, no apparent interest was expressed in discovering who these immigrants were, what they had lost, how they had survived, and what obstacles they had faced between the end of the war and their entry into Canada. Aside from the series on the workers' project by Bernard Shane, there were only self-congratulatory pieces by Ben Meyer of JIAS and Saul Hayes.[70] This neglect was not limited to the *Chronicle*, but was evident throughout the Jewish press in general.[71] At the Congress plenary in 1949, there was much chest-thumping about the organization's role in orchestrating the orphans' project and its contribution to the workers' scheme, and about its redoubtable role in bringing about changes to immigration policy, but there were no workshops, resolutions, or discussions about the survivors themselves. Indeed, survivors were conspicuously absent from Congress plenaries until the 1960s, and their concerns were not given a hearing until 1965.

Simply put, the experience of the survivors was not a high priority for most of Canada's Jews at this time. The impact of the Holocaust as a defining tragedy for all Jews and a watershed event in modern times was long in coming. As Ben Lappin relates, "We couldn't believe that it happened and they [the survivors] disbelieved that it happened."[72] More importantly, the established community submerged its "unbelief" because it had other more pressing considerations. One was the situation in Palestine. The passage of Palestine from a British mandate to a Jewish state in the years 1947 to 1949 preoccupied the community, and justifiably so.[73] Another priority was the transition that the Canadian Jewish community was undergoing. As we have observed, it was beginning the geographical and psychological move from the immigrant neighbourhoods to the suburbs. Moreover, the war had changed both Canada's Jews and Canadians themselves. The former had served in the conflict, in a higher proportion than the rest of the population, and had returned with the intention of creating a new life that was substantially different from that of their predecessors. Canadian society was also changing, with regard to its institutional policies on Jews. Beginning in the mid-1940s, substantial revisions of human rights legislation succeeded in eliminating the most blatant antisemitic restrictions. Consequently, Canadian Jews, especially those born after 1910, no longer considered themselves to be immigrants but Canadians.

The arrival of Jewish refugees in Canada in the late 1940s was entirely due to changes in immigration policy. These changes were reflective of the economic transformation in the country after the war. There is little evidence that humanitarianism motivated Ottawa's mandarins. The organized Jewish community, while actively lobbying for a relaxation in immigration restrictions, was largely a spectator rather than an actor in the process. Its most noteworthy contribution was in persuading the government to allow the orphans' and workers' projects, which accounted for about 20 per cent of the Jewish newcomers. Upon their arrival, Jewish organizations were faced with the difficulty of absorbing the refugees. The existing infrastructure proved to be less than adequate to meet their needs, and many immigrants were ill-served. On another level, the community was even less responsive to the immigrants. Most Canadian Jews were unwilling or unable to listen to the experiences of the newcomers. This insensitivity was also evident in the absence of survivor voices in the ethnic press and at Congress meetings. It is not surprising, therefore, that a gulf emerged between the newcomers and Canadian Jews. This breach would widen in the 1950s.

3 "Europe's ghosts in Canadian living rooms": The Canadian Jewish Community in the 1950s

Philip Weiss came to Winnipeg in 1948. He had been born in Poland in 1924 and had survived the death camp at Auschwitz. He recalled his first years in Canada:

They were hard years. We had full freedom, but still from a point of spiritual satisfaction, there was a lot to be desired. You had to start anew; you were an immigrant. We didn't have relatives. We were strangers in a strange land. You were not fully accepted, even in Jewish circles. There were barriers between Canadian citizens and those who survived. We were all considered to be greener, and we were to a certain degree ... For a certain period of time everything was dark; you could not be as happy as the Canadian who didn't go through the experiences of the Second World War. It was a tremendous burden which a former inmate carried for a lengthy period of time. Eventually the barriers broke. For me it took a minimum of twenty years.[1]

Cyril Levitt, a third-generation Canadian Jew, born in Toronto in 1946, remembers that when he was growing up, "the Holocaust was never broached directly in my house. It was kind of a disease that one didn't talk about." Regarding the survivors, he recalls that "they were the butt of jokes. At the same time there was this sense that they were all a little bit crazy, that you couldn't really treat them as normal people. [It was] due to partly fear, partly pity, partly a sense of stigma. We called them 'greenies' ... The Holocaust was constantly being swept under the rug. It wasn't until post-1967 that the established community came onside."[2]

Philip Weiss and Cyril Levitt represent two of the faces of post-war Canadian Jewry. Born in different generations, one a Holocaust survivor and the other a child of middle-class Canadians, they describe the contrasting worlds of the survivor and the Canadian Jew and how they each relegated the memory of the Holocaust to the depths of their collective consciousness. Although their viewpoints were dissimilar, their conclusions are not. Until the 1960s most survivors and many Canadian Jews worked and lived side by side but knew little of each other's background. In Toronto and Montreal, and to a lesser degree in smaller cities with sizable Jewish communities, they were two distinct groups. They were separated by their experiences, their perceptions of each other, their languages, their associations, and their position in the ethnic community. The one common denominator for both in the 1950s was their desire to climb the socio-economic ladder.

THE ESTABLISHED COMMUNITY

The Canadian Jewish community in the 1950s was led by the children and grandchildren of immigrants. This cohort, born or raised in Canada in the first quarter of the century, was unlike its parents. It had contributed to the war effort, been educated in Canadian schools, become disproportionately over-represented in the professional world,[3] and abandoned the language and customs of the immigrant neighbourhoods where it had lived. As systemic antisemitism and ethnic discrimination receded in the more liberal atmosphere of post-war Canada, Canadian Jews were no longer preoccupied with fighting the battles of the previous decades. The war was over, immigration barriers had been lifted, economic prosperity and the emerging welfare state had erased the vestiges of the Depression mentality, and Israel had been established as the national homeland for all Jews. These individuals were bent on advancing from the fringes of the Canadian mosaic into the mainstream of Canadian society. They were a community in transition, from the immigrant neighbourhoods to the suburbs, from the plethora of storefront synagogues, union halls, and ideological groups to large-scale congregations and service clubs. Yiddish culture, as represented in the ethnic press, the labour halls, the theatres, and most significantly, in street life, was vanishing in the 1950s, as the Jewish community had gained the acceptance of most Canadians. Jews were becoming part of the process that historian Harold Troper has described as the "whitening of Euro-ethnics."[4]

During this period of transition, the concentration on creating a unified voice and gaining recognition within Canadian society left little opportunity for established Jewry to consider the experiences of the survivors. As for remembering the Holocaust, for most Canadian Jews it was painful reminder of Jewish powerlessness, of submission to unbearable dehumanization without resistance, which disturbed the new image of the confident Canadian Jew who celebrated the apparent miraculous rebirth of the Jewish state as both a historical and a spiritual emergence. The community continued to be committed, with good reason, to the immediate needs of the survivors, but as the 1950s wore on and as the influx of survivors diminished, this concern became less pressing. Simply put, the vast majority of Canadian Jews remained estranged from the memory of the Holocaust.

For four decades, Saul Hayes was the most notable public servant in the Canadian Jewish community. Born in Montreal in 1906 and educated at McGill University, where he earned degrees in social work and law, he was appointed lecturer in social work in 1932 and entered Jewish communal life in 1940 as executive director of the United Jewish Relief Agencies of Canada. Two years later he became executive director of Congress, subsequently upgraded to executive vice-president, a position he would hold until his retirement in the late 1970s. He had spearheaded the community's effort to have immigration restrictions relaxed during and after the war and served on a myriad of committees, especially those devoted to human rights.[5] Saul Hayes was the leading voice of the Canadian Jewish community at home and abroad. No other individual in this century has played as important a role in articulating the needs of the community and in shaping its identity. His speeches and articles as executive director of the CJC addressed the Jewish agenda from the perspective of the mainstream. Although he had his critics, both religious and ideological, he earned the respect accorded him by the vast majority of Canadian Jews.

Three of Hayes's pronouncements in the 1940s and 1950s reveal the main interests and developments in the community in the post-war era. In May 1949 he reported on the state of antisemitism in Canada. While admitting that there was still discrimination against Jewish white-collar workers in banks and that there were no Jews on the Toronto police force and only six in Montreal, he pointed out that no laws, federal, provincial, or municipal, discriminated against Jews or any other identifiable group, except Japanese Canadians. Hayes declared: "Antisemitism does not present an immediate menace to the Jewish community today ... Although there is no immediate cause for undue concern, the resources of the Canadian Jewish community are mobilized currently in the defense of the Jewish position in the Dominion."[6]

In 1953 Hayes extolled the changes that had occurred in the post-war community and reflected upon the challenges facing it. He wrote: "The Canadian Jewish Community, young and small though it is, has matured 'all of a sudden.' The tragic events of the recent war have made Canada the sixth largest free Jewish community in the world." He argued that Canadian Jews could no longer look to Europe as a source of leadership because of the destruction of that civilization and because Israel had become the haven for most of the refugees. Canadian Jews now faced the problem of social integration while maintaining their identity. "In Canada, the Jews are and always will be a small minority of persons individually integrated into the social, economic and political life of the country, while as a group they strive to retain their religious and cultural identity in a democracy which permits them to worship and live their lives in accordance with their establishment of Jewish community councils". But Hayes warned that these councils could not act as substitutes for the national functions carried out by Congress. Despite the growth of the community in the immediate post-war years, he reminded his readers that there were fewer Jews in Canada than in Philadelphia, Chicago, or Los Angeles, and that despite the preponderance of Jewish settlement in urban areas, there were 595 towns and villages that were home to fewer than ten Jewish families.[7]

At the Conference of World Jewish Organizations in 1958, Hayes reported on the state of the Canadian community. He noted that Canadian Jewry had grown by 47 per cent since 1945, but that the rates of immigration had receded between 1953 and 1956 and that there was a relatively low incidence of intermarriage. He stressed that the role of Congress was "the perpetuation of a heritage. The heritage consists of our Canadian way of life, our Jewish traditions, our place in the British Commonwealth of Nations, our New World hopes, our relationships with a homeland reconstituted, our values steeped in age-old legacies." He extolled the role of Congress in urging the postmaster general of Canada to bar the use of the mails for the circulation of antisemitic materials and in the campaign against discriminatory practices in employment, housing, and services.[8]

It is noteworthy that, over the course of almost a decade, Hayes had little to say about the impact of the Holocaust on Canadian Jews, and that he omitted specific reference to the arrival of the survivors in these reports. This neglect was due more to his background and connection with the leaders of the community, who were preponderantly established businessmen and professionals, than to any deliberate evasion of the issue. Saul Hayes was the embodiment of the new Canadian Jew, a charter member of the first generation whose members did not regard themselves as immigrants. The estrangement of this cohort from their European roots insulated them from the grief and emotional needs of the survivors. Certainly, Hayes regarded the Holocaust as a seminal and tragic event in contemporary Jewish life, as witnessed by other speeches and the energy that he devoted to fighting immigration restrictions and sponsoring survivors. Rather, his comments reflect the community feeling at that time – that the Holocaust was not a defining element in Canadian Jewish identity.

The established community did play a role in commemorating the Holocaust on the anniversary of the Warsaw Ghetto Uprising. This was largely a perfunctory effort, since from the beginning the memorial was organized by the Federation of Polish Jews. In the absence of an official ceremony in 1947, the federation informed Congress that it would undertake the organization of the event.[9] In 1948, on the fifth anniversary of the uprising, Congress sent congratulatory telegrams to observances in Montreal, Winnipeg, and Warsaw. In 1952 it joined the JLC and the Labour Zionist Movement in organizing the event in Montreal. A year later, on the tenth anniversary, the Jewish Public Library in Montreal hosted an exhibit of "Jewish Sufferings during World War II"; eight hundred people attended the service.[10]

Noticeably absent from the organizing committee of these early events were the survivors themselves. The Organization for the Warsaw Ghetto Remembrance in Toronto did not include survivors, nor did the committee in Vancouver. Sophie Waldman, a survivor who came to Vancouver in 1951, attended the memorial the following year. She was determined to become involved. "I decided more had to be done; I was the first to call a meeting with my friends. Only two families were survivors and others came during the war, some through Japan. We decided to start a memorial for the Warsaw Ghetto Uprising in 1953 in a synagogue and then in the community centre ... I think we were the first in Canada to have this service ... This is how I got involved in the community."[11] Mrs Waldman would remain chair of the committee until 1986. She may have been the first Holocaust survivor to gain a position of leadership in the Jewish community. At its plenary session in 1959, the CJC resolved "that the Canadian Jewish Congress, in reconfirming the date of 27th day of *Nisan* as the date for the solemnization of the Ghetto *Yahrzeit* [annual commemoration], requests all communities in Canada to observe the Yahrzeit on this date."[12] The resolutions establishing the official date of the commemoration were the only ones dealing with the Holocaust proposed at Congress plenaries in the 1950s.

TRANSITION AND CHANGE

The 1950s saw the largest growth of Jewish population in any decade in Canadian history. Between 1951 and 1961 the community grew by more than 60,000, an increase of 31 per cent.[13] Some 40,000 immigrants arrived during this decade, of whom approximately 36,000 remained in Canada.[14] It is impossible to determine the exact number of Holocaust survivors and their children, since their wartime experience was not a criterion for admission. We do know that between 1945 and 1957, 26,000 immigrants whose country of last residence had been under the domination of the Third Reich arrived via ocean ports. It can be assumed that almost all of these immigrants were Holocaust survivors. A further 26,000 came from other countries or via the United States, a number of whom were survivors.[15] One estimate of 36,500 survivors resident in Canada in 1953 is too high, since it postulates that all the post-war immigrants were survivors, and the contention in another study that 12 to 15 per cent of Canadian Jews in 1951 were survivors is also an overestimate.[16]

Using the data available, I have drawn the following conclusions:

1   From 1945 to 1956 between 30,000 and 35,000 survivors and their descendants immigrated to and remained in Canada, constituting 13 to 15 per cent of Canadian Jews in 1961.
2   Of the "natural increase" of 27,286 Jews between 1946 and 1956, about 4,000 were children born to survivors.[17]
3   Some 6,000 Hungarian Jews immigrated in 1957, most of whom were survivors or their descendants.[18]
4   In absolute terms, the influx of survivors to Canada was small in comparison with the estimated 250,000 who went to Israel and the 137,500 said to have gone to the United States up to 1952.[19]
5   In relative terms, the influx of survivors was high. They represented 3 per cent of the total number of immigrants to Canada in the decade after the war.[20] More significantly, the proportion of 13 to 15 per cent was far greater than the ratio of survivors (approximately 4 per cent) in American Jewry in the same period.

Consequently, the impact of the survivors on the political and social dynamic of the Canadian Jewish community, while muted until the 1960s, was to become increasingly dramatic over time. One estimate determines that 20 per cent of Jewish households in Montreal in 1978 were headed by Holocaust survivors and that there were thirty-one organizations of survivors active there at that time.[21]

The rapid growth of the Jewish population and the proportionately significant number of Holocaust survivors impacted on the demography of the community in the 1950s, but another trend was also significant. The community had changed from a predominantly Yiddish-speaking and urban-based one to one that was English-speaking and suburban. In 1931, 95.4 per cent of Canadian Jews had listed Yiddish as their first language; twenty years later the figure had dropped to 50.6 per cent, and in 1961 it was 29.6 per cent. Meanwhile, of the Jews born in Canada, only 13.5 per cent in 1961 reported that Yiddish was their first language in contrast to 59.4 per cent of foreign-born Jews.[22] The 1961 census also revealed the shift from traditional urban neighbourhoods to the suburbs. In Toronto 49,000 Jews lived in the city in 1941, while only a few thousand were found in the suburbs. By 1961 only 19,000 lived in the city, and 45,000 in suburban North York; these represented more than half the total of 89,000 who lived in Metropolitan Toronto. In Montreal the transition was less dramatic. In 1941, 80.2 per cent lived in the city; twenty years later, of the 103,000 Jews in the metropolitan area, 62.5 per cent were resident in the city. In metropolitan Winnipeg 64.9 per cent lived in the city in 1961, whereas virtually all the Jewish population had been found there twenty years earlier.[23] In Vancouver 44 per cent of the Jews in the metropolitan area lived in the city in 1951; a decade later only 16 per cent were city-based.[24]

The transition was most telling in the changing economic climate, the reorganization of community institutions, the construction of large synagogues and educational facilities, and the concurrent decline of the secular and ideologically based societies of earlier decades. David Rome described the situation in Montreal. The post-war era was "accompanied by a newer Jewish economic structure. The years since Hitler had seen the disappearance of a particular type of ghetto poverty, with the militancy of the garment factories, its independent stores and its host of service outlets in mutually supporting roles. The quiet revolution destroyed that particular labour class ... Many of the younger generation shifted to the professions with newer ideologies. Language [presumably fluency in English and French] was no longer a barrier; it was mastered by ingenious graduates of Baron Byng [high school] and the doctoral students of McGill and of the Université de Montréal."[25] In smaller cities with a sizable Jewish population, such as Winnipeg, London, and Windsor, new synagogues and schools were erected.[26] This growth was accompanied by communal restructuring, whereby smaller welfare groups coalesced into large-scale, professionally administered associations. Examples include the Va'ad Hair (Jewish community council) in Ottawa and the Jewish Family Service in Edmonton.[27]

The emergence of broad-scale community structures and the demise of the traditional neighbourhoods had profound effects on the community. The *Yiddishe Gass* (Jewish street) became extinct, and with it, the battles between communists and socialists, bundists and Zionists, and among other ideological groups disappeared.[28] According to Ben Kayfetz, "the 1950s were a period of transition. The values and traditions were changing the face of Canada. [There was] a Jewish mayor [Nathan Phillips, elected in Toronto in 1954]; officialdom was not necessarily Anglo-Saxon; hospitals, a symbol of discrimination, were taking in Jewish doctors. This was not visible, except by omission."[29]

Two developments had caused this transition: economic prosperity and the ebbing of antisemitism. The first is chronicled in numerous studies.[30] The reduction in antisemitic activity reflected the trend toward legislation against discrimination in employment, housing, and education. Congress was in the forefront in working with federal and provincial leaders in this initiative. In Ontario in 1944, the government of George Drew adopted the Ontario Discrimination Act which banned signs prohibiting minority groups, such as the "No Jews or Dogs Allowed" signs that had been displayed prominently in parks and private facilities in the province. Prodded by the Joint Public Relations Committee of Congress and B'nai Brith, the government of Leslie Frost passed the Fair Employment Practices Code in 1951, opening the door to more laws at the provincial and federal levels. Other organizations, such as unions, churches, the Canadian Civil Liberties Association, the YMCA, and the Canadian Association for Adult Education, played key roles in these initiatives.[31] As Ben Kayfetz relates, "[By the 1960s] Canada had the most advanced anti-discrimination laws (based on race and religion) in the world."[32]

Although the 1950s were the most tranquil decade in this century with regard to overt antisemitism, the virus was still very much alive. In Quebec, Adrien Arcand, while not the force of earlier times, continued to instill his views in a small group of followers. More importantly, antisemitic attitudes had not eroded, although a rapprochement was being established between the Jewish community and some circles within the Roman Catholic Church and the intelligentsia.[33] In western Canada several groups publicly disseminated antisemitic vitriol. The most notable was the Social Credit Party, which had a political stranglehold on British Columbia and Alberta. Percy Young, a delegate to the B.C. Socred convention in 1957, declared, "Zionism has completely destroyed Christianity and it will destroy Social Credit too, unless the people have proper education." B.C. premier W.A.C. Bennett did not disassociate himself from this comment. Writing in the *Dawson Creek Star* on 15 November 1957, Young denounced "Zionists, not Jews." Ernest Manning, the long-time premier of Alberta, refused to act as honorary chairman for Brotherhood Week in 1957 unless "all Jews converted to Christianity." Another group, much less prominent than the Social Credit Party but more persistent in its antisemitism, has been the British Israel Association of Greater Vancouver. For forty years it has kept up the rhetoric that Christian values are being poisoned by "Zionist" subversives.[34] Another source of extreme antisemitism was Ron Gostick, who for four decades (from the 1950s to the 1990s) has been a writer and purveyor of hate literature. Gostick was most notorious as the editor of the *Canadian Intelligence Service*, based in Flesherton, Ontario. His tireless devotion to rooting out the "menace of the international Jewish conspiracy" has been a long-running irritant to the Jewish community, and it contributed to the antisemitic movement of the 1960s.[35]

Antisemitism had also not been eradicated in the Department of Immigration. Visas were routinely denied to Israelis, and many Jews from Romania and Hungary who applied to immigrate in the 1950s were denied entry obstensibly because at the height of the Cold War they were considered a potentially subversive element.[36] Antisemitic attitudes were still deeply engrained in the Canadian social fabric. An article in the *New Liberty Magazine* in 1957, entitled "How Race-Haters Bait Canada's 230,000 Jews," provided examples of anti-Jewish attitudes and discrimination, ranging from Gostick's publication to the exclusion of Jews from private golf courses, banks, university fraternities, and curling clubs.[37] The age-old canard that they controlled finance and manufacturing was still being given an airing in some circles, even though there were few Jews on the higher rungs of either sector.[38]

Nevertheless, in comparison to the preceding decades, antisemitism was insignificant in the 1950s. While opportunities for advancement to the highest echelons of the power structure were limited, restrictions elsewhere were rapidly disappearing. Jews born and raised in Canada in the pre-war era were finally passing as "ordinary Canadians." For many, this development was enough to cement their bond to the present and distance them from their immigrant background. It also meant that the destruction of the Jewish world in Europe a decade earlier was receding from their collective memory.

Jewish organizations nevertheless maintained their commitment to press for restitution to the survivors. Assistance was given to victims of Nazi persecution in applying for indemnification from West Germany and Austria. In 1953, following negotiations between the World Jewish Congress and the West German government, the United Restitution Organization (URO) was established; in Canada it came under the aegis of Congress. Its director was Manfred Saalheimer, a German immigrant who had served the CJC in various capacities since 1942.[39] URO offices were established in Toronto, Winnipeg, and Vancouver, and the head office in Montreal. During its first three years of operation, URO Canada assisted 8,900 persons, of whom an estimated 95 per cent were former DPS. Over $2 million was distributed to 2.000 claimants in that period. In the next three years a further $8 million was collected, and of the 11,600 claimants, 6,500 files were still active. URO Canada employed thirty former European lawyers as clerical personnel and translators. The Congress committee was chaired by Saul Hayes and included Sol Kanee, a future vice-president of the World Jewish Congress and president of the CJC in the early 1970s.[40]

About 40 per cent of the claimants lived in Toronto. In 1953 an average of 40 applications were made weekly, and with changes in indemnification laws in West Germany, the numbers increased. By the end of 1954, over 1,600 new cases were on file. The monthly costs of operating the Toronto office came to $1,300, not including the time spent by Saalheimer and Executive Director Ben Lappin and his staff.[41] These costs were offset by the decrease in other aspects of immigration relief. One example was the expenditure on immigrant Jewish youth by the Jewish Family and Child Service, which between 1948 and 1952 was $356,477. By contrast, the total JFCS budget in 1955 was only $46,770. Another example was aid provided by JIAS. The society's report of March 1952 showed that 151 families were getting assistance. A year later only 41 individuals were on the rolls. At the JIAS regional plenary in 1956, the only mention of immigrant aid was to restitution claims.[42] Most of the Holocaust survivors had arrived by then, and most no longer need for economic assistance.

LIFE IN A NEW LAND

For the survivors, the 1950s were also a period of transition. Many had created new lives for themselves in the refugee camps and cities of war-ravaged Europe prior to immigration. Some had married or remarried and borne children, resumed their education or learned new skills, and prepared themselves for integration into North American society before they left Europe. Upon their arrival in Canada, they were preoccupied with finding accommodation and employment and establishing communal networks with other survivors. For the most part, they were not concerned with relating their experiences to Canadian Jews, especially since their memories were so fresh and painful. For those who did speak, the response ranged from shock to incomprehension to derision. Many had difficulty discussing their experiences even with their families.

Donia Clenman was a survivor of labour camps in Poland. She came to Toronto, married a Canadian Jew, and raised a family. A gifted poet, she recalls those years in her work.

Sometimes
I am a stranger to my family
for I bring Europe's ghosts
into the well-lit living room
of Canadian internationalism ....
I was no child on arrival
and yet, so well assimilated.
Even my verses are native,
and I dream in good English too.[43]

Although it has been more than half a century since the first survivors came to Canada, both Canadian Jews and survivors have retained sharp images of those first years. Individual experiences and personal viewpoints colour each witness's memory of that time, but a pattern emerges with little variation. From the standpoint of Canadian Jews whom I interviewed, the predominant perspective is that the immigrants were a welcome addition to the community. Joseph Kage, the demographer and historian of Jewish immigration, remembered that the community's attitude was "very receptive from the beginning." Canadians "had to deal with the shock of the Holocaust" at first, but by the 1950s they were ready to reflect upon the tragedy. Sydney Harris, who was president of Congress in the mid-1970s, recalled that although "the survivors (were) a fairly contained group, the established community was glad that they had come." Kalmen Kaplansky of the Jewish Labour Committee, himself an immigrant, stated: "I can speak only of our group. [We had] open arms; it was a tremendous experience; we [the JLC] used to organize all sorts of things ... If not for them Jewish life would have been very much impoverished, they contributed to the Yiddish-speaking element ... [It was] a period of great excitement that lasted for a couple of years, until they became indistinguishable. What is the difference, after a while; you're here five years or fifteen years in the country. In '47 I was seventeen years in the country, in '57 they were here for ten years."[44]

The influx of the newcomers was not felt equally by Canadian Jews. Philip Givens, who became mayor of Toronto in 1964 and then a member of Parliament, was born in Toronto in 1922. He was an only child of parents who lost relatives in Europe. Yet when the immigrants arrived, he said, "you didn't notice them. It was almost imperceptible; you didn't see it. So I didn't know how I felt. The only family out of scores that came was my mother's sister with five kids. Slowly I became conscious of the fact because I was fluent in Yiddish." Larry Zolf, a writer and CBC journalist since the 1960s, was a schoolboy in Winnipeg after the war. His memory of the war and contact with the immigrants was more direct. His family were considered immigrants in the teeming North End, but he did not feel himself to be a *greener*. He was the son of Labour Zionists, his father was a Yiddish teacher, and the horrors of the war were never far from his ears. "I had nightmares of being caught [by the Nazis] ... but the enormity [of the event] ... What did mass murder mean? It would be silly [to say] that I knew it." When the refugees arrived, he immediately became friendly with those at his school because he spoke Yiddish.[45]

Another perspective that emerges is the feeling that the refugees were not that different from earlier Jewish refugees who had to flee persecution before and immediately after World War I. Moreover, many Canadian Jews felt that some of the refugees had already achieved financial stability prior to their arrival, unlike the penurious immigrants of earlier times. Harry Gutkin, an artist and historian of Canadian Jewry in the west, opined that "the Jews who ran away from the pogroms in Kishinev in 1903 or 1905 were no different than the Jews who ran away from the Holocaust." He states that some immigrants came before the end of World War II: "the wealthier ones came here and started the Manitoba Sugar Company as they did in B.C. in the lumber industry ... They got in because money talks." In contrast, "ordinary people came when King relaxed the immigration laws."[46]

Kalmen Kaplansky contrasts the survivors with those immigrants who came, as he did, in the 1920s:

Many of the people who came did not survive the Holocaust but came from Russia and returned to Poland and then to the German camps. When the people came many of them did extremely well, they went into business ... Many of them landed jobs in the clothing business, they became contractors... How was the reception? It was very difficult. There was an established gradation in Jewish circles; there were the *greeners* and the *gayle* ... My first job [the boss's] favourite nickname for me was the *"greener tuchester,"* the green asshole ... I had friends years later who were jealous of my success who said, "You made it and I was born in this country," and that was before the Holocaust ... This is the human trait of being superior to your neighbour, feeling more secure ... I can understand what they went through ... People are people.[47]

The predominant memory of survivors of their first years in Canada was not of acceptance but of rejection. They saw themselves as double outsiders, estranged both from Canadians and from Canadian Jews. This feeling stemmed from two roots: their experience as survivors and their reception in Canada. Philip Weiss describes the pain and dislocation of the first years:

The customs were different, the way of life was different, the language was different. We were strange people in a strange country, even those who spent the years in the Soviet Union [outside of German-controlled Europe], and the ones who spent the years in the labour camps and the concentration camps were definitely different. It took a long period of time to reverse that period of negative remembrance into constructive remembering. The [experiences] left a certain imprint within the body, mind, and soul of the person. And definitely in your communication; with others you expressed yourself in a certain way; even without disclosing intimate parts of your experience, you still disclosed a certain tragedy within your system. They [Canadians] didn't experience the Holocaust; they couldn't understand the scope of the tragedy, and that is to be understood today by me, but not then.[48]

The distance between the survivors and Canadian Jews was primarily due to the experience of the Holocaust; secondarily, it was the result of misperceptions that each group had about the other. One such misperception was that Canadian Jews assumed that the newcomers were backward since they came from a society that was remembered as being primitive, rural, and traditional. Adult Canadian Jews in the 1950s had either come as children or been born to immigrant parents and grandparents. Their vision of Jewish life in eastern Europe was framed by the stories and images passed down by family and friends. Life in the late nineteenth and early twentieth centuries had been marked by poverty, orthodoxy, the enmity of Christian neighbours, and underdevelopment. Most of the immigrants at the turn of the century came from *stetlach* (small towns; *shtetl* in the singular) in the Jewish pale of settlement in the Russian empire. The memory of that society, caricatured in *Fiddler on the Roof*, became engrained in the collective memory of North American Jewry thereafter, and to a degree, it remains so.

The world of interwar European Jewish society, however, was markedly different. Most Jews lived in urban areas. In 1939, 10 per cent of Poland's 3.3 million Jews lived in Warsaw, and another 40 per cent in cities with more than 12,000 Jews. Urbanization was even more widespread for the Jews of western Europe. With urbanization came embourgeoisement. Almost all Jews before World War II were fluent in at least one European language, knowing several was not uncommon, and most spoke Yiddish as well. Most young adults had been educated in public schools and considered themselves to be loyal citizens of their nation-state.[49] European civilization in the major cities before the war was far more cultured, with respect to the arts and letters, than were the cities of North America, with the exception of New York. Yet few Canadian Jews recognized the social and demographic transition that had occurred in the generation or more since they had emigrated from Europe. They anticipated that the refugees would be like their predecessors and that, like them, their transition into the community would take many years. The refugees, on the other hand, anticipated that their arrival would be occasioned by an outpouring of understanding and tolerance and that the Canadian environment would be similar to that of pre-war Europe. Further, they were not content to don the mantle of impoverished immigrants, but were determined to climb the socio-economic ladder. Both groups were bewildered when their preconceived notions were dashed.

Gerda Steinitz-Frieberg came to Canada in 1953. When she and her family rented their first flat in Toronto, she invited her husband's cousins for tea. She had bought a set of Rosenthal dishes in Europe after the war. For her, it was a tangible link with her middle-class past. When tea was served, she recalled that "the cousin turned over the cup and said, 'Do you know this is Rosenthal?' This is the way they felt about survivors." Krisha Starker arrived in Montreal in 1951. In her first home, a room rented from a Jewish family, she was shown how to turn on the light, flush the toilet, and dial the telephone. "Before the war, I lived in Warsaw, and after the war in Stockholm, Brussels, and Munich ... I think that there was this double view, that those who came earlier swallowed up the view of the eastern European Jew as the pariah – the pariah who was in a camp surviving by being only a double pariah ... They came from small towns and remained small-town. We came from big cities; we went to high school; so there was absolutely no common ground except for Israel." Steinitz-Frieberg echoed this view: "I think the worst experience was when the Canadian Jews asked how come six million were murdered, how come you survived? I had to justify my survival ... The other notion that came through clearly was 'you must have been a collaborator that they let you live.' They almost resented our survival." Lou Zablow concurred: "I preferred to keep my mouth shut as far as my as history in the concentration camps ... It didn't sound right ... 'Why was I in the camp? I must have done something' ... [There was] a lack of understanding .... [They complained that] 'there was not enough meat, there were chickens, but meat was rationed' ... They told us where the toilet paper was, how to pull the chain on the toilet, while Lodz was a city the size of Montreal ... I was already fluent in English from high school, so it was not a case of not speaking the language."[50]

Most of the survivors came with their spouses and in some cases with children born in Europe after the war, but a significant minority were teenagers or young adults. Some were orphans, while the remainder arrived with one or both parents or were too old to be housed with foster families. The orphans had each other, but this second group had to create a social life for itself, and most had great difficulty in doing so. Eighteen-year-old survivors in 1948 had lived through a different world from their Canadian counterparts. With limited language skills, with a formal education that had been disrupted in elementary school, and with the trauma of their experience, they had no common ground with young Canadians Jews. Most entered the work force, and the rest went back to school. The experiences of two young men are characteristic of the problems that they faced and the strategies that they used to adapt to their new existence.

Twenty-year-old Nathan Leipciger came to Toronto with his father in 1948. He spent two years in high school and then studied engineering at the University of Toronto. When asked, "How did people react to you as a survivor?" he replied:

Well, like somebody with three heads ... It was very difficult to be, to form any type of social communication, any type of social life because I was a D.P. A D.P. was a dirty name in those days. You know, everybody was afraid ... I made very few friends, which in a way helped me because I could devote myself 100 percent to my studies and on the other hand, even with the kids that I was in school with who were 18 or 19, I didn't have anything in common. I couldn't talk about the things they talked (about) .... [I was] in Germany for three years so it was completely different, as a 20 year old man I was completely in a different level than they were as far as social interaction was concerned ... There were some mothers that didn't allow their daughters to go out with a D.P. and I was just as eager to get away from that label.[51]

By the time he went to university, Leipciger had mastered the language, but not his discomfort. "I never told anyone my story: I never told anybody where I came from. In university I spent four years with guys who had absolutely no inkling [about my past]. I didn't wear short-sleeved shirts because I didn't want them to see my number. This was the price I paid."[52]

Leipciger touches upon a central theme in this study – the terminology used to describe the immigrants. For many years after the war, they were DPs, a term that both they and Canadian Jews adopted. It was a pejorative label inasmuch as it both described their statelessness and stripped them of their dignity as the *shaerit hapleita* (in Hebrew, the phrase means the surviving remnant) of a thousand-year-old civilization. The immigrants accepted the term because many came from displaced persons' camps, but more importantly, because they did not feel accepted in their adopted country.[53] It was not until they achieved a measure of financial security and status within the Jewish community that they began calling themselves "survivors." This term elevated their status, and as their contributions mounted and the Holocaust entered the collective memory of the community, it was adopted by other Canadians.

Mendel Good arrived in Ottawa in 1948 at the age of twenty-three. Alone in a city with a small but close Jewish community, he was one of the few survivors there in those years. He immediately found work and became part of the community. He recalled, "This was the poorest neighbourhood. Most of the people where I lived were peddlers; they made me feel so at home. They would invite me in their homes. I knew nobody there. I was the only survivor in my family." Yet Good did not talk about his experiences because there was no common ground and because it was uncomfortable both for him and for his neighbours. "I don't ever recall anyone [asking], either not wanting to know or not to hurt my feelings ... They knew ... many times I wondered about it [the lack of dialogue]." His only outlet was corresponding with friends whom he had made in the DP camps. "One of them said, 'Life was given to struggle, and if you can't adjust, you're a coward.'" His adjustment was to become active in the Jewish community, something that was much easier in Ottawa than for survivors in Montreal or Toronto. "The main reason for the difference was that because there was such a small group [of survivors in Ottawa], we Canadianized much quicker than those concentrated in the big cities ... I was grateful that I was not there."[54]

The arrival of the 1,100 war orphans provided a different set of challenges for the newcomers and their hosts. Most of the orphans were not children but teenagers, and most were not adopted but lived in group or foster homes.[55] There was no uniformity to their experiences during their first years in Canada. Some were able to adapt easily and others took years dealing with their trauma; some were ill-treated by their host families and others became adopted children of loving families.[56] A few examples illustrate the range in the reception of the orphans. Howard Chandler came to Toronto at the age of eighteen. He recalled that "first of all, you left (Europe) a young person with an old mind. It affected you, it affected me, because you left without parents. You had to find your own way in, in life which, if given a chance, I don't find it too hard. What I most feel affected by is lack of family and lack of education. I had three grades of education and this is all the education I ever got ... If you miss it in your formative years, it's very hard if not impossible to make up. You can make do, but cannot make it up."[57]

Eighteen-year-old Musia Schwartz came to Montreal in 1948. Her first foster home was in well-to-do Westmount. "I wasn't miserable; there were certain disagreeable things that survivors first encountered ... I remember when the lady of the house said to me after taking a bath, 'You didn't stay up to clean or help, and by the way, in your ghetto, or wherever you were, did you take a bath too?' I had a different upbringing; I was on my own since I was twelve, I was my own parent, my own disciplinarian ... There were many people who came at the turn of the century, who came in the thirties, who thought that those who came now [after the war] sort of left behind what they left behind." Shortly after, Schwartz married. Her husband's boss's secretary, upon meeting her, remarked, "Look at her, she barely stepped off the ship and she walks like a princess."[58] Leo Lowy was one of six orphans who arrived together in Vancouver. He was sixteen years old. He was fortunate to be placed with a Yiddish-speaking family, "so I almost felt at home. I was very shocked that they heard of the Holocaust. They read about it in the newspapers, but to get information first-hand, everything was new to them ... These people were so warm I accepted them as foster parents ... I was in heaven."[59]

In Winnipeg the arrival of 106 orphans by the end of 1948 required a community-wide effort at fund-raising in order to provide the necessary services. For the most part, the orphans were received warmly and quickly integrated into the community. They even founded a soccer club, Hagibor, in their first summer in the city.[60] The most notable orphan in Winnipeg turned out to be John Hirsch. He arrived in 1947 at the age of sixteen. He completed high school in one year, although he did not speak English at first. After graduating from the University of Manitoba, Hirsch became one of Canada's leading theatrical personalities. He was a co-founder of the Manitoba Theatre Centre, head of drama at the Canadian Broadcasting Corporation, and artistic director of the Stratford Shakespearean Festival. During his first years in Winnipeg he was welcomed into the Jewish community, and more significantly, he became part of his adopted family. In interviews and articles, Hirsch has described those years.

I came to Canada under the scheme of the Canadian Jewish Congress, I didn't know where Winnipeg was, or what Winnipeg was ... When I was asked whether I wanted to go to Vancouver, or Montreal, or Toronto, or Halifax, I asked for a map of Canada and Winnipeg being in the middle of it and having been involved in so many extreme situations just the mere fact that Winnipeg was in the middle of the continent I pointed to Winnipeg and I said that's where I want to go, it looks safe.

I was placed in the home of the Shacks, Sybil Shack and Mrs. Shack and Mr. Shack. They were the most exceptional people I have ever come in my life.

My adopted mother, Mrs. Shack ... if I could pick a model for the kind of person I would like to be I suppose it would be the kind of person she is ... Remarkable person, my sister Sybil Shack. They mended me. They really put me together and they did it with the only glue that can put human beings together. They did it with love and concern.

It's difficult to find roots in an ever changing world, especially when you live the kind of gypsy life dictated by my profession. Coming back to Winnipeg on family visits gives me a great deal of strength. As the years go by, I realize more and more just how valuable and enriching this connection is. Every time I come back I recognize how fortunate Winnipegers are. There are few places anymore where you can find this sense of community, a sense of belonging.[61]

By the mid-1950s, survivors and Canadian Jews were adapting to the new dynamic in the Jewish community. The survivors were no longer surprised at the mixed reception they received, at the relative cultural backwardness of Canada, or at obstacles they faced in finding employment, housing, and education. Canadian Jews were also shedding their preconceptions of the newcomers. For the survivors, the expanding economy that marked the post-war era was an incentive to acclimatize themselves to their new environment. Their first economic consideration was finding employment. Once this hurdle was cleared, learning or improving English and/or French became obligatory. Some survivors were able to deal quickly with these challenges, and a minority became self-employed by the mid-1950s. Within that group, a handful became prosperous.

The process of adaptation and integration occurred on three planes: in the wider community, within the family, and among other survivors. In general, it was easiest in the first case, more complex in the second, and tremendously difficult in the third. Adaptation to the wider community essentially meant achieving economic security, taking advantage of educational opportunities, and gaining acceptance by other Canadians. While these were monumental challenges for most survivors, they were ones that could be met. After all, they had to deal with far more formidable obstacles during the war. They then had had to rebuild their lives in the DP camps or the cities of wartorn Europe. The challenges of learning Canadian customs, coping with the language, dealing with recalcitrant employers, and scraping to save for a house or a business were daunting, but they could be overcome.

Leo Lowy bought a tiny store with a small inventory in New Westminster at the age of eighteen, two years after he arrived in Vancouver as an orphan. He married a Canadian Jewish woman and was accepted by her family and friends. Mendel Good purchased a small store, which he converted into a haberdashery. His clientele was not confined to Ottawa Jews, and he integrated into the wider community. Nathan Leipciger graduated in engineering from the University of Toronto in 1954. A year later he married a Canadian Jewish woman and moved into a non-Jewish community. "I didn't want to be ghettoized ... I separated myself from the Jewish mainstream." Musia Schwartz also managed to adapt quickly. She continued her education, eventually earning a doctorate in comparative literature at McGill. She recalled that "very early on my friends weren't only survivors or Jews. There was great diversity [in Montreal]; integration was never a problem; it was never my aim to be a total insider ... Canada was an ideal environment for me precisely because it left me alone. It was almost like a balm." Robert Krell was born in 1940. As a child survivor growing up in the 1950s, he felt that it was important "to show your stuff, making it in this new world." Doing so meant that he had to deal with being an outsider. "What you're aware of is that you belong to the immigrants, an affiliation to other *greeners*." The most immediate path for Krell in escaping estrangement was mastering English. He eventually enrolled in medical school and became a professor of psychiatry at the University of British Columbia.[62]

Far more difficult than economic advancement for survivors was coping with the losses and memories within their families. Most older survivors, that is, those in their forties, had lost their spouses and children in the Holocaust. They had remarried after the war and were raising young children in Canada. Younger survivors, those in their twenties and thirties, were also raising young families with spouses who were either survivors or Canadian Jews. The dilemma for many was how to communicate their experiences to their children. For some survivors, it was just too painful to talk about the war, the loss of family and home. For Pola Granek, "it took me more than 25 years. I couldn't talk about it, not even with my children, with my children especially." Clara Forai related, "I couldn't speak about it, to my daughter, to anyone." Mike Englishman remarked that he could not speak about the Holocaust, "no, not even in my house," even though he was married to a survivor. Yet, Granek, Forai, and Englishman eventually overcame their demons and became active in the community; but they did so only after their children had grown up.[63]

Other survivors were determined to speak to their families about their loss. Perhaps it was their desire to teach their children about their heritage, or perhaps it was a way of dealing with their pain. One should not rule out the possibility that speaking about the Holocaust was also a vehicle for instilling hatred in others toward the oppressors. After all, many children of survivors were warned not to buy anything manufactured in Germany or to be wary of gentiles. Freda Kupfer stoically accepted her situation. "It was better to work hard and to ask nobody for anything. Children had to know the hard way. They knew." Eleanor Posner was adamant: "I'll never forget them [the perpetrators]. And I can never forget. Never until I'll die. And everything that I went through, my children know ... I don't hide nothing from my children. Why should I protect them? Let them know. Because they didn't come face to face with anti-semitism yet." Howard Chandler, who has been active as a speaker in Toronto since the late 1970s, recalled, "I never sat down formally or tried to explain to them [his children]. If they asked me questions, I answered them but no more, no less. I don't want to make them feel that they should feel sorry for me or I should give them any complexes." Interestingly, Chandler's wife, Elsa, is also a survivor and has been active in municipal politics as a school trustee. Yet she was unable to speak about her experiences until recently. Chava Kwinta was one of the first survivors in Canada to write a book about her experience. She stated: "I have three daughters. If they came home and they asked questions I answered. I tried to explain to them the truth. I never covered up anything. I encouraged them to read as much as possible and to find out for themselves ... They read my book, not much later than I wrote it, when they were like 16 years old."[64]

A common experience for many survivors was the constant feeling that they were outsiders in the Jewish community. In her reminiscences of those years, Gerda Steinitz-Frieberg was unsparing: "The worst thing that happened to me in the 1950s [occurred because] I didn't know that you had to buy tickets for services on Rosh Hashana. On Yom Kippur I walked down to the Shareii Shomayim [a major synagogue in Toronto] with my mother to say *yiskor* [the portion of the service for remembrance of lost family], so I came to the synagogue and the guy at the door said, 'Where is your ticket?' I said, 'Look, I'm a Holocaust survivor and all I want to do is say *Kaddish* [the prayer for the dead] for the entire family that I lost. He said, 'I'm sorry, you can't come in.'"[65]

Krisha Starker recalled similar experiences. "I heard people asking, 'What did you do to survive? I withdrew; I didn't go to work on April 19 [the anniversary of the Warsaw Ghetto Uprising] and lit six candles and set fresh flowers. It was my way of commemorating. I had to apologize to survive. It was hurtful." For Musia Schwartz, the memories of her experiences are intertwined with her post-war life, yet are surreal. "I wrote my memoirs, which I didn't publish, in the late fifties ... They are sitting in a drawer somewhere ... I sometimes look at these things and I myself am not certain if this is fictionalized; did it actually happen to me? The things we impose on memory we edit in a conscious way, in an unconscious way."[66]

The most difficult problem facing survivors in the 1950s was dealing with their memories. This problem still has not been eradicated for many. As with their dilemma over discussing their past with their children, no consistent pattern emerges with respect to how survivors have coped. For some, suppression was the way to deal with memory. For the majority, social interaction with other survivors provided an outlet for their innermost conflicts. Nathan Leipciger was hurt that Canadian Jews did not want to know or learn about survivors' experiences. "They weren't interested in listening, and we weren't prepared to talk. [Therefore] survivors spoke with one another, [but] that was another reason why I tried to avoid survivors, because every time they got together, that's all they talked about." More typical was the route taken by Philip Weiss; for him, social interaction with other survivors became the norm. In the small survivor community of Winnipeg, it became customary to spend Sundays with families and friends in parks and at picnics.[67] In Toronto and Montreal, socialization took place in a more formal setting. There survivors from the same city or region joined *landsman-shaften*, which became the focal points for discussion and the outpouring of memories.

One leading *landsmanschaft* was the Radomer society. Radom, a city in central Poland, had over 30,000 Jewish inhabitants in 1939, representing one-third of the city's population. Less than two months after the German invasion of the country, it came under German civil administration. In the succeeding months the Jews of the city and district were concentrated, and a ghetto created. Transports from the ghetto to the extermination camp at Treblinka began in August 1942, and were followed by transports to other killing centres. The last major transport took place on 13 January 1943. Those who were not selected for the transports were recruited as slave labourers. The handful who survived this ordeal were liberated in Germany in the last weeks of the war. According to the census taken at the end of 1945, of 79,000 inhabitants in Radom, only 299 were Jewish.[68]

The Radomer Mutual Benefit Society of Toronto had been created in 1925 by *landsleit* (people from the same town or district); its counterpart in Montreal was established in 1941. The Toronto organization founded a relief fund for Radomer Jews in need in 1929 and a credit association for its members in 1933, at its offices at 210 Beverley Street, in the heart of Toronto's Jewish neighbourhood. The society was affiliated with the World Jewish Congress and the Federation of Polish Jews. When survivors from Radom came to Toronto, they gravitated to the society, which had about two hundred members at that time. Most of the survivors were secular Jews, that is, they were not religious, but they celebrated the holidays. Many had come from non-religious families in pre-war Europe. According to Professor Adam Fuerstenberg, who arrived in Canada as a young boy and whose father was an active member, "they used the Radomer society as a means of Jewish cohesiveness." Although there were ideological divisions among the survivors, they were incidental to the general operation of the society.[69]

The arrival of Radomer survivors in Toronto created a new dynamic in the society. It was being run by many of the same individuals who had started it a generation earlier. The society had its established traditions and practices, and the arrival of the newcomers was both a welcome and an unsettling experience. The survivors were much younger than their Canadian counterparts and had different objectives. Their main goals were the preservation of the memory of Radom, which entailed both commemoration and education about the Holocaust and support for Israel, especially for Radomers there. These goals were at odds with those of the traditional membership, which was most concerned with local needs. Consequently, the survivors formed an informal component of the society, which they called B'nai Radom (the sons or children of Radom) in about 1954.[70]

This group had about thirty members. Their goals were a catalyst for the formation of the group, but there was a more pressing reason for its formation. Henry Rosenbaum, one of the founders of B'nai Radom, remembered: "We felt much better among survivors. We had something in common to talk about. When I came, I was a stranger here and had to establish a new social life and felt more comfortable with people my age [he was twenty-six] than those twenty-five years older. To them we were strangers. We wanted to be equal to them; to be equal to them, we had to establish our own group."[71] What united the survivors in spirit was their memory; what transpired was activating that memory into something tangible.

The first project of B'nai Radom was to hold its own *yiskor* (remembrance service). The society had had a *yiskor* for years, but it attracted a handful of people and had little meaning for the survivors, since it did not commemorate their own loss. B'nai Radom held its first *yiskor* in January 1955, on the anniversary of the liquidation of the ghetto. The old-timers resented this intrusion and continued to hold their own for another two years before relenting.[72] The other major project for B'nai Radom was building a monument for the victims of the city at the society's cemetery plot. Again, there was some opposition from the established members. But when the survivors, several of whom had become wealthy, threatened to buy their own plot, the society accepted the proposal. The monument was unveiled on 2 September 1962. It was the first monument to victims of the Holocaust erected in Toronto.[73]

B'nai Radom was a remarkable example of the traditional self-help organizations that had proliferated in Jewish communities for centuries. It supplied survivors with a link to the Canadian Jews most like themselves – those who shared the need to maintain a connection with their origins. Of greater significance, it provided the opportunity for the small remnant of survivors from one city to establish a group with a common purpose and reinvigorate old friendships. Most survivors in Toronto and Montreal joined *landsmanschaften*. They were successful in reclaiming the memory of their old life and in finding a mutual understanding of their shared loss. Ultimately, the *landsmanschaften* were a basis for the recognition of the Holocaust as a defining point of Jewish identity a generation later.[74]

A DIVIDED COMMUNITY

Leslie Hulse was the first scholar to argue that there were two distinct groups within the Jewish community after the war. She based her findings on interviews conducted with survivors active in Toronto in the 1960s. While there is little dispute about her conclusion, the supporting documentation is flawed by her narrow focus on a small group in one city and her collapsing of the events of the 1960s and early 1970s. Jean Gerber, who studied the survivor community in Vancouver, maintained that "survivors integrated into existing patterns established by the host Jewish group." Unfortunately, she does not account for the feelings of the survivors and the fact that what the host community took for acceptance was not seen that way by many of the survivors.[75] Nevertheless, her argument helps us understand the complexity of the survivor-Canadian relationship in mid-sized Jewish communities.

A case in point is the post-war Jewish community in Winnipeg. Larry Zolf argued that "there weren't two communities, not like here [Toronto]. We had a rabbi, Kravitz, who was a survivor .... The integration was strong, I saw no tension." Zolf's view was coloured by his family's proximity to survivors, both because it lived in the old neighbourhood of the North End and because of his father's interest in Jewish affairs. Zolf remembers that survivors did not talk about their experiences to him, but did so to his parents. "If you were a survivor, it depended upon the kind of Jew you found here ... If you found S.C. [a prominent Jewish leader] he was a *bissele goy* [verging on gentile]. If you found someone like my father, why wouldn't you talk to him. He knew the geography, the history. We had visitors, some had tattoos." The opposite perspective is presented by Harry Gutkin. He maintains that there were two communities in Winnipeg. "They couldn't find themselves. In the first twenty years, they were concerned with economic factors ... [Living in the North End] it was insular, as it would be with all newcomers ... They were really a group that lived within themselves, and it wasn't until they themselves came forward to preserve the Holocaust on a continuing basis [that the situation changed.]"[76]

Another example of this divergent view is seen in the Vancouver community. Sam Rothstein feels that the survivors merged "very readily" with the wider Jewish community. He points to the Warsaw Ghetto Commemoration and the Kristallnacht Commemoration as examples of two events that brought the community together.[77] Sophie Waldman, the chairperson of the Warsaw Ghetto Commemoration from 1953 to 1986, says that in the initial years the Canadian Jews took little interest.[78] Although she and her husband were professionals (she a medical technologist after receiving a degree in pharmacy in Poland before the war, her husband an engineer), "we had very few Canadian [Jewish] friends. Actually nobody asked me questions about my past .... We were left absolutely to ourselves."[79]

Vancouver and Winnipeg had a relatively small proportion of Holocaust survivors in the 1950s. Vancouver had several hundred, representing less than 5 per cent of the Jewish community. Winnipeg had approximately 1,000, slightly more than 5 per cent. By most indications, despite the fact that many survivors lived in the same neighbourhoods as Canadian Jews, there was little integration. Survivors were totally absent from established organizations. Given the small number of survivors, the possibility of integration and acceptance in Winnipeg and Vancouver would appear to have been greater than in Toronto and Montreal. Although barriers may have eroded more quickly in mid-sized communities than in the two main centres, barriers still existed.

The economic success of some survivors was not unnoticed in the established community. In fact, it was almost expected. Cyril Levitt, a child at that time, remembers that attitude. "Very often these *greenies* did very well. You heard their ethics were suspect. A more generous interpretation was 'they're not afraid to take chances, they have nothing to lose, the *greenie* has seen it all. You can't hurt him because after you go through the camps, losing a few bucks is nothing.'"[80]

Ben Lappin recalled that by the mid-1950s the survivors had recreated their own lives and the focus of community life had shifted to other concerns. The rehabilitation of the newcomers, which had been central in community affairs earlier in the decade, was over. As the survivors adapted, the memory of the Holocaust receded further in the organized community. Lappin states that "both sides were numbed."[81] At Toronto's Beth Tzedec Synagogue, Canada's largest congregation, the Holocaust was purposely omitted from the curriculum because it would "traumatize" the students, according to psychologists.[82] Canadian Jews not only did not want to be reminded of the horror, but also they resisted any efforts at introducing the topic into Jewish schools. In Vancouver the Jewish schools emphasized the "more positive elements" of recent Jewish history, such as Israel, and it was not until the 1960s that the Holocaust was discussed there.[83] This view, however, did not resonate within certain sectors of the community. The left-wing Jewish People's School in Montreal, for example, stressed the importance of the Holocaust, and many of the teachers were themselves survivors. Similar emphasis was found in other ideologically based institutions, such as the Borochov School in Toronto, which I attended. It represented the Labour-Zionist perspective.[84]

In the ethnic press, the Holocaust and the integration of the survivors continued to be judged as not worthy of investigation. The English-language journals ignored the topic, and the Yiddish-language newspapers provided little information. When Sam Lipshitz, manager of *Der Vochenblatt*, was asked whether his paper devoted any analysis to the Holocaust or the adaptation by survivors to the community, he replied, "Not overwhelmingly. There was a tendency on the part of the survivors to see the Canadian establishment as [being] uninterested in their lives." He recalls that the publications of *landsmanschaften*, in which survivors played a prominent role, were the exception, but their readership was limited and could not be considered significant in the ethnic press in the 1950s. Lipshitz maintained, however, that one should not generalize about Canadian Jewish attitudes. "There was very great sympathy; there were very great relations with the tailors, furriers, etc ... There wasn't one solid attitude; there were different attitudes."[85]

All in all, the 1950s were a decade of profound and lasting change in the Canadian Jewish community. Its population grew by 35 per cent, of whom one-half were Holocaust survivors. Economic prosperity and the decline of systemic antisemitism also contributed to the transformation. The decade was marked by the transition from the traditional immigrant inner-city neighbourhoods to the suburbs, accompanied by the erosion of traditional structures, religious and secular, that had cemented the community for decades. In their stead, large congregations emerged, the social services became professionalized, and long-held ideological positions that had provided the vitality and culture of the community evaporated. For the first time, some doors were opened to Jews in employment, education, and housing, and most took advantage of this situation. Young adults did not follow their seniors into the factories and shops, but availed themselves of the opportunities now open to them and became disproportionately represented in the professions and in graduate schools at universities. They were the first Canadian Jews to adopt English as the language of the home and workplace exclusively.

These changes brought a new perspective, a distinct Canadian viewpoint, to the community. Connections to the European past became more hazy. The arrival of the Holocaust survivors only served to cloud that faded memory. Contrary to the preconceptions of Canadian Jews, the survivors were different from earlier immigrants. Marked by a tragic past, the witnesses of the greatest inhumanity of recorded history, they experienced a pain that was not comparable to the humiliation felt by the immigrants who had fled from the pogroms of earlier times. Their suffering was one aspect of their distinctiveness. Another was their upbringing in the cities of interwar Europe. Canadian Jews could relate neither to their tragedy nor to their advanced education and culture. Consequently, two communities emerged in Toronto and Montreal, with little to unite them but support for the state of Israel and the desire to make good in the flourishing post-war economy. In mid-sized communities such as Vancouver and Winnipeg, there was more interaction in the workplace and neighbourhoods, but survivors there for the most part felt the same sense of rejection as did their counterparts in the larger cities.

With an emphasis on turning themselves into ordinary Canadians, established Jews were abandoning the connection to their European roots. In so doing, they were neither prepared to mark nor interested in marking the Holocaust as an event with which they could identify. They may have lost family members of whom they had little memory, but for the community as a whole, the Holocaust was not a significant issue. In fact, discussion of the event or learning about it through the survivors and through the few available books was discouraged. It was a blot on Jewish history. Some Canadian Jews even felt that the survivors had to have "done something" to live, implying that survival might have been achieved through collaboration or deceit. Moreover, the rapid economic success of a handful of survivors stimulated envy among some Canadian Jews, further reinforcing the belief that these were people who were not to be trusted. In response, most survivors isolated themselves socially, finding a release for their memories in association with other survivors, thus increasing the separation between the two groups. The Holocaust was relegated to the past, a tragedy outside the lives and beyond the comprehension of most Canadian Jews. As long as their security was not threatened, there was little reason to commemorate the terrible events that had taken place a decade earlier. That comfortable position would be disturbed by events in the 1960s. As the Holocaust took on a more immediate meaning in that decade, the collective memory of the community began to change.

4 "The disease of anti-Semitism has again become active": The Community and the Hate-Mongers in the Early 1960s

On 9 May 1965 Prime Minister Lester B. Pearson spoke at a ceremony on Parliament Hill to mark the twentieth anniversary of the end of World War II in Europe. The occasion was sponsored by the Association of Former Concentration Camp Inmates/Survivors of Nazi Oppression, an organization founded in Montreal in November 1960. Pearson, in his address, observed:

Twenty years ago the guns stopped firing ... It was also 20 years ago when the pitiable and few survivors stumbled out of the concentration camps. The nightmare ended then, but the memory still burns of the horror and the tragedy of the degrading and terrible demonstration of man's inhumanity to man ... Much of the tragedy we remember, and the emotion and sorrow it evokes, is centred on the Jewish race. How often, throughout man's blood-stained history, has the still sad music of humanity been a Hebrew melody which hymns not only the despair, but the hope, of mankind, that hope which lies in the value – immeasurable and eternal – of the humblest of human lives, of the little peoples of glory and greatness on whose sacrifices man is given the chance to move upward to something better ... You are commemorating this anniversary at the shrine of Canadian liberty – its Parliament – where men meet together – the men chosen by you – to make the laws that maintain freedom within the bounds of dignity and decency. Those bounds do not include organized and directed propaganda which, in other places and other times, led to the horrors of 25 years ago; or the advocacy of the degradation and elimination of a race or a people ... Your Association is on guard against these dangers – while it reverently perseveres for all times the memory of their victims in the past. Your vigilance and your purpose is a recognition that the ageless cry, "Lord God of Hosts be with us yet," must not only be voiced, but be backed by our own action and resolution. It is not enough to say, "It can't happen here." We must be on guard to make sure it doesn't happen here – or there, or anywhere.[1]

The prime minister's address was symbolic of a turning point in the Canadian public's consciousness of the Holocaust and the turbulent debate regarding its significance in the collective memory within the Jewish community. That there was some awareness of the Holocaust in general and that a debate existed within the Jewish community in 1965 was in marked contrast to the lack of knowledge and discussion five years earlier. At the end of the 1950s the Jewish community was secure in its belief that Jews had become Canadianized and that systemic antisemitism had been largely expunged. Survivors were becoming acclimatized to their new environment but had not yet been admitted into the traditional community's organizations and institutions because they had not gained acceptance by the mainstream and still lacked the skills and motivation to challenge the establishment. Consequently, they were not prepared, nor did they consider it essential, to reconfigure the community's historical memory of the Holocaust or its ignorance of its European roots. By 1965 this situation had changed dramatically.

The participation of Canada's political leadership in a ceremony on Parliament Hill sponsored by a survivors' association was indicative of the current of events that had changed the public's awareness of the Holocaust in the preceding five years. Pearson's address was significant for three reasons. First, it was the first acknowledgment of the Holocaust by a prime minister. Second, it specifically referred to the Jewish tragedy, and in so doing, it used the term "survivors" to define the Jews who had been liberated. Not only did this speech recognize the particular oppression suffered by Jews, as distinct from other victims, but it conferred status upon the survivors because of the association's role in organizing the ceremony. Third, Pearson's address underscored the legislation that was being considered to criminalize the distribution of hate propaganda.

In these respects, the address was one of three events the same month that reordered the Jewish community's approach to the Holocaust. The others were the CJC plenary, held from 20 to 24 May in Montreal, and a riot at Allan Gardens in Toronto on 30 May at which the self-styled leader of the Canadian Nazi Party was to have spoken.

The central factor for the sudden prominence given to the Holocaust by Canadian Jews in the early 1960s was fear of the revival of antisemitism in Canada and abroad. The community reeled from one antisemitic incident to another in those years, and the unrestrained pressure on the community disrupted the relative tranquility of the preceding decade. Just as Canadian Jews were becoming comfortable with their achievements, a handful of racists, both native and foreign, succeeded in reinvigorating the antisemitism that had been dormant since the war. Canadian Jews began to feel vulnerable because they had become unaccustomed to this behaviour. Initially, the organized community acted as it had in the past. It urged restraint, reiterated its confidence in the legal system to take the necessary action, was concerned about offending civil liberties, and lobbied politicians and law enforcement officials behind the scenes. Survivors, however, were accustomed to antisemitism, but not to the Canadian way of dealing with hate-mongers. A small contingent of survivors, dissatisfied with their leaders' quiescent approach, sought other means to deal with the antisemites and advocated a more forceful public stance. Their actions represented a stirring of political activism that originated within the survivor community in Montreal. By the mid-1960s their protests had gained momentum and caused Canadians to take notice. Certainly, the ability of the Association of Survivors to recruit the prime minister to speak on Parliament Hill was indicative of their growing strength and political skills. Concurrent with the revival of antisemitic outrages was the publicity surrounding the trial of Adolf Eichmann. Together these developments put the Holocaust on the community agenda.

Two points need clarification. First and foremost, the main challenge for the Jewish community in these years was how to deal with antisemitism, rather than commemoration and education about the Holocaust. The catastrophe was not, in and of itself, the primary item on the agenda. Rather, the strains in the community over how to effectively mitigate antisemitism in time led to an awareness that the Holocaust was a defining point of identity for Canadian Jews as well as for survivors and their families. The second clarification to be made is that antisemitism in this period was not a practical threat to the community. The most virulent antisemites, the purveyors of hate literature and the poseurs who preached neo-Nazism, were a minuscule group on the margins of society without any mainstream support. Rather, there was a perception that antisemitism might become widespread and acceptable. That this perception was credible was due to the tremendous publicity afforded to antisemites and racists, together with the coverage of international events that harked back to the darkest days of the Holocaust. It was this perception, rather than the reality, that alarmed the survivors and disquieted Canadian Jews.

ANTISEMITISM IN 1960

For the first three decades after the war, there was one official voice in the Jewish community on matters relating to antisemitism – the Joint Public Relations Committee. It had been formed in 1938 and formalized in 1947 with a sponsoring agreement between the two main bodies in the Jewish community, Congress and B'nai Brith, to protect Canadian Jews from discrimination and attack. Congress was the umbrella organization for the myriad local federations, and B'nai Brith an international service organization with a central administration that oversaw dozens of local lodges. B'nai Brith's Anti-Defamation League was the main Jewish body in the United States dedicated to anti-discrimination. By 1964 B'nai Brith Canada had 15,000 members or about 10 per cent of the adult Jewish population. Many prominent leaders in the Jewish community served as officers in both organizations. The constitution of the JPRC, signed by both bodies on 3 September 1947, stated that ten members from each organization were to constitute the national committee. The JPRC had a Case Division, "whose function it shall be to institute and supervise a program of action in cases of personal assault, or malicious attack, against Jews, and in respect to antisemitic movements." It also had a Law and Social Action Division, "whose function it shall be to institute and supervise programs making full use of law, legislation and social action to eliminate discriminatory group practices." The constitution articulated the principles adopted when the committee was formed in 1938. The national body, the National Joint Public Relations Committee, in its statement of policy of 22 April 1950, declared in article 1 that "the principle [sic] objective of the NJPRC should be the protection of the civil and human rights of the Jewish community as an integral part of the Canadian community."[2] In the early 1960s the name was changed to the Joint Community Relations Committee. B'nai Brith's participation ended in 1980, but it was not until the mid-1990s that the word "Joint" was dropped from the renamed Community Relations Committee.

On Christmas Day 1959 a number of synagogues in the Federal Republic of Germany were smeared with swastikas. In a matter of days, an epidemic of similar desecrations swept over other western European countries. By New Year's Day the plague had crossed the Atlantic. In the United States approximately one hundred communities in thirty-one states were hit. Canada was not exempt from the virus. Numerous synagogues and Jewish institutions across the land were marked with the offensive symbol of Nazi tyranny. In Ontario alone, synagogues were defaced in Toronto, Sudbury, Kingston, Kitchener, Cornwall, and Galt. The onslaught ended abruptly on 13 January 1960. According to the American Jewish Congress, Jewish buildings in twenty-five countries had been desecrated. A report by the Vancouver Civic Unity Association in April noted that there had been over five hundred incidents in 240 communities in thirty-four countries. Six of the communities were in British Columbia.[3] No group or individual took responsibility for these actions, there was no evidence that the scourge had been planned or organized, and no charges were laid. It appeared to have been spontaneous and imitative. Without knowledge about the identity of the perpetrators, we can argue that those who carried out these actions, at least in Canada, may not even have known that the swastika was a symbol of the most virulent hatred in history.

The immediate response by the Jewish establishment to the outbreak was to preach caution. The JPRC recommended the following approach at to a meeting of the national executive of Congress on 9 January: first, there was no cause for panic or hysteria; second, all cases of swastika daubings were to be reported to the police and Congress; third, the community should not provide any unnecessary publicity; and fourth, all vigilante action was to be opposed.[4] A day earlier, all the Toronto synagogues had been put under police protection. On that day a confidential letter to the officers of Congress and to Abraham Arnold, editor of the *Jewish Western Bulletin* in Vancouver, was received from Maxwell Cohen, dean of the law school at McGill University and an adviser to Congress. According to Cohen, "these disgraceful exhibitions are in some cases probably planned, but in most cases outside of Germany are likely to be merely imitative hooliganism. Nevertheless, all people of good will of every denomination will want to condemn them, and I am hoping that leaders everywhere will be putting into words our feeling of abhorrence for what is taking place – although one must not exaggerate these incidents and must keep a sense of perspective."[5] Cohen's appraisal of the outbreak as "imitative hooliganism" became the operative response by Congress. According to the *Canadian Jewish News*, Congress regarded the perpetrators as a lunatic fringe and demanded that the police apprehend those responsible.[6]

Its cautious attitude did not sit well with survivors. For the first time, survivors in *landsmanschaften* challenged the organized community. Typical was a letter from the Piotrkow, Tomashov and

Belchatov Landsmanschaft of Toronto to Ben Kayfetz, the executive director of the JPRC. It demanded to know why Congress was not taking more aggressive action. Kayfetz responded by reiterating the course of action formulated at the meeting of 9 January.[7] Because the outbreak had stopped as quickly as it had started and because there were no suspects, the demands for a more vociferous response by Congress ceased. Nevertheless, the desecrations received tremendous media publicity. Survivors were not the only Canadians alarmed by the epidemic. The swastika was anathema to most Canadian adults. An article by Joan Seager in the *Burlington Gazette*, of Burlington, Ontario, typified the revulsion felt by ordinary Canadians. "It is important that we should remember these things [the horrors of Nazism] – so that they don't happen again. The swastika sickness that has flared across the world recently is a warning ... When I worked in a newspaper office I occasionally received chain letters and other garbage from anonymous sources which 'proved' that the Jews were responsible for – among other things – all the wars in history, the weather, strikes, Edward the Eighth's abdication, sexy movies and cancer ... I could feel the hate dripping off the paper."[8]

The legacy of the swastika daubings lingered in the public mind for several months. For the first time in the post-war era, Canadians expressed their outrage over the possible re-emergence of a mindset that they had fought against in a global conflict. Leon Crestohl, the only Jewish member of the House of Commons, demanded imprisonment for those guilty of antisemitic activities.[9] Jewish and labour groups organized a public meeting called "Anti-Semitism – A Threat to Democracy" in Montreal on 3 February. The guest speakers included Hazen Argue, the CCF leader in the House of Commons, and Roger Provost, president of the Quebec Federation of Labour. On 26 February Louis Segal, of the executive of the World Zionist Organization, decried the re-emergence of antisemitism and urged Zionists to pressure other Jewish organizations to take action. On 3 March an editorial in the *Canadian Jewish News* deplored the mild rebuke given to West German neo-Nazis in a white paper commissioned by the government. The featured speaker for the annual commemoration of the Holocaust in Toronto on the anniversary of the Warsaw Ghetto Uprising was Meyer Gasner, chairman of CJC Central Region. This was the first time that the leading officer in Congress had been asked to give the keynote address. He stressed that one-quarter of world Jewry lived in potential danger. A few weeks later, Gasner wrote about his visit to Auschwitz, the first piece about the camps written by a Congress officer since the Caiserman-Lipshitz delegation in 1945.[10] These responses were significant insofar as a link was made between the desecrations and similar antisemitic activities in the 1930s that had preceded the Holocaust.

The outrage was not limited to Canada. Ten thousand people demonstrated against the swastika incidents in West Berlin. Dr Gerhard Riegner of the World Jewish Congress[11] issued a report on 15 February declaring: "These events have revealed a latent aggressive mentality of frightening extent in one half of the world – a mentality we believed belonged to the past. We are faced with a social disease which must be suppressed and whose seeds must be removed. No country is *a priori* safe from the germs of this social peril which may once again lead to persecution of all sorts of minorities and who knows – to the gas chambers."[12]

The swastika outbreak set the course of events for the next several years. An eruption of antisemitic agitation or an event abroad that focused on hatred of the Jews or a public display of antisemitic or racist rhetoric precipitated reactions from the Jewish community. There was no respite: as soon as one incident ended, another one arose. The revival of antisemitism lent a heightened importance to the commemoration of the Holocaust that was held in various communities in conjunction with the observation of the anniversary of the Warsaw Ghetto Uprising of 19 April 1943. These ceremonies had been of interest to some survivors and few Canadian Jews until 1960, but they now turned into events which stressed the necessity to respond to the new threat to Jews.[13] While the fires ignited in the community by the swastika outbreak lessened in the spring of 1960, before the embers had died, they were stoked by new developments.

Referat IV B4 of the Reich main security office at Gestapo headquarters had been the section dedicated to Jewish affairs and evacuation. From December 1939 to the end of the war, the director of the section was Adolf Eichmann. He was entrusted with implementing the "final solution," and he reported directly to Heinrich Himmler, chief of the ss. A fanatical antisemite, Eichmann had worked with industriousness and thoroughness in carrying out his task. Even after Himmler ordered a moderation in the mass murder toward the end of the war, Eichmann diligently and scrupulously orchestrated the deportation and murder of more than half a million Hungarian Jews in Auschwitz and the killing of thousands of others in the death marches to Germany in the winter of 1945. After the war he found a haven in Buenos Aires. Of all the war criminals loose in the post-war era, aside perhaps from Martin Bormann, Hitler's secretary, Eichmann was the most notorious.[14]

He was tracked down by Israeli security agents on 2 May 1960 and abducted to Israel nine days later. The episode dominated the world's media. The immediate impact in Canada was no less explosive than in any other country, except Israel and West Germany. The first issue of the *Canadian Jewish News*, after the announcement of the capture and abduction, ran a one-inch headline that read: "Monster Eichmann behind Israeli Bars." The accompanying article declared that "[this is] the most startling news since the establishment of the State ... [His] apprehension by Jewish police in the Jewish state ... symbolized the redemption of Israel."[15] The next issue documented Eichmann's capture. The newspaper continued to refer to him as a "monster."

Meanwhile, a controversy regarding Eichmann's capture and secret abduction was brewing. Editorials in the West questioned whether these actions contravened international law. The *Daily Star* in Toronto left no doubt as to the question. It opined: "Snatching Eichmann was a breach of international law. His trial in Israel will smack also of extra-legal procedure. For Eichmann broke no law of Israel – the state and its law were not then in existence. There is also the ticklish issue of whether Israel can appoint itself to punish people for admitted crimes against Jews who are not Israeli citizens, committed outside Israel. The question, then, is not whether Eichmann should be punished for his monstrous crimes. He should be. It is whether his case is so exceptional – and any man who murders six million people is truly an exceptional case – that all consideration of law and legality can be brushed aside in guaranteeing that he is called to account."[16]

An editorial in the *Globe and Mail* stated that Israel had violated Argentina's sovereignty,[17] even though that country had dropped its demand that Eichmann be returned. This controversy, relating to the most significant news about the Holocaust since the Allies had entered the camps in the last weeks of the war, unsettled Canadian Jews. The community was proud of the ability of the tiny state of Israel to infiltrate the sovereignty of another country to capture and abduct an enemy of the Jewish people. It felt that imprisoning a leading Nazi in an Israeli jail was a fitting end, and that it provided an iota of retribution for the crimes of the Nazis against the Jews. Consequently, the community was disturbed about the editorial opposition of some leading publications to the episode. For some Jews, this was an indication that Canadians would never understand that the horrors of the Holocaust went beyond international boundaries and protocol. If Israel had broken international law, they reasoned, this was nothing in comparison to consigning an entire people for extermination.

After a relatively tranquil summer, the country was shocked to learn that a "Nazi Party" had been formed in Canada with direct links to the infamous American Nazi Party. On the CBC television program *Newsmagazine* on 30 October Norman Depoe interviewed George Lincoln Rockwell, the leader of the American party. Rockwell was already notorious for expounding his racist and antisemitic views in the American media. Sitting in a chair, wearing a Nazi uniform, smoking a corncob pipe, and backed by his acolytes standing sternly in their Nazi regalia with a swastika flag as a backdrop, Rockwell defined the situation. He told Depoe: "In Canada we have two fairly large sections of the Nazi Party. We have the Canadian National Socialist Party in Montreal and a Hungarian section in Toronto." Rockwell revealed that the Montreal contingent was headed by André Bellefeuille from Sorel, Quebec. Bellefeuille was a follower of Adrien Arcand, the septuagenarian godfather of neo-Nazism in Canada. His "party" never contained more than a handful of followers, and it expired shortly after its creation. Interviewed by Depoe, he told him: "We are antisemitic ... I will have to do it [establish political concentration camps] because there is so much Communism."[18]

Bellefeuille, a federal civil servant, was suspended after Rockwell's revelation and then reinstated when the movement collapsed.[19] Some survivors found out that Rockwell was staying at the Berkeley Hotel on Sherbrooke Street in Montreal. They staged a protest there, the first public demonstration held by survivors in Canada. The broadcast was condemned by the premiers of Ontario and Quebec and by federal officials. In the immediate fallout after the interview, the RCMP deported Rockwell. [20]

Other organizations also criticized the broadcast. In a press release on 3 November the Canadian Labour Congress stated: "Canada contains many persons who have been victims of the brutal atrocities committed by the Nazi Party and its followers in Germany. These people, who have come here at our invitation, now subscribe to our economy and progress ... We can imagine their anguish when they are confronted with evidence that such movements also exist in Canada. The knowledge of the feelings of these victims of Nazi horror should spur all peoples and organizations to fight unremittingly to wipe out the traces, however small, of Nazism in Canada."[21]

Nine days after the broadcast the Canadian Jewish Congress issued its own press release. It maintained the organization's long-held principles that racial hatred should be dealt with by the political and law-enforcement authorities, and that while public pronouncements such as those made by Rockwell and Bellefeuille must be condemned, they did not present a menace to society. "We believe that incitement to violence by fomenting racial hatred should be outlawed and in the past we have made representation to Parliament to this end and — fully cognizant of the need to preserve freedom of speech and communication — we will continue our efforts towards this goal. We know that the law enforcement agencies are aware of Fascist activities that are being promoted in our midst ... Fascist activity of whatever dimension and wherever promoted is of course a serious matter and a potential threat. While the activity revealed constitutes no imminent threat to Canada and its institutions, nevertheless it would be mischievous to underestimate its significance or ignore its existence."[22]

In its report to the Congress plenary in 1962, the JPRC outlined its policy following the Rockwell revelations. "Congress has since this time been in close touch [with] two ministries: The Department of Citizenship and the Department of Justice. With the former we have discussed the threat of anti-semitic and neo-Nazi activities among unnaturalized residents, and with the latter, the possibility of legislative remedy against hate-mongering ... Similar discussions have also been held with the Postmaster-General on the postal aspect of this matter. A meeting was also held with CBC management on the question of the neo-Nazi exposes and the implication of such broadcasts."[23]

Congress's belated press release did little to satisfy some Montreal survivors. Isaac Piasetski recalled that he went to see Saul Hayes. "[I said] something should be done; [let's do] something together. Hayes said, 'There are special conditions here; [it's] not like during the war.'" When he and Aba Beer saw the swastikas on television, "we were shocked." When told by Hayes that it was totally legal for Rockwell to spout his views in public, they felt "that the rest of the Jews didn't give a damn; [that] here it can never happen." Lou Zablow also met with Hayes. He was told, "There's nothing we can do about it, it's a free country."[24] Dazed by the legal prerogative of free speech and rebuffed by the Jewish establishment, a small core of survivors, including Zablow, decided to establish their own organization. In November, they formed the Association of Former Concentration Camps Inmates/Survivors of Nazi Oppression. The association's constitution had two central aims – preserving the memory of the Holocaust and the victims and counteracting the resurgence of Nazi movements. Although the association was born because of the survivors' frustration with Congress, it did not see itself as a rival but as a complementary organization. Article 9 of the constitution read, "Try, whenever possible, to act in co-operation and conformation with the activities of the Canadian Jewish Congress and other affiliated organizations representing the voice of the Jewish Community here."[25]

The association's first public act was a march commemorating the Holocaust and Liberation along Dorchester Street in downtown Montreal in May 1961. Zablow invited Hayes and other dignitaries to join the march. Hayes responded, much to Zablow's amazement, that "Jews never marched on the streets of Montreal before." Zablow, retorted, "[During the war] I thought you [would] lay down [sic] on the steps of Parliament [to protest the treatment of Jews in Europe]." He later recalled that none of the Jewish leaders appeared at the march.[26]

The editorial response in those media critical of the apprehension and abduction of Eichmann, like the CBC's decision to provide Rockwell with a national forum, caused consternation in the Jewish community. These incidents fuelled fear that antisemitism was alive and well and that the national media were negligent, at best, in not recognizing the threat. Congress's attitude remained consistent: do not sow panic, disavow any vigilante action, work with the authorities, and assuage the anxieties of the survivors. For a handful of survivors, this approach was inadequate and short-sighted. They were distressed that most Canadians did not understand the gravity of the situation and were more perturbed that their own leadership was also unenlightened. The events of 1960 were an initial breaking point in the Jewish community because of the internal divisions created by the response to incipient antisemitism both in Canada and abroad.

THE EICHMANN TRIAL

The indictment against Adolf Eichmann was registered in the district court in Jerusalem on 21 February 1961. He was charged with fifteen counts of "crimes against the Jewish people," "crimes against humanity," "war crimes," and "membership in a hostile organization." The trial began on 10 April. The world learned the details of the trial immediately through live television coverage. Eichmann sat impassively in a bulletproof glass booth throughout the proceedings. His defence was that he could not receive a fair trial in Israel, that he had been kidnapped from Argentina, that the Nazis and Nazi Collaborators Law was post factum; and that the offences listed had occurred before the founding of the state of Israel. These arguments were rejected by the court. The prosecution produced documents – and more important, eyewitnesses – to buttress its case. This evidence was of overwhelming significance for most of the television viewers knew little about the specific details of the Holocaust. The trial did more to raise awareness of the catastrophe in the general public than any other event up to that time. A Gallup poll taken in the

United States in May showed that 87 per cent of the sample knew of the trial, 71 per cent thought that it was a "good thing" to be reminded of the camps, and the same proportion thought that Eichmann was getting a fair trial.[27] He was found guilty on all counts on 15 December and sentenced to death. He appealed the verdict, but the appeal was rejected on 29 May 1962, and Eichmann was hanged at midnight 31 May. His body was cremated and his ashes scattered at sea.[28]

In Canada the trial dominated the media for several months. As it opened, the key consideration was whether Eichmann would be tried impartially. However, as the witnesses presented their testimony, the focus shifted to the horrors which had been inflicted upon the Jews. The *Canadian Jewish News* sent its editor, M.J. Nurenberger, to Jerusalem. In his front-page editorials, Nurenberger excoriated the "civilized world" for not protesting the Holocaust and the United Nations for censuring Israel for abducting Eichmann. He glorified the Jews who had revolted against the Nazis and the state of Israel as the defender of the Jewish people. The six million were recast as martyrs, especially the children. "The million and a half murdered Jewish children whose clothing and toys were saved for the little Michls and Gretchens had no defenders, for at that time there was no sovereign Jewish state to act on their behalf. In our civilized world these tots were not important enough for the preservation of their lives to be considered an Allied war objective."[29] In the non-Jewish press, coverage of the trial had its sensationalist side as well as sober reflection on the events. *Maclean's* ran an article titled "I Worked for Adolf Eichmann," in which a Toronto woman wrote about how she had helped to "process Jews" for Eichmann in Czechoslovakia. The *Star Weekly Magazine's* feature was called "The Trial of the Century."[30]

Prior to the trial, the JPRC and the United Zionist Council created a special subcommittee "to consider and advise regularly on the public relations aspect in Canada of the Eichmann trial." In a statement to "Jewish Community Leaders," the committee declared that "while the facts surrounding Eichmann's capture and forthcoming trial are a stirring and dramatic background for many kinds of program there is a much higher duty in the interests of the community and the people of Israel as well that demands restraint and self discipline. The committee, therefore, advise all groups, clubs and organizations to adopt a very judicious attitude and to refrain from panel discussions, lectures, legal opinions, mock trials and any public discussion at least until the trial is over."[31] The committee was undoubtedly referring to a front-page article in the *Globe and Mail*, which described a mock trial at Beth Jacob Synagogue in Hamilton. The trial had asked whether executing Eichmann would fan the fires of neo-Nazism and link Israel with totalitarian regimes in a disregard for legal process, and whether Eichmann could be tried impartially. The audience wept as evidence was presented about the Holocaust. The "jury" was spared the task of bringing in a verdict.[32]

The subcommittee, reviewing the state of public opinion about the trial based on editorials and letters to the editor following the publication of the Gallup poll, concluded: "The majority of editorial opinion has come around to the view that the major purpose of the trial has been served. The feeling is that the record is being clearly set forth on what was done not only to a people but to humanity at large." The subcommittee also noted that letters to the editor were five to one in favour of the view that Eichmann was receiving a fair hearing, but it was distressed at the deluge of antisemitic publications which claimed that Eichmann had been "framed" by "Zionist Jews", and pamphlets that cited "the falsehood ... about the 6,000,000 Jews said to be gassed by Hitler."[33]

One notable exception was the *Globe and Mail*. Its lead editorial on 11 April made the same arguments as Eichmann's defence attorney. It went on to argue that the trial would become a television spectacle and asked whether the trial could "assure the Jews of anything except a moment of vengeance." It maintained that the "Nuremberg" trials had failed to establish a system of international justice, but it then contradicted that point by contending that a world court, rather than an Israeli one, was the proper venue for the proceedings. When the trial ended, the *Globe* claimed that Eichmann had been kidnapped and that the trial had focused on "one particular kind of persecution and on the misdeeds of one particular people, the Germans," blurring the atrocities committed by other regimes in the 1930s and 1940s. The *Globe*'s narrow editorial interpretation was not shared by some writers in the paper. John Gellner, a military and international affairs analyst, pointed out that the trial had failed to make Germans realize the enormity of the crimes. It had triggered a spate of belated prosecutions of Nazi war criminals, but he denounced the German public for viewing this development with apprehension.[34]

The trial had a deep effect on Canadian Jews. Survivors had provided eyewitness accounts of ghettoization, deportation, mass murder, and Jewish armed resistance. The eloquent testimonies of Zivia Lubetkin and Abba Kovner, leaders of uprisings in Warsaw and Vilna, were stirring and detailed. Viewers were brought face to face, via television, with these and other survivors and with one of the architects of the destruction of European Jewry. Nathan Leipciger recalled: "My [Canadian Jewish] friends asked, 'Did it really happen,' and that's the first time we started to talk about it to our immediate friends. The Eichmann trial had a profound influence on the survivors, on how to talk about it, and [to] their families as well. The stories coming out from Jerusalem [made] us spectators." Lou Zablow credited the publicity over the trial with bringing "the survivors out." It was one factor in the growth of the Association of Survivors. Sophie Waldman borrowed a television, and she remembered that watching the trial "was painful to me."[35]

Yet it did not have the same impact on survivors as native displays of antisemitism did. According to Ben Kayfetz, the trial did not stimulate survivors to press Congress for the prosecution of war criminals, nor were there rallies and demonstrations such as those inspired by the appearance of neo-Nazis in public. It only confirmed what the survivors already knew from bitter experience, but it did arouse the desire on the part of some Canadian Jews to learn more about the Holocaust. One spark for this interest was the campaign by the *Canadian Jewish News*. By this time, the CJN had replaced the *Jewish Chronicle* as the main English-language newspaper in the community. During the trial it had published an article on the Ringelblum archives, hidden during the war, which documented the story of Warsaw Jews under Nazi occupation. Next to this article was an editorial urging readers to participate in a "mass observance" commemorating the Warsaw Ghetto Uprising. Over the next several weeks the paper published excerpts from *Young David's Diary*, an account of ghetto life; an article announcing a public lecture by ghetto fighter Zivia Lubetkin, followed by an account of the event, which drew an audience of a thousand; and Meyer Gasner's article on his visit to Auschwitz.[36] The trial was not a factor in dividing the community, unlike the events of 1960 and those of the next few years, since it could only stand by and watch the proceedings. Aside from monitoring public opinion, there was no direct action that the organized community could take.[37]

COMING TO GRIPS WITH ANTISEMITISM

In late February 1962 the European executive of the World Jewish Congress created a committee to collect information about the spread of antisemitism. A year later it published its findings. The incidents included the cutting of swastikas into the bodies of Jewish youth in Argentina and Uruguay, organized neo-Nazi demonstrations in Trafalgar Square in London, and attacks on Jews in Rome. The main concern was the proliferation of extreme right-wing groups. There were a dozen such groups in Britain, seven in France which produced twelve periodicals, and thirteen international organizations headquartered in Austria, Belgium, and Switzerland. The report remarked on the attraction of such groups for youth. The leaders of the two main extreme right-wing parties in Britain, for example, were under the age of forty. The report of this committee appeared in the *Jewish Standard*, a Toronto weekly. The article concluded:

reports from various countries show clearly that the disease of anti-Semitism has again become active. Like a contagious plague, it has spread across frontiers and oceans. Its successful growth in one country has stimulated its emergence in others. It may well be that the situation and prospects are even more menacing, for the reports do not cover the whole of Europe, but only a selected number of countries, and they are based, to a large extent, on press reports and other published material. They do not contain information which the Nazi and anti-Semitic organizations have been able to conceal ... Past experience in dealing with anti-Semitism must be re-examined in the light of present conditions and new approaches made in the spheres of information, legislation, education and Christian religious teaching to children and adolescents ... Intensive efforts will be required to arouse public opinion on the national and international levels to the danger which the evil of anti-Semitism bodes for democracy, for liberty and the freedom of the individual.[38]

In four CJC plenaries held in the 1950s, there had been only two resolutions relating to the Holocaust, both in reference to the commemoration of the Warsaw Ghetto Uprising. The plenary of May 1962 was held against the backdrop of the execution of Eichmann and the exposure of widespread antisemitic actions. Those events were a catalyst in the adoption of three resolutions related to the Holocaust. The most significant resolution dealt with hate-mongering and Nazism. Clause *a* stated: "That the Canadian Jewish Congress continue to seek ways and means which will make it possible, without infringing on the democratic freedoms of Canadians, to take all steps necessary to bring about amendments to the Criminal Code which will make it a criminal offence to practice genocide and race hatred." Clause *c* stated: "That the Canadian Jewish Congress take steps to encourage educational institutions in the provinces of Canada to introduce in their teaching of modern history an understanding of the background and repercussions of Nazism in the 1930's and 1940's, and that the true lessons of race prejudice not be overlooked in the curriculum." This resolution was a landmark because it made public the intent to pressure the federal government to respond to hate-mongering and it recognized the need to include the Holocaust in public education. Nevertheless, there was a specific emphasis on not infringing upon the freedom of speech, a key concern of many members of the NJPRC.

The second resolution dealt with the integration of "newcomers" into the structure of Congress, and the third one was yet another resolution recommending that "every center of Jewish population in Canada carry out an annual event marking the Uprising in the Warsaw Ghetto."[39] The Association of Survivors claimed a large measure of credit for these resolutions. Six of its members were given delegate status. The association had submitted six resolutions for consideration whose language was much stronger than in those adopted. One example was the resolution on education. It had originally read: "To introduce into all public and high schools of this country a thorough study of the evil results of race prejudice in all its manifestations throughout history. This special sickness capable of spawning such collective crimes as Nazism, must be studied for future generations, in the classrooms of our children across Canada."[40]

Resolutions do not automatically result in policy. They are often merely statements of intent or are designed to please certain groups, without any commitment toward their realization. Congress did pressure the federal government to enact changes to the Criminal Code, but it did nothing with respect to education. Three years after the plenary there were still no "newcomers" on the Congress executive. A resolution on the commemoration of the uprising was mere window dressing, as such events had been held in the largest centres for many years. When asked about the discrepancy between the resolutions and their enactment, Lou Zablow responded that "in the early years, they hated our [the survivors'] guts."[41] Despite the bitterness still felt by Zablow and some others more than thirty years later, the plenary did confer delegate status upon members of the association and did respond to the perceived rise of antisemitism for the first time in the post-war era in its campaign to have hate propaganda criminalized.

In the early 1960s the "disease of anti-Semitism" was the primary concern of the Jewish community. The Eichmann trial had been a rude jolt, not because the information that it produced was new, but because the knowledge of the events that it brought to light had receded from the collective memory of the community and because not many Canadian Jews had heard first-hand about the horrors of the Holocaust from the survivors. Continued antisemitic incidents, mostly confined to Toronto, together with reports about the outbreak of antisemitic organizations abroad, heightened the tension and created discomfort in the community. The founding of the association by a small core of survivors and the creation of another Montreal group, the Bergen-Belsen Survivors Association,[42] marked a dramatic shift in the politicization of the newcomers. No longer content with the CJC as their sole advocate, its members sought to prod Congress by working within the umbrella organization to step up the public campaign against antisemitism and to preserve the memory of the destroyed civilization and the two-thirds of its members who had died. In the general community there were some indications of a growing understanding of the survivor experience, but in the main, the gap between Canadian Jews and the survivors remained.[43]

The spread of antisemitic propaganda increased in 1963. The centre of neo-Nazi activity was Toronto. Beginning in April, more than twenty incidents were recorded. They included graffiti stating that "Hitler Was Right" and "Communism Is Jewish." Pamphlets and leaflets were stuffed in mail boxes and distributed on the streets and in stores. They were published by several extremist groups, notably the American Nazi Party, the National Socialist Movement of London, England, the World Service of Birmingham, Alabama, and the Christian Education Association of Union, New Jersey.[44] Aside from Toronto, there was little antisemitic activity in Canada. One exception was in Winnipeg, where during the summer a synagogue was desecrated, and antisemitic insults were hurled at Jews at Winnipeg Beach. These events were not linked with any particular group.[45] One factor for the rise in antisemitic activity at this time was the civil rights movement in the United States. As a backlash to the movement, racists redoubled their efforts, creating new groups and reinvigorating established ones. Jews were targeted as the secret force behind the civil rights movement. The CBC continued to provide a forum for the racists. On 25 August *Sunday Magazine* interviewed Rockwell on the eve of the "March on Washington,"[46] the central event of the movement. Other factors included the growth of fascist elements in West Germany, the spread of neo-Nazi groups to other European countries and to Latin America, antisemitic rhetoric masquerading as anti-Zionism among both left-wing and right-wing extremists, and the distribution of literature such as the notorious "Protocols of the Elders of Zion" in the Arab world and the USSR. Yet another element was the contention that the assassination of John Kennedy was the work of a Jewish conspiracy that had employed Jack Ruby as the trigger man.[47]

Ben Kayfetz recalled that, after the accusations that Jack Rubinstein (Ruby) "'killed our president,' it was something new every day. There was a rain of leaflets at King and Yonge that was frightening. I had the impression that there was a highly organized, well-trained, numerous operation in Toronto, but in speaking to Stanley years later, he said that it cost about $25 with a handful of people, giving the impression of a highly organized operation which fooled me.

That was when we decided to go public."[48] Kayfetz was referring to an incident that occurred in downtown Toronto on 11 November 1963, (before the Kennedy assassination) when leaflets reading, "Communism Is Jewish" and "Hitler Was Right" were scattered in large quantities from the upper floors of buildings. The leaflets had been published by the American Nazi Party in Arlington, Virginia.[49] David Stanley was a twenty-year-old disciple of George Lincoln Rockwell and John Ross Taylor, the éminence grise of the neo-Nazi movement. Taylor had first emerged as a disseminator of antisemitic material during the Depression. He had briefly acted as Adrien Arcand's representative in Toronto in 1937.[50] For the next half-century Taylor continued his antisemitic activities; they would only end with his death in 1996. He was a mentor for many notorious purveyors of hate, including Ernst Zundel. Stanley was also influenced by the materials written and distributed by Ron Gostick from his centre in rural Ontario.[51]

In 1964 there were more than a score of documented incidents of antisemitism in six provinces. Ontario was once again the main target. Some of the happenings there surpassed earlier ones in their severity and extent. The worst occurrences were the sending of leaflets by mail to all persons in Toronto whose name began with "Rosen"; the mailing of cards with a swastika and the words "THITH ITH THE END" to members of the Jewish community in Toronto and Hamilton on 7 and 8 September, the Jewish high holy days; and the distribution of the "Protocols of the Elders of Zion" in Sault Ste Marie.[52] Stanley was the mastermind behind many of these episodes. He received hate materials from American and British neo-Nazi and white supremacist organizations.

The tension and concern in the Jewish community over these overt displays was heightened on 25 October. The most watched public affair program on television in the mid-1960s was *This Hour Has Seven Days*. It tackled controversial subjects with a panache that was out of keeping with the staid image of the CBC. Its hosts, Warner Troyer and Laurier Lapierre, combined a scholarly, investigative approach with a dash of humour and derring-do. They were ably abetted by a core of young reporters, including an irreverent Winnipeg Jew, Larry Zolf. On the evening in question, the program interviewed George Lincoln Rockwell. Not shying away from the controversy over the interview with Rockwell four years earlier, the CBC ventured into Rockwell's headquarters in Arlington Virginia. In the preamble to the interview, the program explained why it was being broadcast. "We believe that the best way to deal with extremists is to expose them, not to pretend that they don't exist. These are the facts: the growth and influence of the far right in the last five years ... Jews and others are receiving hate literature ... To ignore his [Rockwell's] very real existence will not reduce the threat he presents and may well assist him. We believe it must be shown."

Rockwell was then given the opportunity to expound at length. He said in part, "[We are] out to liquidate Communist traitors, not Jews ... We are racists, devoted to preserve the white race ... Deport the Negroes who agree, keep the rest on reservations ... About 80 percent of Jews are Commies or traitors – death by trial ... Hitler is lied about more than any person than Christ ... It's a lie that six million were gassed ... I'm the Lenin to Hitler's Marx, the St Paul to Hitler's Christ ... Martin Luther Coon ... I'd rather gas queers than anyone else. A lot of Jews and liberals are also queers." As he had in the interview in 1960, Rockwell sat wearing his uniform, smoking his pipe and protected by his guard, who stood impassively, with their arms folded.[53]

Understandably, the broadcast was met with an outcry from the Jewish community. The Association of Survivors presented a memorandum to the Board of Broadcast Governors, the public regulatory body. In it the association stated that "the Rockwell interview was conducted in a way constituting a flagrant violation of all acceptable standards of good taste and human decency." The memorandum continued, "Enlightened opinion, newspaper editorials, Members of Parliament who spoke on the subject in the House of Commons on October 27, agreed that the producers of the program had stooped down to cheap, vulgar, yellow journalism."[54] Rabbi N. Fredman, in a letter to the editor of the Winnipeg dailies wrote: "There are three reasons for protest. First, Rockwell is no more demented than Hitler; Canadians are no more virtuous than Germans ... Second, Rockwell's anti-Negro jibes were in part fed him by his questioners ... Third, to expose Rockwell as a freak to be laughed at, a nut to be pitied, or an extremist to be exposed, avoided, or reviled is to forfeit hope in humanity."[55]

Less than three months later, *This Hour Has Seven Days* entered the fray once again. This time David Stanley was accosted as he handed out antisemitic leaflets on a street corner in downtown Toronto. His appearance was a contrast to Rockwell's. Here was a young, clean-cut fellow, articulate, holding a briefcase, and with a quiet, persistent demeanour. He told Zolf, the interviewer, that he was "exposing a certain element in this city – a Commie and Zionist element. Not all of the Jewish community, a majority, is treasonable." Stanley said, "I can see the interviewer is Jewish." World War II was "useless ... the six million Jew thing ... there were no gas chambers." A crowd began to swell around Stanley. One person called him mentally defective, and Stan-

ley responded, "90 per cent of Commies in the U.S. are Jews, are traitors." A Jewish survivor from Radom demanded, "What do you
know?" Following this segment, the program interviewed Minister of
Justice Guy Favreau, who had announced the establishment of the
Committee on Hate Propaganda earlier that week. He observed that
"our problem is to strike a proper balance of dignity of the citizen and
the maintenance of freedom of speech." Within a year, Stanley had
dropped out of the scene. Kayfetz bumped into him years later, and
Stanley told him that he had disavowed his youthful ideology.[56]

After the Favreau interlude, the program interviewed John Ross Taylor at his retreat in rural Ontario. He stated that he had distributed literature for thirty-one years "because it's the truth" ... the time has been
ripe since 1962 ... due to a whole series of factors ... [with] an increase of
5,000 per cent in the last twelve months of distribution and printing ...
this is a religious war; Communism is a religion ... This is symbolized
by international Jewish finance, for example, the CBC ... Jews have to be
dealt with as a people ... Hate literature is the Talmud ... Jews and Commies are the same." Taylor appeared an older version of Stanley – well-
spoken, quiet, wearing a business suit, sitting in front of a window that
captured the peaceful landscape outside.[57] Zolf remembered meeting
Taylor in the early 1960s. "He said that he would only eat Jewish food
because they poisoned the world's food supply. Taylor was a meticu-
lous, boring man; Nazis are boring." Kayfetz described Taylor as coming from a well-to-do family that manufactured Fairy brand soap. "He
had deep-set eyes, with a ghost-like intent look about him. He was
influential with the true believers, not the general public."[58]

Three days later a radio station in Winnipeg announced that it
would carry an interview with Rockwell which had been broadcast
in the United States. A delegation headed by Heinz Frank, the executive director of CJC Western Region, persuaded the station to abandon
the project.[59] Meanwhile, Michael Garber of Congress wrote to R.C.
Fraser, vice-president of the CBC, protesting the airing of the Stanley-
Taylor broadcast. Fraser's response was unsatisfactory. Garber wrote
again to Fraser, concluding, "If you, forgetting your official position,
can contemplate your having been a Canadian Jew listening to these
harangues, you will have a better answer to your letter than I can
give you."[60]

HATE PROPAGANDA AND
THE COHEN COMMITTEE

Guy Favreau's announcement on the CBC that a committee on hate propaganda was being established by the Department of Justice was the

result of long-term lobbying by Congress and pressure from some members of the Liberal caucus.[61] Bill C-21 had its first reading in the House of Commons on 20 February 1964. Called "An Act respecting Genocide," it was a private member's bill introduced by Milton Klein, the Liberal member for Montreal-Cartier, and seconded by party whip James Walker of Toronto-York Centre, as a response to the proliferation of hate propaganda and incitement to racial hatred of the preceding four years. Klein had met with Lou Zablow on several occasions in 1963 over the issue. The degree to which these meetings influenced his decision to introduce the bill is unclear since there had been so much opposition to racism, especially antisemitism, in the early 1960s.[62] Moreover, Congress was changing its lobbying tactics, and had decided to drop its backroom "quarantine approach" (so called by the JCRC). It sent a public deputation to meet with the ministers of justice, the post office, and customs and presented unsolicited resolutions from church leaders, lawyers' groups, veterans' associations, and a national women's federation urging the government to take action.[63] Klein's bill, supported by Walker, an influential member whose constituency had a large Jewish population, was in line with the philosophy of Lester Pearson's Liberals. The prime minister, speaking on Brotherhood Week earlier that month, stated: "Brotherhood calls for more than resistance to the violence that hatred inevitably begets. It must also reject just as resolutely, the moral cynicism and hush-hush social discrimination which are the roots of more violent bigotry."[64]

The Klein-Walker bill was rooted in the United Nations Convention on Genocide, signed by both houses of Parliament in March 1952. It called for the criminalization of acts in which the victims were targeted because of their nationality, ethnicity, race, or religion. The death penalty was to be imposed for killing a member of such a group, a minimum of ten years imprisonment for causing physical or mental harm, and five years for publications or speeches that were injurious to such groups or exposed them to hatred, contempt, or ridicule.[65] The bill was given second reading on 10 July 1964, and the debate was carried, by unanimous consent of the House, on 17 July. Walker spoke in support of the bill that day. He referred to editorial endorsement from *Dimanche Matin*, the *Toronto Telegram*, and the Toronto *Daily Star*, and reported that according to the attorney general of Ontario, no provincial legislation existed that would outlaw hate propaganda. His speech is indicative of the mood at that time and of the input of the Jewish community on the issue.

I have not tackled this problem from the viewpoint of its being just a problem of my Jewish constituents. To me it is a matter which concerns every

Canadian citizen regardless of his race or creed because it was in an atmosphere of hate and distrust that the late President Kennedy was assassinated. I think all Canadians must do more clear thinking about what is right and what is wrong, what is good and what is evil. As far as I am concerned, the current hate campaign is a very evil thing and I am committed to fight against it from the very beginning, before it has a chance to produce the conditions which allow would-be Hitlers and Stalins to gain a foothold. People who forget the past are sometimes condemned to relive it ... These enemies of society, these wreckers and destroyers of other people's lives use freedom of speech to destroy other freedoms equally important – freedom from fear, freedom from persecution. The next step is the use of democracy to destroy democracy ... The rationalizing has gone on long enough. For years the Canadian Jewish congress has presented briefs to various governments asking that action be taken. They are doing a job for all of us ... We heard the Prime Minister today in his statement to the house upon his return from the commonwealth prime ministers conference, stress the need of an immediate beginning toward the solution of human and race relationships within the commonwealth. At this moment Canada is generally free of this problem, but there is a cloud on the horizon and I believe it should be dispelled now before it cast an ugly shadow across our beloved land.[66]

Bill C-21 was reintroduced as Bill C-30 on 8 April 1965.[67] It died on the order paper when the House was adjourned for the summer recess and not recalled until after the federal election held on 8 November. It was significant, nevertheless, because it addressed the issue in uncompromising terms. The bill took a maximalist position, which disturbed even Walker; he opposed the automatic death penalty yet urged the House to refer the bill for study because "the purpose and intent of the bill is clear."[68] In addition, the debate put Congress into the public arena for the first time with respect to this issue. It may be argued that the CJC had no option, since the Association of Survivors had taken the tack of public protest first, but there can be little doubt that without the pressure from Congress, there would have been less incentive for Klein to introduce the bill.

In the meantime, the association continued its campaign for inclusion in Congress decision-making. Despite the adoption of the resolution at the 1962 plenary to integrate "newcomers" into the organization, no steps had been taken two years later. On 17 May 1964 the association proposed a resolution, based on the need to "enlist the maximum amount of support in dealing with this issue [the problem of neo-nazism and hate incitement]," to "revitalize" the JCRC "by endowing it with a true representation of the entire spectrum of opinions within the Jewish community."[69] The association wanted to be both an independent voice in the community and a partner with the JCRC. From the standpoint of Congress, this was an untenable position. The association had lobbied Klein at the same time as Congress had shifted from private to public advocacy. Although there is no evidence of a discussion at the national level of the association's resolution, the fact that Congress did not offer a position on the NJCRC to officers of the association indicates that it was not prepared to "integrate the newcomers" at the main decision-making level at that time.

Congress was not content to send a token public delegation to Ottawa and to receive an endorsement in Hansard from Walker. It had been meeting with the postmaster general to urge him to amend the Post Office Act by making it an offence to use the mails for the distribution of hate propaganda. It argued that section 153 of the Criminal Code, which makes it an offence to "use the mails for the purpose of transmitting or delivering anything which is obscene, indecent, immoral or scurrilous," be judicially interpreted to prevent the spread of hate literature.[70] A board of review undertook this task and passed a interim order on 29 September 1964, which prohibited the forwarding of mail from the National States' Right Party, publisher of the periodical the *Thunderbolt*. As a result of this interpretation, the postmaster general barred the delivery of mail to David Stanley and John Ross Taylor. [71]

Congress also was making headway in its discussions with the Department of Justice. Maxwell Cohen, Congress president Michael Garber, and Saul Hayes met with Guy Favreau on 17 October 1964. They suggested to the minister that he establish a committee to "study in depth the problem of possible effective legislation to control or eliminate the publication and distribution of 'hate' materials." [72] A few weeks later, in an address to a B'nai Brith lodge meeting in Montreal, Favreau announced the appointment of a "special committee of experts to study the problem." [73] Not surprisingly, the first two experts chosen were Cohen, as chair, and Hayes. On 10 January 1965 Favreau announced the appointment of the other members. They were James Corry of Queen's University, Father Gérard Dion of Université Laval, Mark MacGuigan of the University of Toronto, Shane MacKay of the *Winnipeg Free Press*, and Pierre Elliott Trudeau of the Université de Montréal. The committee was extra-parliamentary in its personnel, which meant that it could survive general elections and present its report to the next minister of justice.[74]

When later asked about the creation of the committee, MacGuigan, a Federal Court justice at the time of the interview, responded: "There was a great deal of relatively underground circulation of anti-Jewish hate material. There was corresponding pressure from the Jewish community of Canada to do something about that and various proposals in Parliament to deal with it ... I don't know precisely what the trigger was ... one might have thought that it was Trudeau, but he wasn't in government until the fall." MacGuigan had been surprised that the committee was created in such haste. "The government doesn't usually respond so quickly to things that happen in society. It usually takes a much longer period before something happens. My guess is that CJC was very much involved in it because Saul Hayes was made a member of the committee, which is rather unusual ... It leads me to believe that they were the principal reason for the committee and that it was set up to satisfy them."[75]

Although the proliferation of antisemitic and racist materials and the public rhetoric of the early 1960s acted as a catalyst for the Klein-Walker bill, the amendment to the Post Office Act, and the formation of the Cohen committee, these initiatives must be viewed in the wider context of domestic and international developments. Congress had been working quietly since the late 1940s to have teeth put into legislation that barred discrimination on the basis of religion, race, or ethnicity. It was one force in successfully pressuring provincial governments to adopt fair employment practices acts. The second Diefenbaker administration had also played a vital role in the process when it passed the Bill of Rights in 1960. In the United States, beginning with the Supreme Court decision in 1954 to overturn the barriers to racial integration, the effort to change the laws was gaining steam, in response to the civil rights movement and the determination by the Johnson administration to eradicate barriers against "Negroes." In 1957, Ghana became the first black African nation to win independence from Britain. Over the next seven years the rest of the British Empire in Africa, as well as most of the French Empire, gave way to the independence movement. As the new Commonwealth was shedding the remains of the empire, Canada was regarded as the leader of the "white" nations in the battle against racism by third-world members of the Commonwealth, and Pearson, who became prime minister in 1963, eagerly accepted the mantle.

That the Jewish community was instrumental at the initial stage of legislation outlawing hate propaganda is undisputed, but the degree of influence of the survivors, notably the Association of Survivors, as distinct from Congress, is difficult to determine. It may be argued that the association's tactics forced the CJC to react more quickly than it would have otherwise and might have been a factor in its decision to go public in February 1964. Yet the central reason for these developments lay with the racists themselves. Their actions necessitated a vocal response from the Jewish community and created the animosity towards them that resulted in condemnation by all elements of the Canadian public.

CONCLUSION

It is somehow fitting that Rockwell, Stanley, and Taylor were partially responsible for enlightening the Jewish community about the Holocaust. The revival of antisemitism disturbed the mood of ethnic complacency. The unrelenting pressure of native antisemitism, in combination with international displays of antisemitic behaviour and the Eichmann trial, created the perception that there were pockets of individuals and small groups who were prepared to do more than merely speak and publish. While there was evidence that this behaviour would not be tolerated, as editorials, letters, and articles and the protests of non-Jewish organizations demonstrate, Canadian Jews were alarmed about the proliferation of hate and the unabashed public display of the racists. Many could not understand why the CBC would provide a national forum on the most popular public affairs program to hate-mongers or why the esteemed *Globe and Mail* and other leading newspapers would question the actions of the tiny state of Israel in apprehending and trying a man who had personally directed the murder of millions of Jews.

In context, the discomfort felt by the community was understandable. These five years witnessed the height of the civil rights movement in the United States, of which the Canadian public was overwhelmingly supportive. Canadians fancied themselves as being tolerant of their minorities and fortunate in not having to bear the burden of a legacy of slavery and segregation. The actions of white supremacists, the murder of white civil rights workers, the bombing of black churches where children were killed, and the defiant stand of state governors on the steps of state universities to prevent the registration of black students were condemned by most Canadians. There seemed to be a real threat of civil disorder south of the border, especially following Kennedy's assassination. While Rockwell's boast that Barry Goldwater (the most right-wing mainstream candidate for the presidency in memory as the Republican nominee in 1964) would win the 1968 election but then "betray" the country, leading to Rockwell's election, was fanciful, there was a fear that extremist elements were gaining ground in the backlash against the civil rights movement. That was one significant factor in the uneasiness felt in Canada, particularly among Canadian Jews, about the spread of racism and antisemitism.

Another factor for this feeling was the revitalization of antisemitism in Europe, the Middle East, and Latin America. It became apparent that the "disease of antisemitism" was spreading and that attacks on Jews, both physical and verbal, were part of the problem. Moreover, the anti-Israel propaganda centred in the Arab world and the Soviet Union was gaining momentum. Jews in the diaspora were concerned about these developments. The revival of antisemitism was outside the experience of many Canadian Jews who had reached adulthood after the war. For the older generation, it harkened back to the interwar period. Of greater significance, the public displays of antisemitism were a shock to the survivors, who had not expected such activity in their adopted country. Such feelings of victimization were not uncommon at the time. Other minorities in North America were also publicly voicing their pain and seeking recognition of their suffering.

At issue was how to respond to these activities. The JCRC, an amalgam of leaders of Congress and B'nai Brith, determined that the proper authorities could handle the immediate outbreaks while the committee quietly lobbied for legislation to counter hate literature. It relied on its contacts with politicians and was confident that its success in influencing governments after the war to enact legislation banning discrimination in hiring and housing would continue in the 1960s. The problem was that the wider community was either not aware of its initiatives or dissatisfied with them. A small core of survivors in Montreal, not content with the "tranquil" approach, became politicized. In so doing, they became adept at creating publicity, influencing politicians favourable to their cause, and irritating the established powers in the Jewish community. As antisemitic incidents proliferated, the differing approaches in dealing with the crisis further divided the community, first in Montreal and then in Toronto. Congress had to change its tactic by publicly lobbying for legislation in February 1964, partially in response to the pressure exerted by the survivor organizations. This was one factor in the decision by Klein and Walker to introduce their bill and in Pearson's decision to allow Favreau to establish the Cohen committee.

By early 1965 a new dynamic was glaringly apparent – there was a serious split in the Jewish community. On the one hand, Congress, in response to antisemitic activity, promoted a vocal, public presence within the norms of accepted civil liberties. On the other hand, a nucleus of Holocaust survivors, confident and emboldened by their success and recognition at the highest levels of officialdom, as demonstrated in Pearson's address on 9 May, advocated a more aggressive attack against the hate-mongers. The clash between these two forces would reach its apex a month later.

5 "A cleavage in the community": The Toronto Jewish Community in the 1960s

On Monday, 31 May 1965 a two-inch headline in the *Globe and Mail* screamed, "Mob Beats Suspected Nazis in Outburst at Allan Gardens."[1] The news in the nation's media that day described an anti-Nazi demonstration that attracted, according to the *Globe*, five thousand people, of whom nine were arrested when the demonstration deteriorated into a riot. Protesters had gathered at a park on the eastern edge of downtown Toronto to oppose an announced rally by the Canadian Nazi Party, at which John Beattie, the self-styled leader of the Nazis, was to have spoken. Ironically, despite police protection, Beattie did not have an opportunity to speak because he was attacked by the protesters as he entered the park. Moreover, he did not have a permit from the parks department for the rally; only a few of his supporters appeared, and the victims of the mob violence, apart from Beattie, were not neo-Nazis. Had he been allowed to mount the podium, he would have been arrested for public mischief, and the riot might have been averted.

At face value, the demonstration and riot were an extreme overreaction by an enraged citizenry to a tiny group of misfits who posed little threat to law and order. The rally would have been an isolated event that would hardly have disturbed the calm of a pleasant spring afternoon. That it was over within fifteen minutes without serious injuries was due to the rapid response of the Toronto police and because only a handful of the anti-Nazi demonstrators participated in the violence. At a deeper level, however, the riot in Allan Gardens was profoundly significant. It was arguably the seminal event in Toronto's Jewish community in the post-war era.

By 1965 some survivors had attained the confidence to cast aside their cloaks of silence in order to denounce the antisemitic epithets of homegrown Nazis. They and their supporters created a counterforce to the CJC Central Region. Congress was responding to local neo-Nazis through surveillance, by working with local authorities, and by cautioning against "vigliantes," but survivors rejected these actions as a passive attempt to dismiss a malicious force. They had become politicized to the degree that they could infiltrate the perceived enemy, sway community opinion, and influence politicians, journalists, and the police. The riot was an unfortunate consequence of this disparity. In its aftermath, Congress recognized the necessity of providing an outlet for the survivors' concerns. Until that realization was reached, however, the gap in Toronto's Jewish community between the established forces and their critics threatened to destroy the fragile unity that had been created in the previous decades. For that reason, the riot in Allan Gardens was a watershed for the Toronto Jewish community.

INFILTRATING THE NEO-NAZIS

On 19 April 1964, on the anniversary of the uprising in the Warsaw ghetto, Sydney Harris, the vice-chairman of the JCRC Ontario Region gave the keynote address at the community's commemoration of the Holocaust. He was a prominent Toronto attorney and a symbol of the gains made by Canadian Jews. Born in 1917, he was the child of parents who had themselves been born in Toronto, a fact that made them "pioneers" among the Jewish community. Harris graduated from Osgoode Hall law school in 1942 and quickly gained a reputation as a bright and energetic individual. By 1964 he had served in leadership positions in the principal Jewish organizations and in the Canadian Bar Association. He would be elected president of Congress in 1974.[2] Harris's address before 1,500 Torontonians at Beth Tzedec Synagogue marked a departure from Congress's traditional method of counteracting antisemitism. He stated: "We have come into the possession of certain facts which identify the cowards who have crawled through post office boxes into our homes and lives, who have scrawled obscenities and indecencies on envelopes and postcards, who have littered streets and apartment lobbies with incredible repetitions that 'Hitler was Right,' who have created a mythical Col. Fry to induct people into a foreign white supremacy political party." Harris then proceeded to identify "these scum" – David Stanley, John

Beattie, and Neil Carmichael – and he gave their addresses and the names and addresses of their supporters.[3]

For decades, the main Jewish organization in Canada had worked behind the scenes in combatting antisemitism. It rarely publicized its efforts to the general public, preferring to deal with politicians and law-enforcement officials to urge them to clamp down on the activities of antisemites, much to the consternation of more militant individuals and groups in the community. Harris openly broke with this tradition in his address. "First, we have for the time being abandoned the policy that has said 'Don't publicize the hate-monger.' We have done so not only because he is so insignificant in stature and in meaning that we must know what small and futile enemies we now have, but also because the ever widening tidal waves of his influence, if unchecked by the barriers of public disavowal, disfavour and illegality, may spread to inundate our society before we recognize the disaster." Harris maintained that the prime avenue for combatting the neo-Nazi groups was through changes to the law, for which Congress had been lobbying without success for several years. "It is our continued and firm belief that the activities of the group we have exposed tonight ... are immoral and should be clearly defined as illegal by amendments to the present provisions of the Canadian Criminal Code ... We now repeat our request for amendments to the law as it now stands so that society may be protected against these branches of that precious freedom of expression which none of us wishes to see sacrificed on the altar of license."[4]

This important address should have removed all doubt that Congress was moving away from the *sha shtil* (don't rock the boat) policy of the past. Harris warned that "it is no longer a time for us to be silent – it is a time for us to speak, to speak to our government and to the world, to speak to the tiniest spreaders of the typhoid germs of hatred and to the largest oppressors of racial and religious minorities in the same voice ... We must ensure that the sacrifice for freedom made by the brave fighters in the Warsaw Ghetto uprising, whose *"Yahrzeit"* [annual commemoration] we observe tonight, need never be repeated."[5]

Nevertheless, the decision to disclose information about the neo-Nazis was not unanimous, nor was it taken quickly. According to Harris, "we [the JCRC] had been fighting for a long time on the *sha shtil* approach, and there was a large element in the community that said, 'Don't make a noise.' That did not wash well with me ... was never an ideal that appealed to me. Now [at the time of the riot] we were accused of that mentality, but if anyone looks at the record, they would know. We had vetted these things [the Nazis and their supporters] and we had inside information."[6]

Harris's address was a public indictment of those who had been spreading antisemitic hatred in Toronto in the preceding months. The most important individuals were David Stanley and John Beattie, who were in touch with George Lincoln Rockwell and Colin Jordan, the leaders of Nazi parties in the United States and Britain respectively. Neil Carmichael allowed them and a tiny group of followers to meet at the headquarters of his Social Credit Action Party at his home in central Toronto. Posters and leaflets were pasted on billboards, dropped from the roofs of buildings, left in apartment buildings, and distributed outside schools in predominantly Jewish neighbourhoods.

This campaign understandably outraged the Jewish community. The JCRC (Ontario Region) successfully infiltrated the fledgling neo-Nazi group early on, and thus it was able to gather the information that Harris made public. The information was attained through an informer who, according to Harris, provided the material "for a 'consideration' ... before we decided to give that speech ... Once we had it, enough was enough; the best way to shut him [Stanley] up was to shine a bright light on him. It didn't shut him up, but it certainly satisfied the community."[7]

Harris was correct on one count: public exposure did not lessen the activities of the neo-Nazis. Their distribution of hate literature continued. The white supremacist groups in the United States continued to gain notoriety, and Rockwell and the American Nazi Party were provided with wide exposure to the Canadian public on the CBC in the fall of 1964. This publicity heightened the tensions within the Jewish community. Survivors and their supporters were outraged. The National Joint Community Relations Committee responded in traditional fashion. It worked with a board of review created by the postmaster general, John R. Nicholson, and headed by Mr Justice Dalton Wells, which was established to look into denying the National States' Rights Party the use of the mail to send its literature to Canada. Doing so would cut off Stanley's main source of hate propaganda. The NJCRC representatives also met with NDP member of Parliament David Orlikow, who had introduced a private member's bill on this issue that was referred to the House Standing Committee on External Affairs.

The NJCRC made a submission to this committee.[8] In addition, it lobbied the minister of justice to amend the Criminal Code to indict neo-Nazis and publicly protested the airing of the Rockwell interview.[9] Congress, however, misjudged the mood of some elements in the community who were not "satisfied" by the change in the organization's tactics. In the months following Harris's address, some survivors, displeased with the apparently tame response to Stanley, Beattie, and Rockwell, began to take action themselves. The rising militancy among a vocal and active group of survivors and their supporters in the winter of 1964–65 marked a break in the Toronto Jewish community. They challenged Congress to take a stronger line and countered the neo-Nazis with their own brand of action.

In early 1965, JCRC's surveillance of the neo-Nazis was boosted when a young man "of Italian ancestry" came to the office of Myer Sharzer, the executive vice-president of Central Region, offering, together with two of his friends, to infiltrate the Beattie group. After attending a meeting at Carmichael's house, the informant contacted Sharzer to report on the group's plans. He stated that Beattie and Stanley had split because the latter had stopped supporting Rockwell. Beattie had only a few active followers at this point, mainly young men in their late teens and early twenties. In a confidential memo written on 18 February 18 Sharzer reported, "M. [the code name for Beattie] says that he is going to be the leader of the Canadian Nazi Youth Party, which he is forming, and which will come 'into the open' on April 20. (Why April 20? We must find out)."[10] Sharzer was apparently unaware that 20 April was the anniversary of the birth of Adolf Hitler. The insignificance of Beattie's group was reinforced by a report received after the riot. In an article written by John Garrity, a private detective hired by Ben Kayfetz, the venerable executive director of the JCRC, in October 1966, the detective revealed that "early in 1965, when there was just Beattie and a couple of teenagers, Jack DeCock [J. de C. in Sharzer's memo] and Peter Riedel, in the Nazi business, they ... caused riots and demonstrations just by declaring themselves Nazis ... 'Just think,' Beattie once told me, 'three or four kids, that's all we were, and we had the country up in arms.'"[11]

Meanwhile, survivors were also becoming involved. Until the early 1960s the survivor community in Toronto, smaller and less politicized than the one in Montreal, had been content to yield the arena of anti-racism to the JCRC. Survivors were either apolitical with respect to the Jewish community or had joined *landsmanschaften*, Zionist groups, or ideological movements in the city, a pattern that tended to reinforce their insularity. While not comfortable with the apparently passive approach of the established organizations to the spread of antisemitism, they were not yet ready or confident to take public action themselves. One survivor, Mike Englishman, who had emigrated from Holland in 1952, had not been involved in communal affairs for the first decade of his life in Canada. He recalls that one day,

Irv walked in [to his store]. [He asked] if I would be interested to know that a new Nazi party was being planned in Toronto. I never found out why Irv came to see me. [I replied], "you must be stark raving mad." ... He said, "I have proof". From that point I was interested. Irv and I, just the two of us ... went to the Yonge Street meeting place. One of the back doors was unlocked ... We heard them. They were planning to form a fascist party ... Now I got my back up and went to the Jewish Congress. Ben Kayfetz said, "we know all about it." [I asked], "what are you going to do about it?" [Kayfetz said], "no sir, we're not going to give them the publicity. We're not getting the Jewish people upset." I said that the *Judenrat* [the Jewish councils appointed by the Nazis in the ghettoes] did exactly the same thing as what you're doing right now.[12]

Another survivor, Mike Berwald, had emigrated from Hungary in 1952. When the hate literature began to proliferate, he met with fellow survivor Charles Wittenberg and then with two Canadian Jews, Rabbi David Monson, who had been a chaplain in the Canadian army during the war, and Harvey Lister, of the Jewish War Veterans, Wingate Branch. Berwald remembers that "we had to do something. [We] met Kayfetz, Harris, and [J.S.] Midanik [chair of JCRC Central Region], and they said not to do anything, it was their job; not to stick our noses in it, [they were] doing everything possible."[13] These meetings took place before Harris's address. Rebuffed by Congress, Englishman and Berwald decided to take matters into their own hands.

On 24 January 1965 about forty people met at the headquarters of the Hakoach Soccer Club, of which Berwald was president. They watched a movie on the rise of Nazism, organized themselves to confront Stanley, who was holding a rally that night outside the CBC studios, and elected an executive. One week later the group met at the same place. After some deliberation, it chose N3 as the name of the nascent organization. Suggested by two university students at the meeting, the name referred to Newton's third law: To each action there is an opposite and equal reaction. Berwald remembers that "we came out with the name N3. I didn't even know what it meant. The university students named it." At the meeting various viewpoints were expressed. Sam Zeldin pointed out "that they had full respect for what Canadian Jewish Congress was doing in this field. It was their view that the function of congress was to work towards legislation while they themselves had another role to play." Alex Dymant made "an impassioned plea that he was sick and tired of our community taking a beating, and that he wanted his children to grow up in a community free of David Stanley and his leaflets ... He also stated that Syd Harris ... was doing a good job." After the formal meeting, about twenty people met and volunteered for action groups, and were divided into cells. Berwald led one of the cells. They had lists of thirty-five neo-Nazis. It was noted that at least three independent vigilante groups were already in existence.[14]

The newly formed executive committee of N3 met on 3 February. While there was still no clear-cut direction in the organization, Wittenberg, who eventually became its president, recommended that it should be a public organization with a defence element. N3's next meeting five days later attracted sixty-five people. A tape recording of a meeting of the neo-Nazis at Carmichael's home was played, and the group discussed a protest against the German Statute of Limitations for Nazi war criminals. Ironically, the source of information about these meetings was a JCRC informer who reported directly to Kayfetz. Kayfetz then relayed the news to Midanik and Harris. Thus the JCRC had infiltrated not only the neo-Nazis but also its own most active critic in the Jewish community. Berwald claimed that N3 officials knew the meetings were bugged. He explained, "We went to New York to buy a bugging device [to infiltrate the neo-Nazis] ... and this equipment picked up Congress's bugging device, so we knew."[15]

In response to the neo-Nazis, N3 opened a second front within the Jewish community whose membership was unique. Berwald and Wittenberg were among a small core of survivors who had emerged as spokesmen outside the established organizations. N3, however, was not strictly a group of disgruntled survivors. Unlike in the *landsmanschaften*, survivors from many different European countries joined the group, thus both allowing a wider representation from the survivor community and determining that English, rather than Yiddish, was to be the language of operation. Further, many members of N3 had been born or raised in Canada. Disenchanted with Congress policies and enraged by the rising tide of antisemitism, they were not content to be relegated to the sidelines.

This union of survivors and their supporters led to two types of response. On a public level, N3 orchestrated a protest demonstration and march to the West German consulate in opposition to the Statute of Limitations on the prosecution of Nazi war criminals and the decision by the West German government to stop exporting arms to Israel. More than 1,500 people participated in this protest on 28 February.[16] The so-called defence element, the other avenue of response, bugged the meetings at Beattie's home on Rhodes Avenue in the east end of the city.[17] According to Berwald, he was the leader of this "underground group, not officially part of N3."[18] In addition, Max Chikofsky, a member of N3, contacted John Garrity, the private investigator subsequently employed by Kayfetz, and asked him to infiltrate Beattie's cadre, which he succeeded in doing.[19]

Meanwhile, Mike Englishman and his acquaintance Irv were also infiltrating the neo-Nazis. Englishman went to Carmichael's residence on the pretext of applying for membership. While Carmichael was distracted, he loosened the deadbolt on the back door. Later he and Irv returned, kicked in the door, and removed the membership files. "As soon as that was done, nobody came to that building anymore ... That threw the party into shambles ... They killed themselves from any further support." Another meeting place for the neo-Nazis was the apartment of Henryk Van der Windt on Admiral Road in central Toronto. Englishman, posing as a Hydro inspector, gained the layout of the apartment.[20]

At the same time, yet another anti-Nazi group was created. Canadian-born Jewish students established the Canadian Organization for the Indictment of Nazism (COIN). Its aims were to "instill an acute awareness of the menace ... of anti-semitic groups in the Jewish Youth of Toronto; to inform of the many incidents and actions which have occurred ...; to initiate an all encompassing organization of Jewish Youth; to work ... with other organizations."[21] Cyril Levitt, one of COIN's founders, remembered that the leaders had first contacted Ben Kayfetz. "[We] had the backing of Congress for a rally that we wanted to hold in Toronto at the YMHA [on 2 May 1965]. [We] contacted most of the Jewish youth organizations ... Over 1,000 showed up ... It [the auditorium] was packed from wall to wall ... [We] tried to keep channels of communication open between those who favoured a strong response, even a violent response, and those that preferred to do it through the *stadlanist* [the traditional approach], working behind the scenes, and we did that. I can recall a meeting within the N3 that was more extreme ... [I also met] Mike Englishman and Irv, who were interested in more strong-arm things."[22]

Levitt, however, admitted that "we decided to run the organization on two levels, that there would be a public face ... and then there would be a much smaller group that could work with people who favoured more direct kind of action." As with N3, this "defence element" was not officially part of COIN. It gathered intelligence about the Nazis with the help of three non-Jewish students at the University of Toronto. They contacted Van der Windt, who by this time had become a double agent, and were allowed to photograph Beattie's files, which had been entrusted to Van der Windt by Beattie. They included correspondence with Colin Jordan and George Lincoln Rockwell.[23]

This low-level espionage by amateur sleuths in the Jewish community was high-level surveillance in comparison with the stupidity, carelessness, and naïveté of the neo-Nazis. The contacts between the surveillance teams and their prey had some bizarre moments. Sydney Harris tells a story about monitoring a meeting outside Carmichael's house (probably while Englishman and Irv were eavesdropping at the back door). He was slouched in his car with other leaders of the JCRC, and "as we were making notes about who was coming out, some drunk came careening up Yonge Street and crashed into my car and drew everybody's attention." On another occasion, the JCRC learned that the homes of Jewish community leaders who lived on the same street, including the Harris residence, would be daubed with swastikas. Having alerted the police, who were hiding in the bushes, Harris waited for the perpetrator. "What happened was that my house was the last to be decorated ... We had a dog, who had to be let out at 11 p.m. We purposely stayed home that night. At 11 it appeared that nothing had happened. I let the dog out, and as I opened the door, this stupid bugger appeared on the verandah. The dog tore after him, he tore down the street, the cops chased after him, and they grabbed him ... In any event he was charged with mischief and convicted to three months ... I think it was Stanley."[24]

At least four groups – JCRC, N3, Englishman and Irv, and COIN – had apparently succeeded in infiltrating the neo-Nazis. Even if, thirty years after the events, the recollections of the actors tend to exaggeration, the reality is that more outsiders had information about the neo-Nazis than those within the movement itself. Further, aside from some co-operation between the defence element of COIN and N3 and Englishman, there was no communication between the organizations and presumably little awareness that each group was gathering the same information. In the winter and spring of 1965, the distrust between the JCRC and its critics in the Jewish community was palpable and growing. The JCRC justifiably felt that it had the inside track and the political connections to take appropriate action when it was called for. N3, the militants in COIN, and other so-called vigilante squads had the same information, but they were alarmed by it and felt that only a strong, public display against the neo-Nazis would act as a deterrent. This distrust deteriorated into open competition when word circulated that Beattie was to speak at a public rally at Allan Gardens on 30 May.

THE RIOT AT ALLAN GARDENS

On 20 April, Beattie had announced the formation of the Canadian Nazi Party. Ten days later he publicly declared that he would hold a rally, with fifty supporters wearing swastika arm-bands, at Allan

Gardens on 30 May. According to a city bylaw passed in June 1963, anyone had the right to speak in public on condition that he or she received a permit from the commissioner of Parks and Recreation. Only the time and place was to be stipulated by the parks department.[25] The JCRC immediately contacted City Hall. Philip Givens, the mayor of Toronto, was an active member of the Jewish community, having served as a president of a B'nai Brith lodge and as a member of the JCRC, among a host of organizations.[26] He recollected that "the parks department could only regulate the time of the permit, but not the subject, and [we] could not refuse [Beattie]. [It] was hard for me to explain to Sharzer and Kayfetz and the community that we could not deny him a permit." When asked about petitions from survivors, Givens replied, "I couldn't do things that were extra-legal. I couldn't do that."[27]

In mid-May the Ontario Region of Congress was preoccupied with the upcoming triennial plenary in Montreal. In planning the plenary, Kayfetz lamented to Harris that the Toronto Jewish community had not learned from Harris's speech the previous year at the commemoration of the Warsaw Ghetto Uprising. Kayfetz wrote:

For many years we pursued the quarantine technique with certain kinds of agitators. This is called the silent treatment but that is a misnomer for it gives the impression of non-action, when in actuality it involves very definite action of a certain kind ... We knowingly dropped the quarantine method in relation to the neo-Nazi agitation of the past year and a half for a number of reasons: 1. their kind of agitation (e.g. sprinkling leaflets from the air) commanded [the] public and could not be suppressed. 2. If we were going out on an intensive campaign for laws we had to tell the public-at-large about this hate-material and could not do so under the quarantine treatment ... What about the so-called 'sha-sha' policy? There are some people in our midst who feel that if one is not marching in the streets with placards and pickets, forever manning the barricades, one is doing less than one's duty. Anything short of this constant 'demonstration' is a dereliction.[28]

On 28 May, Congress issued a statement with respect to the planned rally at Allan Gardens. "Toronto apparently faces the gross provocation of a public Nazi demonstration some time this weekend. The Canadian Jewish Congress feels that the very threat of attempting such a demonstration ... is insulting and provocative to the great majority of the citizens of this city. It indeed poses a threat to the peace and good order of the community .... For the citizens of Toronto, there can be only one response: to condemn completely and unreservedly the acts of the self-styled Nazis, and to bring to bear the weight of an outraged public opinion against the provocations they plan."[29]

The position of the CJC was somewhat ambiguous. Did complete condemnation mean that a counter-rally would be supported? Or did it imply that the public authorities had the sole responsibility to prevent the Nazi rally from taking place? Seeing that City Council could not legally stop Beattie from holding the rally, what was Congress advocating? Sydney Harris said, "[we were] still hoping that our people would practise restraint, that we would be going as observers, that none of the leadership of the community would participate in the affair, but we were there."[30] The Congress statement did not deter its critics. In the days leading up to the rally, N3 sent letters to Jewish organizations and synagogues urging mass attendance at the Beattie rally.[31]

On the day of the rally, one leaflet distributed by some *landsmanschaften* implored supporters:

Where Is Our Pride!
Where Is Our Dignity!
Where Is Our Self-Respect!
Come to Allan Gardens.
Experience Nazism In All Its Flourishes.
See If You Can Maintain A Calm And Dispassionate Attitude.
Join Your Fellow Citizens In A Non-Violent Demonstration Against This
　　Cancer In Our Midst.[32]

Another leaflet was addressed "To All Jewish Youth." It stated: "On May 27 they [the neo-Nazis] received a permit from the city to speak and demonstrate from 2 P.M. to 5 P.M. You are required, as a citizen of Toronto and as a Jew, to be there no questions asked by parents ... Your lives are at stake ... Your parents' generation has failed you."[33]

In fact, Beattie was never granted a permit because he had failed to apply for one. This omission was known by Congress and N3 two days prior to the rally. Beattie had asked Garrity to go to City Hall for the permit, but Garrity had "conveniently" forgotten.[34]. On 29 May, Mike Berwald went to City Hall to implore Givens to revoke the permit. The mayor, who was honorary president of the Hakoach Soccer Club, told Berwald, "He hasn't got a permit, and he never got a permit." Berwald recalled, "I knew that at that time he could have had a permit."[35] Nevertheless, neither Congress nor N3 informed the public of this fact. If Beattie had tried to speak, he would have been charged with public mischief. Instead, the city was inflamed that weekend by the news that the rally was to be staged, and the temperature was further raised by public service announcements in the media urging citizens to demonstrate against the rally.

Allan Gardens is a small green space, one large block square, in a seedy area on the edge of downtown Toronto. For decades its denizens have been down-and-out alcoholics, drug pushers, addicts, prostitutes, and the hopeless and homeless. On 30 May, on a glorious spring day just after noon, a crowd began to form in and around the park. By 1:30 it had swelled to between 1,500 and 5,000 people.[36] At one corner of the park a group of teenagers from the Habonim Zionist Youth Organization were dancing to Israeli folk music. N3 later claimed that two hundred of its members, specially trained in demonstration tactics, were strategically placed throughout the park. The crowd was made up of Ward 8 residents (Beattie's neighbours) who had formed an anti-Nazi group, curious onlookers, gentiles whose families had been persecuted by the Nazis, Jews, the regular patrons of the park, and passersby. A radio report at between 1:30 and 2 p.m. stated that all was calm at the park. Fifty of Toronto police officers, headed by Sergeant of Detectives Harold Adamson, were there to keep order. Mayor Givens and Alderman David Rotenberg, both of whom are Jewish, were the only municipal politicians present.

Shortly after 2 p.m., six youths, one wearing a black leather jacket, were stopped by police on Gerrard Street on the southern end of the park. A crowd of several hundred gathered, and when the police let the youths continue, the crowd swelled. Some people began to attack the youths and were urged on by others who yelled, "Kill them. Get them." Meanwhile, Beattie had appeared, alone and under police protection. Nevertheless, he was recognized immediately and attacked despite the police cordon, but was hustled into a waiting paddy wagon before any serious injury could be inflicted. Through a loud-hailer, Adamson and Rotenberg appealed for calm. Rotenberg told the crowd that there were no Nazis among them, not realizing that Beattie was present. The mayhem lasted no more than fifteen minutes, and the police soon rescued the victims. The crowd milled around for two hours before leaving. A tragedy had been averted by the quick response of the police and because only a small portion of the crowd had resorted to violence.[37]

In the immediate aftermath of the riot, the city was in shock. In the civil, conservative climate of "Toronto the Good," a riot in a public park seemed outrageous. Eight of the attackers had been arrested, and although none of them were on the N3 executive or appear to have been connected with the organization, N3 put up their bail; all eight were Jewish. Beattie was also arrested. They were all charged with creating a public disturbance, one with assault, one with possession of a starter's pistol, and Beattie with unlawful assembly. One of the Jews and Beattie were convicted of the first charge; Beattie was acquitted on the second charge because there were no other persons assembled to act in concert with him.[38] The victims of the attack turned out to be members of a motorcycle club from northern Ontario who happened to be passing by.[39]

The respected journalist Robert Fulford wrote a perceptive analysis of the event. He opened his article by stating that when "the people who disgraced themselves ... attacked some innocent bystanders they turned their effort at rough justice into a grotesque comedy." He went on to say that "our only real protection against the poison of racism lies in law and order." Fulford, however, displayed a sensitivity to the survivors in the community which was uncommon at the time. "We need to be reminded often of the fact that there live among us thousands of men and women who are the scarred survivors of the greatest crime of all the centuries ... If I had lost my family to the Nazis, or my whole generation, I might never again believe in the virtues of orderly and respectable society, or in the process of law." He then quoted Alexander Donat, whose *Holocaust Kingdom* had recently been published. Fulford concluded: "It is proper that [the] rioters be punished. But those who give the lectures and administer the punishments should try at least to guess at the agony of the people they confront; should try, anyway, to imagine the quality of the nightmares which live among us."[40]

Another commentator, Rabbi W. Gunther Plaut, writing in the *Globe and Mail*, also expressed compassion for the survivors. "To them a public Nazi rally meant the possibility of a repetition of what they had barely lived through; gassings, inhuman treatment, murder and rapine mutilation, starvation and torture." He laid the blame for the riot on the police, who "should have made it clear that in the circumstances no Nazi meeting could have been held at Allan Gardens," and on the media, which made "newsworthy people out of the Nazis." Plaut declared that the Jewish leadership and the government would have to assure the survivors and the wider community that they must not take the law into their own hands, and that the government must deal appropriately with the distribution of hate literature.[41] Arnold Bruner, a reporter for the *Toronto Daily Star*, laid the blame on the media, "anti-Nazi groups" who distributed the leaflets, the CJC for its statement the day before the rally that the event was "a threat to the peace and good order of the community," the police for not being prepared, Givens for not speaking to the crowd, and Rotenberg, who spoke only after the riot began. Curiously, Bruner did not condemn the Nazis or their supporters.[42]

The shock waves were understandably most apparent in the Jewish community. Berwald recalls: "We [N3] were very disappointed ... total strangers did it attacking innocent people ... It hurt us in the Jewish community with the *landsmanschaften*."[43] Cyril Levitt remembers that "it was pandemonium, it was bedlam, it was jammed. There were all kinds of rumours floating about."[44] An issue that gripped the community in the immediate aftermath was whether the violence had been spontaneous or premeditated. One report stated categorically that "from all the evidence, the anti-Nazi groups did NOT plan last Sunday's 10 violent minutes in Allan Gardens." Quoting Max Chikofsky, the report contended that, at a meeting of N3 on 28 May, three hundred people "unanimously voted that there should be NO violence – that there should be a turnout for a silent protest."[45] Berwald stated: "Period. No violence was planned ... We wanted to get a big demonstration, wanted to have a crowd ... That's why we had the kids dance the Hora [the Israeli folk dance] ... Our plan was not to let Beattie speak .. The only thing we wanted to do was to take the sign [swastika]."[46] Mike Englishman concurred: It was "totally spontaneous; nobody was actually prepared for violence ... People started to run after them more a chasing party than a violent party, then the police came ... definitely not a planned way for physical action."[47]

Cyril Levitt provided another perspective. He recalls that the riot was both planned and spontaneous: "Both, absolutely both. I think that groups within the N3 planned to get this guy. Even within COIN people were prepared to do that ... As far as I know, none of them were involved ... but much of the emotion was spontaneous. People were working themselves up to a pitch."[48] Beattie's appearance and the unfortunate bikers were the emotional outlet for some of the demonstrators. They had been the targets of public antisemitic outrages for five years. The anti-Nazi groups may not have planned the violence, but neither did they call off the demonstration when their leaders knew that Beattie did not have a permit. They were prepared for a confrontation. For them, the issue was not the legalities of municpal bylaws but the unfurling of a swastika in a public park in their adopted haven.

THE AFTERMATH OF THE RIOT

The riot was a major setback for Congress. It had undone the years of goodwill that had brought the Jewish community into the Canadian mainstream. Despite its surveillance of its critics, Congress could not control them. Tragically, the riot justified its decision not to work with the militants (or vigilantes, as they were called in Congress correspondence). According to Sydney Harris, "N3 wouldn't talk. They weren't interested in us, and didn't give a damn what the general Jewish community thought was right. I don't think they were being fair in calling us the *Judenrat* ... they were not ready to accept the fact that there was a different climate in Canada than in the old country."[49] Givens echoed this sentiment. He told the survivors that "this is not the old country. I told these persons that our police operated under democratic institutions and were prepared to preserve the law."[50] For Harris and the other leaders and staff of Congress, the riot was proof that the community had not understood that the "quarantine" approach of earlier times had been abandoned, and that Congress had done everything in its power to inform the community about the neo-Nazis and to prepare for the rally. Nevertheless, Congress did not have a clear strategy. It also did not inform the public that Beattie did not have a permit, and it was not prepared to address the crowd. Its leaders were at Allan Gardens as observers and not as representatives of Toronto's Jewish community.

Congress's frustration exploded with its "Report on Neo-Nazism and Hate Literature," released on 8 June 1965. The report, also referred to as a "communiqué," created unanticipated tremors in the Toronto Jewish community that threatened to destroy any pretence of unity, because of its language, its untimely public release, and the vitriolic reaction to it by both militant critics and hitherto moderate supporters of the established community.

The report was a four-page document reviewing the formation, structure, and support of the Canadian Nazi Party, the current situation regarding hate-propaganda legislation, the Allan Gardens Incident, and – the most contentious section – "vigilantes." It was signed by Jacob Finkelman, national vice-president of the CJC, Meyer Gasner, chairman of CJC Central Region, Sydney Harris, vice-chairman, and J.S. (Sydney) Midanik, chair of JCRC Central Region. Harris had written the report. With respect to activities of the Canadian Nazi Party, the report stated: "The volume of this [hate] propaganda was such that the 'quarantine' technique of refraining from publicizing this activity was no longer effective and we had to confront and expose the distributors," a reference to Harris's speech of 19 April 1964. The party was "absurdly small" and was marked by "financial instability." Regarding the "vigilantes," the report declared:

Some of them sincerely avow non-violence, others pay lip-service to non-violence but from their actions seem bent on violence. During the few days before the event, meetings were held and irresponsible leaflets circulated all of which helped whip up some groups within the Jewish community to the pitch of fear and frenzy that assisted in creating the atmosphere that led to the mob violence ... The Canadian Jewish Congress accuses these persons and groups of irresponsibility creating a tense and inflamed situation which involuntarily was bound to erupt into violence and which unfortunately did so erupt ... There are some individuals — fortunately very few — of these self-appointed *shomrim* [watchmen or defenders] who have mistaken noise for action and rabble-rousing for militancy ... Our firm and aggressive policies both in opposition to neo-Nazism and in support of legislation will continue. We must above all exercise that restraint and self-discipline that is absolutely indispensable if we are to avoid the climate of terror, mob-rule and intimidation which can only serve the purposes of the neo-Nazis.[51]

On reading the report thirty years later, Harris commented:

What upset them most was that if there were any self-appointed *shomrim*, it was us, forgetting that we were the representatives of the total community ... we were speaking on behalf of the community. Perhaps it was an infelicitous phrase; today I might have phrased it differently, I don't know. There's no question in my mind that I wrote it, but I'm only one of the four signatories; the other three cannot be accused of irresponsibility in community affairs, and as I read it now, I think it's a calm and reasoned explanation of what was happening at the time. The 'self-appointed *shomrim*' was a bit of hyperbole that I could have done without, not so much as *shomrim*, but as self-appointed, because the truth cuts close to the bone.[52]

The inflammatory wording of the report was bound to upset organizations such as N3 and other critics of Congress. Unfortunately, the report was leaked to the press prior to its release to community organizations. This faux pas significantly exacerbated hostility toward the CJC and widened the split within the community. The bulk of the report had been written prior to the riot. It was then edited to reflect the position of Congress after the riot and was to have been sent out by mail to the Jewish community on Tuesday, 8 June. Ralph Hyman of the *Globe and Mail*, and a member of the JCRC, knew of the report, asked for a copy, and was given one. Unfortunately, the other copies did not arrive until Friday or the following Monday, while the *Globe* printed excerpts of the letter the next day (Wednesday) on its front page. The headline read, "Jewish Congress Blames Jews for Fomenting Mob Violence," focusing on the section of the report that discussed "vigilantes."[53] The article was picked by other newspapers and received prominent exposure. Headlines in Ontario newspapers proclaimed: "Jewish Congress Denounces Riot" (Brampton), "Jews Asked to Show Restraint, Discipline" (St Thomas), "Jewish Congress Accuses Jews for Anti-Nazi Riots" (Oshawa), and "Our Own People Helped Incite Riot" (Peterborough).[54] Thus not only did the Jewish community first learn of the report denouncing Jewish vigilantes from the press, but the rest of the country did so as well.

Immediately, criticism of Congress reached unprecedented proportions. Linda Silverberg wrote to Gasner: "I don't like violence, but if violence will help us rid ourselves of Nazis, let's get violent! ... your Congress is against the Jewish people and their views. We need an organization who thinks with us and for our best interests. The Jewish Congress has shown that they will only voice a 'safe' opinion." The Zaglembier Society, an important *landsmanschaft* that heretofore had been a supporter of Congress, wrote a "Letter of Protest" to the Central Region office. It stated:

We Protest that the C.J.C. chose publicly to call those Jews Irresponsible Vigilantes ... We do not have to be pitched to Fear and Frenzy, as a group of Nazi Concentration Camp survivors we do not need anymore sympathy. It is action we want ... We say Nazism is not a Political party and speaking about genocide against people and in particular Jews, is NOT FREEDOM OF SPEECH. As long as there are no laws against these things, we shall be "SHOMRIN" for all the Jews. The Jewish "Judenrat" had orderly waited in Germany for a law since 1923. They got a law passed in 1935. We shall NOT wait that long again ... We respect and are proud of the C.J.C. and its leaders in all their actions. We are however sorry that we have to protest and disagree with this action you have taken. Our bitter experience tells us that you are wrong. Our past has prepared us for today and proved to us that we have to be on guard as long as it is not too late.[55]

Rabbi Gunther Plaut, a member of the JCRC, wrote a resolution on behalf of the United Zionist Council that "deplores the release of the letter of June 8th. to the press ... [and the] intemperate wording on vigilantes in this letter ... [and] urges a broader representation on this committee."[56]

The Association of Former Concentration Camp Inmates/Survivors of Nazi Oppression of Montreal, the earliest and most important organization of survivors in Canada, wrote a nine-page "Open Letter to the Jewish Community of Canada." It referred to 9 June as "'Black Wednesday' for the Jewish Community in Canada."

The blame is laid on the Jews and not on those poor Nazis of whom only a pitiful three wanted to hold a harmless little rally! Indeed, their statement means that, in this instance, *the Nazis were right, the Jews were wrong* ... Let it be stated categorically that this is *the first time* in the history of the Jewish Community in Canada that a statement by or in the name of the Canadian Jewish Congress, condemning and insulting a segment of the Jewish population, has been made in public ... It is indeed sad and tragic that a people who barely survived the worst holocaust in its long and painful history and which devotes so much of its energy to protect itself against outside enemies, should be plagued by such unfair and damaging actions from within ... It is imperative that a full investigation be conducted by the National Executive into the channels through which this communique was processed and that Messrs. Finkelman, Gasner, Midanik and Harris be removed from their functions in Congress, and that the National Executive in its own interest and for the benefit of the entire Jewish Community should at once proceed with their dismissal, or request their resignation as may apply to their individual positions.[57]

Editorial opinion in the Jewish press regarding the controversy over the report was mixed. The Yiddish-language *Kanader Adler* (Canadian Eagle) wrote: "They [the rioters] went too far and ... the mass attack on the racists was beyond all proportion to their number and importance ... We are, therefore, inclined to believe that the Canadian Jewish Congress behaved properly with its public rebuke ... Perhaps this rebuke was a little too sharp but it was in the proper time and place." The English-language *Canadian Jewish Chronicle* disagreed: "It seems to us that the Central Region of the Canadian Jewish Congress acted with undue precipitancy and dubious wisdom ... It is our impression that someone in the Toronto leadership of the Canadian Jewish Congress panicked, and we doubt that Congress as a whole is behind the statement ... The inescapable fact is that after what happened in Hitler's Europe, Jews are in no mood to react with polite indifference those who call for the revival of policies that caused six million Jewish deaths. After what happened in Europe, Jews do not feel reassured by the statement, it can't happen here."[58]

For the Jewish community of Toronto, the CJC report and the reaction to it marked the nadir of community relations in the post-war period and perhaps in the history of the community. By the mid-1960s it was clear that the membership of the JCRC was not representative of the community, and that in some ways it had lost touch with significant segments of Toronto Jewry. A socio-economic profile of the committee members who attended a meeting on 24 June is illuminating. Of the thirty-one members, eighteen are listed in the 1964 edition of *Who's Who in Canadian Jewry*, the most comprehensive description of the community leaders ever published. Two were the editors of the two largest English-language papers in the Toronto Jewish community; five were lawyers (and another three, not listed, were queen's counsel); one was a doctor; two others were professionals; two were rabbis, from the same synagogue; two were politicians; and three were industrialists. Thirteen had been born between 1900 and 1920, and only eight had been born in Europe, the most recent immigrant having arrived in 1926. There were no survivors, no small businessmen, no tradesmen, no women, no one under age thirty-five, and no representatives of the Orthodox community.[59] Nevertheless, the committee was divided over the riot and the report, and its leaders, chairman Sydney Midanik and vice-chairman Sydney Harris, had to defend Congress's response.

At a special meeting on 18 June, Midanik reviewed the circumstances leading to the events. In the following discussion, David Newman said that "to go to the press to condemn the people seems as if you go to the *goyim* [gentiles] in order to do some public relations in the community. It seems that the primary concern was ... [more] about what the goyim say than the feelings ... of a Jewish minority or majority." Rabbi Abraham Feinberg, past chairman of the committee and regarded as its most anti-establishment figure, declared, "Congress through this committee reserved its most eloquent and its most vitriolic polemic for Jews .... [It] suggests that every individual and group in Toronto maintain silence and turn over to the Canadian Jewish Congress without question a determination of policy in regard to Jewish interest ... This [the report] is a flagrant act of disservice." Harris replied to the criticism: "I do not see a blanket condemnation of the people who participated in the violence and frenzy. What is condemned is the action of individuals and organizations ... who stirred up people to the pitch, taking poles, two by fours, weapons that were later discovered ... CJC has a duty to say to Jews and non-Jews that this was violence." Harris then explained the errors that had led to the release of the report to Ralph Hyman.[60] Commenting thirty years later, he said: "I was as outraged as everybody else that it had gotten to the *Globe* before ... I think it was by accident. They didn't like to read in the newspaper that they were being blamed ... They were absolutely right – there was no excuse for it and it shocked me as well as everyone else."[61]

Six days later, on 24 June, following the publication of the "Open Letter" from the Association of Survivors and the editorial in the *Canadian Jewish Chronicle*, another special meeting of the JCRC was held. Midanik began by stating that if the majority of the committee wished to dismiss him, they could freely do so. The matter died on the floor since no one had any intention of asking him or any of the other officers of Congress to resign. Nevertheless, criticism of the report within the committee went on unabated. David Newman recommended that the committee make a statement of apology since the message "We are beyond reproach" was not acceptable. Julius Hayman, editor of the *Jewish Standard*, supported such a letter to the community. He indicated that while the "establishment" was concerned about Beattie and the neo-Nazis, what should concern it more was "the cleavage in the community ... We stand a chance of ending up after some time finding that we do not have one community but two: the newcomers and the old-timers." Harris replied that the suggestion "that this committee created the cleavage in the community is not so; this was created by individuals who said that they would do what they please and do not care one bit what the leadership said." Donald Carr was of the opinion that "persons who *do understand* the English language did misinterpret the letter." He suggested that the executive explain the purpose of the letter in monosyllabic terms, in clear, unequivocal English and in Yiddish if necessary. Rabbi Plaut responded that, whether the English language was badly used or badly read, the impression was that Congress was principally interested in pleading the case before the general community and only secondarily before the Jewish community. It was the communication that was faulty by providing the impression that the committee was taking the Nazi peril too lightly. He ended the discussion with four points, the most important one being that "the JCRC needs considerable broadening of membership. The community is not widely enough represented on this body."[62]

The debates at the JCRC meetings speak volumes about the mindset and composition of the established community in Toronto twenty years after the end of World War II. Clearly, Julius Hayman was correct in stating that a cleavage had occurred in the community. What is astonishing is that it had taken so long for Congress to recognize this fact. The arrival of the survivors in the late 1940s and early 1950s, their adaptation to Canadian society in the following decade, and their concern and then outrage over domestic and international events that threatened to resuscitate the evil of Nazism were outside the experience of the established majority. Even though the threat existed more in the minds of the survivors than in reality, it was the seemingly tepid response by Canadian Jews to the events that was most hurtful. They (Canadian Jews) had gone blithely on with their own affairs, though mindful and somewhat aware of the growing antisemitism in a few isolated circles of Canadian society, without reaching out to the survivors. It was only the shock of the riot and the after-effects of the report that awoke some members of Congress to the realization that there were two elements in the community. Harris was correct in stating that the JCRC had not created the cleavage. The split was the result of almost two decades of separation between two groups who had different experiences. As for Plaut's recommendation that the JCRC needed wider representation, one only had to look at the socio-economic profile of the committee to see that he was right.

THE COMMUNITY ANTI-NAZI COMMITTEE

Plaut's recommendation did not go unheeded by Congress. Within two weeks, it was determined that "an active and vigorous anti-Nazi program in the Toronto area" should be implemented to continue and intensify the campaign for laws against hate propaganda; to plan political action toward this end, to secure the co-operation of the widest sections of the Canadian public toward these ends, and to establish the "Special anti-Nazi Committee."[63] On 22 July a steering committee under the aegis of CJC Central Region and the JCRC decided on the composition of the special anti-Nazi committee. There were to be eighty representatives, chosen by congregations, labour, ideological groups, women's societies, B'nai Brith youth, the JCRC, and members "at large."[64] Congress had committed itself to rectifying the error of attacking its critics publicly. Of greater significance, the leaders of the established community had recognized that the rupture in the community had widened to such a dimension that whatever mandate they had been given was rapidly eroding. To heal the rift, it was incumbent upon them to create as inclusive a group as possible, no matter how diverse and fractious it might be, to advise Congress on matters relating to incipient antisemitism. The birth of what was called the Community Anti-Nazi Committee (CANC) was the first step in bringing survivors and their supporters into the corridors of power in the Toronto Jewish community.

The formation of CANC was not universally applauded. In retrospect, Mike Berwald felt that the committee was "in the front of the Jewish community, to sweep it [concern about Nazism] under the rug ... They [the CJC] wanted to stop the lobby [N3] ... They didn't do anything."[65] Cyril Levitt, who was COIN's representative on CANC, states:

At the time, [I felt] it was a kind of sop that the established community had thrown, a kind of bone thrown at the survivors .... Today I don't think so ... I thought that essentially the established interests in Congress thought of these people as a potential embarrassment to the community ... I'm not saying that it was completely Machiavellian; I'm not suggesting that Congress was not concerned about Nazism. There was a kind of view that they [the survivors] don't really understand how Congress works, that they weren't socialized into a democratic polity; they don't understand that this is not Poland in 1940. In a way, the anti-Nazi committee was an attempt to sidetrack what Congress thought was a potentially embarrassing direction. There was this sense of condescension ... [that] these guys can do nothing but trip over their own feet and get everybody into trouble ... In retrospect, I'm a little more sympathetic to Congress. The passion of the survivors got in the way of realizing what the reality was.[66]

Other members of CANC are more lenient in their judgment. Mike Englishman felt that "it was an effective committee because lines of communication were open between the two groups". Sydney Harris maintained that "it was not a sop. It was a reaction."[67] When the committee was created, Charles Wittenberg, the chairman of N3, wrote a letter addressed to Dr Alex Lipson, first chairman of CANC. It began, "We welcome the establishment of your special Anti-Nazi Committee which has finally given proper recognition to the menace of neo-Nazism." And the letter continued, "N3 now as in the past ... is prepared to listen and work with every active anti-Nazi group interested in an active fight against neo-Nazism, but in addition expects that our point of view must be listened to and taken cognizance of."[68] Lipson, in fact, was not the chairman; that position was held by Max Shecter, who was a prominent community leader involved in both Congress and B'nai Brith.

CANC was an active committee of Congress for several years, but its most significant work was done in 1966, its initial year of operation. While the anti-Nazi group acted only in an advisory capacity to the JCRC, its function was primarily to bring a wider representation to Congress – to, as Englishman states, open the lines of communication and act as a sounding board for the range of views presented. For the first time in the post-war Jewish community, representatives on the same committee brought different agendas, backgrounds, and experiences to the table. This assemblage included the brilliant young lawyer Alan Borovoy, counsel to the Canadian Civil Liberties Association, who took a strong line on the dangers of preventing Beattie and his followers from exercising their right to expound their noxious views; militant survivors such as Jacob Egit and Wolf Rosenblatt, who warned Congress about pursuing a timorous and weak-kneed line in combatting antisemitism; and former radicals such as unionist Max Federman and journalist Sam Lipshitz, whose anti-establishment criticisms had been tempered over the years. The ultimate value of CANC was that it provided a forum where contentious debate could take place before decisions were made by Congress. Whether one takes the view that Congress co-opted its critics or that it seriously sought an avenue for discussion of the problems facing the community, CANC was an important first step in the healing process. Its representatives provided a wide public voice against antisemitism and ultimately for the integration of the memory of the Holocaust into the consciousness of the community.

Two issues dominated CANC's agenda in 1966. The first was the application of pressure on the federal government to proceed with legislation outlawing hate propaganda. The second was to convince Toronto City Council to amend the parks bylaw in order to prevent Beattie from holding further rallies. In January the Cohen committee on hate propaganda, created by the minister of justice, was due to present its report. CANC recommended that a delegation from Congress meet with Prime Minister Lester Pearson during the Christmas recess, before reopening of the House. On 11 January 1966, ten representatives, including three from CANC, met with Paul Martin, the acting prime minister, who promised that the matter would be brought up in the House after the Cohen report was translated but would not make further commitments. On 24 January the executive of CANC recommended that a mass demonstration in Ottawa be organized as part of the campaign for anti-hate legislation and that the Toronto park bylaw be reviewed. At its meeting two days later, the JCRC discussed the first recommendation. Sydney Harris felt that organization of the march in Ottawa should proceed quickly and that it must reflect the belief that this was a problem for all of society, not merely a Jewish issue. Myer Sharzer, the executive director of Central Region, concurred. Caution was expressed by the most of the discussants, and the question was left unresolved.[69]

On 3 March the march, now dubbed the Ottawa Cavalcade, again dominated the JCRC agenda. CANC had resolved that a march should be organized for May, following the first reading of the Cohen report in the House. Harris now withdrew his support for the idea, citing the close monitoring of neo-Nazis and the view that the emergency situation which had gripped the community a year earlier was unlikely to recur. Discussion ranged from abandoning the project, to preparing for a march if the situation changed. Paraphrasing Mackenzie King, Harris supported "a march if necessary but not necessarily a march."[70]

The proposal for the march lost its momentum in the subsequent months, as the more pressing issue of the parks bylaw dominated the agenda. It resurfaced in the summer, however, in another guise. CANC had become increasingly concerned with the question of Nazi war criminals in Canada, and it recommended that a rally be held in Ottawa to publicize the problem. The rally was proposed for 18 October but as with the march to hasten the anti-hate law, the idea was not pursued.[71]

As noted, the second issue of importance for CANC and the JCRC was the Toronto parks bylaw. The existing bylaw regarding public addresses provided for the approval a permit for any application, with the commissioner of Parks and Recreation only stipulating the time and place.[72] Beattie and seven supporters, in the meantime, had entered Allan Gardens in a silent protest march on 25 July 1965. They were attacked and were subsequently charged with unlawful assembly, but the attackers were not charged.[73]

City Council had created a chaotic situation. Beattie's repeated applications and the contradictory decisions by the municipal authorities again put the Jewish community to the test. At first, CANC resolved that "it would not be politic to become embroiled in this issue as it would distract from the main goal of national legislation and would present us in the image of preventing free speech."[74] This hands-off approach was abandoned when the city Parks and Recreation Committee discussed changes to the existing bylaw. The issue for Congress was whether to take a public position on the question. Several views were expressed at the JCRC on the matter. At a meeting on 10 March 1966 Sydney Midanik argued that the Jewish community should not be involved in matters which would limit free speech. Alan Borovoy went further by stating that intercession in the political process would put the community in the position of denying free speech. Albert Rose opined that abolishing the "quarantine treatment" had not achieved anything, and that the Jewish community should ignore Beattie. Several members disagreed with these views, stressing that a letter should be sent to City Council outlining Congress's position and that non-Jewish support be enlisted. Wolf Rosenblatt took a hardline view. He stated that a minority would not accept compromise at any price even if it meant violence, and he would not submit to a *sha sha shtil* policy. A motion to solicit non-Jewish support, and if that failed, to take a public position, lost by a vote of 7 to 12. Another motion advocating that Congress support the bylaw as long as the propagation of genocide was prohibited was also defeated. Finally, a motion that no action be taken before City Council met was carried.[75]

The JCRC's reluctance to take a public stance on the bylaw deliberations outraged some members of CANC. At a meeting of CANC later that day, Harvey Lister expressed his concern that the JCRC, instead of CANC, had called a meeting on the issue and then had adopted its traditional wait-and-see position. Jacob Egit asked that the executive of Central Region openly press for a postponement of any change in the bylaw. As at the earlier meeting held that day, there was no unanimity on the issue. Finally, it was determined that "Congress is apparently of the opinion that independent action is obviously something it would give its blessings to with any public proclamation," and if Federman and Lister of CANC proceeded to enlist outside support, "it might be effective."[76] In other words, Congress would not take a public stand, but it also would not deter unofficial representatives of the organization from appealing to the wider community to lobby the municipal authorities.

Two significant points can be made about these deliberations. First, there was a diversity of opinion among community leaders about how to deal with the perceived neo-Nazi threat and the appropriate manner to appeal to the municipal authorities and the general community. Despite the inclusion of survivors and their supporters in the JCRC, the traditional approach of moderation and a low public profile remained in effect. Second, there was open competition between CANC and the JCRC over "ownership" of the issue. Not surprisingly, given the mandate of CANC as an advisory body to the JCRC, it was the latter committee that ultimately recommended policy to the Congress executive.

CANC's existence did not stifle the work of N3, even though the anti-Nazi committee was designed to be a vehicle for diffusing criticism of Congress. CANC had allotted one seat on its committee to an N3 member (although there were N3 supporters from other organizations on the committee) on the understanding that it "had undertaken to submit to discipline."[77] While the JCRC refrained from lobbying City Council during the deliberations on the bylaw, N3 had no such qualms. In a brief to City Council, it wrote: "Incitement to hate, the whole area of racial hatred ... cannot be considered or set aside as deserving of different valuations ... because it is essentially the fountainhead of the most serious menace to our enjoyment and practice of all freedoms. Moreover, it leads to civil disturbances, to violence, even to war and genocide."[78] After months of debate, City Council finally determined on 25 May 1966 that the original bylaw would stand, but with a subsection stating that "profane, indecent or abusive language ... that is likely to stir up hatred" was illegal.[79]

Meanwhile, Beattie had obtained a one-hour permit to speak at Allan Gardens for 5 June. Although drowned out by a crowd estimated at 4,000, he ranted for twenty-five minutes in his first public speech in a Toronto park. Two weeks later, on 19 June, he spoke again, protected by two hundred police officers, to a hostile crowd of

1,200. The next day a furious James Mackey, chief of police, wrote to Mayor Givens urging that Beattie not be allowed to speak again. Five days later, after listening to a tape recording of the speech, Mackey charged Beattie under the new subsection dealing the promotion of hatred.[80] Charles Wittenberg, chairman of N3, contemptuously referred to the two rallies as "'lawful' by our current standards."[81] For N3, Mackey was a hero and William Archer, the controller who had voiced opposition to the subsection, a villain.

The subsection still had to be approved by the Board of Control, the executive of City Council, at its meeting on 6 July. Congress and N3 had each sent delegations to meet with members of the board. Upping the ante, N3 organized a demonstration in Nathan Phillips Square, outside the council chambers, the night before the board meeting. Harvey Lister told a cheering crowd: "We will never forget or forgive the Nazi atrocities! That will never happen in this country!"[82] Archer, who refused to speak at the rally, likened the mobs at Allan Gardens to "any vigilante group." At its meeting the Board of Control "voted to initiate a policy that no person charged under the parks by-law for inciting racial hatred would be granted a permit to speak while his trial was pending," effectively excluding Beattie from speaking for the next several months.[83] Despite this minor victory, the established leaders were not amused by N3's tactics. Sydney Harris stated that N3 had no place on a Congress committee if it planned its own activities. Others maintained that "N3 and survivors have another approach and this is why they exist."[84]

Even though Beattie was silenced by municipal authorities, the affair was kept in the public eye as a result of exposure of the neo-Nazis by John Garrity in *Maclean's* on 1 October 1966.[85] Garrity was the private investigator who had infiltrated Beattie's group at the behest of N3. When he found himself at loggerheads with N3's leaders after the riot, he was hired by Ben Kayfetz to continue his sleuthing for the JCRC. In the article he referred to N3 as a "lunatic fringe" and "the Jewish mafia" and an organization "who, in their attempts to destroy Beattie, provide him with most of the publicity he craves." The Nazis were "misfits" but "the most visible part of a growing right-wing movement in Canada which, I have come to believe, could represent a threat to our national stability." Beattie himself was unemployed and bereft of funds, and had been evicted from five apartments for nonpayment of rent. He had been careful to stay within the law, and it was Garrity's hope that legislation outlawing hate literature would limit his capacity to spread his propaganda. Nevertheless, Garrity was far more sympathetic to his prey than he was to N3. He concluded: "I have spent so much time with

Beattie in the past 16 months, that I've felt pangs of disloyalty ... But he, or rather what he stands for – must be destroyed. To Beattie I can only say, 'I'm sorry, John, but you deserve it.'"[86]

Garrity's revelations stunned most members of the Jewish community, who had not been aware of the minute surveillance of the Nazis carried out by Congress and other groups. The *Canadian Jewish News* excoriated Garrity for minimizing the threat posed by Beattie and the Nazi Party and for proclaiming the movement as the visible vanguard of a dangerous right-wing threat. The CJN also strongly criticized the CJC for splitting the community, for acting as "ghetto police," and for publicizing Garrity's revelations to gain favour with its constituents.[87] In reality, the Garrity article and the CJN rejoinder had little effect on the dynamics within Toronto's Jewish community or on the fortunes of the Canadian Nazi Party. By the fall of 1966 the rift between the CJC and its more moderate critics had been paved over, and the community's concern with Nazis, antisemitism, and remembering the Holocaust were now focused on the proposed Statute of Limitations for Nazi war criminals in West Germany and the coming visit of the leader of a German neo-Nazi party to Toronto.

Beattie and his coterie were neutralized by the Board of Control's decision that an individual could not apply for a permit to speak while awaiting trial. His trial, stemming from his speeches in June 1966, began on 18 October, and he was acquitted on 7 December. The acquittal was based on residual power given to the federal government under section 91 of the British North America Act and reinforced by the Bill of Rights. Simply put, once Beattie had been given the right to speak, there could be no restriction imposed by City Council on what he said. As Mark MacGuigan, professor of law at Osgoode Hall and a member of the Cohen committee, wrote at the time: "With the utmost good will, whatever the Toronto City Council tried to do seemed to turn out badly. Perhaps this suggests that a municipality is not the proper forum in which to grapple with the problem ... It is important that such legislation be at the national and not at the local level ."[88]

Over the next two years, Beattie continued to speak at Allan Gardens, but with little publicity from the media or response by Toronto's Jews. On 30 June 1968 he addressed about 125 people, who jeered and heckled him. Aside from 12 members of the JCRC, there were almost no Jews in the crowd. Ben Kayfetz reported that "the Jewish community again stayed away en masse. This time the media gave it the smallest attention yet, the radio and two of the three Toronto dailies not mentioning it, and TV giving it minimal attention."[89] By 1970, Congress files on Beattie, N3, and CANC were empty.

CONCLUSION

The evaporation of John Beattie, David Stanley, and the Canadian Nazi Party into the ozone layer of local history is not surprising. The group never numbered more than fifty, and the hard-core activists were only a fraction of the movement. A poor orator, Beattie had no organizational skills, published nothing, and was totally naive about security, surveillance, and infiltration. Other right-wing elements in the country, such as the racist fringe of the Social Credit Party and Ron Gostick and his *Canadian Intelligence Service*, had little connection with the neo-Nazis and probably viewed them as a hindrance because of their visibility and the hostility that they engendered. While Beattie was able to work around municipal bylaws with some success, his most enduring achievement was providing a catalyst for the emergence of those in Toronto's Jewish community who had heretofore been excluded from the centres of communal power.

The cleavage in the community was widened because of tactics, misconceptions, and a contest of wills. There was no division, however, over the fury felt by Toronto Jews about the neo-Nazis and their brazen antisemitic activities. Holocaust survivors, Canadian Jews, and many non-Jews would not countenance Nazis in their midst. The events of the early 1960s, from the swastika daubings of 1960 to the Rockwell broadcast in 1964, had so angered the community that the appearance of Stanley and Beattie on the local scene necessitated an immediate response.

Congress had little alternative but to respond on two fronts – pressing local authorities and undertaking its own surveillance. The information that it gained determined its decision to disclose the racists publicly. Disatissfied with this response and angered by the CJC's rejection of their pleas to do more, survivors used their considerable organizational skills to mount their own counterattack. The riot in Allan Gardens was predictable, given the swelling tension. The events there were not, however, inevitable. The demonstration could have been averted had community leaders, from both Congress and the anti-Nazi organizations, informed the community in advance that Beattie did not have a permit.

One view is that the riot could have been avoided if the Nazis would have been disregarded. Thirty years later Sydney Harris still felt that "if we had simply ignored these guys [the Nazis], they would have died ... But in the climate of opinion people couldn't care less about them in the general community. But unfortunately the Jewish community didn't feel that way. The net result was that we got them all the publicity that they wanted through our own actions, and that's why the whole Allan Gardens thing was an unnecessary situation."[90]

But the Nazis, however inconsequential they may have been, could not have been ignored. In "the climate of the day," community leaders, whether elected, appointed, or self-appointed, had their own agendas. In retrospect, if the riot had not taken place, the established forces would not have had to confront the reality that there was a cleavage within Toronto Jewry, that it had existed for years, and that it had now widened to such a degree that only by bringing the discordant elements together could the healing process begin. For this reason, the riot was arguably the most significant event in the postwar Toronto Jewish community.

6 "The Jewish Emptiness": Confronting the Holocaust in the Late 1960s and Early 1970s

At the plenary of the Canadian Jewish Congress in 1965, there were two resolutions regarding the Holocaust. One of them, dealing with the endorsement of legislation prohibiting hate propaganda, had been opposed by several members of the executive. Despite their objections, the resolutions committee voted to present the resolution. On the floor, representatives of the Association of Former Concentration Camp Inmates/Survivors of Nazi Oppression presented an amendment to the legislation to make it more effective; the result was a nasty quarrel between opponents of the resolution and supporters of the amendment. Although the amendment passed, the ill feeling between some established leaders and the survivors was palpable.

Nine years later the Congress plenary adopted four resolutions on the Holocaust without opposition. The recently formed Holocaust Memorial Committee held a meeting with over one hundred plenary delegates in attendance, including Sol Kanee, the outgoing president of Congress. Ten pages of reports on the activities of local Holocaust memorial committees were included in the plenary minutes.

The contrast between the two plenary sessions marked the emergence of the Holocaust within the collective memory of the Canadian Jewish community. Between 1965 and 1974, information about the Holocaust had become widespread, heightening the community's consciousness of the event. A number of factors were responsible for this development. One was the public debate over legislation to curb hate propaganda. After the release of the Cohen Committee's report, most of Canada's Jews were united in their desire for legislation. Two developments in West Germany also served to heighten public awareness: the proposed imposition of a Statute of Limitations for Nazi war criminals and the rise of a neo-Nazi party. A fourth factor was the increasing politicization of Holocaust survivors and their supporters in the community. They were successful in holding commemoration services that drew wide audiences and extensive media coverage and raised their profile in mainstream organizations. Fifth, Israel's insecurity, highlighted in the 1967 war, alarmed Canadian Jews. Increasingly, the Holocaust was invoked as a reminder of the need to support the Jewish state. Lastly, the postwar transition of the community from one made up of working-class immigrants and their children to one where members had achieved an elevated socio-economic standing as "Canadians" had been accomplished, producing a new generation that was increasingly estranged from its roots. In response, many Canadian Jews born in the 1930s and 1940s, in searching for self-definition, appropriated the destruction of European Jewry as an element in that identity.

The memory of the Holocaust now drew a more responsive hearing from some Canadian Jews than at any other time, but commemoration of and education about the event, and attention to related issues, such as antisemitism and the presence of suspected Nazi war criminals, were not at the top of the community's agenda.[1] Priority was given to support for Israel in light of the military threat to its existence and its diplomatic isolation at the United Nations, and to the status and security of Jews in foreign lands, mainly in the Soviet bloc and the Arab world. This was a period of transition for the community regarding the Holocaust. While interest and awareness of the event grew at a rapid pace, it would not be until the next decade, 1975 to 1985, that its impact was fully realised.

THE COHEN COMMITTEE REPORT

The fourteenth Congress plenary was held in Montreal on 20-24 May 1965, two weeks after Prime Minister Lester Pearson spoke on Parliament Hill on the twentieth anniversary of ve day and one week before the riot in Allan Gardens. At the time, the Cohen commission on hate propaganda was in its second month of hearings. The cjc, led by Saul Hayes and Michael Garber, presented the following resolution at the plenary:

HATE INCITEMENT & NEO-NAZISM

WHEREAS it is of paramount importance to the people of Canada and to the Canadian Jewish community in particular, that the spreading of race hatred be curbed by every legal means, and

WHEREAS it is imperative that the Canadian Jewish Congress take the initiative and render leadership at every level of our society in order to realize the widest freedom consistent with peace, order, and good government in Canada,

THEREFORE BE IT RESOLVED THAT the 14th Plenary Session fully endorse the brief presented by the Canadian Jewish Congress to the House of Commons External Affairs Committee, and directs that efforts be pursued towards the adoption of legislation incorporating:

a) effective measures against the propagation of race hatred and group libel ... and,

b) effective implementation of the United Nations Convention on Genocide.[2]

Congress's endorsement of the government's initiative was attacked from two sides – by civil libertarians in the national executive, and by survivors and their supporters. The majority of the executive overrode the opposition of the former group in presenting the resolution, but had not counted on resistance from the latter. Twenty-one members of the Association of Survivors were granted delegate status to the plenary, including Milton Klein, the MP who had introduced the private member's bill in the House of Commons in 1964. According to Lou Zablow, president of the association, they were at first denied entry. However, when they threatened to demonstrate outside the Queen Elizabeth Hotel, the headquarters for the plenary, they were allowed inside. They persuaded the resolutions committee to include a clause referring to group libel in the original resolution. When the civil libertarians insisted that the burden of proof be placed on the Crown, arguments broke out on the floor. The association's delegates hammered out a compromise resolution by incorporating a reservation by Congress of "the right to recommend any amendments or the deletion of any defences ... should such defences prove to render the legislation ineffective." The amendment passed by a wide majority.[3]

The actions of the Association of Survivors must be considered a major triumph for the group. It was able to push through a more strongly worded resolution, and in so doing, it overcame opposition within the establishment. Yet for some survivors this victory was insufficient. Sabina Citron of Toronto, writing in the *Voice*, the annual report of the association, criticized the opponents of the resolution. "Some are so afraid to change the status quo, they are paralyzed into inaction, incapable of dealing with the needs of the day, forgetting that laws written a hundred years ago could not possible [*sic*] provide for situations then unforeseen ... And if the survivors of Nazism seem a little impatient, please remember that we have been to hell and back. We are the living witnesses of a destruction unprecedented in recorded history."[4]

Perhaps Citron was unaware of what the leadership of Congress actually desired, which was similar to the position of the survivors. In a letter to the National Executive Committee on 6 April 1965, Saul Hayes had written:

The general purpose of the Criminal Code makes it eminently proper that it be the vehicle to express the national concern for the harmonious co-existence of different ethnic, racial and religious groups in Canada and that it underscore this concern by properly drafted provisions looking to the elimination of acts and practices which produce or promote injurious discord. The Canadian Jewish Congress is fully aware that any such provisions must be consistent with protection of the democratic character of our society ... The Jewish people of Canada share with the rest of the Canadian people a determination to preserve those freedoms which are deeply rooted in the traditions of our country ... However, we do *not* believe ... that the preservation and maintenance of these essential freedoms requires us to give license to those who would arouse hostility between different racial, religious or ethnic groups ... Conduct of this character undermines democratic rights, sabotages the national welfare and destroys national unity. It exploits our democracy for evil ends.[5]

Hayes's position was not different from that of the association when it wrote that "there is no freedom for expression which jeopardizes national security or is seditious."[6] As had been the case for several years, the differences between Congress and the survivors were based more on misperception than on reality.

In those months, the Cohen committee was receiving briefs and holding meetings with a wide range of Canadians. Mark MacGuigan, a member of the committee, remembered that there was a representation from the Jewish community, but he did not recall any from survivor groups.[7] The committee's report was submitted to Lucien Cardin, the minister of justice in the Pearson administration, on 10 November 1965. He introduced it in the House of Commons in the spring of 1966. The report stated that there were three possible courses of action: not changing the law, minor changes to offer a remedial response to the situation, and new legislation to amend the Criminal Code. The committee recommended the third option.[8] The report reviewed the spread of hate propaganda in Canada and its social and psychological effects, surveyed the existing law in Canada and elsewhere, and presented conclusions and recommendations. There were five specific conclusions. First, there was a serious problem, but it was not a crisis or a near crisis; nevertheless, the potential psychological and social damage was incalculable. Second, there were inadequate legal remedies to deal with the situation. Third, only through legislation could the situation be addressed. The committee noted that "democratic society no longer accepts ... the notion that freedom of expression is an absolute right" (precisely the position taken by Hayes, a member of the committee, *and* the Association of Survivors). Fourth, freedom of expression must be given preference, but not when it "colours the quality of liberty." Fifth, the new legislation should forbid the advocacy of genocide, the incitement to hatred of groups that would breach the peace, and group defamation.[9]

The committee recommended that the promotion of genocide should be an indictable offence punishable by five years' imprisonment and that the incitement of hatred or contempt against an identifiable group in a public place leading to a breach of the peace, or the communication of such statements, be punishable by two years' imprisonment. There would be no convictions if a person could prove that the statements were true or where they were made for the "public benefit".[10] This last point was crucial.[11] Cohen was committed to writing a report that was unanimously accepted by all the members. MacGuigan, a member of the Canadian Civil Liberties Association, stated that he would not accept the report if it allowed for acquittal when the person believed the statement to be true. Hayes opposed him on this issue. Cohen's solution was to put the burden of proof on the accused, and this approach was accepted. According to MacGuigan, "[I] have a great deal of recollection of that. It was the turning point of the committee because they wanted to have a unanimous report and that was the bottom line as far as I was concerned. To me it was intolerable that people could be convicted of saying something that was historically true."[12]

Following the presentation of the report to the House, a bill based on it was referred to a special joint committee of the House of Commons and the Senate. The report was not fully endorsed by the media or in the House. In a survey of editorial opinion, Congress found that twenty-seven newspapers supported the legislation and fifteen were opposed.[13] Michael Garber wrote to the prime minister on 5 May supporting the report, without mentioning the differences of opinion among the leadership of the Jewish community. Pearson replied that the government was "proceeding as expeditiously as is possible."[14]

Meanwhile, Hayes informed a meeting of the NJCRC that the matter did not have high priority on the government agenda, while Ben Kayfetz, the executive director of the JCRC, said that MacGuigan had told him that there were thirty other matters ahead of the report on its list. Hayes stated that a representation from the CJC would be meeting Pearson, the solicitor general, and the minister of justice on 16 May 1966. Divisions within the NJCRC prevented the body from adopting a direct tactic. It could not decide whether to write its own draft of a bill, promote a campaign of mass endorsement for the report, or confine itself to the letters and brief that had already been presented.[15]

Congress's dilemma was solved when a bill based on the report was introduced in the Senate in November 1966. The bill adopted the recommendations of the report exactly. Ben Kayfetz remembered that the JCRC was surprised by the report and the bill because its proposals went beyond what had been advocated by Congress, "which until then had restricted itself to posing laws against incitement to violence."[16] Kayfetz also remarked that the government brought the bill before the Senate first because of opposition in the House.[17] Congress expected that the legislation would proceed forthwith. After all, Pearson had said as much at a press conference in August.[18] That expectation was not fulfilled: the legislation would not be on the books until 1970.

NEO-NAZISM IN WEST GERMANY

In the late 1960s, as the hate-propaganda bill was winding its way through the legislative process, other incidents arose which reminded Canadian Jews of the Holocaust. Any development in the Federal Republic of Germany after the war which smacked of neo-Nazism or exculpation of the Nazi past was a lightning rod for the Jewish world. Two such events in the second half of the 1960s were particularly alarming. The first was the proposal by the West German government that a Statute of Limitations on prosecuting suspected Nazi war criminals in Germany be invoked. The second was the emergence of the neo-Nazi Nationale Partei Deutschland (NPD), which contested seats in state elections.

According to an official declaration by the German minister of information, a statute to limit judicial punishment to twenty years was to go into effect on 8 May 1965. If passed, the legislation would allow those suspected of crimes against humanity to live freely in Germany, including individuals who had escaped to other countries after the war. This announcement, coming on the heels of the execution of Adolf Eichmann, the revelation that Martin Bormann, Alois Brunner, and other important figures in the Nazi party were allegedly living in safe havens abroad, and the proliferation of neo-Nazi groups in Germany and in other western European countries, prompted widespread protest. France, Britain, and Israel appealed to Bonn to reconsider its decision, and demonstrations were held at the German consulate in New York. In Canada, opposition was spearheaded by the Jewish Labour Committee. It began with an appeal from its president, David Orlikow, the NDP member of Parliament, to the German ambassador;[19] this was followed by a conference of trade union leaders on 19 January 1965, a memorandum to the consul general in Montreal,[20] and finally a public protest on 25 February which drew six hundred people.[21]

Bonn caved in to the pressure and extended the period of judicial punishment to 1969. This change did not assuage the Jewish community, however. Congress, in a resolution on the "Warsaw Ghetto Event – Communal Unity," presented at the 1965 plenary, included a protest against the imposition of any Statute of Limitations.[22] The following year a submission by Saul Hayes and Michael Garber on behalf of the CJC to Prime Minister Pearson requested that "at all levels of international diplomacy and at the forum of the United Nations it [Canada] foster the view that war crimes and crimes against humanity must have no time limitation as to prosecution."[23]

Four years later, as the term for prosecutions was drawing to a close, the Jewish community began a new round of protests. Again Bonn wavered over its decision. It apparently intended to extend the term for another decade, to 1979, but a differentiation would be made between those who had acted willingly and those who had not participated out of "base motives," This decision did little to diminish the opposition. A mass meeting organized by the Central Region of Congress was held in Toronto on 9 June 1969 . It was accompanied by a resolution condemning the statute and appeals to Bonn to withdraw it, to the Canadian government to put pressure on the West German authorities, and to the United Nations to intervene.[24] The extension did, however, satisfy the World Jewish Congress. In a letter to Sydney Harris, Gerhart Riegner, president of the WJC, wrote: "It is unlikely that new relevant facts would come to light after that date [1979] and that proceedings would then still be initiated against potential defendants, if for no other but 'biological' reasons." The WJC did promise, nevertheless, to support the Central Council of Jews in Germany in its effort to have the differentiation clause eliminated.[25] Although Riegner's assessment that by 1979 additional information about war criminals and the discovery of surviving murderers was unlikely proved to be short-sighted, the issue was shelved for yet another decade when Bonn rescinded the differentiation clause.

On 22 January 1967 Canadians sat glued to their television sets watching the CBC news program *Sunday*. After weeks of anticipation that Adolf von Thadden, the leader of the NPD, would be visiting Canada, it was revealed that he was not coming. The NPD had 25,000 members and had received 11 per cent of the vote in two state elections in 1966. Von Thadden had been a member of the Nazi party while serving as an officer in the Panzer division of the German army during the war. Meanwhile, the CBC had sent a television crew to interview von Thadden at his home. When news of the interview was made known, the Canadian Jewish community was enraged. The affair had begun when Department of External Affairs had informed Congress that von Thadden had been invited to appear on *Front Page Challenge*, a popular CBC program. The NJCRC, at a meeting of its officers on 8 January 1967, discussed the matter and recommended that Saul Hayes contact External Affairs, Immigration, and the CBC. It also endorsed a demonstration at the CBC studios in Toronto at the time of the program to be organized by Central Region.[26] Five days later, at a meeting of the executive committee of Central Region, the demonstration was organized for 29 January, when it was anticipated that von Thadden would appear, not on *Front Page Challenge*, but on *Sunday*. At the meeting there was debate about whether the CBC had the right to air the program. Most of the officers agreed that it was less a matter of von Thadden's appearance than of how he would be treated and whether opposing opinions would be presented.[27] A press release by Congress on 16 January stated: "We would have no complaint about a program presented in depth and in perspective which examines the resurgence of political extremism of a neo-Nazi type in West Germany in the light of current and past history. But we do take serious objection to a program built around the figure and personality of Adolf von Thadden ... Were von Thadden to come to Canada on his own, no sizable or responsible organization would give him a platform. Unfortunately, the CBC is affording him, in the words of its producer, an audience of two and a half million who would not otherwise be reached."[28]

Because of the uproar in the community, the CBC decided at the last minute to interview von Thadden at his home in Hanover and to broadcast the program on 22 January. Journalists Bob Hoyt and Larry Zolf, who had added spice to the controversial *This Hour Has Seven Days*, were sent by executive producer Daryl Duke to conduct the interview. Von Thadden contested assertions that he was a Nazi and that the party was extremist and a threat to democracy. He stated: "I never was a Nazi, and there's no reason why to become a Nazi now. The party is not a neo-Nazi party, it's a normal right-wing party. The percent of ex-Nazis in the NPD is not greater than in other parties. National socialism was unique; it died with Hitler. Hitler was not a hero, but a man of German history. It was a terrible tragedy for our people." Regarding racial hatred and the Holocaust, von Thadden contended that "antisemitism is not a problem because there are no Jews. There is no Jewish problem in Germany because we haven't got them ... We heard about the camps ... I saw things in Romania, but they were done by Romanians ... Antisemitism is not a German phenomenon."[29]

The interviewers were at first taken aback by von Thadden. He spoke impeccable English, looked and dressed like a small-town banker, and was surrounded by his children, neighbours, and pets. Zolf chose to use irony in the interview. At its conclusion, he remarked that anyone who loved kids and dogs could not be all bad. A Winnipeg Jew who had grown up with child survivors, Zolf was excoriated by the Jewish community. Three decades after the interview, he remarked: "I was a journalist. If I cannot interview Adolf von Thadden, who else can I not interview?" But he also regretted his decision to employ irony. "I made a stupid mistake. I let my sense of irony get me into trouble ... I went off to Germany and I spent hours with the guy ... a boring, fatuous ass ... there was nothing to him." Ben Kayfetz concurs with Zolf's assessment. He says, "Zolf made the fatal mistake of using irony, and people did not understand irony."[30]

The Jewish community had little time to prepare a protest. The date of the program was not revealed until the day before it was aired. Nevertheless, a telephone chain was organized and the CBC was flooded with several thousand phone calls, and a silent vigil that drew three thousand protestors took place outside the studios. One week later the mass demonstration against neo-Nazism in West Germany, organized by Max Shecter of CANC and publicized by the JCRC Central Region and N3, was held at the Coliseum in Toronto. It attracted a capacity crowd of six thousand people. One of the speakers was David Lewis of the NDP, who stated that Zolf should be fired.[31] The journalist now responds, "Fired for what?" Zolf determined that he would "fight this myself, so I accepted any invitation to debate the 'infamous von Thadden interview' in synagogues and I would lose each time when a Holocaust survivor said that I had said, 'He ain't all that bad.' I couldn't win. I said, 'I don't own the CBC.' Thirty years later a survivor saw me and said, 'you did the von Thadden interview.'"[32]

Reaction to the interview was not confined to Toronto. In Winnipeg, a mass meeting of five hundred people at Rosh Pina Synagogue presented and approved a resolution calling on "all people and organizations who join with us in recognizing the dangers of neo-Nazism" to be vigilant, to commemorate the victims of Nazism, and to "inform and instruct young people" about fascism. The meeting was reported in the *Winnipeg Free Press*, in which a panel composed of editorial writers from that paper and the *Winnipeg Tribune* were joined by a representative of the Canadian Institute of International Affairs.[33] In Montreal the Jewish Labour Committee aligned with the Canadian Labour Congress and the Quebec Federation of Labour and sent telegrams to the prime minister, the ministers for external affairs and immigration, and the secretary of state. The press also gave its opinion on the von Thadden affair. *Le Devoir* quoted *Le Monde*, which stated that "everybody considers von Thadden's party to be neo-Nazi except that very party alone." *La Presse* reported that eighteen members of the party's executive were former Nazi leaders. Similar views were expressed in the English-language press.[34]

Outrage over the Statute of Limitations and the von Thadden affair was shared by most of the Jewish community. The demonstrations in 1965, 1967, and 1969 were planned by the JLC in the first instance and Congress in the other two, but involved other organizations, both Jewish and non-Jewish. For the most part, survivors were included in the planning of these protests, thereby negating any potential opposition on their part. This united front was indicative of the feeling that when it came to neo-Nazism and West Germany, there was no room for appeasement. This was especially true in the context of other developments. Antisemitism was still viewed as an active element in Canadian society, although the incidents had decreased in comparison with the first half of the decade. Together with the debate in Parliament over hate propaganda and the overwhelming events in Israel, the developments in West Germany kept the spotlight on anti-Jewish activities.

In retrospect, the controversy over the Statute of Limitations and the airing of the von Thadden interview caused the expenditure of a great deal of energy and emotion over issues that did not merit this degree of concern. The statute must be viewed as part of the compulsion in Konrad Adenauer's Germany to recreate historical memory in light of its embrace of democracy and the economic rebirth that was taking place. At the time, West Germany was intent on depicting the Nazi era as an aberration of German history. Moreover, the country was the West's bulwark against Soviet expansion. Therefore the issue of Nazi war criminals was not a pressing one for the government. West Germany had paid lip service to world opinion by holding trials of former Nazis in the 1950s and 1960s. Those found guilty had received light sentences. The fuss that erupted over the statute spoke more about a heightened consciousness of Jewish historical memory than about the possibility that former Nazis could emerge triumphant. The von Thadden affair was even less important. Von Thadden was an nonentity, a man without charisma or vision and with few devotees. He and the NPD had vanished into the sinkhole of historical memory by the end of the decade.

In both instances, the Jewish community in Canada, and in the West in general, was genuinely upset with the public attempt to minimize the Nazi era in West Germany. Neo-Nazism there was a red flag for Jews, whether survivors or those born and raised in their adopted country. These events did not create an upsurge of identification with the Holocaust as a defining event for non-survivors, but they did contribute to a growing understanding that the spirit of hatred that had led to the Holocaust would not be tolerated a second time.

OTHER FACTORS IN A CHANGING SELF-IDENTIFICATION

Other factors, less tangible than the West German issues, also contributed to the changing attitude toward the Holocaust in the Jewish community in the late 1960s. These included alarm and concern about the threat to the existence of Israel, random displays of anti-semitism, mostly in Manitoba, and an unease within the community about its self-definition.

In the spring of 1967 President Abdel Nasser of Egypt ordered the United Nations peacekeeping forces out of the Sinai Peninsula and closed the Strait of Tiran. These actions led to the Six Day War in June between Israel and the Arabs. The war was Israel's greatest military triumph to date and caused an unparalleled upsurge of pride among most Jews in the West. It did not bring peace, jowever, and the situation grew more unstable during the War of Attrition (1967–73), the Yom Kippur War (1973), the anti-Zionist resolutions of the United Nations General Assembly, and the oil embargo. The pressure was eventually relieved somewhat by the peace treaty signed with Egypt in 1978.

What effect did these events, especially the 1967 war, have in raising consciousness about the Holocaust among Canadian Jews? This question is difficult to answer. Minutes of organizational meetings deal with specific current events and not with how those events reflect or evoke historical memory. There was no discernible swing to commemoration and education about the Holocaust because of the threat to Israel's security. Yet in the minds of most Canadian Jews, that threat brought home in some measure the reality of the Holocaust – that Jews had to be vigilant, that antisemitism was a palpable threat, and that Jews must never allow themselves to become captive to totalitarian regimes based on racial or religious exclusion. The Six Day War necessitated an unprecedented campaign to raise funds. The Canadian Jewish community was more than up to the task, and survivors were in the forefront of the effort. As a result, they were recognized for their contribution, and this appreciation paved the way for their entry into the wider community, encouraging more of them to become involved in mainstream organizations.[35]

For Canadian Jews who were involved in community affairs at the time, the threat to Israel was of great importance. For Sam Rothstein, president of the Vancouver Jewish Community Centre in the early 1970s, the 1967 war was one of the most "earth-shattering" events of his life and was the one development that led to a commitment by community organizations to become more involved in Holocaust commemoration. Professor Moe Steinberg, chair of the Pacific Region of the CJC in the late 1970s, concurred. He saw Holocaust remembrance and support for Israel as inseparable.[36] For younger Canadian Jews who became active in community affairs, the feeling persists that 1967 was a watershed in helping to heal divisions between Canadian Jews and survivors. Stephen Cummings, the founder of the Montreal Holocaust Memorial Centre, said that "consciousness [of the Holocaust] has changed. Jews are much more proud, and that's a post-1967 [phenomenon]. It was the event that gave Jews around the world confidence." Professor Cyril Levitt, who as a student was involved in the anti-Nazi alliance in Toronto in the mid-1960s, feels that the conflict between the established community and the newcomers eroded after 1967. "It wasn't until post '67 that the established community came onside."[37]

Jacob Neusner, the noted American theologian, has written that the war was a turning point for American Judaism also. He argues that the third generation, those who had been born in the the United States and who emerged in the post-war era, found their memory and their hope as American Jews in the weeks leading to the Six Day War and in Israel's victory.[38] In a recent and provocative study, Peter Novick writes that "it's harder to locate a single decisive moment" than the Six Day War in explaining the cementing of the connection between American Jews and Israel, and by extension, the Holocaust and Israel.[39] These arguments are compelling but insufficient to describe the Canadian experience. June 1967 was a watershed for Jews around the world, but for the Canadian community, it was only one factor in a series of events during the 1960s that contributed to a collective consciousness of the Holocaust.

Concern within the community over issues related to the Holocaust dominated the JCRC report to the Congress plenary held in Toronto from 16 to 20 May, 1968. The report discussed the bill on hate literature, the rise of anti-Zionism, the anguish expressed by some Christian groups for having inculcated antisemitic attitudes over the centuries, the von Thadden and Statute of Limitations affairs, the upsurge of antisemitism in Poland, the activities of racist groups operating in Canada, including John Beattie's Nazi Party, and observances commemorating the anniversary of the Warsaw Ghetto Uprising.[40] This preponderance of attention to anti-Jewish activities was unprecedented in plenary sessions. Nevertheless, Congress did not see the necessity of creating a standing committee on issues related to the Holocaust, despite resolutions on commemoration and education. The feeling persisted that the Holocaust itself did not merit special consideration as an ongoing aspect of the Canadian Jewish agenda; rather, issues related to the event were best left to the purview of the JCRC.

In the late 1960s, public expression of antisemitism was most prevalent in Manitoba. A great number of incidents there between 1967 and 1970 created concern in the Jewish community. In January 1967 Ron Gostick was invited to appear on local radio and television programs. His reputation as a writer and disseminator of scandalous anti-Jewish literature, including "The Protocols of the Elders of Zion," was well known. Protests were launched by the Western Region of Congress and the Communications Office of the United Church of Canada.[41] Gostick had already appeared the month before at a meeting of the "Friends of Rhodesia," a cover for local right-wing bigots, whose chair was John Belows, the mayor of Assiniboia, a suburb of Winnipeg. When challenged at a town council meeting about his association with Gostick, Belows replied that Gostick's name did not appear in the Cohen committee report and that he had known him for fifteen years. The television program was aired on 19 January on the local CBC affiliate. Charles Huband of the Canadian Council of Christians and Jews confronted Gostick, who admitted that the "Protocols" might be a forgery. Columns and editorials in the Winnipeg dailies condemned Gostick's views. Letters to the editor, however, defended him and Belows. Among them was one which was found to have been written by the person who had arranged Gostick's presentation at the "Rhodesia" meeting. In a related event, Eric Butler, Gostick's counterpart in Australia, visited Winnipeg in the spring of 1966 and spoke at another "Rhodesia" meeting.[42]

Butler was again invited by the Rhodesia group, over the signature of Belows, in the spring of 1967. A report in the *Winnipeg Free Press* stated that his publications were "a brand of anti-Semitism that is more dangerous than low brow literature." A year later, Butler was scheduled to speak to the Winnipeg Canadian Club. This engagement was cancelled, in part because of the disclosure a day earlier by the Manitoba Human Rights Association that Butler had published a tract entitled *The International Jew – The Truth about the "Protocols of Zion."* The association was aided in its research by Congress, which issued a "Draft Report on Eric Butler's Visit to Winnipeg."[43] What was particularly galling to the Jewish community was the coincidence of these appearances with swastikas and other antisemitic daubings on synagogues, Jewish businesses, and the Manitoba legislative building between April 1966 (on Passover) and February 1968. Two men were arrested in connection with these incidents and were found to have membership cards in the Canadian Nazi Party. Other racist literature denigrating "Negroes," Native Canadians, and Doukhobors were also distributed in this period. On 10 November 1968 monuments in the Jewish cemetery in Winnipeg were defaced. The following year, hate literature from Elnar Aberg, a Swedish racist who had been exposed in the Cohen report, was distrobuted in the community. One response to these acts was a brief submitted by the Manitoba Human Rights Association to the Senate Committee on Hate Propaganda in 1969.[44]

Two further incidents heightened concern by the Winnipeg Jewish community. A travelling production of a Passion play in the "Oberammergau tradition" was sponsored by the Women's Catholic League. Passion plays had been staged in the Middle Ages and had depicted Jews as the killers of Christ. Cardinal Flahoff responded to Congress's protest by stating, "I find sympathy with the views you express"; but the play was staged nevertheless.[45] In 1970, the *Canadian Farmer*, a Ukrainian-language paper, published a series of articles which contained assertions that Jews had oppressed Ukrainians. The series was stopped as a result of protests by the CJC.[46] One positive outcome of this local expression of antisemitism and the insensitivity in some parts of society to the harm being done to Jewish-Christian relations was the elevation of the Shaareth Hapleita Committee from its position as the planning body for Warsaw ghetto commemorations to a new role as the architect for all activities related to the Holocaust. As such, the committee became one of forty-four organizations affiliated with the Winnipeg Jewish Community Council in 1970.[47]

Local antisemitic incidents in Winnipeg, the events in West Germany, the debate in Parliament regarding hate propaganda – these issues were important to many Canadian Jews at the end of the decade. Yet they expressed only some aspects of the situation facing the community. Saul Hayes had been the spokesperson for Canadian Jews for thirty years. In addition to being the community's voice, he was in some ways its conscience. In "The Changing Nature of the Jewish Community," an article published in *Viewpoints*, a quarterly on Jewish affairs, in 1970, he addressed the predicament of Jewish identity. He raised a number of points in support of his claim that the community had changed since the war. Among them was an acknowledgment that the immigrants of the thirties[48] and forties were different from their predecessors, that there was an absence or marked decrease in the importance of religion, and that a "ghetto life" had been discarded by the Jewish diaspora. Hayes's most provocative point was that "the younger element....are 'fed up' with established institutions and community leadership or, worse, are apathetic to them." He dwelt on the community's increasing identification with Israeli affairs: "One changed situation from former periods is that at one time concern for a homeland for the Jewish people was the *'hazokah'* [concern] of the zionist organizations. Today Israel is everybody's business." Hayes related this development not only to the threat to Israel's existence but to another factor. "A very interesting thing is happening to American Jewry. The Jewish Emptiness in the lives of so many of the present generation is an emptiness not endemic to Jews, but an epidemic affecting all. If emptiness persists, it could be very damaging to the Jewish psyche. It is being filled, but not by a return to customs and practices with which other generations were familiar. 'La recherche du temps perdu' is not for the new breed. Large segments of the Jewish people are finding in Israel a real substitute for their former identification."[49]

Hayes's insight was prescient, but it provided only a part of the story. Israel was the most telling substitute for a community that was searching for an identity. But the "business" of Israel was a necessary but insufficient surrogate. The post-war generation of young adults born in the 1930s and 1940s tried to remember what their parents had tried to forget. They did not have a memory of pre-war Europe or of immigrant life in Canada. According to Neusner, this cohort experienced a crisis of identity and commitment. Its members required a myth, although to them it was a fact, which would serve as an explanation of their ethnic identity.[50] There had to be something that spoke to the new generation about their own vulnerability as Canadian Jews while connecting them with their roots – roots that had been abandoned or not passed down to them by their parents. Thus the murder of the European Jewry became the "Holocaust," the embodiment of all evil, the greatest suffering by any group at any time in history. As they learned more about the destruction of Jewish civilization in Europe a generation earlier, as they heard and read more about war criminals and hate propagandists, and as they experienced the activities of racists and antisemites in their midst, they came to see the Holocaust as one marker of their own identity. Were Hayes to have written the same article a decade later, he might have concluded that both the Holocaust and the establishment of the state of Israel signalled a return of Jews to their history; together they provided two of the bulwarks of Jewish self-definition to counteract the feeling of Jewish emptiness.

THE HATE-PROPAGANDA LEGISLATION

The predominant issue in the Jewish community in the late 1960s was the hate-propaganda legislation, which took three and a half years for the bill to become law. One aspect was whether the bill would be passed on its own merits or whether it was meant to appease the Jewish community. At the outset, Hayes had stated his position on this question at a conference of B'nai Brith leaders. "If members of Parliament decide to vote on the grounds that the Jewish community is making a lot of noise, or that it will make the Jewish community feel better, I'd rather they vote against it."[51] Despite this pronouncement, the community devoted much effort to monitoring the deliberations on the bill and was instrumental in pressuring the government to pass the legislation.

The Central Region of the JCRC was the guiding body for the community's program of action. At a meeting on 7 September 1966 it discussed a proposal to hold a demonstration in Ottawa. Sydney Harris moved that the demonstration be postponed but not cancelled, and the motion passed. In fact, the demonstration never materialized.[52] The JCRC asked its legal committee to monitor editorials and comments on the Cohen report and present its findings to the JCRC.[53] The legislation was introduced in the Senate on 11 November as Bill S-49. In a letter to the JCRC following second reading, Hayes expressed concern that opposition to the bill was building. He recommended that Mark MacGuigan be contacted about writing an article in support of the legislation; MacGuigan agreed. His article, "Free Speech Right Not Absolute," appeared in the Toronto *Daily Star* on 15 December.[54]

The parliamentary session ended in 1967 May with S-49 still on the table. In the next sitting the bill became S-5, and it received second reading in November. Congress submitted a brief to the Senate committee studying the bill in February 1968. It argued that the proposed legislation did not present a threat to freedom of expression. "If a defamatory statement is deliberately made about an identifiable group within the definition of the Bill, and the person issuing this statement can show no reasonable grounds to believe it true, and if its public discussion is not for the public benefit – what possible protection is owed to such gratuitous and malignant sowing of hatred? If a person knows his tale is false and does not care a whit for the repercussions of the statement, if it has no relevance to the public interest and brings hatred and contempt upon a racial, ethnic or religious group – surely he should face the consequences of this act?" The brief cited wide support for the legislation, beginning in 1964, from bodies as diverse as the Manitoba and Ontario legislatures, the Canadian Federation of Mayors, the Canadian Bar Association, the United Church of Canada, and the Canadian Legion. It concluded: "We appear before you today in support of the legislation embodied in Bill S-5 which we feel, subject to the comments we have made in several respects, is on the whole wisely conceived and drafted. The danger of hate propaganda, as has been stated, lies not in its quantity or volume but in its intrinsic quality, a quality which undermines the climate of our public life."[55] A few days later the government was defeated on a money bill, and the session ended in April. Kayfetz wrote that the brief was "little more than a dress rehearsal" since there would be no further action in the aborted session.[56] Nevertheless, this was the only brief that the Jewish community presented during the years of deliberation.

Parliament resumed in September 1968 with a new prime minister, Pierre Trudeau, and a majority government for the first time in six years. In the interval between the prorogation of Parliament and the new administration, the Jewish community actively lobbied for the legislation. Trudeau was courted by the Association of Survivors, some of whose members had been delegates to his first nomination meeting in Mount Royal in 1965. The association prided itself on its first-hand connections with the new leader.[57] During the election campaign, Congress, utilizing the NJCRC, swung into action. It wrote 150 letters to candidates in Ontario and received 33 responses, all of them positive. Of these candidates, eighteen were elected. Its Western Region lobbied candidates in the Prairies with similar success. Personal meetings were held with Donald Macdonald, the outgoing minister of justice, James Walker, who had seconded the private member's bill in 1964, and Dalton Camp of the Conservatives. Hayes met with Senators Paul Martin and John Conolly, who were of the opinion that the legislation would be passed. Trudeau made statements favouring the legislation on three occasions during the campaign.[58] On 9 June the day after the election, N3 sponsored a public meeting on the issue in Toronto, with Walker as the featured speaker.[59]

In a letter to Hayes on 6 January 1969, Kayfetz wrote that the JCRC was identified in the public mind as the most active agent against neo-Nazism. The community, he said, looks to the JCRC as its "spokesman" and "protector."[60] At this time, Kayfetz was expressing the obvious. Survivor organizations such as the Association of Former concentration Camp Inmates/Survivors of Nazi Oppression and N3 had lost the initiative over the issue. Congress had the contacts and the prestige. The association continued as an important voice, but it was working more with Congress over the issue than on its own. N3's raison d'etre rested on combatting the proliferation of anti-semitism. Following the Beattie fiascos, however, antisemitic activity had diminished considerably, and by 1969 N3 had become moribund.

The bill was reintroduced in the Senate as S-21 on 29 February 1969. Arthur Roebuck, a long-time proponent of civil rights and now over ninety, chaired the committee. He, like MacGuigan and David Lewis and Andrew Brewin of the NDP, were supporters of the bill despite being members of the Canadian Civil Liberties Association. During the deliberations, Congress met with Robert Stanfield, the leader of the Opposition, John Diefenbaker, who had originally supported the bill but now led the critics in the House, and Marc Lalonde, Trudeau's executive assistant. It met with Trudeau and twelve of his ministers on 25 May.[61] The Jewish Labour Committee was also active in lobbying the government. Its president, Michael Rubenstein, wrote to Roebuck, and the JLC presented a brief to the committee. The CCLA also submitted a brief citing its opposition to the bill. Nevertheless, the Senate passed tbe bill, adding religion as a characteristic of an identifiable group.[62]

"An Act to amend the Criminal Code" was introduced in the House in the fall of 1969 as C-3.[63] Five years after the legislation was first presented, the government was finally making it a priority item. Trudeau wrote to David Orlikow on October 22: "I wish to assure you that it is the firm intention of the Government to proceed with this bill during the course of the second session of the Parliament."[64] The bill was guided through the House by Minister of Justice John Turner. It was passed on 13 April 1970 by a vote of 89 to 45, with 127 members absent. Two Liberals opposed it, as did most of the Tories and several NDP members. The bill was sent back to the Senate, where it passed by a vote of 40 to 22 on 5 June.

What did the legislation mean in practical terms? Would it, in fact, be a deterrent to hate propaganda? Two commentators at the time offered their views. Professor Stephen Cohen of McGill University argued that the legislation created a social norm to reassure minority groups, rather than promoting the ideal goal of eliminating hate. Ben Kayfetz agreed with this assessment. Although the law might be "unworkable," he wrote, it was necessary.[65] As events unfolded, throughout most of the 1970s, hate propaganda waned, but whether it was because of the legislation or other circumstances is difficult to determine. The law has not proved to be a deterrent from the late 1970s until the present, partially because provincial attorneys general have been reluctant to invoke it, for reasons discussed in chapter 8.

And what did the process signify? First, there was a demand by a substantial segment of the public that something be done to curb the hate-mongers. Whether this demand forced the Liberals under Pearson and Trudeau to move the process forward is debatable. Both administrations responded to the public concern and set the tone of the debate. Five justice ministers, Favreau, Cardin, Trudeau, Macdonald, and Turner, were supportive, as were prime ministers Pearson and Trudeau. Yet legislation on the issue did not become a high priority until the fall of 1969. Second, the Jewish community for the most part coalesced over the need for legislation after 1966. Led by the JCRC, a concentrated campaign was undertaken to pressure the government, but only after the more strident civil libertarians on the committee were overpowered and the more militant survivors had lost ground. The more moderate survivors were now working with Congress, even though many still felt that the organization was moving too slowly and did not give them their proper due.

Finally, what did the legislation mean with regard to raising consciousness of the Holocaust as a defining point for the Jewish community? In specific terms, the Holocaust was not mentioned in parliamentary debates or in the briefs and meetings between Congress and the legislators. Rather, the emphasis was on the Canadian situation, namely, that the issue was not solely the protection of the Jewish minority but the provision of legal redress for all groups and individuals against defamation. It was significant, as Maxwell Cohen pointed out, that the government was willing to take a moral stance that hatred would not be tolerated. This position was in direct contradiction to what had happened in Nazi Germany and what the community feared was evident in the anti-Israel diatribes and anti-semitic activities of the time. Jews were in peril in some countries and the security of Israel was problematic but Canadian Jews at least knew that they were protected, in contrast to their situation a generation earlier.

COMMEMORATING THE HOLOCAUST

Until the early 1970s the only tangible connection to the memory of the Holocaust by the community was the annual commemoration service held in the cities with the largest Jewish population. This practice had begun in Canada in 1944, on the first anniversary of the Warsaw Ghetto Uprising. For the next two decades, the programs usually featured a speaker, readings from Holocaust literature, memorial prayers, and a candle-lighting ceremony. They were held in English and Yiddish, and most of the participants and attendees were survivors. The memorials were organized on a local basis by committees that were either independent of or had a quasi-association with local federations. Few Canadian Jews or young people showed interest in the commemorations.

During the 1950s, Congress plenaries passed two resolutions urging local Jewish communities to observe the event. Otherwise, the Holocaust was not referred to in plenary addresses or in regional and committee reports. However, as the incidents of antisemitism proliferated, and as the internal debate about hate-propaganda legislation pitted survivors against some of the established community, these annual commemorations assumed a new significance. They were an occasion not only to mourn the victims but also to indict hate-mongers. The most notable example was Sydney Harris's exposure of neo-Nazis in Toronto in 1964. For the next decade, these annual commemorative events in cities with a sizable Jewish population emerged as forums for the Jewish community both to remember and to learn. In so doing, they attracted a wide audience and spawned other programs geared toward educating the community about the Holocaust. By the early 1970s the annual commemoration of the catastrophe had become a fixture in the calendar of the largest Jewish communities in Canada.

In Winnipeg the commemoration had been organized since 1944 by the Shaareth Hapleita Committee of the Winnipeg Congress Council. In 1963 the event was extended from a single day to a week and featured lectures and movies. The focal point of activity was the Bnai Abraham Synagogue, whose rabbi, Peretz Weizmann, was a survivor. Three years later the commemoration was proclaimed by Mayor Stephen Juba.[66] In 1972 Juba and Edward Schreyer, the premier of Manitoba, designated a city block on Memorial Avenue to be renamed the Avenue of Warsaw Ghetto Heroes, a tradition that still continues although the venue has changed.[67] Featured speakers in the late 1960s and early 1970s included Holocaust scholars Eliezer Berkovits and Richard Rubenstein, Mark MacGuigan of the Cohen committee, and Yigal Allon, deputy premier of Israel. Allon's visit attracted an audience of one thousand people. Community programs included an exhibit of *Churban* (Holocaust) literature and one depicting the concentration camp at Terezin.[68]

In Toronto a committee charged with the responsibility for organizing the commemoration came under the auspices of the CJC Central Region, but it was not a standing committee of Congress. It was renamed several times: in the early 1960s it was called the Warsaw Ghetto Uprising Committee. Its programs, held in the largest synagogues in the city, were drawing audiences of two thousand people by the middle of the decade.[69] In 1969 Elie Wiesel was the featured speaker. By this time the organizing body was called the Arrangement Committee of the Warsaw Ghetto Uprising Memorial.[70] A year later the program, now under the auspices of the Shoah Arrangements Committee, was expanded to three events, including an Auschwitz Memorial Service and a ceremony marking the twenty-fifth anniversary of Liberation.[71] In 1972 the Central Region renamed the committee the Holocaust Memorial Observance Committee. It was deemed to be a "projects committee" but not one of the twenty-five "standing committees."[72] The following year the budget for commemorative activities in Toronto was only $2,000. No other funds were targeted for Holocaust-related activities.[73]

Two themes emerge from the Toronto experience. One was that there was much hand-wringing on the part of officers of Central Region over the inadequacies of the program. They pointed to the lack of interest by the city's youth and the overuse of Yiddish, which most of the community did not understand. Survivors felt that more attention should be paid to education. In the meantime, the commemoration was drawing the largest audience of any such event in North America, according to one unofficial survey. The second theme, revealed in the frequent name changes, was that commemoration of the Holocaust was an important event on the community calendar, but not important enough for the organizing group to be given the status of a standing committee. Rather, the event was arranged by an ad hoc committee of survivors and some Canadian Jews which had limited autonomy and was under the scrutiny of the Education Committee of Central Region. Not until 1972 would the yet-again-renamed Holocaust Memorial Committee, chaired by Paul Goldstein of the Association of Survivors, receive the status of a permanent committee.[74]

Elsewhere in Ontario, Holocaust commemorative programs became annual events of significant proportions. They were held in London, Kitchener, Hamilton, St Catharines, Windsor, and Ottawa.[75]

The growth of these programs stirred Congress to adopt a resolution at its plenary session in 1971 calling for "consideration to the establishment of a permanent national memorial to the Holocaust." This was one of four resolutions relating to the Holocaust. The others dealt with action to be taken on Nazi war criminals in Canada, the development of education programs, and representation to the West German ambassador to discuss the rejection of restitution claims.[76]

The catalyst for these initiatives was the survivor community. From its formation in 1961, the Association of Survivors was the single most important voice in preserving the historical memory of the Holocaust in Montreal's Jewish community. Yet its relationship with established Jews was rocky. At times the association and Canadian Jews were adversaries, especially in the first stage of the effort to have the distribution of hate propaganda criminalized, and the furor over the Allan Gardens riot. On other occasions they worked together, as in the protests over the von Thadden's interview and in fund raising for Israel. While relations with Congress improved, especially after the 1971 plenary, there remained a strong feeling on the part of the association that it was outside the mainstream, and that its message about historical memory and the need to educate the community about the Holocaust was not shared by most of Montreal's Jews. This perception was born out in February, 1972, when the Saidye Bronfman Centre of the YM/YWHA decided to stage *The Man in the Glass Booth*.

The play was to be directed by Marion André, a Polish-Jewish émigré who had been hidden in Poland as a child during the war. He was something of a maverick, with a reputation as a brilliant, inventive director given to avant-garde and experimental theatre. *The Man in the Glass Booth* was to be part of a year-long series on the Holocaust, with speakers, films, and exhibits at the centre. It was a parody of the Eichmann trial, scripted by Robert Shaw as an adaptation of his novel. In the play, Eichmann is given the opportunity to defend himself, and he declares that the Jews were responsible for their own demise. Critics pointed to the shallowness of this argument and to the crude stereotypes of the Nazi perpetrators and of the Jews as willing accomplices to their own destruction, but they defended the right of the organizers to stage the play. Survivors did not share this view. For them, not only was the play antisemitic and a desecration of the memory of the victims, but the decision to perform it in the cultural centre funded by the largest Jewish community in Canada, where more than ten thousand survivors had found a haven, was intolerable.[77]

The association launched a vigorous campaign to have the play banned. Directors of the centre were equally vigorous in defending their position. Each side increased the pressure. The association had no trouble in getting support from the various Zionist organizations and from other survivor groups such as the Bergen-Belsen association. But it also managed to get support from the Eastern Region of Congress. In a flyer that was distributed widely, the association and its supporters asked, "Why is the Saidye Bronfman Center Ignoring Public Opinion?" The flyer called the play "an insult to the 6,000,000 Martyrs of nazi barbarism and to the Jewish people everywhere." It encouraged the community to "HELP STOP THE DESECRATION OF THE MEMORY OF THE SIX MILLION MARTYRS. DON'T CROSS THE PICKET LINES. DON'T ATTEND THIS PLAY."[78]

In response, Jack Engels, president of the Y, claimed to have received an endorsement of the play from Gideon Hausner, the chief prosecutor in the Eichmann trial. It turned out that Engels was stretching the truth. In a taped telephone conversation with Lou Zablow of the association, Hausner stated that he had said to Engels, "'I am not particularly enthusiastic about the play' ... I suggested to him to replace it by another play." When Zablow told Hausner that an article in the *Canadian Jewish News* had reported that "Gideon Hausner approved the play and actually urged all the Jews to see it," he replied, "No, that is entirely untrue. I never said so. On the contrary." Hausner reiterated his position in a letter to the editor of the *CJN*.[79]

On the eve of the production's opening, the Y backed down, and the play was not performed. André did not mince his words about this decision: "I have nothing but deep feelings of compassion for the victims of the Nazi Oppression. I know their pain. But I also know that no one is the sole bearer of truth and no one has an exclusive monopoly on suffering ... The play was condemned 'in absentia,' without an open trial. The judgment was rendered 'in camera'; the public was denied the right to judge for itself. But ultimately one fact remains, it is the curtailment of freedom."[80]

The reversal made by the Y received mixed reviews. The *Montreal Star* supported the decision. Michael Ballantyne wrote: "The point in this case is that we are dealing with a situation – the terrible fact of the Jewish holocaust – where tolerant and otherwise natural liberal attitudes tend to break down. In a word, if the survivors of the Nazi death camps feel that a particular play is offensive to them and to the memory of the six million dead, who is to say they're entirely wrong?" A dissenting opinion was expressed in an editorial in the *Suburban*, a Jewish community paper. "We can only hope that there will never again be a repetition of such a shortsighted decision. We owe it to all the future generations of Jews to have the courage of our convictions, to pursue the enlightenment and perpetuation of the history of our people. The holocaust is our history. It is an integral part of our survival."[81]

In March 1972 the play was to be performed in Toronto by the Tarragon Players. The JCRC Central Region passed a motion stating that "we suggest that the play not be proceeded with," with an amendment that "this community does not purport to act as a censor but we are of the opinion that the performance of the play will give rise to serious community problems because of the serious trauma still persisting among survivors of the Holocaust."[82] This motion did not sit well with Sydney Midanik, a long-time member of the committee and at one time its chair. A staunch member of the CCLA, he had been opposed to the hate-propaganda bill and the anti-Nazi demonstrations in Toronto against Beattie because they violated the principle of free speech. In protest, he resigned from the committee.[83] The play was staged, but picket lines were mounted outside the theatre by survivors and their supporters. The demonstrators had a less-legitimate grievance than did the opponents of the Montreal production. There the play was to have been staged in the Jewish Community Centre, whereas in Toronto it was performed in a more public venue.

In the aftermath of the *Glass Booth* affair, the Eastern Region of the CJC created the Holocaust Memorial Committee in May 1972. Its chair and vice-chair were Aba Beer and Isaac Piasetski, two of the most politically active survivors in Montreal. Subcommittees on commemoration and education were immediately established. Activities for the 1972–73 year included an exhibition of Holocaust literature at the Saidye Bronfman Centre in conjunction with the "Literature on the Holocaust" theme of Jewish Book Month;[84] a month of commemorative activities in April 1973 featuring an exhibit from Yad Vashem that was viewed by ten thousand people at several locales in Montreal;[85] teach-ins at Jewish summer camps in 1973;[86] a proposal for a memorial at the new community building of the Allied Jewish Community Services;[87] and plans for teaching the Holocaust "at all school levels."[88] The Central Region followed suit in the fall of 1972 by establishing a similar committee chaired by Paul Goldstein, a survivor who had come to Toronto from Montreal and had been active in the association. Survivors on the committee were concerned that, with "only" two thousand people in attendance at the commemoration, the memory of the Holocaust would perish with the survivors. They pointed out that this figure represented a mere two per cent of Toronto's Jewish population. Contrary opinions were expressed by non-survivors.

Although the first meetings of the Central Region's committee were devoted to widening the commemorative programs, a motion to create five subcommittees, including education, was defeated, signalling divisions between survivors and non-survivors on the committee.[89]

On 15 April 1973 the national executive of Congress established the CJC Holocaust Memorial Committee, with Aba Beer as chairperson. The committee (later renamed the Holocaust Remembrance Committee, or HRC) maintained that its primary objective was that "Holocaust considerations should not be limited to Yom Hashoah observance but should be a year-round programmatic consideration for the community." On 3 December it proposed to the National Executive Committee that a documentation centre dealing with the Holocaust and containing testimonies and other materials be created at the Samuel Bronfman House Museum in Montreal. This proposal was accepted. By the end of 1973, Holocaust memorial committees had been established in most cities in Canada with a sizable Jewish population.[90]

At the CJC plenary held on 15–18 June 1974 there were four resolutions related to the Holocaust. The first was that the 27th day of Nisan be "a Day of Remembrance and Observance, to be commemorated in our homes, synagogues, schools and other appropriate places of assembly in memory of the heroic deeds of our people in the European catastrophe." The second resolution was that an annual meeting of the National Holocaust Memorial Committee be held "in various areas of the country." The third was a protest against the arrest and incarceration of Beate Klarsfeld, a French woman who had worked to get Nazi war criminals arrested. The fourth resolution was to "produce Holocaust Memorial programs in every Jewish community in such a way that every Jewish child receives proper knowledge of the Holocaust, through a continuing program in each and every Jewish school, throughout the entire year."[91]

Why was there such a flurry of activity at the highest levels of the CJC in the two years following the tumult over *The Man in the Glass Booth*? According to the architects of the protest against the Montreal Y, the established Jewish organizations had decided that it would be in their best interests to join forces with the survivors. The first to capitulate was the Quebec Region; it was followed by the Central Region and then the national executive. The formation of the National HRC, they argued, was proof of that decision. Lou Zablow remembered that following the controversy over the play, his group had met with the CJC, and "we suggested that there be a Holocaust Committee of CJC, and they said, 'It's a good idea,' and that's how the committee was started. And what prompted it was *Man*." In recalling those times, Aba Beer and Isaac Piasetski agreed with Zablow's appraisal.[92]

In retrospect, the furor over the play was a last attempt by some elements of the established community to determine the agenda. It must be recalled that the play was to be part of the season's program on the Holocaust. The directors of the Saidye Bronfman Centre did not intend to downplay the importance of the tragedy; indeed, the opposite motivation seems to have driven the decision to stage the play. But, the insensitivity shown by the officers of the centre and their inept public relations forced them to cancel the performance. Congress's decision to establish the regional and national committees may have been spurred by the controversy, but this was not the CJC's main intention. For a decade, Congress had been moving toward those interests which had voiced concern over the absence of historical memory of the Holocaust among Canadian Jews. The movement had begun with Harris's address at the commemoration of the Warsaw Ghetto Uprising in 1964. It gained momentum with Congress's determination to pressure the government to enact legislation against the spread of hate propaganda. Congress's support of protests over the Statute of Limitations and the interview with Adolf von Thadden solidified its interests with those of most of the survivors and their supporters. Although Congress and local federations did not establish standing committees on the Holocaust until 1972, they supported the proliferation of local programs and directed the initiatives by local groups to stage meaningful commemorative activities. The urgency of Holocaust commemoration and education was not shared by much of the established community, but there were few obstacles placed in the way of the limited goals of these groups. Thus the creation of the regional and national Holocaust remembrance committees and the attention given to them in the debates and resolutions of the plenary assembly in 1974 were the logical outgrowth of a decade's development.

The period from 1965 to 1974 was one of transition with regard to the inclusion of the Holocaust in the community's collective memory. Canadian Jews now recognized that antisemitism was a scourge that had to be confronted by action and legislation, that the rise of neo-Nazism outside Canada was not to be tolerated, and that the military and diplomatic attacks on Israel were part of an anti-Jewish animus that harked back to the Nazi era. This comprehension, however, served as a necessary prerequisite, but not as the explanation, for an appreciation that the Holocaust was a seminal event in the formation of an ethnic identity. It would take more knowledge of the event and more estrangement from their traditions – what Saul Hayes had termed the "Jewish Emptiness" – for Canadian Jews to accept the memory of the Holocaust as a symbol of their ethnic identity.

7 "Were things that bad?" The Holocaust Enters Community Memory

On 17 April 1978, when I was in my seventh year of teaching history, I was walking down a hall at North Toronto Collegiate Institute to teach a grade twelve class on the rise of the Nazis. I was joined by two students, who asked if I had watched the NBC miniseries *Holocaust* on television the previous evening. I replied that I had not. They were surprised, given my background and my vocation. They remarked on the horrible scenes that had been shown and asked, in complete innocence, "Were things that bad?" I was stunned. I had read previews of the program that had dismissed it as a trivial, sugar-coated project designed to sell products for its advertisers. It had not dawned on me that children born in 1960 who had no familial connection with World War II had little or no idea of what had happened to European Jews. As we entered the classroom, the rest of the students joined in the discussion. I had rarely seen such keen interest in a historical event. Students asked what they could read and requested that more class time be devoted to the subject. When I went to the school library, I was surprised to find that there was little information available. Certainly the course text mandated by the Ontario Ministry of Education was of no value. In time, the other teacher of the course and I put together some materials, and the following summer we worked on developing a few lessons for the coming year.

My students' experience was not unique. Thousands of high school students in Ontario and elsewhere first learned of the Holocaust that week. The miniseries was a catalyst in the raising of awareness about the catastrophe, a process that had been building for several years.

There were three factors that contributed to this development. The first was a commitment by the Jewish community to Holocaust education and commemoration. By 1975 the community had, with some reluctance, acceded to the demands of Holocaust survivors that the legacy of the tragedy be part of the community agenda. The National Holocaust Remembrance Committee, established by Congress, begun its activities in 1973. Local HRCs quickly sprang up in a number of Canadian cities. Through a process of trial and error, and despite some opposition from local federations, these committees succeeded in developing programs, most significantly in education. It was largely through the efforts of the survivors, some of whom had been in the forefront in confronting the established community in the 1960s over its apparent inaction regarding neo-Nazism and antisemitism, that these endeavours took place. In time, many survivors who had been silent about their experiences or unwilling to become involved in community affairs took the courageous step of speaking publicly.

When they first told their stories in an open setting, they were astounded at the reception they received. Most survivors had shut their experiences inside the closet of their memories. They had not been asked about their lives for thirty years, and they had been unwilling to speak out. According to Gerda Steinitz-Frieberg, "the main reason survivors didn't speak is that they had a real problem with recalling the terrible memories. They tried to push it [sic] out of their lives. They tried to live their normal lives, not realizing that speaking about it made it easier to cope with. They knew they were third-class citizens; [they] didn't have the courage to speak up, so [they] withdrew into survivor communities."[1]

By the mid-1970s this attitude was changing. Survivors had shed their immigrant mentality and now considered themselves Canadians, and some were no longer embarrassed about discussing their past. As well, after more than a decade of witnessing the revival of antisemitism, they were no longer willing to remain silent. This was especially so in the late 1970s, when Holocaust denial began to attain notoriety. Their most receptive audience was students. Philip Weiss of Winnipeg began talking because he felt the responsibility to speak "for those here and those who perished. [I was accepted by the students] with open arms. They listen, they want to know, they are passionate." Leo Lowy of Vancouver first spoke at the first Holocaust seminar for secondary school students in Canada in 1976. He recalled: "The inner feeling was that I had a story to tell, and for one reason or another, I never told my children. They knew that I survived the camps. We never discussed it ... I relived my life to the point that I didn't realize the impact that it had on my psyche ... I just had to go back to describe to these kids the emotions, the feelings, the behaviour that I had at that age." Nathan Leipciger of Toronto broke down the first time he was interviewed on a local television program, but in time he developed a strategy to overcome his emotions. "I could talk about it and detach myself from the story, almost as an observer. It helped me isolate that period and put it as a separate part of my life. While I still felt it emotionally, I could express it without becoming emotional. I really appreciated the interaction and the satisfaction ... This became the means of me dealing with my own feelings, reliving my own experience, being able to vocalize things ... I always have nightmares before I'm going to talk, not after I talk."[2]

The second factor was the explosion of research and media coverage about the event. In the 1960s a monumental study, *The Destruction of European Jewry*, by Raul Hilberg, constituted the acme of scholarship on the subject. The scope and language of the work, however, made it inaccessible to most readers.[3] More readable were the novels of Elie Wiesel, based on his experiences and reflections,[4] and a Canadian work, *Child of the Holocaust*, by Jack Kuper, a fictionalized account of the author's life during the war. The most widely read book was, and remains, *Anne Frank: The Diary of a Young Girl*. Meanwhile, scholars were carrying out research in archives in Washington and Germany and at Yad Vashem, the memorial institute in Jerusalem. The collective outpouring of scholarly works, fiction, and memoirs aroused growing public interest. This focus was accentuated in the 1970s with such works as Lucy Dawidowicz's readable, though flawed, account *The War against the Jews*.[5] By 1980 a field of research had been firmly established that encompassed history, literary analysis, and the social sciences. Concurrently, university courses on the Holocaust, scholarly conferences, and professional development programs for educators were underway.

Of greater import was the depiction of the Holocaust in the popular media. One example was the attention devoted by Hollywood. Between 1962 and 1978 there had been few films that had Holocaust-related themes. But in the next decade at least twenty-three feature films and thirty-four documentaries on the topic were made in the United States.[6] Together with novels, plays, memoirs, and collections of stories, poems, and articles, a veritable library of Holocaust literature was becoming available and accessible to a wide readership.

In Canada, with the publication of *None Is Too Many* in 1982, the revelation of this country's shameful immigration policies created a national response. Its authors, Irving Abella and Harold Troper, appeared on national news programs and spoke at universities, commemoration services, and book fairs across the country. The book was a wake-up call for the Canadian Jewish community. It made them mindful of the fragility of their position by documenting Canadian antisemitism for a new generation. For the wider community, *None is Too Many* questioned the Canadian myth of tolerance and acceptance. It contributed to a new examination of immigration policies and ethnicity.[7] The publication of the book coincided with the second decade of official multiculturalism. Whereas the first decade had stressed the accomplishments and contributions of ethnic and racial groups to the Canadian mosaic, the emphasis in the early 1980s was changing to the empowerment of ethnic communities.[8] This development had ramifications in a number of areas, most notably education. As the Jewish community was instrumental in developing materials and methodologies for teaching the Holocaust, educators found that the event could be used as a vehicle for anti-racist awareness.[9]

The third factor in the growing awareness about the Holocaust in the 1970s was the nebulous one referred to in the previous chapter. A generation of young Canadian Jews, born during and after the war, found themselves disengaged from their roots in the Jewish community. Unlike their parents and grandparents, they had no traditional neighbourhoods, secular organizations, or Yiddish to tie them to each other and to their past. Many of them felt rootless. For some, re-establishing the connection lay in a return to religious observance. For others, it meant becoming involved in Jewish causes. In the post-1967 period, these causes included support for Israel, opposition to anti-Jewish policies in the Soviet bloc, and combatting antisemitism. In combination, they created the perception, whether real or imagined, that Jews were vulnerable. It was not a long stretch to reach back three decades in order to understand that vulnerability might lead to extinction. In the 1970s a small but influential group of young Canadian Jews seized on the legacy of the Holocaust as a defining element of their identity. They transformed this appreciation of the tragedy into practical ends. Working together with survivors and their children, they were instrumental in pushing the established community to adopt Holocaust programs and erect memorials to the event. As a result, the institutionalization of the Holocaust was an unmistakeable aspect of Jewish ethnic identity by 1985.

THE NATIONAL HOLOCAUST REMEMBRANCE COMMITTEE

In the mid-1970s the locus of activity regarding Holocaust education and commemoration was the National Holocaust Remembrance

Committee of the Canadian Jewish Congress. After its formation in 1973, it assumed the reins as the coordinating body for local programs that were already underway and sponsored new committees. Its goals were "to further Holocaust education and commemoration, and to sensitize the public to the issues and lessons emanating from that tragic era." It sought to achieve these goals through commemoration, education, and political awareness.[10]

The NHRC was most successful as a liaison between local Holocaust remembrance committees, in part because of the publication *Zachor* (Remembrance), a quarterly newsletter which described the activities of the national and local committees and international events. By 1976 there were active Holocaust remembrance committees in twelve Canadian cities: Calgary, Montreal, Ottawa, St John's, Vancouver, Winnipeg, London, Victoria, Halifax, Hamilton, Windsor, and Toronto. In 1978 the newsletter had a circulation of five hundred.[11] The NHRC had moderate success in some of its commemorative, educational, and political initiatives. These included a programming kit for Yom Hashoah, an oral history project, a campaign to have the Statute of Limitations for Nazi war criminals resident in West Germany annulled, the recognition of Raoul Wallenberg for saving Jews in wartime Budapest, and travelling exhibits.[12] The committee had little success in achieving its plans for a national monument and a national resource centre and in the campaign for legislation against war criminals resident in Canada.

The first goal of the NHRC was to commemorate the victims. Several commemorative projects were contemplated. One was to erect a Holocaust memorial at the site of the national headquarters of Congress in Montreal. Its purpose was twofold: as a "reminder of the difficulties our people have faced throughout history" and as an educational tool "to strengthen the identification of our youth with our values and traditions."[13] But by the early 1980s the project had been abandoned, perhaps because of the erection of the memorial at the nearby Jewish Community Centre and the plans for memorials in Toronto, Ottawa, Winnipeg, and Vancouver.

Another undertaking was to document the names and experiences of victims as part of the Pages of Testimony project sponsored by Yad Vashem, the authority responsible for Holocaust commemoration in Israel. Its purpose was to "preserve the name of every Jew who perished so that his memory will never be erased." Approximately six thousand names were provided by the Canadian Jewish community.[14] Another early project was the creation of a kit of resource materials for planning Yom Hashoah programs. The kit included poems, testimonies, audiovisual materials, songs, and prayers in English,

Yiddish, and Hebrew. It helped to promote the commemorative services, and local committees reported that attendance and interest had increased, in part as a result of this endeavour.[15]

The NHRC served as the Canadian coordinating organization for survivors' conferences. These meetings were a significant development in the period since they provided a forum at which survivors and their descendants could meet, many for the first time since the war. Survivors were thus afforded a voice, further enhancing their stature within the Jewish community. The conferences also served an educational function since scholars presented their research to a wide audience. The publicity arising from the promotion of the conferences necessitated appearances by politicians, who were only too eager to lend their voice to the proceedings. The first conference was held in Israel in 1976. A Canadian delegation attended under the auspices of the NHRC. Aba Beer, the chair of the committee, and Lou Zablow were elected vice-presidents of the World Federation of Holocaust Survivors, and three other Canadians were chosen to sit on the executive.[16] A second world gathering was held in Israel in 1981 and was one of two major events in the calendar of the NHRC, the other being the implementation of the Holocaust Documentation Project.[17] In 1982 a conference of the second generation (children of survivors) was held in New York. A year later the committee sent representatives to the American Gathering of Holocaust Survivors in Washington, DC, on the fortiethth anniversary of the Warsaw Ghetto Uprising. This meeting provided the spark for the creation of the Canadian Gathering, held two in 1985.

By 1978 the NHRC had hired a part-time executive director, and by 1982 its membership had grown from a nucleus of about 10 people in 1973 to 102. The committee listed five areas of activity: Yom Hashoah programs, the creation of memorial centres, educational programs, liaison with Yad Vashem in Israel, and pressure on the Canadian government to bring suspected Nazi war criminals to trial. Its budget from Congress was $15,700; this amount seems somewhat insignificant, given the scope of the committee's work, but most of the programming was carried out by local committees, which received funding from their federations and from community campaigns.[18]

The second goal of the national committee was to disseminate knowledge. It determined that only through education was there a possibility of maintaining a historical memory of the destroyed civilization of European Jewry. While this aim was laudable, the committee did not adopt a systematic approach. The most ambitious educational endeavour launched by the NHRC was the Oral Documentation Project. It began modestly in 1976 with audio tapes being made of survivors' testimonies in Montreal, Toronto, Winnipeg, and Ottawa. Two years later the national committee published a guide for interviewers and began to make arrangements for tape storage, duplication, and distribution.[19] It pointed out the urgency of the task in a report of activities in June 1978: "The number of survivors, pitifully small to begin with, is diminishing daily as age and illness take their toll; and the Committee feels it is vital, for the sake of future generations, to record the individual story of each one, so that the personal dimension of the Holocaust be perpetuated amidst impersonal numbers and statistics."[20]

For the next two years, the project continued on a local basis, until Congress was persuaded to support an application for a grant from the federal ministry responsible for multiculturalism for the filming of testimonies. This support occurred as an outgrowth of two resolutions at the 1980 plenary calling for the promotion and expansion of Holocaust studies.[21] The grant was for financial assistance to videotape the experiences of survivors, liberators, "righteous gentiles," and other eyewitnesses and have the tapes deposited in the Public (now National) Archives of Canada, Yad Vashem, and Holocaust documentation centres and for the editing of twenty videotape programs, together with teaching guides.[22] An initial grant of $25,000 was provided; this was followed by a further grant of $154,000 on 8 October 1981.[23] A committee of consultants was established which included Emil Fackenheim, the noted philosopher and theologian, and Paul Trepman, a survivor and educator.[24] A professional film crew was hired, and two experienced interviewers, Josh Freed and Paula Draper, provided their services. Taping was done with the help of local committees. The interviews were completed in 1984, with sixty-nine testimonies culled from hundreds of potential interviewees. Ninety hours of material was collected in all, and the tapes were stored in the Congress archives in Montreal.[25] A further $95,000 was needed for writing, testing, and marketing the teaching guides.[26]

This last aspect of the project was not completed according to the initial design. Instead, Congress decided to underwrite the production of a documentary on the Holocaust as seen through the testimonies of seven of the survivors interviewed.[27] The result was *Voices of Survival*, a fifty-five-minute film produced by Montreal filmmaker Alan Handel in 1989, which was first purchased by TVO (the educational television service of Ontario) and subsequently sold to other educational television authorities in Canada and abroad. The film was also marketed as a videotape to educational institutions. In 1989 the CJC hired two educators, Sharon Weintraub and me, to write a teaching guide to accompany the video.[28]

The Oral Documentation Project aspired to record the experiences of Canadian witnesses to the Holocaust and to deposit the finished product with the National Archives. It was successful to a degree. Congress was able to get significant funding from the Multiculturalism Directorate at a propitious time. The Canadian government had established "official multiculturalism" as a priority, and in the early 1980s it was willing to fund projects congruent with this emphasis. Only sixty-nine interviews were recorded, however, at a cost of almost $200,000. This was a very modest return on a large investment, especially given the NHRC's determination to make the project large-scale. Further, the transfer of the tapes to the National Archives did not materialize, and they are still held in the Congress archives. As a result, they have been underutilized, although *Voices of Survival* drew positive reviews and was widely shown. But the true measure of success of the project was the ability of the NHRC, under the auspices of the CJC, to fund the project with public money. It thus indicated a growing appreciation of the Holocaust as an epoch-making event on the part of Canadians.

Numerous other educational projects were directed by the national committee. It sponsored travelling exhibits such as *Holocaust and Resistance* from Yad Vashem and *Image Before My Eyes* from the Institute of Jewish Research (YIVO) in New York.[29] It launched educational guides about Janusz Korczak, who had run an orphanage in Warsaw and had accompanied his charges to their death at Treblinka, and on Raoul Wallenberg, the Swedish businessman who had saved Jews in Budapest.[30] The committee distributed a kit for Jewish summer camps with programming suggestions,[31] and a guide to accompany the *Holocaust* mini-series in April 1978 was issued to local committees.[32] A catalogue of resource material was produced and an annotated bibliography published in 1980.[33] The committee also began began, but did not complete, a curriculum guide for public high schools across Canada.[34]

After a decade of intensive programming on the educational front, the national committee presented a resolution to the 1986 CJC plenary. It read in part:

WHEREAS our country, Canada, prides itself on its multicultural heritage ... [and]
WHEREAS ... the Canadian Jewish Congress believes that Canadian students should be informed intelligently about the Holocaust in order that they may develop an understanding of that human catastrophe conceived in racism and hatred ...

THEREFORE, be it resolved that the Canadian Jewish Congress request the provincial and territorial ministries of education to incorporate a unit on the Holocaust ... [and]

THAT the Canadian Jewish Congress endorse and actively support a professional development program for school teachers who wish to teach Holocaust studies.[35]

To date, this resolution has not been implemented. Only one province, New Brunswick, has a mandated unit on the Holocaust.[36] Starting in September 1999, the new Ontario history curriculum for grades nine and ten has "specific expectations" relating to the Holocaust.[37] But there has not been a program of professional development on a national level. One cannot fault the NHRC for aspiring to goals that exceeded its grasp in the area of Holocaust education. Although the curriculum guide did not materialize, the smaller projects enhanced the teaching of the event. The relatively minor impact of the NHRC educational initiatives must be put into the wider context of Holocaust education in the period from the mid-1970s to the mid-1980s. The most successful programs were engineered by local committees. The NHRC acted more as a coordinating body for these committees than as a catalyst and implementor of educational projects. That is where its value was most evident.

The national committee's third goal was to raise political awareness. Its most successful ventures in this field were in aiding the campaign to have the Statute of Limitations for war criminals in West Germany repealed and in the recognition by the government of Canada of Raoul Wallenberg's heroism. It had little success in persuading the Trudeau administration to adopt legislation to pursue suspected Nazi war criminals resident in Canada.

As we have seen, in 1969 the West German government, under international pressure, had extended the period for the prosecution of its citizens suspected to be war criminals for another ten years. As 31 December 1978, the new date for the Statute of Limitations to come into effect, approached, a renewed international campaign was waged to have any time restrictions removed. The Canadian government was prodded by the national committee, under the auspices of Congress, to lend its voice to this campaign. In a letter to the ambassador of the Federal Republic of Germany in Ottawa, Alan Rose, executive vice-president of Congress, stated that since West German law prohibited the extradition of its own nationals, the Federal Republic could become a haven for war criminals resident elsewhere.[38] In addition, with the passage of the Statute of Limitations, the information centre on war crimes in Ludwigsburg would be closed, preventing further international investigation. Rabbi Gunther Plaut, who was elected president of Congress in 1977, also became actively involved in the protest. A native of Germany who left while a university student for a haven in the United States, he had returned in 1944 as a chaplain with the American army and was a liberator at the infamous slave-labour camp at Dora Nordhausen. Plaut was the first Congress president for whom the Holocaust was a priority item on the community agenda. He was prescient enough to link the tragedy to contemporary violations of human rights. In an article in the *Globe and Mail*, he wrote: "But once you shut the door of remembrance over the killings of millions, what happens to justice? Tomorrow we will begin to wonder whether the terrible tragedy really happened at all, and meanwhile the termites [neo-Nazis] will be busy."[39]

Plaut led a delegation to meet with the consul in Toronto on 4 December 1978 and with the West German ambassador three days later.[40] This was part of a coordinated campaign in which the NHRC played a role. Aba Beer, the NHRC chair, met with the press attaché of the embassy, and the committee orchestrated a letter-writing protest.[41] Beer, Rose, and Paul Trepman accompanied Plaut to the meeting with the ambassador. Before the statute was to come into effect on 1 January 1979, the West German government again succumbed to international pressure. The statute was abolished, and the time restriction was waived in perpetuity.[42]

Hungary had been the last country to fall under German occupation in World War II. It had been an ally of Germany but had not participated in the transport of its Jewish citizens to the death camps. In 1944 Germany occupied Hungary, and Adolf Eichmann carried out the plan for the deportation of more than 600,000 Hungarian Jews to Auschwitz. To help protect the Jews of Budapest, the Swedish legation, which was neutral, sent a young businessman, Raoul Wallenberg, to Budapest. He issued "protective passports" and arranged for safe houses. Wallenberg's cool demeanour and dogged pursuit of his mission afforded approximately 100,000 Jews a haven in the eye of the storm. He was arrested by Soviet authorities in January 1945 when Budapest was liberated and was never heard from again. For more than thirty years the Wallenberg case remained closed. Then scholars unearthed the story of his heroism. Sweden led the way in inquiring about Wallenberg's whereabouts. In 1979, following the death of his mother, international pressure on the USSR to reveal his whereabouts mounted.[43] Elie Wiesel, at a conference in Montreal, asked, "Why did it take so long for his legend to become popular?" He answered his own question with the following: "He disturbed the enemy during the war, but he also disturbed people after the war. His story became an irritant ... he demonstrated that it was possible, even under the worst and cruellest circumstances in recorded history, to oppose the oppressor and side with his victims. In other words, the tragedy was *not* unavoidable."[44]

The Wallenberg saga was one of the central themes on the NHRC agenda. The committee capitalized on publicity about the young hero who had saved more lives than any other individual or organization during the Holocaust. He had defied the Nazis and been captured by the Soviets, the two most hated regimes of recent memory. His story could be utilized in educational programs and in the political arena. At the 1980 CJC plenary a resolution was passed calling upon the Soviet Union "to permit an impartial international review of this case." The national committee then published an information booklet on Wallenberg and organized a letter-writing campaign to the Soviet embassy. It persuaded the Canadian government to raise the Wallenberg case at the Madrid Review Conference of the Helsinki Final Act, which dealt with human rights. Meanwhile, the interest in Wallenberg was growing. Articles appeared in the *Globe and Mail*, the *Toronto Star*, the *Montreal Gazette*, and *Saturday Night*. A documentary by David Harel was telecast, and John Borman, the author of a biography of Wallenberg, was the keynote speaker at the first Holocaust Education Week in Toronto in 1982.[45] On 4 October 1980 the municipality of Toronto proclaimed Raoul Wallenberg Day. At the 1983 plenary the Atlantic Region presented a resolution that there be an annual Wallenberg Day, that a sermon about Wallenberg be given during a significant Jewish holiday, and that the story be included in the curriculum of Jewish day schools and Sunday schools.[46] In 1985 a resolution presented by David Kilgour, MP for Edmonton-Strathcona, making Wallenberg an honorary citizen of Canada, was passed by the House of Commons. Wallenberg is the only individual to whom Canada has given this distinction. The idea for Kilgour's resolution arose as a result of discussions with the Generation After Group of the Edmonton HRC and consultations with Alan Rose, executive vice-president of Congress, and Aba Beer, chair of the NHRC.[47]

The relative success of the NHRC was a reflection of the adoption by the Jewish community of the Holocaust as a defining point in its identity. The national committee's key contribution was to act as the umbrella group for the local Holocaust remembrance committees. It recognized the primacy of education, while establishing commemoration on the 27th day of Nisan in the calendar of the wider community. It did not recoil from entering the political arena, prodding Congress and adding its representative to Congress meetings with politicians. The most important reason for the national committee's considerable impact was the dedication of survivors. Their work was aided by the publicity generated by scholars and the popular media, the antisemitism of neo-Nazis who began masquerading as Holocaust revisionists in the late 1970s, and an alliance with young Canadian Jews who were searching for a connection with their people's past. It was up to local committees, however, to initiate programs that helped to link the search for values and traditions by Canadian Jews with the memory of the Holocaust. Fittingly, Montreal was the first community to undertake this agenda.

HOLOCAUST REMEMBRANCE IN MONTREAL

In the 1970s Lou Zablow, a founder of the Association of Former Concentration Camp Inmates/Survivors of Nazi Oppression and the first survivor on the Congress executive, occasionally met Saul Hayes for lunch. Hayes had not been particularly receptive to the survivors' concerns in previous years. When asked later why the two men got together, Zablow responded that, although they had not agreed on Congress's response to the antisemitic incidents of the 1960s, there was no personal animosity between them. On the question of why Congress had acceded to the resolution at the 1971 plenary that had led first to the creation of the HRC Quebec Region and then to the national committee, Zablow commented: "It was strictly a practical political decision. It was better to have a Lou Zablow in than out."[48]

While pragmatism may have been the guiding principle underlying the inclusion of the survivors in the established community, within a decade this expedient had outgrown its original purpose. The reality was that commemoration and education about the Holocaust had become institutionalized in Monteal's Jewish community. This was a logical development given that in the 1970s the city had the largest Jewish community and the largest survivor community in Canada, proportionately the largest survivor community of any city in North America, and the headquarters of the Congress. The process of making Holocaust remembrance an integral part of the community's agenda, however, was not assured. Some community leaders were reluctant to carry out the construction of a Holocaust centre within the federation building. Concerns about costs and design may have masked a greater reluctance to yield territory to survivors, who wanted their story told. But the mood of the community was in contrast to the hesitancy shown by the establishment. The commitment of survivors, their children, and young Canadian Jews was more persuasive than the reluctance of some leaders in the community.

In the early 1970s, Holocaust programming in Montreal was neither systematic nor centralized. The Hillel Student Society (an organization of Jewish students on university campuses) at McGill University, under the sponsorship of the Eastern Region of Congress, hosted a three-day teach-in on the Holocaust in 1970. Invited speakers included Raul Hilberg, Irving Greenberg, and Richard Rubenstein, three pioneers of American scholarship on the subject.[49] In May 1972 the HRC of the Eastern Region was established. Its mandate was restricted to Holocaust education in the community, including at summer camps. Commemoration services were still sponsored by the Warsaw Ghetto Committee. But in 1975 the latter committee merged with the HRC, and from that point, Yom Hashoah services came under the HRC's purview.[50]

The first education seminar organized by the HRC was held in that year. It was designed for academics, students, and community professionals and featured workshops for CEGEPs and universities, high schools, elementary Jewish day and afternoon schools, and camps. Several recommendations emerged from the seminar, including the establishment of a speakers' bureau and an education resource centre to collect materials.[51] These recommendations mirrored the initiatives of the NHRC. Indeed, at this early organizational stage there seems to have been little difference between the aims, structure, and leadership of the national committee and those of the regional committee in Montreal. Education, however, was not restricted to the HRC. The Hillel Student Society held another conference on the Holocaust in 1975, sponsored by Hadassah-Wizo Canada, a Jewish women's organization.[52]

The stiffest challenge facing the promoters of Holocaust education was in initiating programs in the French-language schools in Quebec. An article by Gerard H. Hoffman, a professor at Vanier College, notes that most textbooks in history and the social studies completely ignore the Holocaust. At best, one writer mentioned the event in discussing the "horrors of Vietnam, Biafra, etc." Hoffman felt that part of the problem was that younger teachers were sympathetic with the anti-Zionist rhetoric of the New Left (which viewed Zionism as imperialism) and that the erosion of the education department's inspectorate meant that teachers were free to teach what they wanted.[53] Given this distance from the majority of Quebec's students, the regional committee limited itself to educational programs designed for Jewish and post-secondary students.

To commemorate the Holocaust, the HRC of the Eastern Region distributed the kits prepared by the national committee, conducted a teach-in, and held a memorial observance at which Emil Fackenheim gave the keynote address. Other activities included a weekend retreat, camp programs, sending women survivors to speak to students, an essay contest for students, and intensive seminars for students at Vanier College and Sir George Williams University (now Concordia) in 1976. [54]

In 1971 the local Allied Jewish Community Services (AJCS) established a committee to look into the creation of a Holocaust memorial. The committee floundered for seven years. Its efforts were obstructed by the Jewish Public Library (JPL), in whose basement the memorial was to be housed, and by conflicting initiatives articulated by the NHRC and the HRC Quebec Region. One officer of the Jewish Public Library reportedly exclaimed, "I don't want horror chambers."[55] At the AJCS there was concern about funding the capital costs of the project and finding money for its operation. There were also questions about the design and purpose of the memorial. Was it to be a shrine to victims? Was it to be a place for research and study? Was it to be an exhibition hall? The NHRC had presented a resolution at the 1974 CJC plenary that a permanent memorial be erected. Was the memorial at the JPL a duplication of this project or a replacement for it? If the memorial was to have an educational function, would it supplant the mandate assumed by the regional HRC to promote educational materials and seminars? These questions hobbled the committee. Yet the memorial was opened as the Montreal Holocaust Memorial Centre in October 1979. In a period of less than two years, some of the obstacles that had beset the project were overcome, funds were raised, a design was accepted, construction proceeded quickly, and the first Holocaust centre in Canada was established.[56] Most of the credit for this achievement is owing to a small group of individuals, whose personal background was far removed from the horrors of wartime Europe.

Stephen Cummings was the driving force behind the creation of the centre. At first glance he was a most unlikely candidate for the job. In 1976 he was in his mid-twenties, the son of an influential and well-established Westmount family. He had been raised in affluence, without much contact with survivors or knowledge of the Holocaust. His first exposure to the tragedy occurred during the Eichmann trial in 1961. "I was just stunned ... all of a sudden this was not a tragedy that happened somewhere else in the world. It became very personal ... From that point I became more tribal." As a undergraduate student in the United States, Cummings became disilllusioned with the civil rights movement because of the increasing alienation between Jews and Blacks. In 1976, shortly after the birth of his first child, he went to Israel. Cummings remembered that while visiting Yad

Vashem, "[I] was overwhelmed by power and powerlessness and the sense of being a parent and not being able to protect your children ... I came back to Montreal thinking, 'I've got to talk about this, got to teach people.' As a Jew I have that responsibility to myself and as a human being. The Holocaust is the worst example ... There is something unique about a cultured Europeanized civilization having manifested so much evil ... There's something that really resonates here. This is something we should have in Montreal."[57] Stephen Cummings was a notable example of his generation among Canadian Jews. Estranged from their European roots and unable to find meaning, as Jews, in other causes, they looked to the recent past. In many ways, the legacy of the Holocaust fulfilled several needs: the link with their forebears, the imperative of Jewish survival, counteracting dehumanization and racism, and the necessity to commemorate and to educate themselves and their children.

In the fall of 1976 Cummings and approximately twenty other young Montrealers approached Michael Greenblatt, chair of the AJCS Holocaust Committee. Greenblatt recorded: "This group asked me and other members of the committee if they could be given the authority to implement and carry out such a Project to completion. In view of the foregoing, the fact that these young men and women were so vitally concerned, interested, and might have funding potential, the group was given the authority to move ahead with the suggestion that the original committee be kept informed."[58] Cummings and his group knew that they had not only to keep the committee informed but also to include it in their plans. The committee was made up largely of survivors who for fifteen years had been through the battles with the established community. For Cummings, the problem was immediate. "The Holocaust Committee was not accomplishing its goals ... I said, 'Look, we'll do it together' with a group of younger people, most of them born here, mostly in their 20s and 30s. [We] combined that group with survivors, most from the Association of Survivors ... we essentially told the powers that be in Federation that they had to let us run the committee ... not to be snotty; [we didn't want] the survivors to think that we were this month's fad, and we were able to come together as a group."[59]

The reconstructed committee first met in Lou Zablow's den. He remembers that it was "the young people working with us" that ended the deadlock with the federation. At the time, it was an uncommon alliance – the children of established Jews, who had largely disregarded the survivors and felt that the Holocaust was a tragedy that did not affect them directly, and survivors, a generation or more older than their fellow committee members. But the reality, as Cummings remembers, was that the committee was effective because "our common denominators were much stronger than our differences. Credibility began to develop. We were able to gain their trust which was not an easy thing. Sometimes it was a pain in the ass for us and for them. It was a passionate issue, and many times people said unfortunate things."[60]

The committee settled on the mandate, design, and budget for the centre in 1978. It was to have a dual function. First, it was to be a memorial with a place for contemplation, and second, it was to house two kinds of exhibits, one permanent and the other consisting of special projects. A capital fundraising campaign was established to meet the projected cost of construction, which was $215,000, and an operating budget of $39,900 in the first year, with a 10 per cent increment for the second year.[61] The "Resolution of Principles" stated: "The goal of the Centre is to become the focus of Holocaust awareness and programming in the community by co-ordinating and implementing educational activities; by maintaining an archival repository for exhibits and research; and by establishing resources that encourage current and future Holocaust scholarship.The Montreal Holocaust Memorial Centre fervently believes that by actively remembering the past we can ensure the future. In the words of George Santayana, 'those who do not learn from history are condemned to repeat it.'"[62]

The centre opened on 15 October 1979. Subcommittees dealing with finance, community liaison, volunteers, and program were established. As a result, the centre received widespread publicity. A comprehensive article in the *Montreal Gazette* described the layout and permanent exhibit. The first two special exhibitions were *The Jewish Child before the War*, which opened on 31 May 1980, and *Spiritual Resistance*, beginning on 5 October that year.[63] Yet in a short time, problems regarding the centre's status became apparent. There was no written commitment from the AJCS to support the centre on a long-term basis. The committee was relatively powerless within the federation and had no written regulations and procedures guaranteeing its perpetuity. A special Task Force Committee recommended to the larger committee that the centre become affiliated with the JPL, and this recommendation was approved.[64] Negotiations with the JPL for affiliated status hit roadblocks, however. The centre continued to be part of the AJCS and received most of its operating budget from this source, the remainder came from fundraising. Affiliation with the JPL would not end this relationship. The merger between the centre and the JPL was formalized on 31 August 1982. On the surface, the centre now appeared to have a permanent home. A full-time director was to be hired, and an evaluation of the agreement would take place on an annual basis for the first two years.[65]

While the centre was being built, the regional HRC continued its programming. It produced an educational kit to accompany the *Holocaust* miniseries in 1978, a seminar and materials on Janusz Korczak the following year, and another seminar for high school teachers on moral issues in 1982.[66] As with their earlier initiatives, these programs were either duplications or offshoots of projects developed by the national committee. The committee also continued with earlier programs, including the Yom Hashoah commemoration, essay contests, resource acquisitions, and teachers' seminars. It managed to carry out these projects on a minuscule budget. In 1981, for example, its expenditures totalled $15,500.[67] When the centre opened, its programming mandate was limited because of the latitude allowed the regional committee. Meanwhile, an independent organization in Toronto, the Canadian Centre for Studies in Holocaust and Genocide, which had existed with minimal impact for several years, provided a seed grant of $75,000 for the production of *Dark Lullabies*, a documentary about a survivor's return to Germany, by Montreal filmmaker Irene Lilienheim Angelico.[68]

The merger between the centre and the JPL lasted for only two years, from 1982 to 1984. While the centre was responsible for presenting a budget and program, all decisions during that time were subject to approval by the JPL officers. The centre's first full-time director, Krisha Starker, was hired in 1983. She described those first two years, "The library wanted to swallow the centre, so it was fight, fight, fight. There was division [as well]. Yom Hashoah belonged to the CJC [HRC Quebec Region], education belonged to the CJC, survivor testimony as well. Here was the centre. What the hell do you do? For me it was a responsibility to do a job. I had to protect the centre so that it would not become a subcommittee of the programming committee of the library." When asked why the JPL insisted on this imbalance in the relationship, Starker cites the fact that the centre had not been able to deliver its services adequately in the first few years because of inefficienct resources, fundraising problems, and the wide mandate given to the HRC.[69] In the first three and a half years of operation, there was little outreach, no educational plan, and no systematic recording of subcommittee minutes. Further, only 2,500 students visited the centre during that period, a single exhibit was launched in 1981, and none was organized the following year.[70] The centre was reinvigorated in 1983, with Starker at the helm. But it was not until the affiliation with the JPL ended in the early fall the following year that the centre was given a wider scope. It entered in a new arrangement with the AJCS, which proved to be more amicable and equitable. In 1984 the centre hosted a special exhibit on the Lodz ghetto, which was eventually displayed at the Gathering of Holocaust Survivors and Their Children the following year in Ottawa.[71] A few months later the HRC yielded its control over education, and an education subcommittee chaired by Professor Frank Chalk, a historian of comparative genocide at Concordia University, was established.[72]

In the early 1980s, according to one estimate, there were 30,000 survivors and their descendants in Montreal, or almost one-third of the Jewish community. In the late 1970s the children of survivors became active participants in community affairs. One important issue for them was continuing the memorialization and knowledge about their families, who had perished in the Holocaust. Second Generation groups were established across North America, and their first conference was held in New York in 1982. The Montreal group published a newsletter, *Montreal Second Generation*. Its third issue articulated the legacy taken up by the children at the gathering of survivors in Jerusalem in 1981. It read in part: "WE TAKE THIS OATH! Vision becomes word, to be handed down from father to son, from mother to daughter, from generation to generation." The "acceptance", stated in part: "WE PLEDGE to remember." [73] Morton Weinfeld, a sociologist at McGill University and a student of the Montreal survivor community, put it this way. "I only made peace with the Holocaust at a deeper level when my daughter was born. In this way the generation process was being carried on and in some sense I was 'undoing Hitler.' I felt a certain self-confidence about the future that I had not felt prior."[74] Stephen Cummings, whose family background was far removed from Weinfeld's, expressed a similar view. "When I look into a survivor's eyes, I see these are the eyes that have seen more than me. I felt that these were my people ... I just felt I could unabashedly embrace them. I felt respected. The adults [his parents' generation] reacted differently [to the survivors] than Jews would react today ... It was a more hostile environment ... 'Don't rock my boat.' If Jews truly understand Auschwitz they would have spoken because it was so overwhelming. I became involved because this was one of my ways of expressing myself as a Jew ... It was important to make a difference as a Jew."[75]

CONTROVERSY AND DIVISION IN TORONTO

By 1980 Toronto's Jewish community was larger than that in Montreal. It was relatively wealthy and close-knit with a high proportion of synagogue members and community volunteers, and was renowned in the Jewish diaspora as, per capita, one of the greatest contributors to Israel. Toronto had become one of the primary magnets for Jewish immigrants to North America. It had a burgeoning population of newcomers from the Soviet Union, Israel, and South Africa and was the destination for most of the Montreal Jews who were leaving Quebec in the wake of the Parti Québécois's electoral victory in 1976.[76] Yet, as was the case in Montreal, when it came to imprinting the Holocaust on the collective memory of the community, some leaders were reluctant to take the initiative. It was the wider community, led by survivors and the generation born in the 1940s and 1950s, whether the children of survivors or not, and non-Jews, that provided the impetus for the project. These efforts, however, did not come without controversy. Two major splits in the community, one concerned directly with the politicization of Holocaust memory and the other with organizational primacy, meant that by the mid-1980s there were several organizations articulating the need to remember and learn about the tragedy.

After several incarnations, the Holocaust Remembrance Committee in Toronto was finally established as a standing committee of Toronto Jewish Congress (TJC), the federation of local agencies, in 1972. Its place within the organizational structure remained clouded however. Despite its name, TJC's sole affiliation with Congress was that it was one of the myriad organizations under the umbrella of, but in no sense subservient to, the CJC. But the HRC of TJC was also connected to the Central Region of Congress. When its first director was appointed in 1976, she was employed by the region and not by TJC. The region determined the parameters of the HRC, and TJC enforced them. This confusing situation reduced the efficacy of the HRC. For example, as a committee of the local federation, it could not conduct programs outside Metropolitan Toronto. Yet it was a provincial body, the executive of the Central Region (formerly the Ontario Region) of Congress, to which the chair of the HRC reported. Given this confusing state of affairs, it is not surprising that in its first five years the HRC's activities were restricted. The committee was not entirely ineffectual however. Its focus was on three areas: commemoration, responding to neo-Nazi groups, and education.

The annual Yom Hashoa commemoration had become an important event in the community calendar by the 1970s. Until late in the decade most of the HRC's programming and expenses were devoted to the event. Held in the city's largest synagogues, the commemoration featured prominent Jewish scholars and non-Jewish political leaders. In 1977, for example, Professor Howard Roiter of McGill University, an early advocate of Holocaust studies, was the keynote speaker.[77]

The next year Emil Fackenheim was featured, together with Roy McMurtry, a member of the provincial legislature.[78] The committee was also instrumental in establishing ties with the non-Jewish community. In 1976 it sponsored a lecture by Dr Douglas Young entitled "A Christian View of the Holocaust" and a presentation by Giorgio Bassani on the movie *The Garden of the Finzi-Continis*.[79]

In the 1976–77 fiscal year the HRC was granted a half-time staff person. Ruth Resnick, a long-time employee of the local federation, was given the position. Her kind-heartedness and determination were central to the success of the committee for the next decade. The operating budget of the committee was $15,900 in 1976–77, but this was reduced to $13,687 the following year. In 1978–79, the committee was disbanded and then reconstituted; it undertook a wider range of programming, and the budget was raised to $29,462.[80]

With the demise of John Beattie and the Canadian Nazi Party in the late 1960s, the perceived threat of right-wing extremist groups in Toronto had diminished but was not extinguished. In February 1967, Donald Andrews founded the misnamed Edmund Burke Society. While not outwardly antisemitic or proto-Nazi, its program was influenced by the John Birch Society, the largest extremist group in the United States. Andrews was joined by Paul Fromm, an articulate university student who remains active in extremist groups. Fromm formed the Western Guard, Toronto's most prominent radical right-wing organization in the 1970s.[81] Andrews and Fromm in those years were expounding racist but not overtly antisemitic views. The community had difficulty countering this problem. The hate-propaganda legislation did not offer much promise as a deterrent to racist activities. The first person charged under the legislation was Armand Siksna, who was accused of posting "white power" placards in 1974. He was acquitted because of insufficient evidence. Jewish leaders were frustrated by this development, fearing that the provincial attorney general would be unwilling to test the legislation again.[82]

For the first few years of its existence, the HRC did not respond to extremists since doing so was not part of the committee's mandate. This situation changed in 1977 when its chair, Harry Wolle, resigned and was replaced by Helen Smolack. A Canadian Jew, she was part of a more vocal group within the HRC, constituting of survivors and Canadian Jews, who wanted the committee to venture into anti-Nazi endeavours. Its attempt to expand its mandate was obstructed by the JCRC, however. On 20 January 1978 the parent body resurrected the Anti-Nazi Committee (formerly CANC), which had ceased operation in 1969. Its task was to respond to extremist groups. The Nationalist Party of Canada was the newest radical right-wing organization to gain prominence, as a result of its recruitment of students and its attempt to gain tax-exempt status by declaring itself a political party in Ontario.[83] The Anti-Nazi Committee met with Arthur Wishart, attorney general of Ontario, to discuss the party's activities, and Wishart turned down the party's application because of irregularities. The committee took credit for this decision.[84] The Anti-Nazi Committee's focus, however, was soon diverted by events in Skokie, Illinois.

For months the American Nazi Party had been seeking permission to hold a march in Skokie, a suburb of Chicago in which many survivors had established homes and businesses. The publicity given to the town was widespread, especially following a showing of a docudrama on network television starring Danny Kaye. The HRC, seeing the controversy as an opportunity to become actively involved, planned to send a large delegation to Skokie to join American Jews in a counter-demonstration. In preparation, it held a protest at Nathan Phillips Square in front of the Toronto City Hall, in conjunction with the thirty-fifth anniversary of the Warsaw Ghetto Uprising. Franklin Littell, a theologian from Philadelphia, pledged that Christians would stand with Jews in Skokie. Congress president Rabbi Gunther Plaut stated that he expected Canadians to go to the Illinois community. Other speakers at the protest included John Roberts, the federal secretary of state, Larry Grossman, Ontario's minister of consumer and commercial relations, and David Crombie, the mayor of Toronto. The HRC launched a petition to the federal government urging that "Nazi War Criminals still among us be brought to justice and the Nationalist Party of Canada be denied legitimization." This petition subsequently gathered 30,000 signatures.[85]

The Anti-Nazi Committee regarded the HRC activities as an intrusion on its mandate. To mollify the HRC, the ANC sponsored a rally at Earl Bales Park in North York on 25 June 1978, the same time as the Skokie march was held, at which Rabbi Plaut was the main speaker. The rally attracted 3,000 people, according to the *Toronto Star*.[86] It was judged by the committee to be a successful compromise between sending a large delegation to Skokie and doing nothing. Yet within the Anti-Nazi Committee the divisions between proponents of action and milder voices, led by committee chair Harry Simon, returned. Jacob Egit declared that "survivors will not stand back and will fight them [neo-Nazis] whenever and wherever." Simon replied that the Chicago organizers had told him that the march was to take place on 25 June, but that there were no facilities in Skokie for outside protestors, and if a delegation was to come, it could be there for only half an hour. The committee, lukewarm to pressure from the HRC to sponsor a large contingent, used this information as a pretext for sending a symbolic delegation instead.[87] Simon, still upset, responded that "we were not responsible for the Skokie decision. It was made by their [the HRC] community. We were reacting to it in a moderate way."[88]

For the HRC, moderation was a code word for passivity. The new guard in the HRC, led by Helen Smolack, Rose Ehrenworth, and Sabina Citron, had been frustrated for years by Congress's apparent unwillingness to counteract the neo-Nazis. In addition, it was outraged that the CJC had not been adamant in pressing the federal government to bring suspected war criminals to trial.[89] According to Citron, the only survivor among the three women, "they [Congress] never touched the issue of war criminals, and when they did it was too late. It wasn't a question of acceptance [of survivors]; it was a question of not doing anything."[90]

TJC was not about to tolerate the HRC's excursion into uncharted waters. Congress had been quietly lobbying the government for decades about war criminals, and the Anti-Nazi Committee was countering the racist propaganda of the neo-Nazis. At first, TJC, under the leadership of Rose Wolfe, tried to accommodate the frustrations of the HRC. At an officers' meeting on 6 July 1978, with Smolack present, she stated, "It was necessary for any responsible community organization to work in a disciplined manner." She then read a resolution which concluded, "The Holocaust Remembrance Committee is advised that it issue no public statements in respect to social and political action and it conduct its activities and affairs within the purview of the defined purposes."[91]

The resolution was adopted by TJC on 17 July, but Smolack refused to accept it. At a meeting of the HRC on 9 August, she read a telegram from committee member Celia Airst which condemned the actions of the officers of TJC. A recommendation that representatives be selected from the HRC to patch up relations with TJC was rejected. The division between Smolack and her supporters and a group urging reconciliation was growing. In a report on the meeting to Irwin Gold, the director of TJC, E.Y. Lipsitz, the executive director of Congress's Central Region, wrote, "Mrs. Smolack is biased and hostile which makes her unfit to chair this Committee."[92] She was asked to resign, but she refused.[93] Finally, the executive committee of TJC dissolved the HRC.[94]

A front page article in the 23 November issue of the *Canadian Jewish News*, stated, "Toronto Jewish Congress Vote Oust Anti-Nazi Group in Controversy." Letters to the editor opposed the TJC decision. One reader wrote: "It may well be that some group in the Toronto Jewish Congress is doing some work to combat our enemies, however, the effect weems [sic] to be minimal if any." Rose Ehrenworth stated: "The words 'never again' embedded in the hearts and minds and on the lips of Jews everywhere, have no meaning whatsoever unless they are translated into action." In a letter to the *Jewish Standard* entitled "PROGRESS OR CONGRESS," Arnold Friedman, another member of the HRC, wrote: "The action of the Toronto Jewish Congress in disbanding the Holocaust Committee ... is tantamount to 'Shooting the Messenger' if you don't like the message."[95]

TJC reconstituted the HRC in the winter of 1979. Some of the old members decided to remain, but the leaders on the new committee were mostly younger Canadian and second-generation people. Meanwhile, Smolack, Citron, and a number of their supporters created their own organization, the Holocaust Remembrance Association (HRA). For many years, it was affiliated with the Toronto Zionist Council. Smolack became the association's first chairperson.[96] Although the HRA and Congress have locked horns on a number of issues, the feeling in the community is that they have worked toward common goals. Since 1980 the most prominent leaders in the HRC in Toronto have been Nathan Leipciger and Gerda Steinitz-Frieberg. Leipciger served as chair of the local HRC from 1981 to 1988 and since then as chair and co-chair of the NHRC. Steinitz-Frieberg was chair of Congress's Ontario Region in the early 1990s. Yet they demonstrate no rancour toward the Smolack-Citron group. Leipciger commented: "I always supported Sabina Citron. Although I was in Congress, I became a member of the HRA. I believe that Sabina should act on her own. She was a free agent. She didn't have to go to the president. She could act independently and quickly ... So officially she was not supported, [but] personally many survivors supported her." Steinitz-Frieberg said that the ouster of the committee was unique in the history of TJC. It showed, she said, "the insensitivity of the community." Citron responded, "I really have no animosity with respect to anyone, but I feel bitter that nothing was being done about war criminals. I can't say that I hate anyone. People were misguided and they acted on what they believed."[97]

The dissolution of the HRC and the creation of the HRA were indicative of the divisions that still existed in Toronto between the established "old guard" of Canadian Jews and the survivors and their supporters. It would be fair to state that while not all survivors who were becoming politically active in these years took as strident a stance as the nascent HRA, most were supportive of their criticisms of the traditional leadership. The split was unfortunate in that the various positions held by community leaders regarding the mandate of a local Holocaust committee could not be accommodated within one body. The splintering of the community over the ownership of Holocaust memory became a feature of ethnic politics in the early 1980s.

Another manifestation of the split in the Jewish community took place at this time. Since 1947 B'nai Brith Canada (BB) and Congress, together with the Canadian Zionist Federation, constituted the NJCRC and the regional JCRCs. But in the mid 1960s the relationship between BB and the CJC began to be strained.[98] Ultimately, in 1981 the CJC decided to restructure the NJCRC without BB. The events leading to the rupture were complex and controversial. What follows is a short history of those events to explain how BB became involved in Holocaust remembrance and education under its own aegis.

With 15,000 members in 1964, BB was the largest Jewish service organization in Canada. Its role in community affairs was overseen by a special committee, the Anti-Defamation League (ADL) of District 22, modelled on its American counterpart. On 21 June 1971, BB replaced the ADL by creating the League for Human Rights (the League) of B'nai Brith Canada. This change was approved by the JCRC Central Region.[99] Problems arose later that year, however, when BB refused to send delegates to the CJC plenary. The organization stated that its lodges were prevented by the Supreme Lodge from being members of other organizations. In fact, in many instances, especially in smaller communities, the same individuals served on both organizations. In response, Sydney Harris, the outgoing chair of CJC Central Region and the incoming president of Congress, accused BB of "isolationism" and "parochialism."[100]

Throughout the 1970s, tensions between the two organizations increase . Congress viewed BB's entry into anti-Nazi activities and its comments about Israeli affairs, Soviet Jewry, and war criminals as an attempt to stake out territory outside the NJCRC. BB, for its part, felt increasingly shut out of the decision-making process on the joint committee, and it saw the committee as impotent, since final decisions were made by the CJC.[101] Harvey Crestohl, president of BB, in a letter to Frank Diamant, the executive vice-president, wrote: "I am sure that I am not alone in believing that as it presently exists, the JCRC is a mere shadow of what it was intended to be, and of what is [sic] once was, and of what it should be again."[102]

On 13 September 1981 the officers and executive of CJC passed a motion to "reconstitute and expand the JCRC," code words that effectively expelled BB from the committee. This decision was made executory in a letter from Congress to BB four days later, which gave notice of the former's termination of the partnership.[103] In essence, the position of BB and the decision by the CJC indicated that each organization was asserting its claim to speak on behalf of Canadian Jews. The struggle came at a price. As the editor of the *Jewish Standard* put it: "Now the partnership is coming to an end and the Jewish community looks on at the disruption with dismay. Cooperation must yield to competition and competition to confrontation."[104] By the early 1980s, this unfortunate development had created fissures in the Toronto Jewish community over organizational primacy. One of these was a power struggle over how best to respond to expressions of antisemitism and the legacy of the Holocaust. The principal players were the HRC of TJC, the HRA, and the League.

TEACHING THE HOLOCAUST IN ONTARIO

When the Toronto HRC was formed in 1972, it had identified three areas of primary importance: remembrance, combatting antisemitism, and education. Commemoration of the victims of the tragedy had begun even before the Holocaust ended. Commemorative services were relatively easy to organize. They required a venue and a program, and the audience was ready-made. Combatting antisemitism was much more difficult from a strategic and organizational perspective. The traditional approach of backroom diplomacy employed by the established community had been challenged by survivors and their supporters since the 1960s. Conflicts between these two groups over exerting pressure on the government to legislate against war criminals and deniers of the Holocaust was a constant in the Toronto community until 1985. When it came to education, however, a different set of obstacles had to be overcome. There was little division in the Jewish community over the necessity to teach about its recent past. Essentially, the problems were pragmatic rather than philosophical. How could the Jewish community convince educational authorities that the curriculum should include the Holocaust? How could the event be taught without adequate resources or teacher training? Who should be the primary target – students in Jewish schools, students in public schools, Jewish adults, or the community in general? Where would the funding come from? Would learning about the Holocaust not reinforce the feeling that Jews were a people forever slated for exclusion? How could learning about the tragedy not cause trauma?

These practical problems meant that education was the last frontier to be conquered. In the mid-1960s the frontier seemed impassable. The problems were manifold: insufficient public awareness and consciousness; a Jewish community preoccupied with responding to antisemitism; and, most important, an antiquated, Anglocentric education system. A decade later, the frontier was being explored. Interest in and knowledge of the Holocaust was rapidly increasing; the Jewish community was better organized; tentative programs for students and teachers had been inaugurated; and educators had been freed from the constrictive teaching model of decades past. By the mid-1980s the frontier had been crossed. In Ontario the Holocaust was on the provincial curriculum; two curricula had been written for the two largest school boards in the province; student and teacher training was growing; a Holocaust education and memorial centre had opened in Toronto; and adult education programs were proliferating. The impetus for Holocaust education in Ontario emanated from the HRC of TJC, but the League for Human Rights also played an important role, as did groups outside the mainstream organizations. It was this interest and involvement that most clearly illustrated the appropriation of the Holocaust as a defining point of ethnic identity by the Jewish community in Ontario.

The Modern Age, first published in 1963, was the sole textbook for the compulsory history course in grade twelve in Ontario. Its author was an outstanding professor of education who had trained a generation of teachers. Yet in more than five hundred pages, the only remarks made about the destruction of European Jewry were as follows: "[Hitler] blamed the Jews for many of Germany's troubles ... [in Germany] most of them [the Jews] were slaughtered. They numbered about half a million but they had incurred the hatred of many peoples for their success in business and the professions, and the Nazis delighted in destroying them."[105] A new work, *The Modern Age: Ideas in Western Civilization*, was published in 1987 and became one of the approved texts for an optional course modern history. A book of readings accompanying the text contains sixteen pages of selected readings on the Holocaust, including excerpts from *Anne Frank: The Diary of a Young Girl*, Elie Wiesel's *Night*, Yevgeny Yevtushenko's poem "Babi Yar," Paul Tillich's *The Courage to Be*, and Dietrich Bonhoeffer's *Letters and Papers from Prison*.[106]

The evolution from *The Modern Age* of the 1960s to the similarly titled work a generation later is indicative of the delayed impact of the Holocaust on public education. While the earlier text provided little and erroneous information, the later one utilized carefully chosen primary materials. That all senior students in Ontario in the first case did not learn about the Holocaust and that some students who elected to study modern history a generation later may have learnt a fair amount symbolizes the extent to which the Holocaust had entered into the public discourse.

Ben Kayfetz, the executive director of the JCRC, undertook a one-person campaign for the inclusion of the Holocaust in public education. In 1966 he persuaded a reluctant JCRC to submit a brief to the Hall-Dennis Commission, which was reviewing the provincial education system. He pointed to *The Modern Age* as a prime example of the poor quality of resources available to teachers.[107] The commission did not even send a letter of acknowledgment to the committee. On reflection, Kayfetz, who had been a high school teacher before entering the service during World War II, remarked, "This is a perfect example of the indifference that applied in the sixties to the [teaching of the] Holocaust. I was disturbed by this."[108] Yet the commission made sweeping recommendations in its 1968 report, many of which were adopted by the government. Three years later, spurred by these changes and the release of the federal government's report on official multiculturalism, the Ontario Human Rights Commission funded a survey on bias in Ontario textbooks. The result was *Teaching Prejudice*, by Garnet McDiarmid and David Pratt, two professors at the Ontario Institute for Studies in Education (OISE). With respect to the Holocaust and the treatment of minorities in World War II, they reported that the lack of information was "astonishing". In general, Jews were stereotyped more than other minorities. From my perspective as a teacher, the survey had a major impact on pedagogy in the 1970s. The Anglo-Celtic bias in the curriculum that had dominated Ontario schools since their inception was rapidly giving way to a more universal paradigm.

In the early 1970s the Toronto HRC was captive to the same impediments regarding education as its counterpart in Montreal. It lacked both a systematic approach and a knowledge of the workings of the educational bureaucracy and the needs of students and teachers. Initially, the committee approached the Board of Jewish Education (BJE) of Metropolitan Toronto to inquire about the state of Holocaust studies in its schools; it was not a promising start. Between 1967 and the late 1970s the only mention of the Holocaust, the Nazi period, or anti-semitism recorded in the minutes of the BJE was to an exhibit on the Holocaust on loan from the United States in 1973.[109] Three years later Harry Wolle, chair of the HRC, wrote to Rabbi Irwin Witty, the director of the BJE, requesting that it and the HRC co-sponsor a conference on teaching the Holocaust. Witty surveyed the teachers as to their willingness to devote seminar sessions to the topic in August. They were not interested and stated that teaching the Holocaust was "a low order of priority." Witty maintained, however, that they were not uninterested. Only one school in eighteen did not teach the topic, he said, but there was room for professional development. Yet he rejected the HRC's involvement in such a conference since it "belongs strictly within the prerogative of the Board of Jewish Education."[110] In

1979 the HRC requested that the BJE provide a summary of programs on the Holocaust. There is no indication in the HRC or BJE files of any response to this request.[111]

Jacob Egit was the committee member most concerned with education in the mid-1970s. He had had a long and distinguished career in public service. Born in Poland, he had been a journalist before the war and had survived the Holocaust in the Soviet Union. After returning to Poland, he served as a member of the Central Committee of Jews in Poland and as its organizer in Lower Silesia, where he planned to create a new Jewish presence. This dream was shattered by events in Poland, and in 1958 Egit immigrated to Canada, where he became the assistant director of the Histadrut, an Israeli-based labour organization.[112] In 1975 he put together a proposal for a program "of ongoing activity and education in our community to further the knowledge of the Holocaust and resistance." The proposal had thirteen recommendations, including three involving the BJE. Egit estimated that an annual budget of $15,000 to $20,000 would be needed to carry out the program. The proposal was summarized in the 1976 HRC report to the TJC executive, but without any recommendation that it be considered. This response was hardly surprising. The BJE was not well disposed to the interference of the HRC in the training of its teachers, and TJC had little appetite for spending a large sum on a project that was clearly not a priority for its own Holocaust committee. Egit's proposal, though well intentioned, did not recognize that the frontier lay in the public schools.[113]

Some progress in Holocaust education in the late 1970s occurred at the post-secondary level, partially as a result of the efforts of the HRC, but more significantly because of the rise of interest in the topic in academe. Yehuda Bauer, the noted Israeli historian of the Holocaust, spoke to the Canadian Friends of the Hebrew University at the homes of patrons of the university in 1975. A series of lectures at the University of Toronto sponsored by the Joseph and Gertie Schwartz Foundation featured Bauer, Raul Hilberg, and Emil Fackenheim. York University started the first course on the Holocaust in Canada in 1975, and the University of Toronto followed suit three years later. York's Jewish Student Federation sponsored a Holocaust Remembrance Week in 1977. Henry Feingold, a historian who had written about the American role in the Holocaust, was the keynote speaker. Films and a mobile exhibit were provided by the NHRC; the use of these resources was facilitated by the local HRC. Two months later the HRC co-sponsored "The Second Encounter," a one-day seminar, with OISE.[114] The HRC's involvement in these programs was mainly due to the efforts of its part-time director, Ruth Resnick, rather than the committee members themselves.

Until 1978 the various initiatives taken by the NHRC and the local organization in the field of education were limited in their impact. There was still no systematic framework or policy for dealing with school boards or ministries of education. This was also true of adult education. Despite the continuous outpouring of scholarship, including the publication of some of the documents that had been used in *None Is Too Many*,[115] there was no single catalyst that generated widespread interest. This situation changed over the four nights in 1978 when NBC aired the docudrama *Holocaust*. This presentation, a prototypical Hollowood miniseries based on the *Roots* model, was banal and was excoriated by serious scholars. Historian Henry Feingold commented: "The 'Holocaust' was sold much like toothpaste ... [Gerald] Green, the producer and screenwriter] was not interested in finding some meaning or lesson in Auschwitz ... Thus, while it may be true that the individual incidents are based on fact, the story in its entirety is the most improbable fiction ... I suspect that in a few weeks we will hear very little about 'Holocaust.' The public will be anxiously awaiting the next TV happening."[116] Feingold's review was valid, but his prediction of the program's short-term impact was not. The miniseries was enormously popular and the subject of numerous articles. It did more to spur interest in the Holocaust in Canada, the United States, and western Europe than any other event since the Eichmann trial.[117] For the post-war generation, which had been either shielded from the horror or told that the Nazi era was an aberration, the glossy images of well-fed actors parading as concentration camp inmates had much less impact than the fact that the program opened of old wounds. This was especially the case when it was broadcast in West Germany the next year. The historian and journalist Joachim Fest, writing in the influential *Frankfurter Allgemeine Zeitung*, stated: "What has been said about the triviality of the film remains undeniable; the sensationalism, the sentimentality, the bad taste whereby the gruesome is made entertaining. Despite all this, in the end one is inclined to concur with the undertaking."[118]

Before the miniseries was shown, Congress president Gunther Plaut had contacted the CBC about broadcasting it. The corporation did not do so, but CBC radio devoted a special to the program.[119] Meanwhile, Ruth Resnick enlisted the aid of Professor Roger Simon of OISE to produce classroom materials for Ontario schools. An announcement about the series and the availability of these materials was sent to heads of history departments in Ontario secondary schools. More than one month prior to the screening, over one hundred packages had been sent. In total, almost two hundred were mailed.[120] The response by teachers was overwhelming. John

Baker's letter to Ruth Resnick typified the reaction. "The NBC production, your literature and CBC's *Cross Country Check-Up* have certainly struck a raw nerve! ... I would like more information about the *Holocaust Remembrance Committee* ... I would be willing to attend workshops in Toronto or Kingston, speak to people in my community, donate money, add my name to a membership list, and anything else you think might be useful ... I will strive to include Holocaust in the county curriculum for *Contemporary Canadian and World Concerns* ."[121]

Baker's interest and that of scores of other teachers in the province in learning more about teaching the Holocaust could not be accommodated by the HRC in Toronto until 1979, because of the dissolution of the existing committee the previous September. After the HRC was reconstituted, it embarked on a policy of meeting the needs of Ontario's teachers and students. In the meantime, the League initiated its own foray into Holocaust education and creation of awareness about antisemitism.

The divisions between BB and Congress were so strong in 1979 that the League was unwilling to send a representative to the new HRC. Sandra Wolfe, educational coordinator of the League, in a letter to Resnick, explained that it had been working with schools and school boards "for many years." She went on to say, "Very shortly, the League for Human Rights and B'nai B'rith will be integrating and it is my understanding that a more major emphasis will be given to the specific area of Holocaust Programs."[122] In 1980 the League announced that a bibliography for teachers had been produced, with a section on the Holocaust. Of greater significance, BB hired Yaacov Glickman, a sociologist, to prepare a profile of Ontario history textbooks, with an analysis of the information devoted to the Holocaust.[123] When Glickman's proposal was accepted, he teamed up with Alan Bardikoff, a doctoral student in psychology at OISE, to conduct the research and write the report. Bardikoff was the chair of the Holocaust Education Sub-Committee of the HRC. Despite the rivalry between Congress and BB, Alan Shefman, the director of field services of the League, accepted Bardikoff without hesitation.[124]

The Glickman-Bardikoff study was published by BB as a book rather than as a report. The study found that of seventy-two history textbooks dealing with the modern world that were in use in Canada, half had nothing or less than one paragraph on the Holocaust. Only three books did a "good" job on the topic. Further, of 208 high school students attending a seminar on the Holocaust organized by the HRC in 1981, only 28 per cent had a "good" knowledge of the subject according to their self-evaluation after the seminar.[125] Clearly, the legacy of *The Modern Age* was still alive in Ontario schools. Nevertheless, the commitment by BB to fund the study, and by the HRC to inaugurate an annual student seminar indicate that changes were underway.

The League was active in other areas regarding Holocaust education in the early 1980s. Under Shefman's guidance, it produced a series of materials on different aspects of the event, including antisemitism, Nazi war criminals in Canada, and Holocaust denial.[126] In 1982 the League announced that it would publish an annual review of antisemitism in Canada "within the larger context of racism in Canada." The review relied upon antisemitic incidents reported to the League and an analysis of media coverage of events that might impact on the growth of antisemitism.[127] In 1985 Shefman proposed that fifteen educators from Canadian secondary schools engage in a two-and-half-week study tour of Germany, Poland, and Israel every two years. The first tour took place in 1986, and regular visits have been organized since then.[128] Shefman was not averse to co-operating with Congress on education projects. For instance, the two organizations were among a number of sponsors of the first symposium on teaching the Holocaust in high schools in Toronto, held in 1980. The keynote speakers included Gideon Hausner, the chief prosecutor at the Eichmann trial, Irving Greenberg of the U.S. Holocaust Memorial Council, Professor Irwin Cotler of McGill University, president-elect of the CJC, and Professor Deborah Lipstadt, who would go on to become a noted scholar of the American response to the Holocaust. The conference attracted over two hundred high school teachers from across the province.[129]

Three months after TJC dissolved the HRC, a new committee was established. Its chair was Rabbi Mark Dov Shapiro, a young assistant rabbi at Holy Blossom Temple. He immediately asked Alan Bardikoff to chair an education subcommittee. Bardikoff was only twenty-three. He had been born in Toronto and had no familial connection to the Holocaust. As a teenager, he had read poetry at Yom Hashoah services, where it was "an honour to meet with some of the survivors." He spent a year as an undergraduate at the Hebrew University, where he studied the Holocaust under the historian and educator Ze'ev Mankowitz. Returning to Toronto, Bardikoff became the director of education at Temple Har Zion, where the Holocaust was integrated into the curriculum. When he joined his friend Shapiro, a new spirit imbued the HRC. Unlike earlier leaders of the committee, the two men were young, with no direct link to the event and no political bones to pick with established Jews or with survivors, and they were educators. Bardikoff remembered that "there was a feeling that there was mistrust among the survivor community about the HRC" because of the ouster of the Smolack-Citron group. At the time, "it was clear the Congress [i.e., both TJC and the Ontario Region of CJC, who each had a hand in directing HRC activities] didn't know what to do with us; it was gun-shy. [TJC thought,] 'Would this also become more political than it wanted it to be, more vociferous than it wanted to be?' So there was this element of never really being confident that Congress was really behind the committee."[130]

Bardikoff invited a few teachers in the public boards, including Harold Lass of the Toronto Board of Education, to join the subcommittee. At its first meeting, the new subcommittee limited its mandate to the following: "(1) organizing annually a communal observance of Yom Hashoah; (2) encouraging and promoting educational programs relating to the Holocaust."[131] Its first program was a seminar for teachers in public high schools, held on 28 October 1979. In the interim, Bardikoff and Lass began meeting with bureaucrats in the social studies and english curriculum offices of the Metropolitan Toronto boards of education and spoke at teachers' subject conferences.[132]

Bardikoff's subcommittee was unique in the TJC/CJC superstructure. Its members were all teachers from the public school boards. (I was invited to join the subcommittee in 1980.) Most were not the children of survivors, and several were not Jewish. (At present, about half the members are gentiles, as is the director of the Holocaust Education Memorial, Dr Carole Ann Reed.) Non-Jews were not automatically ineligible for membership on Congress committees. They could be members if they contributed to the United Jewish Appeal, but this fact was not revealed by the committee leaders. Of greater significance, there was no opposition from Congress because, according to Bardikoff, "the committee [i.e., the education subcommittee] had success."[133] Its members, however, were all experienced classroom teachers who had been early proponents and practitioners of Holocaust education. Individually, they conducted professional development workshops for their own school boards and spoke to subject councils, notably in English and history.[134] The subcommittee launched two initiatives. The first was an annual one-day seminar for high school students from southern Ontario. Beginning in 1981, the seminar, held at OISE, presented a morning program of a film and a keynote speaker and an afternoon program of small workshops with speakers on a specific subject and a meeting with a Holocaust survivor.[135] This structure necessitated the participation of more than thirty teachers as speakers and facilitators, and about twenty survivors. Thus the subcommittee enlisted the support of teachers themselves, creating a network of educators and survivors, many of whom had never spoken publicly about their experiences before. Some six hundred students (the capacity of the OISE auditorium) attended the seminar. By the mid-1980s, demand was so great that strict limits had to be placed on the students and schools participating.[136]

The second initiative was an annual one-day seminar for high school teachers. The subcommittee planned the program, and arranged with York University's Faculty of Education to co-sponsor this event, beginning in October 1982. In the morning, faculty members from York, and a keynote speaker delivered papers. In the afternoon there were content sessions, chaired by York faculty and committee members, which dealt with pedagogical approaches. Initially, seventy teachers participated, and by the mid-1980s almost one hundred were attending.[137]

While the education subcommittee was planning these seminars, boards of education in southern Ontario, most notably the two largest boards in the province – Toronto and North York – were being won over to the merits of teaching about the Holocaust. By the 1970s the Hall-Dennis report and the federal government's policy of official multiculturalism, had changed the direction of education. Among the Metropolitan Toronto boards there was a distinct shift from the decades-old Eurocentric approach to history and literature. Now, under the guidance of the provincial Ministry of Education, they were promoting materials dealing with multiculturalism to their teachers.[138] Bardikoff and some members of his subcommittee who were teachers in Toronto and North York seized on this new direction. They held numerous meetings with board officials about developing materials on the Holocaust. As a result, each board in the spring of 1982 decided to commission its own curriculum on the Holocaust. The North York one was written by Bardikoff and Jane Griesdorf, a teacher for the board. It was designed for the language arts in grades nine and ten. Toronto determined that an interdisciplinary approach for all secondary students was preferable. It hired two of its teachers, Barbara Walther and me, to write the curriculum. All four authors were members of the education subcommittee. Drafts were prepared in 1982, but because of bureaucratic snags, the curricula were not published until three years later.[139] As word of the curricula spread to other boards in the province, requests for copies and for in-service training proliferated. Between 1982 and 1987 I conducted a number of workshops for teachers in southern Ontario as part of their professional development. For this work, I was relieved of my teaching duties, and the sponsoring board paid the Toronto board for my replacement. Similar arrangements were made to allow other members of the sub-committee to conduct seminars.[140]

Both Toronto-area boards also undertook a systematic in-service training procedure. North York held workshops for its teachers led by experienced teachers and representatives from Facing History and Ourselves, an educational foundation in Brookline, Massachusetts.[141] The Toronto board established its own Holocaust Advisory Committee, made up of board teachers, including some from the subcommittee, as part of its race relations program. Until the amalgamation of Metropolitan Toronto's school boards in 1998, this committee conducted several workshops annually, the only committee devoted to Holocaust education in a school board in North America.[142]

Buoyed by its success at the board level, the HRC undertook a campaign to convince the Ontario Ministry of Education to include the Holocaust in its revision of the secondary school curriculum in history and social studies. Bardikoff met with Dr Bette Stephenson, the minister of education, late in 1983. A letter was then sent out to those on the HRC's mailing list, which included hundreds of teachers. It read in part: "We believe that in a multi-cultural society like ours it is important for students to understand that extreme acts of racism and genocide have their origins in common behaviours like stereotyping and prejudice. Our endeavours have also been prompted by the generally inadequate treatment the Holocaust has received in public education. While improvements appear to have been made, we feel further effort is necessary to make this event part of our public sector's current curriculum ... We ask that you convey your endorsement for our proposal to Dr. Stephenson."[143] Stephenson responded in a form letter. She wrote: "A review of senior division history is currently underway. As a result of these findings, I anticipate a revision of all history curricula from grade 7 to the completion of secondary school. I am referring your letter to the Ministry official responsible for this revision."[144]

The "ministry official" may have been swayed by the letters sent to Stephenson. He or she may also have been influenced by a resolution passed by the Association of Large School Boards in Ontario in May 1984 that the "provincial and territorial ministers of education incorporate studies of the Holocaust in the History, English and Social Studies curriculum" in order to "foster greater understanding of cultural relations in our schools ... to combat racism ... and to stem the seeming growth of intolerance towards immigrant and ethnic groups." The HRC and the League acted in an advisory capacity to the task force that wrote a report based on this resolution.[145] Ultimately, the ministry, in its revision of the curriculum in 1987, stated that students "should develop an understanding of the background to and scope of the Holocaust" in the course on twentieth-century world history. In another course on modern Western civilization, it declared that a "sample teaching strategy" on democracy should employ "the background, the progress, and the horrors of the Holocaust."[146]

A measure of credit for this development should have been given to the HRC. Congress leaders, however, were ignorant of the efforts made by the committee regarding Holocaust education until after the fact. According to Bardikoff, "the leadership was following the committee rather than leading the committee. This didn't come from the leadership. Regarding education, we went to the Ministry. Congress didn't and didn't know ... that we would have an impact. So they would have to catch up and be pulled along ... The survivor committee made sure that their agenda became part of the Congress agenda.[147]

By the mid-1980s the Holocaust was being widely taught in Ontario's secondary schools. The impetus had come from the HRC and to a lesser degree from the League. They understood that the practical problems of teaching the subject in Ontario schools could only be overcome if teachers saw that the Holocaust could be used as a vehicle for anti-racist education. As Bardikoff related, "from the outset [teaching the Holocaust] was directed toward multicultural-ism and anti-racism ... [this was] the key to success, rather than as a part of Jewish history, or for Jewish students ... Hence the emphasis on racism, prejudice, and stereotypes."[148]

The determination by teachers to undertake the teaching of a difficult topic, however, did not stem solely from this impetus. Rather, the seminars and resources supplemented a more widespread demand by teachers that the curriculum be more meaningful. They had found that students wanted to learn about the Holocaust because of the universal questions it posed. Students asked: How could an advanced society undertake such barbarism? How and why did individuals respond in abnormal situations? What did the Holocaust reveal about intolerance and prejudice in their own society? And students struggled with the question, What was the true nature of humanity? These issues were central in the minds of my students on that day in 1978 when I was asked, "Were things that bad?" In the subsequent decade, in my classroom and in the in-service training that I and other members of the subcommittee provided, the questions had less to do with teaching about the events from 1933 to 1945 than with dealing with universal themes. In seeking answers to these questions, teachers were eager to avail themselves of the services provided by the Jewish community. As the community came to understand the workings of the educational structure by inviting teachers to be part of its work, it was better able to provide these services. Thus not only did the Jewish community become committed to Holocaust education, but its relations with the wider community were strengthened.

There are numerous examples of this process. In 1989 a survey was conducted in the history departments of the public and separate school (Roman Catholic) boards in Waterloo County regarding the teaching of the Holocaust. It revealed that thirteen of the fifteen public schools and four of the five separate schools taught the subject in the only compulsory history course.[149] In 1991, ten years after the first student seminar, the HRC education subcommittee conducted a survey of teachers who had used the resources of the committee. The vast majority responded that their motivation to teach this difficult material was the response by students to questions of human behaviour.[150]

Community outreach became a significant part of Holocaust education in the early 1980s, not only in Ontario but throughout the country. In Toronto the HRC created a Christian Outreach Subcommittee in 1980. The timing could not have been more propitious. For several years some Protestant and Catholic theologians had been reinterpreting the history of Christian antisemitism and the role of the churches, both in occupied Europe and in the West, during the Holocaust.[151] The first program in Toronto was a conference on the Holocaust and Christian education at Holy Blossom Temple, arranged by several Protestant and Catholic organizations, and the Canadian Council of Christians and Jews. Also, the subcommittee helped to program ecumenical services at several Toronto churches to commemorate Yom Hashoah, beginning in 1981.[152]

In order to further community outreach, the HRC established the Holocaust Education Week Subcommittee in 1981. Its mandate was to promote interest in the subject by having community organizations, such as libraries, community centres, synagogues, and churches, sponsor programs for adults on specific topics relating to the Holocaust. The programs were held in early November in conjunction with the anniversary of Kristallnacht. This endeavour was unique in North America. Within two years some thirty sessions had been held. By 1999 there were more than one hundred programs, attended by some ten thousand people.[153]

Rabbi Mark Dov Shapiro had accepted a pulpit in the United States in 1981. The new chair of the HRC was Nathan Leipciger, a survivor who had not been active in Holocaust-related developments until he was drafted by Shapiro to chair the subcommittee on the Yom

Hashoah service. Leipciger's lack of involvement in earlier committees was an advantage, given the divisions among community organizations in the early 1980s. As he put it, "I was completely apolitical. I didn't have any baggage. I wasn't even a member of Congress. My entry card was my ignorance."[154] As chair, Leipciger became embroiled in a campaign for which he was not prepared. A new centre to house the main communal organizations, next to the Jewish Community Centre in North York, was being planned. Two benefactors had donated half a million dollars to erect a Holocaust remembrance centre within the new building, but TJC was reluctant to give its consent to the plan. It was concerned that there would be insufficient funds to pay for the interior design and to maintain the memorial. It was also worried that the memorial would be grotesque.[155]

Leipciger met with a design coordinator and a few members of the education subcommittee. This ad hoc group decided that the emphasis should be on education rather than commemoration, and a fundraising campaign, headed by Gerda Steinitz-Frieberg, was launched.[156] She raised half a million dollars to complete the interior design. TJC, however, would still not give its consent, fearing a shortfall. But when a capital grant $243,000 was received from the Ontario government and another $50,000 came from the West German government following a meeting between Steinitz-Frieberg and Helmut Kohl during a Group of Seven summit in Toronto, TJC relented.[157] The Holocaust Education and Memorial Centre was opened in the Lipa Green Building for Jewish Community Services in 1985. During its first decade, over 100,000 people visited the centre. The vast majority were students who came with their teachers. Each group toured the centre and met with a survivor speaker.[158]

The battle between the building committee and TJC was more than a matter of funds, according to Leipciger and Steinitz-Frieberg. At issue was leadership, focus, and power. Survivors claimed, "We have the funds; we have the plans; the need is immediate." The response was "There is a process that needs to be followed." Would the established community yield some of its space at the top to survivors? Would it allow them to dictate the design and operation of a centre devoted to the victims of the Holocaust – but more importantly, to educating the public – within the new confines of the federation building? To the leaders, the issue may have been more with the autonomy of any one interest group than a disinclination to embark upon the project. In the end the established leaders were outmanoeuvred. The survivors' agenda had become the community agenda as well. As in the Montreal scenario, the Holocaust had become a pillar of ethnic identification for the Jewish community. The proof lay in the memorial tiles, exhibits, and visitors at the Holocaust centre. According to Bardikoff: "With the construction of the centre ... Holocaust issues were no longer second place."[159]

HOLOCAUST REMEMBRANCE IN OTHER CANADIAN CITIES

After Montreal and Toronto, the Jewish community in Vancouver has been the most active in promoting Holocaust education and commemoration. Beginning in 1953, Holocaust remembrance in that city had been under the auspices of the Warsaw Ghetto Committee. By the early 1960s the commemoration had become an important event in the community calendar. Other aspects of Holocaust commemoration and education, however, did not begin until 1975. On 9 September that year a meeting of three survivors and Murray Saltzman, executive director of CJC Pacific Region, concluded that a Holocaust committee of Congress, in conjunction with the Warsaw Ghetto Committee and the Jewish Historical Society, be established, with education as its priority. Shortly after, Saltzman met with Graham Forst, a professor at Capilano College, the Reverend Bob Gallacher of the University of British Columbia, and Dr Robert Krell, a professor of psychiatry at UBC, who had been hidden as a child during the war. They were interested in planning a symposium on the Holocaust for secondary school students. Because Gallacher, Forst, and Bill Nichols, a professor of religion at UBC, were not Jewish and therefore nominally outside the scope of Congress, the group decided to call itself the Standing Committee on the Holocaust. It was independent with respect to fundraising, participation, and programming. Forst became chair of the committee. In point of fact, the HRC of the Pacific Region and the Standing Committee acted jointly, and each had members in the other organization.[160]

The first symposium for secondary students on the Holocaust in Canada was held at the Oakridge Auditorium in Vancouver on 27 April 1976. Speakers included Forst, Nichols, Gallacher, and Professor Rudolf Vrba, who had escaped from Auschwitz and written a report on the camp that found its way to the World Jewish Congress in Switzerland. The following year, the symposium was held at UBC, where it continues.[161] The event in 1980 was covered by the *Vancouver Sun*, which related the stories of several survivors who spoke to students on that occasion.[162] Within a few years, two one-day symposia were held, attracting one thousand students from the lower mainland. The Standing Committee and the HRC undertook other projects as well. An outreach program sent a large core of survivor speakers and materials to schools in the lower mainland, and conducted professional development sessions.[163] An essay contest on the Holocaust began in 1978,[164] and five years later the Standing Committee offered its resources to the Vancouver School Board. The board responded positively and acceded to the request that meetings between representatives of the committee and the board take place.[165] The Vancouver seminar was a model for the one established by the Toronto committee five years later. According to Bardikoff, "We learned from them, and tried to do it better."[166]

Despite this promising start, neither the board nor the British Columbia Ministry of Education recommended that the official curriculum include a study of the Holocaust. This did not sit well with the British Columbia Teachers' Federation. Referring to the Glickman-Bardikoff study and the gaps in the new curriculum designed for the province's schools, the federation commented in its newsletter: "The new social study curriculum bombards students with a wild collection of topics ... What they need is a coherent set of historical perspectives that will enable them to draw lessons from the past. And that can only be achieved if the curriculum faces the record of the past squarely. The stuff of history, after all, is humanity with all its warts, embarrassments, contradictions and wrinkles. When one looks over the bloody record of mankind and the challenges before us, should such a study be any less?"[167]

The HRC Pacific Region had its own programs as well. Its main focus was to conduct the Yom Hashoah memorial. But it expanded its activities into other areas, sponsoring an annual lecture on the anniversary of Kristallnacht, with speakers such as Elie Wiesel. It sent representatives to the gatherings of survivors; videotaped more than seventy witnesses; established an institute of Jewish studies; and provided resources and funds to the Community Hebrew Foundation Council of Greater Vancouver and the "Alternatives to Racism" guide for British Columbia schools.[168]

In 1984 Robert Krell decided that a permanent memorial to the victims of the Holocaust, incorporating an archive and a place for exhibits, should be erected. In a letter to CJC Pacific Region, he cited the success of the Standing Committee and the increasing interest by educators. His primary goal, however, was that the centre should "prove to be an important and lasting legacy of the survivor community of British Columbia to the future generations of its citizens."[169] As a result, the Vancouver Holocaust Centre Society for Education and Remembrance was established. However, survivors first wanted a memorial at the Jewish cemetery before they would commit to building a centre. After the memorial was unveiled in

1987, the community centre was expanded to become the home of the Vancouver Holocaust Education and Remembrance Centre, which opened in 1994. Leo Lowy, a member of the centre society, remarked that there was no resistance from the established community towards these endeavours. Survivors had gained standing in the community through their work in raising funds and speaking to the public. This view was corroborated by Professor Moe Steinberg, who was chair of CJC Pacific Region in the late 1970s. Ultimately, the HRC Pacific Region merged with the centre society, while the Standing Committee remained as an autonomous body with links to the centre.[170]

On the Prairies, commemoration and education emanated from Winnipeg. One feature of the Jewish community there was that, although there were several separate organizations, it was sometimes difficult to determine which one was responsible for a particular event. In many cases, the same people belonged to the Winnipeg Jewish Community Council (WJCC, the local federation), the Jewish Historical Society of Western Canada, and CJC Western Region, which was later renamed the Manitoba-Saskatchewan Region. Until 1975, Holocaust commemoration was carried out by the Shaareth Hapleita Committee of the WJCC, which that year was described as "the most active group in Winnipeg at the present time."[171] The committee then became the Holocaust Memorial Committee of CJC.

An early example of the community's willingness to mark the Holocaust was an exhibit, *Journey into Our Heritage*, created by the Jewish Historical Society of Western Canada. It premiered at the Museum of Man and Nature in Winnipeg in 1970 and then travelled throughout western Canada for two years. The exhibit included interviews with survivors, including Rabbi Peretz Weizmann, theatre director John Hirsch, and community leader Paul Berger. A CBC documentary, *An Hour of Lifetimes*, based on these interviews, was aired.[172] This exhibit resulted more from the efforts of the established community than of the survivors. The survivor community of four hundred families was not yet active, aside from the Shaareth Hapleita Committee. As Philip Weiss related, "The voice of survivors was shut out in most cases either because of lack of education, language skills, and the authority rested with those who could break the barriers of the Jewish community and the legitimate authority of the country [on issues such as war criminals]."[173] But by the mid-1970s, with the formation of the Holocaust Memorial Committee, the survivors' voice was mute no longer.

Two ongoing events were the highlight of the community's observance of the Holocaust. The first was Holocaust Awareness Week, held in conjunction with the Yom Hashoah service. This practice, begun at the instigation of CJC Western Region in the 1960s, was amplified in the next decade. As we have seen, the mayor of Winnipeg proclaimed the week and changed the name of a block on a city street to the Avenue of the Warsaw Ghetto Heroes.[174] In 1975 the proclamation read in part: "I call upon all citizens to participate in this memorial observance and to work together to combat racism and eradicate discrimination wherever it is manifested. In light of continuing harassment, and in many cases imprisonment of Jewish people wishing to leave the Soviet Union, it is urged that those citizens be accorded the rights proclaimed for all people in the Universal Declaration of Human Rights, including the right to emigrate. Steven Juba, Mayor."[175]

The second event was an education program. This program was sometimes designed for students in Jewish schools, as when the first seminar took place in 1975.[176] The next year there was a three-day seminar for the community on recent scholarship. Entitled "I Never Saw Another Butterfly," it included lectures based on the works of the historian Lucy Dawidowicz and the literary critic Lawrence Langer. Its purpose, according to the *Jewish Post*, was "to assure unflagging interest and continued understanding of the Holocaust for what it was, the central, shattering experience of modern history, the releasing of those demonic forces that we assumed forever subdued by the triumph of modernism."[177] In 1980 another three-day session, "Encounter with the Holocaust," was taught by Evita Smordin, a local teacher.[178] Four years later Manuel Prutschi, director of the JCRC Western Region, held a series of meetings with the minister of education, school superintendents, and school trustees about providing resources for teaching the Holocaust. One outcome was that education workshops for public school teachers were inaugurated in Winnipeg on a division (board) basis.[179]

The culmination of the efforts of the Holocaust Memorial Committee and the symbolic recognition of acceptance of the Holocaust in the public consciousness occurred on the grounds of the Manitoba legislature on 16 September 1990. A granite memorial in the shape of a broken star of David, inscribed with the names of 3,200 victims of the Holocaust whose families had migrated to Winnipeg, was erected. The memorial had taken five years from conception to completion.[180]

Elsewhere in western Canada, Holocaust remembrance programs were centred in Edmonton. The local HRC constructed a memorial on the grounds of the Jewish cemetery and conducted an annual Yom Hashoah service. A plaque recognizing and commemorating the contributions made by Jewish communities in Alberta was presented to the community by the provincial government.[181] In remembrance of the plight of Jewish refugees denied sanctuary in Canada, the community sponsored twenty refugee families from Vietnam.[182]

Throughout Canada in the period from 1975 to 1985, activities related to the Holocaust proliferated in smaller Jewish communities as well. Some resulted from outreach programs of the national committee or HRCs in the largest cities or from initiatives launched by the League. Most, however, were conducted by local committees.

The most active of the smaller communities was Ottawa. Although its Jewish population grew at a faster rate than in any other city in Canada in this period, it had a small core of survivors. From their first days in the city, the survivors had become integrated into the wider Jewish community, especially in the old neighbourhood in the market area. The local federation, the Va'ad (Hebrew for community), willingly embraced the survivors, but did not understand their experience or appreciate their suffering.[183] Only after 1973, when the local HRC was formed, did the Holocaust became part of the community's agenda. Even then it took several years and some arm-twisting for the established community to yield to the HRC's requests. At issue was its determination to erect a memorial to the victims at the local cemetery. The Va'ad would only agree to place a plaque in the community centre. Mendel Good, the chair of the HRC, remembered: "[I said that] it was an insult to the memory of the six million. I went to the mayor [Laurie Greenberg, a Jew], who was not supportive. I went to the cemetery committee and they relented." He said that the negotiations were difficult because "you were dealing with nice people. They could not understand ... we could not talk about it [the pain] then." The monument was completed in the spring of 1978 and was unveiled at a ceremony at which Chief Justice Bora Laskin was the guest speaker.[184]

The memorial provided the spark for further activities. An exhibit of artifacts from the Holocaust was held at the Canadian War Museum. Student groups were brought to the exhibit, and with their teachers as a base, an education committee was established. Its first initiative was a seminar for educators.[185] An attempt to convince the Ottawa Board of Education to adopt a curriculum on the Holocaust, however, was not successful. Upon hearing of the request by the HRC and the League, Arab Canadians voiced their disapproval, and the project was shelved. Nevertheless, a small but committed contingent of survivors was regularly invited to speak to students by individual schools. The committee conducted an oral documentation project of witnesses. It was revealed that an immigrant from the Netherlands who had been honoured as a righteous gentile among the nations for having saved Jews was resident in Ottawa.[186] This flurry of activity in Ottawa in the early 1980s illustrated that the community had embraced the memory of the Holocaust as part of its self-definition. It helped the community to gain credibility when it lobbied for permission to host the first Gathering of Holocaust Survivors and Their Families in 1985.[187]

A NEW GENERATION FACES THE HOLOCAUST

The Holocaust entered into the consciousness of Canadians between 1975 and 1985 at two levels. Whereas for the first thirty years, the destruction of European Jewry had been a tragic footnote to the war for most Canadians, in the next decade the term "Holocaust" became part of public discourse. That knowledge of the event was increasing was most apparent among secondary and post-secondary students. A decade after Holocaust education had become a mainstay in Metropolitan Toronto, a survey of two hundred high school students in their final year showed that 89 per cent "knew about the Holocaust and its effect on the Jewish community in Europe."[188] This awareness was in marked contrast to that of my students in 1978, whose first exposure was the television miniseries. Some had learned about the Holocaust in classes, and many others had become conversant with the event because of the attention of the popular media. While there were no surveys on the questions of whether Canadians as a whole knew of the event and what their specific understanding of it was, the publicity generated by the trials of Holocaust deniers, the controversy over suspected Nazi war criminals, and the revelations of Canada's appalling immigration policies during the Nazi era could hardly be ignored by the majority of Canadians.

At a second level, the Canadian Jewish community's response to the Holocaust had changed immeasurably during this period. The tragedy had entered the collective historical memory of most Canadian Jews in the mid-1970s. It was not, however, a defining element of their ethnic identity. By the mid-1980s the situation was altogether different, as issues related to the Holocaust were continually thrust onto the community agenda. In 1985, in its quarterly publication of news briefs, Congress listed nine articles on the Holocaust.[189]

The main reason was the changed composition of the principal volunteer organizations. Until the 1950s the membership had been small and limited to prominent individuals, all male, in the community. Thus the leadership was circumscribed, and while it was nominally representative of the majority of Canadian Jews, it dominated the decision-making process. This closed system began to undergo some modification in the 1960s, in response to the transformation of the community from immigrants and their children to "Canadians," and it was gradually opened further in the next two decades. The most marked aspect of this diversification was the entry of survivors into the organizational mainstream. Their agenda was the same as it had been since the 1960s: remember and teach. But in contrast with their situation in struggling against the community establishment then, they now had formidable allies – their children and the third generation of Canadian Jews. As these people emerged as community leaders in the 1980s, a new myth entered the consciousness of the Jewish community. It was rooted in the belief that the memory of the Holocaust was a pillar of their ethnic identification, even though this was a generation too young to have remembered the war, born and/or raised in Canada, and thus removed from the event.

The transference of this perception into a tangible reality was most apparent in the erection of Holocaust education and memorial centres in the federation buildings in Montreal and Toronto and the plan to do the same in Vancouver. These structures, built with funds raised in the community, the exhibits they displayed, the volunteers who planned and carried out commemative and pedagogic programs, and their impact on both the Jewish and the wider community were testimony to the fact that not only had the Holocaust become engrained in historical memory but its legacy helped to define what it meant to be a Jew in Canada.

8 "A crucible for the community": The Landmark Events of 1985

Shortly after the Progressive Conservative victory in the federal election of December 1984, the new government proclaimed that it would appoint a commission of inquiry into Nazi war criminals in Canada. The decision seemed to emanate from the office of Brian Mulroney, the prime minister, rather than from his cabinet. Yet this determination was the outcome of two decades of public lobbying by the Jewish community. At the time of the announcement, the trial of Ernst Zundel was taking place in Toronto. He was charged with the promotion of false news, including the publication and dissemination of literature that declared that the Holocaust had not taken place. The charge resulted from a campaign by elements within the Jewish community to pressure the Ontario attorney general. Several weeks after Zundel was found guilty, another trial began in Red Deer, Alberta. Teacher James Keegstra was charged with propagating hatred among his students. The attorney general of Alberta laid charges only after an intensive campaign spearheaded by the Jewish community. Keegstra also was found guilty. During his trial, Canadian Holocaust survivors and their children held a national gathering in Ottawa to commemorate the victims, educate the Canadian public, and show their appreciation to the country that had provided them sanctuary.

Although four-fifths of the Jewish community had not been directly touched by the Holocaust, many had appropriated the tragedy as part of their ethnic identification. The coincidence of these events in the early months of 1985 served as the culmination of a collective consciousness that had emerged in the preceding two decades.

During these months the community was surprised at the unexpected announcement of the war-criminal inquiry, outraged at the calumnies presented by Zundel's defence and the insensitive reporting of the trial, united in remembrance at the gathering, and relieved when Zundel and Keegstra were found guilty. That the community was able to withstand these tensions and to mobilize its efforts to meet these challenges was testament to its resolve that the memory of the Holocaust would not be stained and to its determination to pass on the legacy to the next generation.

NAZI WAR CRIMINALS IN CANADA

Antanas Kenstavicius, a police chief in his native Lithuania following the German invasion in 1941, is alleged to have participated in the murder of 5,500 Jews while collaborating with the ss. In 1945 he joined the German army, and after the war, he found refuge in a displaced persons' camp in the British zone. Kenstavicius was on a list of alleged war criminals in DP camps compiled by Jewish organizations in 1948 which was distributed to the Allies. Canadian immigration authorities, although informed by the International Refugee Organization, nevertheless accepted his application for admission to this country. He arrived in Halifax on 24 May 1948, was given a visa to take up residence, and moved to British Columbia. In June the following year the Canadian Jewish Congress received a file with affidavits from Holocaust survivors, who swore that Kenstavicius had carried out the actions against the Jews with zeal. The file was passed to the RCMP for investigation later that month. However, he was finally charged only in 1996. While waiting for a hearing by an immigration tribunal, Kenstavicius died at the age of ninety.[1]

Why was a man like Kenstavicius allowed into Canada, and why did he live in peace here for forty-seven years? At the time of Congress's submission to the RCMP, the Jewish community believed that the federal government would investigate the allegations against Kenstavicius and other suspected criminals whose files had been relayed to the authorities. For the next two decades, Congress made representations to the government under the assumption that progress could be made in having such suspects deported. As Ben Kayfetz related, "We were politely received, but we didn't know then that the government lied to us. [It] was very sympathetic, but no action was taken or could be taken. [The unspoken policy] was 'no action.' It was political conceit."[2]

The unspoken policy had been decided upon in July 1948 when the three major Allied powers had determined that the punishment of war criminals would end. A telegram from the British Commonwealth Relations Office to the seven dominions explained the new policy. "In our view, the punishment of war criminals is more a matter of discouraging future generations, than of meting out retribution to every guilty individual. Moreover, in view of future political developments in Germany envisaged by recent tripartite talks, we are convinced that it is now necessary to dispose of the past as soon as possible."[3] For the Allies the most pressing concern was the Cold War. They had no use for further war crimes trials. A few of the most notorious criminals had been dealt with; of the thousands of others, a small number were apprehended in Soviet-controlled Europe and tried, but the majority were not pursued. The new enemy was not a defeated Germany but an aggressive and expansionist Soviet Union. If suspected war criminals who were avowedly anti-Communist went free, and were even allowed admission to Canada, that was considered insignificant in the larger fight against Soviet hegemony.[4]

From the late 1940s to the early 1960s, Congress quietly but sporadically lobbied the government to investigate certain individuals whose names they had received via survivors' affidavits and from Simon Wiesenthal, the Nazi hunter who supplied evidence against suspects from his office in Vienna. In 1962, Congress asked the government to investigate Joseph Kirschbaum, who had been in the Hlinka guard in Slovakia which had deported Jews to the death camps.[5] Three years later it asked that evidence about alleged war criminal Harold Puntulis in Riga, Latvia, be considered. Both requests were stonewalled. The government hid behind the excuse, as Justice Minister Marcel Cadieux wrote to Saul Hayes, "that no decision to order an inquiry to revoke a person's citizenship could be taken without very substantial reasons for believing that his guilt could be proven." Congress was dissatisfied, but Hayes felt it best to keep this communication confidential. A copy of the letter from Cadieux contains Hayes's hand-written directive "No publicity."[6]

By 1966, survivors were becoming agitated Congress' apparent passivity. At meetings of Toronto's Community Anti-Nazi Committee, they said that Jewish organizations should raise a *shtimmung* (outcry). A proposal by the committee to hold a rally on Parliament Hill was scrapped for lack of support from the JCRC. But N3, the leading anti-Nazi group in Toronto at the time, mounted its own campaign to publicize the issue. It invited Nazi hunter Simon Wiesenthal to speak in the city on 2 April 1967, at a rally which attracted "thousands" of Torontonians, according to the *Canadian Jewish News*.[7] Congress responded to the survivors' concerns by presenting a submission to the Special Joint Committee of the Senate and

House of Commons on Immigration on 22 February 1967, but the government remained unmoved.[8]

Between 1967 and 1977 the war criminals issue remained on the back burner of the community agenda, much to the consternation of survivors and their supporters. I asked Sol Kanee and Sydney Harris, who were CJC presidents from 1971 to 1977, why this was the case. In separate interviews, they responded that there were two overriding issues during this period with regard to community-government relations. One was to lobby for support for an embattled Israel against international censure, between the Six Day War (1967) and the peace accord with Egypt (1978). The other issue was to pressure the Soviet Union to allow Jews to emigrate. Kanee related that discussions with the government over war criminals did take place, but "it was a lot of effort and money, [with] little to show." The government's inaction was, in the eyes of Congress, inconsistent with the perception that the organization had close ties to the Liberal Party and a direct line to prime ministers Pearson and Trudeau. Harris maintained that "every administration of Congress that I know of has pushed, complained, yelled, lobbied, written, but they haven't been successful. The complaint is not that they haven't done anything, but that they didn't succeed."[9]

That the problem was not lack of effort but lack of success became apparent in the growing dissatisfaction with the process by some survivors, especially those in the Toronto Holocaust Remembrance Committee. At Congress's plenary session in 1977, the committee presented a draft resolution that the NHRC prepare and present a brief to the government and that on the day of the presentation demonstrations, including a hunger strike, be organized across the country.[10] The resolution was not passed. Congress maintained that it had kept up the lobbying in its meetings with cabinet ministers John Turner (justice), John Roberts (secretary of state), and Robert Kaplan (solicitor general).[11] The plenary, in response to the survivors' concerns and because of the mounting furor over West Germany's decision to implement a limitation on trying suspected war criminals in 1979, passed a watered-down resolution . "Congress [will] present a brief on the issue, and that the presentation be part of an effort organized across the country to bring this action to the attention of the Canadian public in a dramatic and striking manner."[12] The message was clear: if anyone in the community was to control the agenda on this issue, it would be the appropriate bodies in Congress and not the survivors.

The CJC now felt that the time had come for more forceful action. In a memorandum to Congress vice-president Alan Rose, Saul Hayes, in his last days as executive director, wrote: "I think we have discharged our moral obligations in the academic area. The only thing left is to determine who are the criminals and how we can obtain reliable witnesses to identify them."[13] Despite this resolve, the government remained unyielding. Its position was clearly expressed when Robert Kaplan's private member's bill to deprive war criminals of Canadian citizenship was not adopted by his party.[14]

Why was the Trudeau government adamantly opposed to enacting legislation to try war criminals? Philip Givens, the former mayor of Toronto, who was elected in the Liberal sweep in 1968, was an MP for only three years, largely because of his outspoken views in caucus and his discomfort at being a backbencher after having been in the spotlight in municipal politics. Regarding war criminals, he stated: "When I became an MP ... I went to see Trudeau. So he said to me [parenthetically], 'Phil, this guy's a Pole, this guy's a Ukrainian. Phil, do you realize how many Poles there are, how many people we would be offending? Phil, I've got a lot of other priorities to consider. Do you want to rile up all these people?' I realized that he didn't care about the Jewish people, and that the RCMP, going way down ... didn't have the slightest intention of doing anything about it for the same reasons as Trudeau."[15]

Sol Kanee, a long-time Liberal supporter and a confidante of Mitchell Sharp, the secretary of state for external relations, offered a different perspective. At a dinner at 24 Sussex Drive toward the end of Trudeau's administration in 1984, the prime minister lamented that his standing with the Jewish community was at its lowest point ever. Kanee responded that ten years earlier there had been one Jewish deputy minister and now there were four, in addition to a chief justice, a federal court judge, and an ambassador to the United States, and that this change had occurred under Trudeau.[16] Kanee could have added that Trudeau was the first prime minister to appoint Jews to the cabinet (four in total). Trudeau's refusal to commit his government to act on the war criminal issue was due to political considerations and his often-stated repugnance of ethnic triumphalism masking as nationalism. He had a marginally accurate premonition that trying war criminals would inflame smouldering passions among Canadian immigrants from some European countries, but he misunderstood that the driving consideration was justice. His administration's soft-pedalling of the issue, was not, however indicative of an anti-Jewish bias.

In the last Trudeau administration, from 1980 to 1984, there were three interrelated factors in operation regarding war criminals: the intensification of lobbying by Congress; the response by the justice ministers and the solicitor general; and the opposition to Congress policy and government intransigence on the part of the Holocaust Remembrance Association. Although the question of amending the legal code to prosecute war criminals fell under the purview of the justice department, most of the pressure from the community was directed at Robert Kaplan, the solicitor general, who was Jewish. In 1980 he met Wiesenthal in Washington. Wiesenthal by then was refusing to visit Canada because of its admission of war criminals and its reluctance to prosecute them. He stated that at one time there were as many as a thousand war criminals in Canada.[17] Kaplan disclosed that he intended to establish an interdepartmental committee to examine legal angles which could be used in prosecutions. Congress wholeheartedly supported this endeavour. At its plenary that year it applauded the initiative taken by Kaplan and called upon the federal and provincial governments "to initiate forthwith vigorous and adequately-staffed police investigations of the allegations against alleged Nazi war criminals resident in Canada."[18]

Encouraged by Kaplan's announcement, Congress felt that the momentum was shifting. It initiated a national letter-writing campaign to press the issue. Letters to Kaplan and Lloyd Axworthy, minister of manpower and immigration, met with the response that the government was not prepared to conduct investigations without a proper legal foundation.[19] In addition to writing letters, Congress established a war criminals subcommittee of its Legal Committee. Irwin Cotler, Congress president and a legal expert on human rights, introduced a resolution at the Canadian Bar Association annual meeting in 1981 calling for legislation on the matter. The resolution was passed unanimously.[20] In September that year, the head of the West German Central Office for the Investigation of Nazi War Crimes came to Canada, and his meeting with survivors in Vancouver was covered by the CBC's *National*, the nightly news broadcast.[21] In a detailed letter to Kaplan, with whom he had close ties, Cotler reminded the solicitor general that he had sufficient evidence to proceed and that Kaplan, at an earlier meeting with Aba Beer, chair of the NHRC, had indicated that the government had the political will to do so. Beer had stated that "he could not understand how a government cannot bring to justice the greatest mass murderers in history." Cotler referred to the growing Holocaust denial movement and a meeting between Jean Chrétien, the minister of justice, and Maxwell Cohen, dean ofMcGill University's law faculty and an adviser to Congress. Lastly, Cotler stated that the previous day the war criminals issue had dominated the meeting of CJC national officers.[22]

Yet the government remained intransigent. In response to a question in the House of Commons about the report of the interdepartmental committee that had been established almost a year earlier and had not yet produced its report despite the assurance that one would be forthcoming within three months after its first meetings, Chrétien responded, "We have to deal with the Charter of Rights in this House before deciding whether to proceed with some legislation." The questioner, Svend Robinson of the NDP, retorted, "Madam Speaker, the government knows very well that is just a cop-out for its inaction and the betrayal of the promises it made in the last election."[23] Kaplan, speaking several days earlier in London, Ontario, stated, "I regret to tell you the matter is still before cabinet. It hasn't lost its priority but I am not ready to announce a decision."[24] When the report was finally made public in March 1981, its author, Martin Low, contended that "the evidence was lacking in detail and imprecise or containing factual inconsistencies." As Harold Troper and Morton Weinfeld argue in their analysis of the war criminals issue, "The report left little doubt that government could or perhaps should do nothing."[25]

In the fall of 1982 Mark MacGuigan replaced Chrétien as minister of justice. Congress officials met with MacGuigan, who, Cotler related, was sensitive to the moral aspects of the issue. The minister's concern was not with political will, which he said existed, but with the law. Meetings were also held with Trudeau and Kaplan.[26] The prospects looked bright. For one thing, the publication of *None Is Too Many* in September 1982 had created a national outcry. The government would have to take action if it was not to be compared to the King administration. Yet the war criminals question, despite MacGuigan's assertion to Cotler that the political will existed, had very little priority. Years later MacGuigan could not recall that the issue was brought up in cabinet, although he conceded that Kaplan might have done so. In my interview with him, he elaborated further: "It wasn't high profile ... This is the most important factor. There wasn't a general perception that there were many if any war criminals in Canada, so it seemed a theoretical exercise to the extent that it had any validity at all ... I was lobbied by CJC, but it wasn't a first-rank issue. It wasn't made even by them. We had problems involving Canada's relationship with Israel [over the moving of the embassy to Jerusalem and the invasion of Lebanon]. Those things were front and centre ... I can't say that I ever remember that it was a major thing, and to the best of my recollection, it was not an issue on which I thought I had to make a decision."[27]

In the spring of 1983 the Jewish community again intensified the pressure. Cotler, at the Gathering of Holocaust Survivors in Washington, attacked the government's foot-dragging. A resolution was passed at the Congress plenary in May a to continue vigorously to press the federal and provincial governments to prosecute, under existing legislation or newly enacted legislation all alleged Nazi war criminals resident in Canada whose extradition had not been called for. The NHRC disclosed that a public-action program had been published which called for education, mobilization, organizational and community support, and media support.[28] Milton Harris, the new president of Congress, met with MacGuigan, who assured him that the government would reconsider the issue in light of the deportation of Helmut Rauca to West Germany to be prosecuted for war crimes that he had committed in Lithuania. But the minister was still wary of the legal quagmire and was now devoting his energy to winning the leadership of the Liberal Party in light of Trudeau's resignation. The Jewish community felt that it had been deceived. Although representations and pressure continued, there seemed little likelihood that this administration could be moved.[29] In the election of December 1984 the Liberal Party, led by John Turner, was crushed by the Tories. The Jewish community's efforts to win Liberal support, a struggle that had lasted twenty years, appeared to have been for nought.

Congress's lobbying efforts during the post-war era were unrecognized by the more vocal elements in the Jewish community. Having operated in secret until the early 1960s and without any appreciable success thereafter, the established community was accused of having a *galut* mentality (a term used to describe subservient Jews who grovelled before Russian authority) by the Holocaust Remembrance Association. Shortly after its formation, the HRA had presented a brief to the governments of Canada and Ontario in December 1980 requesting that they implement the War Crimes Act and the Geneva Conventions Act in order to bring the suspects to trial. Accompanying the brief was a petition with 30,000 names.[30]

The HRA sought to establish itself as the authority on war criminals and to oppose Congress's claim to act as the voice of the Jewish community. In a letter to Trudeau, it stated that the brief which called for the extradiction of war criminals had been received positively. The letter went on to say that a brief to be presented by Congress "has really nothing of significance to offer. We have pointed out, and the record speaks for itself, the Canadian Jewish Congress never wanted to institute proceedings against Nazi War Criminals in Canada due to their fear of an 'anti-semitic backlash.'"[31] The HRA's frustration was understandable since Congress had maintained exclusivity in its deliberations with the government and since the Trudeau administration was clearly uninterested in facing the problem. The government's position was evident when Sabina Citron, the association's spokesperson, met with Justice Minister Chrétien. She later remembered, "It was a great disappointment because Chrétien is Chrétien. He didn't address anything, although he had months to read it [the brief] in advance. He seemed very cordial and very pleasant."[32]

Ben Kayfetz felt that, aside from the HRA, there was unanimity in the community on the issue. Unlike the internal debates on the hate-propaganda legislation, Kayfetz maintained, "I don't remember anybody being opposed on the war criminal issue. The major dissenter was Sabina and she was only speaking for her own group." Regarding the meetings with Kaplan, Kayfetz used a Yiddish expression. "It was *aroisgevorfen gelt* [wasted money]." Kaplan, he felt, "wanted to do the right thing as a Jew, as a man of justice, but found himself stymied." The intensity of feeling on the part of Canadian Jews concerning this issue, Kayfetz remarked, was a direct outgrowth of the community's appropriation of the Holocaust as part of its ethnic identity.[33]

With Congress shut out of the decision-making process, there was little hope that the new government, which did not have close ties with the Jewish community, would be more willing to prosecute war criminals than its predecessor. Thus it was an utter shock when John Crosbie, the minister of justice, rose in the House on 7 February 1985 to proclaim that the government was establishing a commission of inquiry into allegations that Nazi war criminals were resident in Canada. The inquiry, headed by Justice Jules Deschenes, was to report to Crosbie by the end of the year.[34]

Why had the government taken this sudden and unprecedented leap in only its fourth week in power? One could point to the startling revelation at that time that Josef Mengele, the notorious ss doctor at Birkenau, might have stayed in Canada in the 1960s, but that fact was dismissed as an excuse and not the cause.[35] Rather, according to Troper and Weinfeld, Mulroney acted on his own without consulting cabinet, the minister of justice, or anyone in the Jewish community. In fact, he was not attuned to the Jewish community. There had been little pressure placed on him by the community while he was leader of the opposition, and there had been little time to do so after he became prime minister. If, in fact, he acted alone, the reason is a mystery. He had no apparent personal conviction or motivation.[36]

Congress was stunned by the news. It was not entirely exuberant about Crosbie's announcement. After all, it had lobbied for legislation, and this was merely a commission of inquiry into what the

Jewish community had known for decades – namely, that there were Nazi war criminals living safely in Canada. Yet Congress could not condemn the announcement. It quickly set out to gain accreditation to appear before the commission, as did the League for Human Rights, the Simon Wiesenthal Center, and the HRA. All but the HRA were accorded status. These organizations had all helped to place the issue before the public. While Sol Littman, Wiesenthal's Canadian representative and an investigator of Nazi activity in Canada, and Sabina Citron may have acted as gadflies to the Jewish establishment, and while Congress and B'nai Brith both claimed to speak for the community, their efforts had a common purpose.[37] Although no organization in the community could claim credit for Mulroney's decision, without two decades of pressure, the issue would not have been on the public agenda in the first place.

Antanas Kenstavicius had not been tried in Europe in 1948 for crimes against humanity because the Allies had believed that they had more pressing problems. Furthermore, his alleged crimes had not prevented him from emigrating to Canada and becoming a citizen. His peaceful life was not disturbed by these allegations because the post-war governments did not have the political will to investigate the information they had received on suspects such as Kenstavicius. Until the late 1960s, Congress had trusted that the government had the intention of investigating suspects. When it became apparent that the Jewish community was being lied to, it united in demanding a concrete response. For survivors and their children, it was inconceivable that they and the murderers of their families should have found haven in the same country. Indeed, the murderers had often found it easier to enter than had the survivors. Madame Justice Rosalie Abella of the Appellate Court of Ontario and the child of survivors, put the issue into the context of the post-war era when she stated: "Nuremberg and I were born in the same year and in the same country. Both of us came from the experience of the Holocaust and, it can be argued, both of us represent a kind of revenge ... But we were not unmindful that behind the Nuremberg curtain were relics of indifference and insensitivity from the very players who wrote the script, directed the actors, and produced the morality play that Nuremberg became."[38]

THE ZUNDEL AND KEEGSTRA TRIALS

A curious incident took place at the Liberal leadership convention in 1968. The individual who finished last on the first ballot was not a Canadian citizen and was unknown to the party. The name on the ballot was "Ernest Zuendel." Ernst Zündel (his real name) had immigrated to Canada from Germany in 1958 at the age of nineteen, and settled in Montreal. There he met Adrien Arcand. By the late 1960s, Zundel was living in Toronto. He was linked to the extremist Western Unity Movement and had become an associate editor of the *Torontoer Zeitung*. He also had begun mailing German nationalist propaganda and neo-Nazi items to small numbers of people, including rabbis in Montreal.[39] Even so, Zundel was not considered to be in the top rank of local neo-Nazis, among such individuals as David Stanley, John Beattie, and John Ross Taylor. Although he was known to Jewish organizations, Sol Littman, executive director of the Anti-Defamation League, wrote, "Zundel appears to be a very small cloud in Canada."[40] When Zundel announced his candidacy in the leadership race, Ben Kayfetz informed Philip Givens, who would be running for a seat in the House of Commons under the Liberal banner. Givens did not pass on the information to the party leadership for fear of creating needless publicity.[41] A protest letter to the Liberal Party from the JLC also had no effect.[42]

The greatest impediment to the spread of neo-Nazi ideology has been knowledge about the Holocaust. Because of the enormity of the event, it has not been easy for followers of Hitlerism to recruit new members. While the trappings of Nazism have held some measure of fascination for the young and impressionable, because of the stigma of Auschwitz, few extremists have had the audacity to call themselves Nazis. But in the 1950s a lie was fashioned to exculpate the Nazis — there had not been a Holocaust. Rather, the event was a hoax fostered by an international conspiracy run by Jews to gain sympathy and to garner support for Israel. This fabrication began in Europe with little fanfare and virtually no support, but it gained credence in some quasi-intellectual circles in France in the 1960s and was appropriated by fledgling neo-Nazi groups that proliferated at that time. By the 1970s, denying the Holocaust, now dubbed "historical revisionism" by its adherents, had become commonplace among North American extremists. Soon they were flooding the market with pseudo-scientific books and pamphlets. By the late 1970s the largest base for publication and distribution of this literature was a house in downtown Toronto, the home of Ernst Zundel.[43]

Zundel eagerly sought publicity. He formed various organizations to defend the honour of German Canadians, who, he claimed, were being maligned by the media, especially in the aftermath of the *Holocaust* miniseries. As his notoriety grew, so did his publishing empire. Needless to say, the Jewish community did not take kindly to Zundel's operation. In 1977 B'nai Brith lodged a complaint to a post office inspector and provided examples of the materials being distributed. No action was taken then, nor was there any response to a letter about Zundel's activities sent by Simon Wiesenthal to Robert Kaplan in 1980. That year the HRA, frustrated by the mainstream Jewish organizations' merely monitoring antisemitism rather than carrying out a proactive campaign, asked André Ouellet, the postmaster general, to revoke Zundel's postal privileges. The post office's investigation led to the granting of an interim prohibitory order on 13 November 1981. Zundel appealed the order to the Postal Review Appeal Board on behalf of his company, Samisdat. Both the HRA and Congress made deputations to the board. On 18 October 1982 it ruled in favour of Samisdat, and its privileges were restored. The ruling was based on the naive view that the case was basically an argument between two ethnic groups, Germans and Jews, living in Canada, and that since there had not been a police recommendation to prosecute, the board had no jurisdiction to uphold the revocation. Its ruling only served to increase the Jewish community's disgust with Zundel's actions and its disappointment with the authorities for not invoking section 281 of the Criminal Code, which prohibits the distribution of hate propaganda. The HRA was particularly infuriated and proceeded to speed up its own attack on Zundel.[44]

Although criminalization of the distribution of hate propaganda had been on the books since 1970, the law had been applied only once, against a minor figure in the neo-Nazi movement who was discharged for lack of evidence. Charges brought under section 281 could be laid only by the provincial attorney general. Although there seemed to be ample evidence against Zundel under this section, and although the JCRC (Ontario region) had been asking for charges to be laid not only against Zundel but also against other purveyors of racist materials, attorneys general were reluctant to do so because of loopholes in the law. At its plenary in 1983, Congress pressed for their closing through amendments to section 281 and other parts of the Criminal Code.[45] When these requests were rejected by the Department of Justice, the only alternative was section 177 of the code, which made it a criminal offence to knowingly disseminate false news that was likely to cause injury to the public interest. Charges under this section could be laid by an individual or group without provincial sanction. Congress had rejected this approach because it would put the Holocaust, as an event, on trial and would put the burden of proof on the Crown, thus making the risk of prosecution too great. The HRA, however, was not so disinclined to take the risk. When it met with Roy McMurtry, the attorney general of Ontario, it received a sympathetic hearing, but the association was told that section 281 would not be invoked. In response, the HRA laid a private complaint against Zundel under section 177 in December 1983. In its attempt to unmask Zundel as a racist, the association, perhaps unwittingly, forced the hand of both the attorney general and the Jewish community. The Crown had either to let the charge drop, effectively exonerating Zundel, which was not a viable option given the public mood and the mountain of evidence against him, or take over the case from the complainant. The Jewish community, unwilling to invoke section 177 and internally divided over whether to give greater publicity to Zundel, was put in a similar predicament. Not only did it have to support the charge, but, as the trial unfolded, it had to assist the Crown.[46]

The trial opened in January 1985. Zundel was tried on two separate counts, based on the publication of two pamphlets. The first was a four-page article, *The West, War and Islam*, and the second, *Did Six Million Really Die?* a thirty-two-page diatribe of Holocaust denial. The trial lasted thirty-eight days, and Zundel was found guilty by a jury on the second count. He was sentenced to fifteen months in prison but freed on bail pending an appeal.

Two salient issues arise with regard to the trial and the Jewish community. The first was the decision by the JCRC and the League for Human Rights to work with the Crown. Manuel Prutschi had been hired as national director of the JCRC in the summer of 1984, upon the retirement of Ben Kayfetz. He had just arrived from Winnipeg, where he had been regional director. Soon after, Prutschi and Alan Shefman, the director of the League, discussed the case. When they spoke with Peter Griffith, the Crown attorney, it was clear that the Crown was out of its depth, according to Prutschi, and justifiably so.[47] It had little knowledge of the history of the Holocaust, few contacts with potential witnesses, and no experience in dealing with sophisticated purveyors of hate on the witness stand. As the trial unfolded, the reluctance by some elements in the community to invoke section 177, because the Holocaust, rather than the denier, would be put on trial, was realized. The Crown had to rebut the calumny that the event had not happened, and to do so required the daily support of Prutschi, Shefman, and their staffs. The HRA, without whom there would not have been a trial, did not have the same clout as the established organizations in working with the Crown. Nevertheless, Sabina Citron considered Griffith to be "a wonderful human being," and she told him that the HRA could get in touch with potential expert witnesses, including Raul Hilberg, who testified as the Crown's historical expert.[48]

The second issue was the effect of the trial on the Jewish community. Zundel and his supporters would walk in a phalanx to the courthouse, and he, wearing a construction hat ostensibly for protection, would make pronouncements to the press. His attorney, Douglas Christie, was an abrasive performer who tried to bully the Crown witnesses, many of whom were survivors. Christie was constantly censured by the bench. He maintained that he had no connection with the ideology of the anti-Nazi movement, but he stayed at Zundel's home during the trial and continues to be the lawyer of choice for other right-wing extremists. Moreover, Christie was directly involved with the radical fringe of the Social Credit Party, for which he ran as provincial leader in his native British Columbia, and its offshoot, the Western Canada Concept. He was often present at meetings of neo-Nazis.[49] The trial received massive press coverage. The *Globe* ran an average of 1.1 stories per day during the trial, a figure equivalent to the coverage in the *Toronto Star* Unfortunately, the newspapers had difficulty distinguishing between facts and lies. One headline in the 12 January edition of the *Globe and Mail* read, "Witness Indecisive – Lawyer Challenges Crematoria Theory." The lawyer referred to was Christie. Another headline, in the 6 February edition of the *Globe and Mail*, read, "No Gas Chambers in Nazi Germany, Expert Witness Testifies", a reference to the testimony of a man convicted and sentenced for neo-Nazi activities in Europe.[50]

The seeming insensitivity of some of the press alarmed Canadian Jews from coast to coast. At the outset of the trial there was a sharp division in the community over the decision to prosecute. Some who were opposed felt that not only would Zundel gain converts with a show trial, but that by invoking section 177 instead of section 281, the Crown had made a grievous error, since there was little chance that Zundel would be found guilty. Other opponents in the community reverted to the freedom-of-speech argument. Most prominent among these was Alan Borovoy, the counsel for the Canadian Civil Liberties Association. He observed, "Freedom of speech is often most important when it creates discontent or disquiet. How in the world can the blunt criminal law distinguish destructive hatred from constructive tension?"[51] Sabina Citron even included Congress among the opponents. In my interview with her, she stated, "Congress was shaking. 'What if we lose this trial?'"[52]

As the trial dragged on, the tension in the community became unbearable. Survivors were berated by the defence attorney, and a certified lunatic, Detlef Felderer, who had been in an insane asylum in Sweden for his fantastic ravings about an international Jewish conspirary, was paraded as an expert witness.[53] Inevitably, detractors and supporters of the decision to prosecute were drawn together. Acquittal would have meant that Zundel had succeeded in hoodwinking the jury and that the media had lost the message among the lies. Of greater significance, it would have meant that after twenty years of lobbying and debate, there was still no law on the books that would effectively constrain the hate-mongers. When the verdict was announced, there was a sense of vindication, of triumph, immediately followed by an almost audible sigh of relief. Yet to those in the community most alert to the trial, it was clear that Zundel had been found guilty because he was a neo-Nazi and not because he had spread false news.

The verdict was announced only three weeks after Crosbie's proclamation that an inquiry into Nazi war criminals would be conducted and only four weeks before the fortieth anniversary of the Warsaw Ghetto Uprising, to be commemorated on Parliament Hill during the gathering of Holocaust survivors. By this time the community was united in its appropriation of the Holocaust as a defining element in its identity. Zundel boasted that he had received a million dollars' worth of free publicity for his cause, but a study revealed that interest in the Holocaust among the general public had increased and that the denial movement's marginal support had declined.[54] Moreover, the Holocaust denial movement created a perverse kind of victory for the survivors. Beginning in the late 1970s, many survivors, infuriated by the lies, had decided that they could no longer remain silent. They became involved in local HRCs and swelled the ranks of witnesses who spoke to students of all ages about their experiences. In interviews conducted with survivors for this study and in earlier research, I found that most of them had two reponses to the Holocaust denial movement. They were alarmed about its apparent growth, its methods, and its appeal to the youth, and they were bound and determined to expose the lies that it propagated. Their reaction was a central reason for the spread of Holocaust education aimed precisely at those who were most vulnerable to the blandishments of the deniers. There can be no doubt that today's youth is far more aware of the event than are those who have swallowed the neo-Nazi message.

During the Zundel trial the Jewish community reached a threshold. The issue was not whether the HRA or the Crown had erred, but how the community would respond. The answer was not long in coming. Long-held divisions and animosities were set aside, as Congress and B'nai Brith worked hand in-hand. The fissures between survivors and Canadian Jews were closed as the interest, passion, and involvement of the community increased during the trial. One small indication of this involvement was the daily lineup of spectators. Each day the line grew longer, and observers hoping for a seat arrived up to two hours before the proceedings started. From my observations at the trial, there seemed to be no distinction between Canadian Jews and survivors among the attendees. Although the trial was held in Toronto, the Jewish community nationwide was caught up in the daily reports in the media. According to Manuel Prutschi, "It [the trial] was felt with tremendous intensity across the country. In one sense, the community was not prepared. There was no premonition of how painful, how emotionally wrenching the experience would be ... When one had the whole assault on the Holocaust, when one had the survivors' experience assaulted by defence counsel, when you had the media reporting it in such an insensitive way because they were not prepared to deal with it, I don't think anyone foresaw what it would involve emotionally ... At times, it was iffy if the community would come through the trial ... In some ways it was a crucible for the community."[55]

The aftershock of the Zundel trial still reverberates. His appeal was upheld in 1987. The Crown than charged him again, with the proviso that judicial notice of the Holocaust was to be taken, so that the defendent and not the event was on trial. He was again found guilty, and this time his appeal was rejected at the provincial level.[56] The Supreme Court, however, overturned the verdict on 28 August 1992 ruling that the "false news" section was unconstitutional. In a confidential document, Prutchi wrote to Gerda Steinitz-Frieberg, chair of Congress's Central Region, that "the whole process was worth it since it put Canada's leading Holocaust denier ... out of commission for seven years and that not only did the law have the effect of deterrence, but it declared that racist speech were [sic] outside the pale, and that the process was an exercise in educating and sensitizing the general public."[57] In 1996 Zundel was charged with violating the Canadian Human Rights Act on his "Zundelsite" Web site on the Internet. The charge was laid by Citron and the Toronto Mayor's Committee on Community and Race Relations. A tribunal of the Canadian Human Rights Commission began its inquiry in October 1997. It was recessed in the spring of 1999 and, as of the time of writing, was expected to resume in the fall of that year.[58]

The Zundel trial was one of two cases of antisemitic hate-mongering before the courts in 1985. The other was the prosecution of James Keegstra, a high school history teacher in Eckville, Alberta. For years he had forced his perverted view of history on his students, who had then to parrot the misinformation back to him. Typical was the following answer of a grade twelve student on a social studies test written on 1 April 1982: "The Nuremberg Trials were insidious and wrong because the complete trial was run by Jews (the enemy) and the German leaders and soldiers were accused of things they did not do. The Jews had no real evidence or witnesses to back them up. The trials went on hearsay. This was where the bit about 6 million Jews came up. They started with 12 million then went through to 9, 5 and down to 6 (when they do this you know it must be a hoax)."[59]

Keegstra was certified to teach auto mechanics not history. His views were based on paranoid fantasies about a Jewish world conspiracy bent on controlling and then destroying Christianity. Although some Eckville parents had complained to the school board for years, the information was not passed on to the superintendent of the Lacombe County School Board until September 1981, and Keegstra was not fired until December the following year. Under intense pressure from the Jewish community in the province in 1983, the attorney general of Alberta ordered an investigation by the RCMP. Keegstra was then charged with promoting hate under section 281. His trial began on 9 April 1985 and ended with a guilty verdict on 20 July. Keegstra was given one month to pay a $5,000 fine or face six months in prison.[60]

How did the Alberta Jewish community respond to the disclosure of Keegstra's activities? According to David Bercuson and Douglas Wertheimer, in 1982, when the gravity of the affair was not widely appreciated, the reaction was disorganized and almost always ad hoc.[61] When Harry Shatz, the executive director of the Calgary Jewish Community Council, first received information about Keegstra's teaching in January, he recommended that the material be sent to the regional offices of Congress in Edmonton, but it was not. It appears that relations between the two communities were strained. Finally, in December he sent the material to Ben Kayfetz, who was outraged and suggested that a common policy be established by the Alberta Jewish community. Yet no such policy was forthcoming, and Alberta's Jews came to learn of the affair through spotty press reports. For many, the lack of action was inexcusable. A rally in Edmonton attracted one thousand angry people. According to sociologist Stanley Barrett, who researched the affair, one young person told him, "'Such weakness is despicable'; he wanted nothing less than direct confrontation, with no apologies to those sitting on the fence."[62]

This lack of response changed when Herb Katz became chair of the Alberta JCRC. He had just read *None Is Too Many* and felt ashamed at the actions of the Jewish leadership in Canada during the war. Katz determined that as much publicity as possible be brought to the affair. His reaction had the effect of mobilizing the Jewish community. Not satisfied with Keegstra's firing, it undertook an intensive lobbying campaign in May 1983 to force Premier Peter Lougheed to take action against race hatred. Its efforts were buttressed by investigative reports in the *Calgary Herald*. Yet Lougheed would not commit himself. He was criticized for his inaction by some media, by James Fleming, the federal minister for multiculturalism, and by Irwin Cotler, past president of Congress. The Edmonton Jewish Federation created an Ad Hoc Legal Committee, which urged the Alberta attorney general to order the RCMP to investigate Keegstra's actions under section 281.[63] This tactic had some effect. The pressure on the government had become too intense. The combined effect of the Jewish community's lobbying and the media exposure forced its hand. The most significant media event was the national broadcast on CBC television of "Lessons in Hate" on 2 May 1983. More than one million Canadians watching *The Journal*, the nightly news magazine, were astonished to hear Keegstra promoting his views in a confrontational interview with Linden MacIntyre.[64] In many communities, seminars and lectures on the affair and the importance of anti-racist education were held.[65] Keegstra's refusal to recant, his appeals for reinstatement to the board of education, and his refusal to resign as mayor of Eckville were also responsible for the decision to prosecute.[66]

The Keegstra affair united Alberta's Jewish community. Once the trial began, the community rallied behind the combined effort of Congress and the League to help the Crown prepare its case.[67] Having established an amicable relationship during the Zundel trial, Manuel Prutschi and Alan Shefman again combined the forces of their respective organizations. Because the trial was held two thousand miles from their offices, they worked with Crown attorney Bruce Fraser on alternate weeks.[68] Prutschi recalled that the trial did not have the same kind of intense involvement by the Jewish community as the Zundel trial had had, because it was held in Red Deer, some two hundred miles from Calgary and Edmonton and because, in contrast with the Zundel trial, the Holocaust was not in question. Thus survivors and expert witnesses were spared the anguish of having to testify.[69]

The Keegstra affair did not end in 1985. Douglas Christie, Keegstra's defence attorney, appealed the verdict on the grounds that his client's freedom of speech had been violated under the Canadian Charter of Rights and Freedoms, and the Alberta Court of Appeal upheld the appeal in 1988. The Crown then appealed the case to the Supreme Court on the grounds of the constitutionality of section 281. In 1990, in a 4 to 3 ruling, the Supreme Court upheld the constitutionality of the conviction and returned the case to the province. The following year, Alberta determined that Keegstra would have to stand trial again. Once again he was convicted and he appealed. This appeal was finally overturned by the Supreme Court in 1994.[70] According to Manuel Prutschi, the ruling was fitting. Keegstra, he claims, had wilfully intended to promote racial hatred, and section 281 provided the perfect laboratory experiment for the case.[71] Mark MacGuigan, a federal court judge, former justice minister, and member of the Cohen committee on hate propaganda, concurred. "Now that the decision has been given, there is a strong weight of precedence in favour. No one who raises that defence in a criminal trial is going to be entertained by the trial judge, and he's not going to have any success if he goes to the Court of Appeal, which is bound by the decision of the Supreme Court."[72]

Stanley Barrett, in his study of the right wing in Canada, distinguishes between the radical right and the fringe right. The former element is composed of white supremacists, often violent individuals strongly connected with American militia groups. He places Zundel in this category because of the reverence in which he is held by right-wing extremists worldwide and because of his blatant neo-Nazi views. Keegstra, however, is a more marginal figure, in Barrett's opinion. He is not violent, is not part of the international network, and thus is considered to be on the fringe. Yet Keegstra's actions were just as insidious – maybe more so – than Zundel's. The Alberta teacher had a captive audience of thousands of young minds for many years. They had no choice but to listen to his lies and regurgitate them in order to pass. They were not given access to accurate historical accounts, and many retained the racist perspective foisted upon them. Zundel's audience, in contrast, has a choice. He can be, and is, rebutted publicly. When Keegstra's students and former students were shown films depicting the atrocities, or attended the student symposium held at the University of British Columbia, or were flown by the League to see for themselves the sites of mass murder, some maintained that these were fakes designed to convince the world of a great hoax. The impact of the Keegstra affair on the Canadian Jewish community hardened its resolve to educate the public about the Holocaust and to use all of its resources to press for legal action against those who would deny that the event had occurred. The most notable example was Congress's efforts to have Malcolm Ross removed from the classroom. Ross, a mathematics teacher in Moncton, New Brunswick, had written books denying the Holocaust and warning of a Jewish conspiracy for world domination. Although he did not preach his views to his students, his presence in the classroom had a chilling effect. After several years of legal wrangling, Ross was finally given non-teaching duties in 1991.

THE NATIONAL GATHERING OF SURVIVORS

At the American gathering of Holocaust survivors in Washington in 1983, several Canadians present decided that a similar event should be held in their adopted country. The idea was taken to a group of the second generation in Toronto, where it was fleshed out. The project was then presented and adopted at the Congress plenary. The gathering was to be held in conjunction with Yom Hashoah and the fortieth anniversary of the liberation of the concentration camps. A committee was established, headed by Aba Beer, the chair of the NHRC. The committee had three issues to deal with: site, funding, and program.[73]

For almost a year, preparations for the gathering were mired in a simmering dispute for primacy within the leadership of the survivor community. For two decades there had been an ongoing tussle between survivors in Toronto and in Montreal over which community had made the greatest contribution. Toronto survivors were proud of their opposition to neo-Nazi groups, beginning in the early 1960s, and their ability to move Congress to take a more public and vocal stance against this scourge. In the early 1980s they felt that Toronto had become the Canadian centre for education about the Holocaust. Montreal survivors were equally proud that they had created the first survivor organization and the first Holocaust memorial, and that they were in the forefront of the NHRC. Consequently, relations became strained over where the gathering should take place and who should be in charge. Ultimately, it was resolved to hold the event in Ottawa. That city was neutral territory, the nation's capital, and a commitment had already been received from the developers of the National Convention Centre to house the gathering. The co-chairs for the event were Nathan Leipciger of Toronto and Mendel Good of Ottawa. Hindy Friedman, of the second-generation group and a professional planner, was hired as director.[74]

At an organizational meeting held in Kingston, equidistant from Toronto, Ottawa, and Montreal, a set of objectives was developed. They were to gather survivors and their children from across the country; to recognize the contribution of Canada in the struggle against fascism; to show appreciation to Canada for providing survivors with the opportunity to build new lives; to raise Canadian consciousness about racism and discrimination; to commemorate the six million; and to express solidarity with the Jewish people and with Israel.[75]

Having set its objectives, the committee now had to raise funds. Traditionally, unless one donor provided all or the bulk of funding for a project, the procedure was to secure a token amount of seed money from an organization and then build on that by going to the community. The committee, as an ad hoc body of Congress, understandably went to the parent organization and asked for $10,000, which would be returned if the event showed a profit. Congress officers initially refused the request, but eventually, under pressure from Milton Harris, Congress president and a supporter of the gathering, the money was provided. Nevertheless, survivors felt offended. As Dr Robert Krell puts it, "I was pissed off because we were a committee of Congress and were denied the money."[76]

The Gathering of Holocaust Survivors and Their Children was held on 28–30 April 1985, between the designated date for Yom Hashoah and VE day. At the convention centre a survivors' village was set up so that survivors and their offspring could meet. Some survivors located people that they had not seen since the war. The commemorative aspect of the program featured Madame Justice Rosalie Abella, who gave the opening address. A ceremony was held at the national cenotaph, where a wreath was laid. Speakers also included Elie Wiesel, Minister of Finance Michael Wilson, John Turner, the leader of the opposition, and Edward Broadbent, the leader of the NDP. Education sessions dealt with the Holocaust and its contemporary implications with respect to universal human rights, Nazi war criminals, and Holocaust deniers. Workshops on these issues were led by community leaders, academics, and teachers. Professor Irwin Cotler, past president of Congress, was the plenary speaker on human rights, and Serge and Beate Klarsfeld, the French Nazi hunters, spoke about war criminals. A cultural program utilized art, music, and dance to depict the Holocaust. The final event was a cultural night, at which music composed especially for the gathering by noted Canadian composer Srul Irving Glick was performed.[77]

The organizers had hoped that 1,000 participants would attend. In fact, 2,700 showed up, representing almost 10 per cent of survivors and their children in Canada. The organizers had also hoped to recoup the $10,000 in seed money which had been grudgingly provided by Congress. The profit, after the money had been repaid, was $66,000. Some eight hundred volunteers worked on the event.[78] The numbers, however, tell only a small part of the story. The gathering was of tremendous significance for two reasons. First, it celebrated the position of the survivors as a force in the community, after a generation of breaking down barriers. Still, there was much work to be done. This fact was eloquently expressed by Irwin Cotler, a child of Canadian Jews, in a commentary addressed to the community.

The first ever – indeed, perhaps last ever – National Gathering of Holocaust Survivors and Canadian Jews must be an act of remembrance and of witness, of fidelity to memory and fidelity to truth. For the *cri de coeur* that finds expression whenever Jews gather, the angst that screams silently in the mind and heart of Holocaust survivors wherever they may be ... is not only that their death would not be redeemed, but that they would not even be remembered; that those who were then indifferent to their fate would now be indifferent to their memory; that the most unspeakable horror in human history would not only be forgotten, but, in a land that one could not contemplate let alone speak of, the Holocaust would be denied; that the murderers of children would continue to go free.[79]

The second important aspect was that the gathering was held during several heady months of anxiety and celebration by the Jewish community. In February the Canadian government had ended forty years of silence and obfuscation about the presence of Nazi war criminals in the country. A few weeks later a jury convicted Ernst Zundel of knowingly disseminating false news about the Holocaust. While the gathering was taking place, a jury was hearing evidence against James Keegstra for promoting racism. Several weeks after the gathering the Toronto community celebrated the opening of the Holocaust Education and Memorial Centre. During these months the legacy of the Holocaust was the focal issue in the Jewish community. It had become part of the community's collective memory by various routes – commemoration of the victims, remembrance of Liberation, education, the conviction of Holocaust deniers, and the investigation of war criminals. Such a focus would not have been possible to the same degree on the thirtieth anniversary of Liberation, and it would have been outside the realm of comprehension on the twentieth anniversary. In 1985, however, the confluence of local and international events, together with the efforts of survivors and their supporters, had mobilized the community. That such an outcome had been achieved was possible primarily because Canadian Jews had embraced the legacy of the Holocaust as one defining pillar of their identity.

Conclusion:
The Holocaust is not Joseph

Now, at the beginning of the twenty-first century, scarcely a day has passed without a reference to the Holocaust. At this time,[1] several issues are in the forefront of world events. The German government is awarding $2.5 billion (U.S.) to survivors of slave-labour camps run by German industries. Approximately half the expected claimants are Jews. In a recent election in Austria, the centrist coalition of socialists and conservatives that had ruled the country for most of the postwar period was overturned by the rise of the extreme right-wing Freedom Party, led by Joerge Haider. Haider, who has praised the ss and whose parents were members of the Nazi party, has rocketed in popularity because of his thinly veiled attacks on minorities and immigrants. The new coalition has roused the condemnation of other Western nations, which claim that Austria has yet to admit its collaboration with the Third Reich, rather than its victimization. Pope John Paul II has just completed a trip to Israel and the Palestinian Authority. At Yad Vashem he decried the role of Christians in the persecution of Jews. This pope has made tremendous efforts to reconcile the two faiths and has consistently atoned for the sins committed by his followers. Yet he did not condemn the silence of the Catholic Church during the Holocaust, and he is sponsoring the beatification of Pope Pius XII, who was notably silent during the terror. In London a charge of libel has been brought by David Irving, a historian of World War II and an apologist for Hitler's role in the Holocaust, against another historian, Deborah Lipstadt, who wrote that he was a Holocaust denier. Irving's claim that his earnings have plummeted and that his career is in jeopardy are being heard by a judge. Reports continue to spill out of Rwanda, the Sudan, and the former Yugoslavia about mass murders against identifiable nationalities in recent years, raising comparisons to the Holocaust.

In Canada a tribunal of the Human Rights Commission is in its second year of hearing charges laid against Ernst Zundel for transmitting antisemitic materials on the Internet. But despite the proliferation of distortions of the Holocaust, awareness of the event is growing. Last year the Ontario government passed a bill proclaiming a day for the memorialization of the Holocaust, an initiative that was copied by the legislature of Prince Edward Island. Ontario's Ministry of Education has included "specific expectations" on the Holocaust in its revised secondary school curriculum. Textbook publishers are feverishly working to add materials that meet these guidelines. In Toronto the Holocaust Education and Memorial Centre is undergoing a major expansion. Its Holocaust Remembrance Committee is actively working with members of the Rwandan community by helping survivors of the genocide of 1994 and their families to adapt to life in Canada. Holocaust survivors have been in the forefront of this project. In Montreal, plans have been unveiled for the erection of a new Holocaust Memorial Centre adjacent to the federation building. The current space, in the basement of the Jewish Public Library, has become unsuitable for the demands placed by the public. The centre refused entry to Haider on his recent, unscheduled visit to Montreal because he would have used the opportunity to remake his tarnished image.

Scholarship in the field has continued to expand. York University in Toronto has announced that a chair in Holocaust studies, the first in Canada, would be forthcoming. A recent issue of the journal *Holocaust and Genocide Studies*, published three times a year, listed approximately 330 new books on the Holocaust,[2] a record that is by no means exhaustive. When I formally began this research seven years ago, nothing had been written on the impact of the Holocaust in Canada or the United States in the post-war era. *The World Reacts to the Holocaust* appeared in 1996, with chapters on twenty-four countries, including these two. The release in 1999 of Peter Novick's *The Holocaust in American Life* and *The Americanization of the Holocaust*, edited by Hilene Flanzbaum has opened up this area further.

The Holocaust has become part of our social discourse for two reasons. First, it is a defining event of our time. Some have referred to it as a caesura – in historical terms, a rupture with the past. In this sense, the Holocaust has shaken our notion of progress in Western civilization and those attributes which we ascribe to modern times, such as democracy and the protection of human liberties. One speaks of a "post-Holocaust theology," the absence of a vocabulary to describe the event, and a reordering of ethics and morals. Auschwitz has become synonymous with the most abhorrent behaviour of individuals and states. In a "post-Auschwitz world" any evil can occur because the precedent has been set. Second, the legacy of the Holocaust is invoked daily in reference to current events. The International War Crimes Tribunal in the Hague for the prosecution of perpetrators of brutality in the conflict in the former Yugoslavia and the Truth and Reconciliation hearings in Johannesburg for the practitioners of apartheid are rooted in the Nuremberg tribunal. Comparisions are justifiably made between the atrocities in Rwanda and the Holocaust, and with less justification in countless other conflicts where human rights are violated. Unfortunately, the word "Holocaust" is also used to describe developments which have nothing in common with the murder of European Jews.

Two questions have formed the basis of this study. The first is, What was the impact of the Holocaust on the Canadian Jewish community? The research has shown conclusively that the community was forced to confront the event. As a result, its historical memory was recreated. The established Jews, defined as those who were born or raised in Canada prior to World War II, had created a historical memory of their European roots that did not account for the advances made by European Jews in the interwar years. Instead, their memory was grounded in what they had experienced or were told about – essentially Jewish life before World War I. Further, they believed that all that the community was capable of doing to aid European Jews between 1933 and 1948 had been done. Lastly, they could not comprehend the enormity of the Holocaust, although they were aware of the tragedy not long after it unfolded. Consequently, a historical amnesia was apparent until 1960.

In the 1960s and early 1970s, however, the confidence of the community was shaken with the resurgence of antisemitism in Canada and abroad, the Eichmann trial, and the Arab-Israeli conflict. In response to these developments, the community took a more forceful and public stand against hate-mongers and increased its pressure on the Canadian government to investigate the presence of suspected Nazi war criminals. Demonstrations, including the infamous Allan Gardens riot, became commonplace. Although the Holocaust was not yet a pillar of ethnic identification, it had been recast in the community's collective memory because it served as a warning that the community had to publicly defy its detractors, be resolute in its lobbying to criminalize hate mongers, and avoid the delusion that it was immune from outbreaks of Judeo-phobia like those occurring in other parts of the world. Once the realization had set in that the legacy of the Holocaust was relevant to the current situation, the community undertook a concerted approach to commemorate and, more significantly, to educate. By 1985, Holocaust programs had become institutionalized across the country. When Canadian Jews were forced to confront the Holocaust, they had two choices: to recoil or to muster the fortitude to deal with the catastrophe. By choosing the latter course, they reordered the community agenda and recreated their historical memory.

The second question is, Why was this impact delayed for a generation? To a degree, the answer to the first question also applies to the second. One fact bears repeating: the community was not psychologically ready to deal with the Holocaust for a generation. What had happened was tragic, but it happened over there; it was not part of the world of Canadian Jews. Other reasons help to explain the delay. One was that their immediate priority was to support the establishment of Israel. A second was that the leaders of the community were still ostracized from the halls of power in the immediate post-war years, and while they may have received sympathetic hearings from politicians, they possessed little clout. This situation began to change in the 1950s. As the social and economic status of Canadians Jews was slowly elevated, they were perceived as "whitened Euro-ethnics." No longer were they the targets of systemic discrimination. The community had moved away from the political margins, as evidenced by the ability of Jewish leaders to persuade the government to launch the Cohen committee on hate propaganda and by Pearson's address on the twentieth anniversary of VE day. In the 1970s there were Jews in the federal cabinet, at the highest levels of the civil service, and on the Supreme Court. These developments were reflective of a community that was far more self-confident and united than it had been a generation earlier.

At the same time, as a new generation was reaching middle age, it faced a crisis of identity and commitment. Yes, the cohort born in the 1930s and 1940s were Canadians, and yes, they were Jews, but what did that mean? What differentiated them from other ethnic communities? In shedding the label of "immigrants" through acculturation and assimilation as "Canadians," they had lost their connection with their past. The traditional props of neighbourhood, language, discrimination by the majority, and institutions catering to specific ideological, religious, or secular needs had disappeared. This generation had no memory of that era and had little success in learning about it from their parents, who were more intent on forgetting the past than celebrating it. But as public displays of antisemitism in Canada and elsewhere proliferated, so did the new generation's sense of vulnerability. In searching for a connection with their roots, its members came to view the Holocaust as the end point of the earlier civilization and therefore a defining event in their lives. In fact, they were creating a historical memory without historical experience.[3] Moreover, the Holocaust had a utilitarian feature: it allowed Canadian Jews to differentiate themselves from other ethnic minorities. Indeed, by the mid-1980s they had created a civic religion based on a historical myth – that the Holocaust was the ultimate obscenity, but that redemption appeared in the creation of the state of Israel.[4]

The most important factor explaining the delayed impact, however, was the emergence of Holocaust survivors as a force in the community. The most politicized ones brazenly pressured community leaders to speak out on Jewish concerns in a forceful manner. Survivors often misread the initiatives taken by the establishment, and they overreacted to the perception that the community was vulnerable to the rantings of antisemites. Nevertheless, their views eventually had to be considered. In time, they were grudgingly admitted into the community mainstream. Once they had established this foothold, they were instrumental in bringing knowledge of the Holocaust to the community and pushing it to have charges brought against hatemongers and suspected war criminals. To summarize, the impact was delayed because of circumstances. For fifteen years (1945–60) the community was unable to confront the Holocaust because the event was too recent and outside its scope of comprehension, and because it was consumed with more urgent priorities. The transition occurred in the next fifteen years because the dynamics of Canadian society had changed, and so had the Jewish community. From the mid-1970s to the mid-1980s the combination of the momentum of the preceding period, the exposure given to the Holocaust, the efforts of the survivors, a more diverse group of leaders, and the search for meaning by a new generation led to the appropriation of the Holocaust as a pillar of ethnic identification. As circumstances changed, so did the collective memory of the event.

The task of the historian is to examine the past and, where appropriate, make connections with contemporary events, but it is not the historian's province to predict the future. Nonetheless, as this study examines the changing nature of historical memory, it is interesting to speculate on how the sensibilities of the Jewish community regarding the Holocaust in one generation may continue (or not) to exert that generation's influence on the next. One source of speculation is those interviewed for this book – individuals who have shaped the response to the Holocaust in the post-war era. I asked some of them to comment on what they foresaw as the legacy of the Holocaust in the beginning of the new millenium. Here are some their views.

Judge Sydney Harris presented the most provocative perspective. "I don't know that the Holocaust defines us. I just think that the Holocaust will become an event in history, such as the French Revolution ... I don't think the world will founder on antisemitism as it did in the thirties and forties ... Events in history are static, and they don't stay with us although generations overlap. But I don't think that the Canadian Jewish community is defined by the Holocaust, and I would be sad if it were ... The Holocaust may well define the European community, but in another hundred years it won't define them either, because there will be a new king who did not know Joseph, and the Holocaust is Joseph."[5]

Sam Lipshitz, the oldest person interviewed and the only one still living who was instrumental in informing the community about the Holocaust, offered this perspective. "It's a matter of seeking for your roots, of trying to find the history of your people, of trying to belong ... by trying some way to be Jewish. They [the young people of today] are trying in some way to associate with the history of the people. As with the Armenians, something that happened in 1915 is an alive issue."

Manuel Prutschi was born after the war. When asked what his grandchildren will remember, he answered: "It's an event of such catastrophic proportions that every Jew in the process of confronting his Judaism almost immediately comes up against the Holocaust and has to intellectually and emotionally deal with that. There's no way that will dissipate. It cannot but shape our attitudes, and it cannot but be ever-present in our minds and our memory."

Three survivors, Lou Zablow, Nathan Leipciger, and Sabina Citron, are among the most prominent orchestrators of Holocaust consciousness. Zablow responded to the question by commenting on three generations of post-war Jews. "I still believe people born before 1920 ... absolutely don't see their lives this way. For Saul Hayes, the Holocaust was as far away as the moon, till he died. It was the young people (the next generation) who changed ... There were a lot of Stephen Cummings ... The grandchildren, they get involved; they have a different perspective; they have no guilt feelings."

Leipciger placed the legacy of the Holocaust historical context. He responded: "I always fought [against the notion] that the Holocaust should be the central point of Jewish identity. I think that the centrality of Judaism has to be religion and Israel. We should not consider ourselves as the people of the Holocaust because I don't think Jews should be victimized by themselves ... I do not agree with Elie Wiesel, who says, 'I don't envy the last survivor because of the responsibility that will be on his shoulder to carry on the memory,' because that responsibility is on all of us, but it should not be the central defining point of our identity."

Citron anticipates that it is not the Holocaust that Jews will identify with, but rather, the lessons which the memory imparts. It is not a commitment to the Holocaust, she states, but "a commitment to justice. We hope that people will understand that above all else every Jew has the same rights as every other person and to stand up for their rights. This to me is crucial, and it's really the only thing worth fighting for."

What place will the Holocaust have in the collective memory of the community in 2020? Awareness of the event has become so powerful that it will not disappear. Although the survivors will have died, the historical record will still exist. In the last twenty years the Holocaust has become one of the most well documented events in modern history, and since 1985 the community's focus on the catastrophe has continued to escalate. In recent years the Jewish community has been sending teenagers and university students, both Jewish and non-Jewish, to Europe to see the sites of destruction. In twenty years they will be middle-aged and their memories will not have faded, although the community's commitment to pass on the legacy may have. To paraphrase Manuel Prutschi, to be Jewish means that confronting recent history is not an option. Despite Sydney Harris's assertion, the Holocaust is not Joseph. Unlike the new king of Egypt, who did not have the benefit of modern scholarship and advanced communication, people will not have forgotten the Holocaust.

This study has focused solely on the collective memory of Canadian Jews, but the pattern of historical amnesia followed by historical appropriation has been consistent with the experience of most other national Jewish communities. In a survey of American Jews taken in the early 1990s, those questioned ranked the Holocaust first as a symbol of Jewish identity. The High Holy Days were second, followed by American antisemitism.[6] In the 1998 "Annual Survey of American Jewish Opinion," the "remembrance of the Holocaust" was the most important activity related to Jewish identity.[7]

A much broader implication of Holocaust memory deserves a final comment. For an ethnic community to wrap its identity around its own victimization is counterproductive to its vitality. This attitude provides an excuse for self-flagellation, for the appropriation of suffering, and for exercising revenge on real and imagined enemies. To reduce Jewish identity to martyrdom would, in the words of Peter

Novick and Emil Fackenheim, provide Hitler with a "posthumous victory ... by making the Holocaust the emblematic Jewish experience."[8] Instead, by adopting the Holocaust as a pillar of ethnic identity, the Canadian Jewish community must utilize the universal lessons of the event to press for all-embracing human rights. Not to do so would be the ultimate injustice to the memory of the victims and to the community's determination to commemorate and learn about the destroyed Jewish civilization. As Robert Wistrich has written, "The Holocaust will remain an inextricable part of Israeli and Jewish consciousness, reinforced by the memory of persecution throughout Jewish history and the intensity of the Middle East conflict, but transforming it into a unifying myth carries with it the danger of isolationism and negative thinking."[9]

Notes

ABBREVIATIONS

CBC	Canadian Broadcasting Corporation
CJCA	Canadian Jewish Congress National Archives, Montreal
IOI	*Inter-Office Information* (CJC)
JCC	Jewish Canadiana Collection, JPLA
JHS/BC	Jewish Historical Society of British Columbia, Vancouver
JHS/WC	Jewish Historical Society of Western Canada, Winnipeg
JPLA	Jewish Public Library Archives, Montreal
MHMCA	Montreal Holocaust Memorial Centre Archives
NA	National Archives of Canada, Ottawa
OJA	Ontario Jewish Archives, Toronto
PAM	Provincial Archives of Manitoba, Winnipeg
ZIH	Zydowski Institut Historyczny, Warsaw

INTRODUCTION

1 Pierre Nora, "Between History and Memory: *Les Lieux de mémoire*," *Representations*, 26 (spring 1989): 8–9; cited in Gedi and Elam, "Collective Memory – What Is It?" 33.
2 Gedi and Elam, "Collective Memory – What Is It?" 47.
3 Friedländer, "Trauma, Transference and 'Working Through' in Writing the History of the *Shoah*," 43.

CHAPTER ONE

1   Quoted in Gutkin and Gutkin, *The Worst of Times, The Best of Times*, 74–6.
2   Interview with Sam Lipshitz, 3 October 1995, Toronto. See also Lipshitz's article, "On a Mission to Poland, Right after the War," in *Voice of Radom – Special Commemorative Issue*, 1992, in the Sam Lipshitz Papers, ZB, CJCA. For the events in Majdanek, see Marszalek, *Majdanek: The Concentration Camp in Lublin*, 188–9. According to Marszalek, the man executed during Lipshitz's visit was on the SS staff, but not the chief of the crematorium. The chief was Eric Muhsfeldt, who was executed in Cracow in 1947. According to H.M. Caiserman, who was the other Canadian in the delegation, the individual was a Commandant Hoffman. See "H.M. Caiserman's Report on Poland," *Congress Bulletin*, Caiserman Papers, DA 1, 4/1, 7, CJCA.
3   Gutkin and Gutkin, *The Worst of Times, The Best of Times*, 74–5.
4   For a comprehensive account of Canada's immigration policies toward Jews and the efforts by Jewish leaders to affect change in those policies, see Abella and Troper, *None Is Too Many*.
5   For the response by the Allies, see Gilbert, *Auschwitz and the Allies*; Kushner, *The Holocaust and the Liberal Imagination*. For the response in the United States see Bauer, *American Jewry and the Holocaust*; Breitman and Kraut, *American Refugee Policy and European Jewry, 1933–1945*; Feingold, *The Politics of Rescue*; Feingold, *Bearing Witness*; Friedman, *No Haven for the Oppressed*; Lipstadt, *Beyond Belief*; Wyman, *The Abandonment of the Jews*. For the response in Britain see Sherman, *Island Refuge*; Wasserstein, *Britain and the Jews of Europe, 1939–1945*. For the response in the Antipodes, see Blakeney, *Australia and the Jewish Refugees, 1933-1948*; Bartrop, *Australia and the Holocaust, 1933–1945*; Beaglehole, *A Small Price to Pay*. For the response in Newfoundland, see Bassler, *Sanctuary Denied*.
     Although these works differ in interpretation and vary in the depth of analysis, several themes are constant. Immigration policies of the Allies were designed to thwart the entry of refugees, especially Jews. The Jewish community in each country was fragmented and rather ineffectual in persuading its political leaders to change immigration policies and pressure the Nazis for a cessation of the initial persecutions and the later systematic murder of the Jews. Further, the communities were timid in taking more strident measures for fear of retribution by their fellow, non-Jewish citizens. In each country there was knowledge about the events several months after they were under way, but an unwillingness grounded in incomprehension for any sustained protest. For a summary of the general issue, see the introduction to Kushner, *The Holocaust and the Liberal Imagination*; for the American response, see the introduction to Feingold, *Bearing Witness*.

6 *Pathways to the Present: Canadian Jewry and the Canadian Jewish Congress* (Toronto: Canadian Jewish Congress, 1986), 8–9, CJCA; "CJC at 75," *Intercom* 13:1 (Spring 1994): 6–7, CJCA; interview with Ben Kayfetz, executive director of the Joint Community Relations Committee of Canadian Jewish Congress, 1947–84, 7 November 1995, Toronto.

7 Bercuson, *Canada and the Birth of Israel*; Bercuson, "The Zionist Lobby and Canada's Palestine Policy, 1941–1948." Bercuson maintains that the community's lobbying was of minor importance in Canada's ultimately supporting the end of the mandate.

8 For an overview of the Jewish community in Canada to 1920, see Tulchinsky, *Taking Root*. For a broader perspective, see Abella, *A Coat of Many Colours*. For general regional studies, the following are representative: Brown, *Jew or Juif?* Chiel, *The Jews of Manitoba*; Speisman, *The Jews of Toronto*. For a systematic demographic analysis of the community in the 1930s, see Rosenberg, *Canada's Jews*. The figures for 1939 are adapted from Rosenberg's data, from the 1941 census, and from Kage, *With Faith and Thanksgiving*, 259–261.

9 Rosenberg, *Canada's Jews*, 29–35.

10 Ibid., 71-9.

11 Ibid., 255.

12 Ibid., 136.

13 Ibid., 214.

14 Ibid., 162.

15 Ibid., 176.

16 Ibid., 185.

17 Ibid., 272.

18 Interview with Kalmen Kaplansky, 11 September 1995, Ottawa. See also Robinson, Anctil, and Butovsky, *An Everyday Miracle*, 11–21. In 1931, in the five wards around Boulevard Saint-Laurent, the Jewish population ranged between 55.9 per cent and 23.7 per cent, and in the city of Montreal, as compared with "greater Montreal," 5.9 per cent of the population was Jewish. In contrast, 7.3 per cent of Westmount and 7 per cent of NDG was Jewish, according to Rosenberg, *Canada's Jews*, 31–3.

19 Abella, *A Coat of Many Colours*, 192–4; Gutkin and Gutkin, *The Best of Times, The Worst of Times*, 15–25; Speisman, *The Jews of Toronto*, 336–40.

20 I have chosen the spelling "antisemitism," rather than conventional spellings (anti-semitism, anti-Semitism), because there is no phenomenon known as "semitism." "Semitic" refers specifically to a group of languages, one of which is Hebrew. Antisemitism, however, is a phenomenon, referring to hatred against Jews and persecutions against Jews because of perceived religious, political, social, biological, and ideological differences.

21 For studies of antisemitism in the interwar period, see the collection of essays in Davies, *Antisemitism in Canada*, especially Stephen Speisman, "Antisemitism in Ontario: The Twentieth Century"; Pierre Anctil, "Interlude of Hostility: Judeo-Christian Relations in Quebec in the Interwar Period, 1919–39"; Howard Palmer, "Politics, Religion and Antisemitism in Alberta, 1880–1950"; and Marilyn F. Nefsky, "The Shadow of Evil: Nazism and Canadian Protestantism." An expansion of this last essay is found in Davies and Nefsky, *How Silent Were the Churches?* For nativist and fascist movements, see Betcherman, *The Swastika and the Maple Leaf*; and Robin, *Shades of Right*.

22 Rosenberg, *Canada's Jews*, 303–5; Abella and Bialystok, "Canada."

23 Abella and Troper, *None Is Too Many*, 5–9. Palmer, "Reluctant Hosts," 309–12.

24 Robin, *Shades of Right*, 87–178; Betcherman, *The Swastika and the Maple Leaf*, 32–44, 99–147.

25 For an analysis of the antisemitism of Groulx and *Le Devoir* in the 1930s, see Delisle, *The Traitor and the Jew*. For a more conciliatory perspective, see Anctil, "Interlude of Hostility," *Antisemitism in Canada*, 156.

26 Robin, *Shades of Right*, 174–8.

27 Anctil, "Interlude of Hostility," *Antisemitism in Canada*, 144–5.

28 Levitt and Shaffir, *The Riot at Christie Pits*.

29 Robin, *Shades of Right*, 179–206; Betcherman, *The Swastika and the Maple Leaf*, 103–12.

30 Speisman, "Antisemitism in Ontario," in Davies *Antisemitism in Canada*, 119–29.

31 Henry Trachtenberg, "The Winnipeg Jewish Community in the Interwar Period, 1919–1939: Antisemitism and Politics," in *Jewish Life and Times*, vol. 3 (Winnipeg: Jewish Historical Society of Western Canada, 1983), 177–85, JHS/WC; Robin, *Shades of Right*, 197–206.

32 Palmer, *Patterns of Prejudice*. See also Robin, *Shades of Right*, 1–86, which focuses on the Ku Klux Klan in Saskatchewan in the 1920s.

33 Palmer, "Politics, Religion and Antisemitism in Alberta," in Davies, ed., *Antisemitism in Canada*, 171.

34 Ibid., 170–3.

35 Stingel, "Social Credit, Anti-Semitism, and Alberta's Jews," 1–2; courtesy of the author. See also Palmer, "Politics, Religion and Antisemitism in Alberta," in Davies, ed., *Antisemitism in Canada*, 172–82.

36 Robin, *Shades of Right*, 207–32; Zucchi, *Italians in Toronto*, 166–92.

37 Robin, *Shades of Right*, 233–64.

38 Abella, *A Coat of Many Colours*, 180.

39 Robin, *Shades of Right*, 109.

40 Anctil, "Interlude of Hostility," in Davies, ed., *Antisemitism in Canada*, 159.

41 Abella and Bialystok, "Canada," 757–8.
42 David Rome, "The National Story," in *Pathways to the Present*, 5–8;
   Report of the Executive Director, "Canada and the Great Catastrophe,"
   in the Congress *Bulletin*, 7:2 (Octobe, 1951): CJCA. Abella, *A Coat of Many
   Colours*, 188–91.
43 The JPRC changed its name to the Joint Community Relations Committee (JCRC) in the 1960s. See Montague Raisman, *Historical Capsule of Joint
   Public Relations Committee*, JCRC Papers, MG 8/S, 51/90, 1–2, OJA; *Joint
   Public Relations Committee and Constitution Agreement*, 3 September 1947,
   BB Papers, MG 28, V 133, 36/18, NA.
44 Abella and Troper, *None Is Too Many*, 9–26, 62–6.
45 Abella, *A Coat of Many Colours*, 191–5. For *landsmanschaften*, see Avrum
   Shtern, "Notes on *Landsmanschaften* in Canada," CJCA. For the Jewish
   press, see Levendal, *A Century of the Canadian Jewish Press*, 55–172. For
   the Jewish labour movement in Toronto, see Frager, *Sweatshop Strife*,
   181–217. For the role of women, see Frager, *Sweatshop Strife*, and Draper
   and Karlinsky, "Abraham's Daughters."
46 Abella and Troper, *None Is Too Many*, 65–6.
47 Quoted in Sefton, "The European Holocaust," 130-131.
48 There is a vast literature on the history of the Holocaust. Some authoritative works in English include Bauer, *A History of the Holocaust*; Dawidowicz, *The War against the Jews*; Gilbert, *The Holocaust*; Hilberg, *The
   Destruction of the European Jews*; and Yahil, *The Holocaust*.
49 Report of the National Executive Director, in "Canada and the Great
   Catastrophe," 10, CJCA. For the press reports in the United States, see
   Lipstadt, *Beyond Belief*. She writes that "by early 1942 it was clear that
   Jews would die not only because of terrible conditions but also as a
   result of massacres. But what the press did not yet know – and could
   not yet know – was that annihilation would not be haphazard but that
   this killing would culminate in a systematic program using 'modern'
   scientific methods and whose victims would include millions of Jews
   from every corner of the European continent" (157).
50 Lipstadt, *Beyond Belief*, 159–75. There is no comparable study of the
   press in Canada, but it may be assumed that the information available
   to American readers was also available to Canadian ones.
51 "Canada and the Great Catastrophe," 11.
52 Ibid., 12; Sefton, "The European Holocaust," 131.
53 Abella and Troper, *None Is Too Many*, 184–8.
54 Raymond Arthur Davies Papers, ZB, CJCA. The report contains some
   inaccuracies. About 400,000 people were killed in Majdanek, of whom
   approximately one-third were Jews. Davies might have been given the
   figures by Soviet authorities, who consistently over-stated the numbers
   of victims in Majdanek and Auschwitz, the two death camps that they

liberated. The killing of 18,000 killed on 3 November 1943 has been authenticated. The massacre's codename was *Erntefest* (Harvest Festival), and the event represents one of the two deadliest days in the Holocaust. See Marszalek, *Majdanek*, 130–3. The other was the massacre at Babi Yar, which killed 33,000 Jews in two days. See Ilya Ehrenburg and Vasily Grossman, *The Black Book*, 3–12. The estimates of 3 million Polish Jews and 5 million total were accurate at the time of the account.

55 Davies constantly harranged Saul Hayes to pay for his extravagant hotel and travel expenses in Moscow, where he was esconsed during the German retreat from the east. After his Montreal lecture, he returned to Moscow, from where he sent a letter asking for $20,000. Hayes replied that the funds could be better used for relief. In 1946 Davies created World News Services out of Toronto, whose letterhead listed offices worldwide. He hired Abraham Arnold as his associate editor. This venture soon expired. In 1954 Davies was found guilty of falsifying information for his Canadian passport. It stated that he had been born in Montreal as Raymond Arthur Davies. His real name was Rudolph Shohan, he had been born in South America, and he had been a member of the American Communist Party in the 1930s. He was sentenced to two years in prison. In 1977 he was implicated in the trial of a loan shark, Willie Obront, during the Quebec Commission on Organized Crime. Davies died in Montreal on 7 July 1985. (R.A. Davies Papers, ZB, CJCA; interview with Abraham Arnold, 30 May 1995, Montreal).

56 The Vrba-Wetzler report is cited in most studies of the Holocaust. See, for example, Yahil, *The Holocaust*, 638, and Bauer, *A History of the Holocaust*, 220. Large sections of the report are reprinted in Gilbert, *The Holocaust*, 376–7, 497–8, 516–7, 528–30, 648–9, 681, 700, 727. The summary is available in the Canadian Jewish Labour Committee, *Underground and on The Ground*, 31 December 1944, JLC Papers, MG 28, V 75, 7/15; NA. For the series of articles based on the report that were made available to the Canadian press, see the letter from Charles Clay, director of the Canadian Research and Editorial Institute to editors, 7 February 1945, and the articles written by Clay – "Nazi 'Death Factory,'" "The Gassing Chamber," and "The Burning" JLC Papers, ibid.

57 Summary Report (1942–1944), Sixth Plenary Session of Canadian Jewish Congress, 13–16, January 1945, Toronto, AB, Plenary Sessions Files, CJCA.

58 "Refugees Released from Camps," Ibid. "Jewish Internees – The Irony of Fate" and "The Japan Refugee Story" in "Canada and the Great Catastrophe," 14, 18, CJCA. An analysis of the interned refugees can be found in Draper, "The Accidental Immigrants" (unpublished PhD thesis). See also Draper, "The Accidental Immigrants: Canada and the Interned Refugees: Parts I and II," and "The Politics of Refugee Immigration."

59 Draper, "The Accidental Immigrants: Part II," 86–7.

60 Minutes of the Convention of the JLC, Montreal, 25–26 November 1944, JLC Papers, MG 28, V 75, 7/15, NA.

61 Shtern, "Notes on Landsmanschaften in Canada."

62 Quoted in Levendel, *A Century of the Canadian Jewish Press*, 163–9.

63 Bauer, *Jews for Sale?*

64 Abella and Troper, *None Is Too Many*, 148, 187.

65 See note 5.

66 Elie Wiesel, *Night*, 12–20.

67 Sloan, *Notes from the Warsaw Ghetto*, 82, 309–44. In the first reference, written on 8 November 1940, Ringelblum stated: "There's been the growth of a strong sense of historical consciousness recently. We tie in fact after fact from our daily experience with events in history. We are returning to the Middle Ages ... The Jews created another world for themselves in the past, living in it forgot the troubles around them, allowed no one from the outside to come in. As for parallels: The present expulsion is one of the worst in Jewish history, because there were always cities of refuge. Someone said to me: 'It's bad to read Jewish history, because you see that the good years were few and far between. There were always troubles and pogroms.'" In the second reference cited, the journal entries are from July to December 1942, during the liquidation of 90 per cent of the ghetto in the death camps. Ringelblum wrote of the murder of 300,000 people (the approximate number transported in those months) and referred specifically to transports to "Treblinki" (*sic*) on Yom Kippur, 22 September (320–1).

68 "News Release: Press Office of Canadian Jewish Congress" (n.d.), CJC Papers, War Efforts, 1933–1950 JCC, JPLA; Egit, *Grand Illusion*, 36.

69 Dobroszycki, *Survivors of the Holocaust in Poland*, 6–8.

70 Interview with Sam Lipshitz.

71 Hayes to Laurent Beaudry, Department of External Affairs, 24 October 1945, 1945, 11/182, ZA, CJCA.

72 Hayes to A.H. Aronovitch, Board of the Jewish Welfare Fund, Winnipeg, 28 December 1945, 1945, 1/12, ZA, CJCA.

73 For Lipshitz's endorsement, see the reports of meetings of the National Executive Committee of CJC, 14 October 1945, and the National Dominion Council on 25 November 1945, 1945, 11/182, ZA, CJCA; interview with Lipshitz.

74 This was the depiction provided by his biographer. Ben Kayfetz, the long-time executive director of community relations for Congress, disagrees. He attributes Caiserman's business success to his wife. Caiserman, according to Kayfetz, had little aptitude for business and devoted his energy to the community (author's discussion with Kayfetz).

75 Y. Medres, "H.M. Caiserman – 10 yor nokh zayn toyt" (10 years after his death), *Dos Vort* (Montreal); quoted in Pierre Anctil, "H.M. Caiserman:

Yiddish as a Passion," in Robinson et al., *An Everyday Miracle*, 80. See also Rome and Figler, *Hannaniah Meir Caiserman – A Biography*. For the mission to Poland, see chapter 25, "Confrontation in Poland," 289–97.

76 Interview with Lipshitz. "Lipshitz, Sam," in Gottesman, *Who's Who in Canadian Jewry*, 408.

77 The May figure is found in the report of the Centralny komitet Zydow Polskich (Central Committee of Polish Jews), tabela no. 1 (15 *czerwa* [June], 1945): 2, Caiserman Papers, 5/4, CJCA. The July figure is quoted in Davies to Hayes, 18 July 1945, CA 23/198 F, CJCA. It appears to be an overestimate. The December figure is found in "Situation of Jews in Poland," Central Committee of Polish Jews – 1944/1945, Caiserman Papers, 4/1, CJCA.

78 Dobroszycki, *Survivors of the Holocaust in Poland*, 5.

79 Steinlauf, *Bondage to the Dead*, 46–8. Bergman, *Jewish Historical Institute*. For the establishment of the committee and its first years of operations, see CKZP Papers, *Prezydium* 1945, 303/1, k.186, ZIH.

80 "Situation of Jews in Poland," "Jego Eminencja Ksadz Kardynal Hlond o tradedji zydowskeij" (His Eminence Father Cardinal Hlond on the Jewish Tragedy) (Posen, n.d., approximately 15 December 1945), Caiserman Papers, 5/4, CJCA.

81 Report, Meeting with the Central Committee of Polish Jews, Warsaw, 17 December 1945, Caiserman Papers, 5/4, CJCA; handwritten notes on the trip, ZA, 1945, 1/12, CJCA.

82 "Situation of Jews in Poland," 3, Caiserman Papers, 5/4, CJCA.

83 Report of the Warsaw Meeting, 17 December 1945 (see note 81).

84 The meeting in Lodz occurred on 27 December 1945, and the one in Bialystok on 18 January 1946; see Caiserman *Papers*, 4/2, CJCA.

85 ZA, 1945, 1/12, CJCA. For the Jewish republic in Silesia, see Egit, *Grand Illusion*, 44–114; for the meeting with Caiserman and Lipshitz, see 56. Kayfetz finds Caiserman's remark perplexing. He remembers him as being an unabashed Zionist.

86 Caiserman to Hayes, 3 February 1945, ZA, 1945, 1/12A, CJCA. The first press release of the trip came from Caiserman's report from London, published in the *Canadian Jewish Chronicle*, 15 February 1946, 2, MG 28, V 63, M4181, NA.

87 "H.M. Caiserman's Report on Poland," *Congress Bulletin*, March 1946, 6–7, Caiserman Papers, 4/1, CJCA. Rome and Figler, *Hannaniah MeirCaiserman*, 294–5, report that Caiserman "brought with him *thousands* of personal letters from the survivors of the massacre to their relatives overseas" (emphasis added). Caiserman's use of statistics is misleading. While only 3 per cent of the pre-war Jewish population were "left" in Poland, another 7 per cent were in other European countries, mostly in the Soviet Union.

88 "J.D.C. Aid Vital to Jews in Poland, H.M. Caiserman, Canadian Jewish Leader, Reports after Two-Month Inspection Tour" (n.d.), Caiserman Papers, 4/2, CJCA.

89 Hurwic-Nowakowska, *A Social Analysis of Postwar Polish Jewry*, 76–85, tables 8 and 9.

90 ZA, 1945, 11/182, CJCA. See also interviews with Lipshitz in the *Canadian Jewish Chronicle*, 8 March 1946, 7, and Caiserman's report in the *Canadian Jewish Chronicle*, 15 March 1946, 6. There is no further mention in the *Chronicle* about the delegation.

91 H.M. Caiserman, "When Canadian Jewry Will Meet in Open Congress" (n.d., approximately May 1947), Caiserman Papers, 3/2, CJCA.

92 A.B. Bennett, "The Last Syllable," *Canadian Jewish Chronicle*, March 22 1946, 5, NA; see also 5 April 1946, 5.

93 Caiserman Papers, 5/4, CJCA. H. M. Caiserman, "A Reply" (n.d.) to Lipshitz's comments, *Montreal Star*, 7 February 1946.

94 Proceedings of the Seventh Plenary, Plenary Sessions Files, CJCA.

95 This assessment of Caiserman's standing in Congress at the time is provided by Janice Rosen, chief archivist of the CJC, and Irving Abella, a historian and past president of CJC.

96 Interview with Lipshitz.

97 For the Kielce pogrom, see Dobroszycki, *Survivors of the Holocaust in Poland*, 20–7; Meducki, "The Pogrom in Kielce on 4 July, 1946," 158–69; and Gilbert, *Atlas of the Holocaust*, 241. For documents and analysis of attacks on Jews, see Cala and Datner-Spiewak, *Dzieje Zydow w Polsce*, 15–74.

98 Marrus, *The Unwanted*, 314–24, 331–39.

99 Paul Trepman, "The Voice of the Remnant of Jewry," in *Unzer Sztyme*, Paul Trepman Papers, box 2, JPLA. For a depiction of the camp, see "Passover in Bergen-Belsen," *Canadian Jewish Chronicle*, 12 April 1946, 13, NA.

100 Interview with Kayfetz, 7 November 1995.

101 Bauer, *Flight and Rescue*.

102 Hayes to King, 17 July 1946, CA, 29/290B–300, CJCA.

103 Abella and Troper, *None Is Too Many*, 190–237.

104 Nancy Tienhara, "Canadian Views on Immigration and Population – An Analysis of Post-War Gallup Polls," unpublished paper for the *Green Paper on Immigration – A Report of the Canadian Immigration and Population Study* (Ottawa, 1974), 59; quoted in Draper, "The Accidental Immigrants – Part II," 11.

105 Adapted from Kage, *With Faith and Thanksgiving*, 260.

106 Proceedings of the Seventh Plenary, Plenary Sessions Files, CJCA.

107 The Workmen's Circle helped trade unionists in Poland and Germany. *Landsmanschaften* and other organizations also aided the relief effort.

Aid was sent by most of these groups, including the United Council of Polish Jews of Montreal, the Federation of Polish Jews of Canada (an umbrella organization of a number of societies), the Radomer Mutual Benefit Society, and the Stashover Young Men's Society. Another example was the Bialystoker Centre of Montreal, which was established in 1943, with three hundred members, when news of the liquidation of the Bialystok ghetto was revealed. It was connected to sister organizations in the United States and Australia and was able to obtain five hundred permits to bring refugees to Melbourne. The extent to which these societies were part of the centralized CJC/UJRA campaign is not clear. See Workmens' Circle of Montreal, Meyer London Branch 151, *Souvenir Book* (Montreal, 1957), ZC, Workmen's Circle Papers; Shtern, "Notes on Landsmanschaften"; Bialystoker Centre Papers, box 1, By-laws, minutes, JPLA.

108 Salsberg was a Labour-Progressive member of the Ontario legislature who went to Germany and Poland in December 1947 on a fact-finding mission. See Salsberg to Hayes, 12 December 1947, CA 29/300, CJCA, and Egit, *Grand Illusion*, 56.

CHAPTER TWO

1 Hawkins, *Canada and Immigration*, 91.
2 Proceedings of the Seventh Plenary, 31 May – 2 June 1947, 43, Plenary Sessions Files, CJCA.
3 Ibid., 38–9.
4 According to Joseph Kage, the demographer of Jewish immigration, 1,100 orphans emigrated up to the end of 1948. Under the Group Movement Plan, 2,136 tailors and 500 furriers, of whom 60 per cent were Jewish, were given approval to emigrate to Canada. Kage further estimates that 300 Jewish domestics gained admission under this plan. The total number who actually arrived is unclear. In his address to the 1949 plenary session of CJC, Monroe Abbey presented the figure of 2,994 Jewish persons, including the families of the workers, who had come under this scheme. Kage fixes the number of displaced persons who arrived between 1947 and 1950 as 98,057, of whom 11,064 were Jewish, the third ethnic group in rank of admissions, after Poles (23,900) and Ukrainians (19,215). In that period, the total number of Jewish immigrants was 17,914, based on the entry via ocean ports and immigration via the United States. This figure refers to the fiscal year ending 31 March. It is not clear how many actually were European refugees, and of these how many were Holocaust survivors. Given the times and the likelihood that almost all of the European refugees were survivors and their children born after Liberation, an estimate of 17,000 survivors

seems reasonable. But not all of the refugees remained. Kage notes that the net Jewish immigration from 1946 to 1956 was 40,066, but when the yearly figures are added, the total comes to 46,053. Therefore, approximately six thousand (15 per cent) of the immigrants left Canada after arrival. Consequently, an estimated 15,000 to 16,000 survivors and their families came to Canada between 1947 and 1950 and remained here. Between 1911 and 1914, 29,362 Jews had emigrated to Canada. See Kage, *With Faith and Thanksgiving*, 124–9, 259, 260, 262. For Monroe Abbey's speech, see Proceedings of the Eighth Plenary Session, 22–24 October 1949, 8, Plenary Sessions Files, CJCA.

5 Rome, *Pathways to the Present*, 8.

6 Hawkins, *Canada and Immigration*, 92–3.

7 Ibid., 81–3; Abella and Troper, *None Is Too Many*, 229–31.

8 Hawkins, *Canada and Immigration*, 84–8; Abella and Troper, *None Is Too Many*, 239–41.

9 "Press Opinion on Immigration," CJC, 3 October 1946, JLC Papers, 16/2, Correspondence, 1946, NA.

10 Speech by Georges Vanier; reprinted in Troper and Draper, *Archives of the Holocaust*, 15: 340–5.

11 Claxton to King, ibid., 351–5.

12 Norman Robertson, director of External Affairs, to the director of Immigration, ibid., 358–62. Hume Wrong, Department of External Affairs, to the minister of Mines and Immigration, ibid., 366–69.

13 Wing Commander J.W.P. Thompson to Colonel Seaman Morley Scott, ibid., 387–8.

14 Louis Rosenberg to Saul Hayes, memorandum on a speech by Liquori Lacombe, member for Laval-Two Mountains, ibid., 386.

15 Nancy Tienhara, "Canadian Views on Immigration and Population"; quoted in Draper, "The Accidental Immigrants – Part II," 11.

16 Abella and Troper, *None Is Too Many*, 246.

17 Bamberg camp, Germany, 10 June 1947, to the Bialystoker Relief Committee in New York, Bialystoker Center Papers, box 1, file By-Laws, minutes, JPLA.

18 "Tragedy Marked Early Efforts to Rescue 1,000 Orphans in 1942," *Congress Bulletin* (Montreal, August 1947), Seventh Plenary, 63, Plenary Sessions Files, CJCA. For an account of the collaboration between French officials and the Germans regarding the deportation of Jews, see Marrus and Paxton, *Vichy France and the Jews*.

19 Lappin, *The Redeemed Children*, 12–14.

20 *IOI*, no. 144A (no date listed, but marked May 1947), CJCA.

21 *IOI*, no. 148 (8 May 1947), 2.

22 *IOI*, no. 170 (12 June 1947), correspondence between Irwin Rosen, head of the JDC immigration department in Paris, and Saul Hayes.

23 Lappin, *The Redeemed Children*, 26–7; "Congress Enlisting Resources of Community Organizations; Accepted Full Responsibilities," *Congress Bulletin*, August 1947, 64, CJCA.

24 "General Features of Planning Project for Immigration, Reception and Placement of 1000 Orphaned Children" (PC 1647), June 1947, *101*, no. 170.

25 Lappin, *The Redeemed Children*, chap. 4; "First Group of Refugee Youths Coming," *Congress Bulletin* (Montreal), August 1947, 63, CJCA.

26 Lappin, *The Redeemed Children*, 144.

27 Ibid., 145.

28 Memorandum of the Jewish Labour Committee to the Canadian Jewish Congress, 11 July 1946, JLC Papers, 16/2, NA; Hayes to Shane, 16 July 1946, ibid.

29 "Shane, Bernard," in Gottesman, *Who's Who in Canadian Jewry*, 434.

30 Joint Brief in Behalf of the Ladies Cloak and Suit Industry of the Dominion of Canada to the minister of mines and resources (Immigration Branch), Ottawa,18 March 1947, JLC Papers, 16/1, NA. See also the plea from David Dunkelman of Tip Top Tailors to Humphrey Mitchell, minister of labour, 23 April 1947, in Troper and Draper, *Archives of the Holocaust*, 15: 397.

31 Correspondence, 17 July 1947, JLC Papers, 16/3, NA.

32 Kage, *With Faith and Thanksgiving*, 126–7; Abella and Troper, *None Is Too Many*, 257–68; Monroe Abbey, "Needle Trades Workers," Proceedings of the Eighth Plenary, 22–24 October 1949, Plenary Sessions Files, CJCA.

33 Interview with Kaplansky. Humphrey Mitchell, minister of labour, authorizing Bernard Shane to work with members of the Department of Labour to select men and women in the displaced persons' camps, 6 September 1947, JLC Papers, 16/1, NA; J.P. Sigvaldason, administrative secretary, Office of the High Commissioner for Canada, London, granting permission for Shane, Gurbst (Herbst), and Solomon to enter the British and American zones in Germany, 18 September 1947, JLC Papers, 16/1, NA.

34 Memoranda of meetings, 21–22 September 1947; Enkin to MacNamara, 19 November 1947, JLC Papers, 16/1, NA.

35 The series appeared between 20 February and 16 April 1948 in the *Canadian Jewish Chronicle*, NA. See also Shane to Moshe Lewis, 4 October 1947, on his findings in Hanover and Bergen-Belsen, JLC Papers, 7/23, NA.

36 Phelan to MacNamara, 11 March 1948, JLC Papers, 16/1, NA.

37 Salsberg to Hayes, reprinted in Troper and Draper, *Archives of the Holocaust*, 15: 394.

38 David Lewis to Moshe Lewis, 8 July 1948, JLC Papers, 16/7, NA. Hayes was also lobbying MacNamara on the discrimination against Jewish domestics. He wrote, "If it is true that Canadian Government officials refuse to entertain applications on the ground that 'Jews do not make

good domestics' or simply 'that Jews are not eligible' then this is either supererogation, or worse – rank discrimination" (Hayes to MacNamara, 5 January 1948, reprinted in Troper and Draper, *Archives of the Holocaust*, 15: 399–400.

39 Kage, *With Faith and Thanksgiving*, 260.

40 Marrus, *The Unwanted*, 323.

41 Abbey, Address to the Eighth Plenary Session, Plenary Session Files, CJCA.

42 Winnipeg Jewish Welfare Fund Papers, 3511/30, PAM.

43 For the JIAS conference, see *Canadian Jewish Chronicle*, 23 January 1948, 12. For the letter from Lewis to Solkin, see JLC Papers, 7/24, NA.

44 In Canada, Kaplansky became involved in the labour movement, the CCF, and the Jewish Workmen's Circle. He was appointed director of international affairs of the CLC in the 1950s and became active in United Nations human rights programes. After his retirement he was appointed to the refugee board, named an adviser to Indian and Northern Affairs, and received an honorary doctorate from the University of Ottawa. Kalmen Kaplansky died in 1998. (Diane Koven, "Kaplansky Was a Leader in Labour Movement," *Canadian Jewish News*, 5 February 1998, 24).

45 Interview with Kaplansky.

46 JLC Papers, 16/10, 16/11, NA; author's unrecorded conversations with Louis and Helen Lenkinski, 1987–95, and with Bob (Berek) Lenkinski, 1999. After arriving in Toronto with no knowledge of English, Louis Lenkinski mastered the language, moved through the union ranks, and eventually became the executive assistant to the director of the Ontario Federation of Labour. He was an adviser on human rights to the premiers of Ontario for four decades, and after his official retirement, he took on many volunteer duties. These included an appointment to the Ontario Human Rights Commission, where he became associate director, membership on the United Way of Toronto, and the presidency of the Joint Community Relations Committee of the Ontario Region of the CJC. Louis Lenkinski died in 1995. (Paul Lungen, "Congress Leader Lenkinski Remembered," *Canadian Jewish News*, 29 June 1995, 4; Manuel Prutschi, "A Deep Commitment to Jewish community," ibid).

47 12,460 Jews came to Canada between 1 April 1947 and 31 March 1949; see Kage, *With Faith and Thanksgiving*, 261.

48 Until recently, there was no study made of this period of transition within the established community. With the publication of Gerald Tulchinsky's *Branching Out*, we have a more comprehensive understanding of these years. See chapter 10, "Post-War Adjustments, 1945–1960," 261–87. I have relied on interviews with Canadian Jews. Ben Kayfetz and Philip Givens from Toronto, Kalmen Kaplansky from

Montreal, and Harry Gutkin from Winnipeg talked about these changes. See chapter 3 for elaboration. See also Gutkin and Gutkin, *The Worst of Times, the Best of Times,* a profile of Winnipeg Jews born between 1910 and 1930, which documents how their lives differed from those of their immigrant parents and grandparents; Robinson, et al., introduction to *An Everyday Miracle,* which touches on the decline of this culture after World War II; Abella, *A Coat of Many Colours,* 214–22.

49 For an expansion on these attitudes, see chapter 3. Silver's comments were reported in the *Jewish Chronicle,* 3 September 1948, 6, NA.

50 H.L. Lurie, executive director, Council of Jewish Federations and Welfare Funds, to the Survey Committee (Saul Hayes, executive director, Monroe Abbey and Lavy Becker of Montreal, and Arthur Gelber and Gurston Allen of Toronto), 13 October 1949, in Mary Palevsky, "Report On Survey of Jewish Refugee Settlement in Canada for the Canadian Jewish Congress," October 1949, JCC, CJC *Papers,* file "War Efforts, 1933–1950," JPLA.

51 I am indebted to Ben Kayfetz for guiding me through this labyrinth (interview, Toronto, 14 May 1996). Ben Lappin also provided essential information in my interview with him.

52 Interview with Kayfetz; Palevsky, "Report On Survey of Jewish Refugee Settlement in Canada," 22, JPLA.

53 Palevsky, "Report On Survey of Jewish Refugee Settlement in Canada," 22–3, JPLA; my thanks to Ben Kayfetz for assistance in interpreting the meaning.

54 Ibid., 10–11, 35–6; Kayfetz, "Ontario Region," in Rome, *Pathways to the Present,* 33–4.

55 Information provided by Ben Kayfetz. For information on the houses purchased see Minutes of the meeting of the Executive Committee of the CJC (Central Region), 23 June 1950, 1–2, Executive Committee Papers, MG 8, A2, OJA. At this meeting it was reported that twenty of the houses had been sold to the newcomers, many of whom were the tenants. This information provides one indication of the rapid economic adjustment made by some refugees to their new surroundings. The remaining houses were transferred for administrative purposes to JIAS under the supervision of the Housing Committee.

56 Minutes of Meeting re Survey on Refugees, Montreal, 19 April 1949, in "Response to Palevsky Report,"ZA, 1949, 1/2, CJCA.

57 Minutes of the Conference of Community and Professional Workers Devoted to Social Welfare, Toronto, 12 June 1949, "Social Services [for Refugees] 1948–1950," CA, 36/355, CJCA.

58 Palevsky, "Report On Survey of Jewish Refugee Settlement in Canada," 2, JPLA.

59 Ibid., 2–8.

60 Ibid., 10.
61 Ibid., 14.
62 Allen to Hayes, 4 November 1949, ZA, 1949, 1/2, CJCA; Hayes's hand-written comments, on each of Allen's points regarding Palevsky's recommendations, ibid., not dated.
63 Gelber to Hayes, 22 November 1949, ibid.
64 Lappin to Hayes, 15 December 1949, ibid.
65 Daniel Drutz, director of UJRA (Central Region), to A.E. Gelber, chairman of UJRA (Central Region), 25 January 1950, Minutes of Central Region Executive, 1950, Central Region Executive Papers, OJA.
66 Interview with Kayfetz, 14 May 1996.
67 Interview with Ben Lappin, Herzliya, Israel, 20 August 1994.
68 This view has been perpetuated in Congress publications. In Rome, *Pathways to the Present*, a survey of Jewish life published in conjunction with the 1986 plenary, a rosy picture is painted with respect to relief, rescue, rehabilitation, and absorption; see 8–9, 14, 32–4, 70–1, 88, 91.
69 One indication of the revivified traditional immigrant self-help network in the early 1950s was the renaissance of the *landsmanshaften*. The first groups of survivors rekindled existing societies or started new ones that helped integrate later waves of survivors. See Giberovitch, "The Contributions of Montreal Holocaust Survivor Organizations to Canadian Jewish Communal Life," 66–102. See also chapter 3 for further amplification of this development.
70 The 1948 issues for the *Jewish Chronicle* are found in MG 28, V 63, vol. 4182, NA. See Ben Meyer, "JIAS Helps Rescue Jewish Remnant," 1 October, 12–13, and Saul Hayes "Congress Does the Immigration Job," ibid., 14–16.
71 In his study of the Jewish press, Louis Levendal, in discussing immigration, does not cite any article on the survivors who came to Canada. An analysis of the *Canadian Jewish Review* (Montreal) for 1947 to 1949, in MG 31, D 172, NA, also finds that there were no articles on the survivors. It is likely, however, that *landmanschaft* publications would have contained such articles. There has been no review of this segment of the ethnic press.
72 Interview with Lappin.
73 This preoccupation has been recorded in a number of studies and in the author's interviews. For studies, see Bercuson, *Canada and the Birth of Israel*, and "The Zionist Lobby and Canada's Palestine Policy, 1941–1948," 17–36. See also David Taras, "From Passivity to Politics: Canada's Jewish Community and Political Support for Israel," 37–62; Levendel's study of the Jewish press, section C, 175–318, is interspersed with issues of the press and Israel from 1946 to 1970. Interviews with Ben Kayfetz, Ben Lappin, and Judge Sydney Harris (Toronto, 13 May

1995) reinforce this position. As Kayfetz relates, "Canadian Jews were put on more of a hot seat than American Jews, who could scream out at the British ... we in Canada were brainwashed in a positive way about England. It [Toronto] was a Tory British town. It was a very delicate situation. It was particularly infuriating that people who survived in Europe should now face this kind of obstacle [the British prohibition on Jewish immigration from Europe to Palestine] who were supposed to be their friends. That's what the big issue was in those years rather than the Holocaust itself. Our attention was diverted to the fight for the rights of Jews to come back to Palestine" (7 November 1995).

CHAPTER THREE

1 Interview with Philip Weiss, chairperson, Winnipeg Holocaust Remembrance Committee 1979–91, Winnipeg, 21 November 1995.
2 Interview with Cyril Levitt, Toronto, 9 May 1995.
3 In 1951 Jews had the greatest over-representation of males in the professional and financial occupation class of any ethnic group in the country (10.1 per cent of Jews vs. 5 per cent nationally). In 1961 the disparity had grown to 7.4 per cent (16 vs. 8.6 per cent). A similar pattern was recorded in males in school attendance between 5 and 24 years of age. In 1951 Jews were over-represented by 11.1 per cent (64.9 vs. 53.8 per cent), and in 1961 by 16.5 per cent (84.8 vs. 68.3 per cent), by far the largest figure for any ethnic group (Census of Canada, 1951, 1961; Dominion Bureau of Statistics, 1961; as reported in Porter, *The Vertical Mosaic*, 86–91, 564).
4 Troper, "As Canadian as Multiculturalism" (quoted with author's permission).
5 "Hayes, Saul," in Gottesman, *Who's Who in Canadian Jewry*, 421. Abella and Troper, in *None Is Too Many*, depict Hayes's efforts between 1940 and 1948 on behalf of the trapped refugees. The authors dedicated their book to his memory.
6 Saul Hayes, "Report on Anti-semitism," JCC, file: Canadian Jewish History – Saul Hayes, JPLA. Hayes was wrong about discriminatory laws. There were still some against Chinese Canadians in British Columbia and federal restrictions against Aboriginal peoples.
7 Saul Hayes, "The Nature of the Community," 1953, ibid.
8 Saul Hayes, "The Jewish Community of Canada," a paper delivered on October 1958 to the Conference of World Jewish Organizations, London, England, ibid.
9 See Benjamin Diamond, national executive director of the Federation of Polish Jews, to Saul Hayes, 25 March 1947, in which he stated, "In view of the fact that ... the Congress is not preparing any meetings this year

in memory of the uprising of the Warsaw Ghetto, I would like to inform you that at our Officers meeting last night, we have decided to hold such a memorial mass meeting" (Federation of Polish Jews Papers, ZC, CJCA).

10 CJC, *IOI*, no. 99 (27 February 1947), no. 353 (17 March 1948), no. 355 (18 March 1948), no. 375 (16 April 1948), no. 379 (22 April 1948), no. 388 (10 May 1948), no. 1297 (2 February 1952), no. 1322 (3 March 1952), no. 1326 (21 March 1952), no. 1353 (5 May 1952), no. 1588 (22 April 1953), no. 1593 (4 April 1953), no. 1596 (4 May 1953), no. 1604 (14 May 1953); Workmen's Circle Montreal, Meyer London Branch 151, *Souvenir Book, Golden Jubilee*, 1957, Workmen's Circle Papers, CJCA. JLC Papers, vol. 25, Warsaw Ghetto Uprising files, NA.

11 For Toronto, interview with Ben Lappin; also interview with Sophie Waldman, 26 November 1995, Vancouver.

12 CJC, Twelfth Plenary Session, 29 October to 1 November 1959, Montreal, Resolution 22, Plenary Sessions Files, CJCA. The first resolution on this issue was adopted at the 1953 session.

13 Kage, *With Faith and Thanksgiving*, 262. In 1951 the population was 204,836, and Kage estimated the 1961 population at 265,000. In proportional terms, the decade from 1901 to 1911 had the highest growth rate – more than 300 per cent.

14 Ibid., 260–1. A total of 40,512 immigrants arrived via ocean ports and the United States. Approximately 10 per cent left Canada during the decade.

15 Hayes, "The Jewish Community of Canada," 2, JCC, file: Canadian Jewish History – Saul Hayes, JPLA.

16 Helmreich, in "The Impact of Holocaust Survivors on American Society," 363, equates "immigrants" with "survivors" in using Kage's estimate of 36,500. Sigal and Weinfeld, in *Trauma and Rebirth*, 6, do the same in employing Kage's figures for their 1951 estimate.

17 Adapted from Kage, *With Faith and Thanksgiving*, 261–2.

18 Ibid, 260; Whitaker, *Canadian Immigration Policy since Confederation*, 18; Whitaker, *Double Standard*, 67.

19 The figure of 250,000 is cited in Peck, "Special Lives," 1151. The figure of 137,500 is cited in Helmreich, "The Impact of Holocaust Survivors on American Society," 381, where the author equates the number of Jewish immigrants with the number of survivors.

20 In the decade from 1946 to 1955, 1,212,319 immigrants came to Canada (adapted from Whitaker, *Canadian Immigration Policy since Confederation*, 2). In that same period, there were 46,053 Jewish immigrants (3.8 per cent of the total), of whom 40,666 remained (cited by Kage, *With Faith and Thanksgiving*, 261–2).

21 Sigal and Weinfeld, *Trauma and Rebirth*, 6–7.

22 CJC, *IOI* no. 524 (15 November 1968), BB Papers, 37/21, NA.
23 CJC *Bulletin*, 16:8 (October 1962), Abraham Arnold Papers, P5136/50, PAM.
24 Adapted from Gerber, "Immigration and Integration in Post-War Canada," 59–60. I have arbitrarily designated 16th Avenue as the boundary between the city and the suburbs in the 1950s.
25 Rome in *Pathways to the Present*, 22.
26 Telephone interview with Joseph Kage, 17 November 1993, Montreal. For London see Rome, *Pathways to the Present*, 48; for Windsor, 55; for Winnipeg, 72.
27 For Ottawa, see Rome, *Pathways to the Present*, 55; for Edmonton, 88.
28 Interviews with Lappin, Kayfetz, Gutkin, and Lipshitz; interview with Judge Philip Givens, Toronto, 10 May 1995 (Givens died two months after the interview).
29 Interview with Kayfetz, 7 November 1995.
30 For example, see the following general studies: Creighton, *The Forked Road*, chaps 6, 9, 10; Bothwell et al., *Canada since 1945*, chaps 8, 9, 15, 16, 19; Easterbrook and Aitken, *Canadian Economic History*, chaps 12, 13, 14; Watkins and Forster, *Economics: Canada – Recent Readings*; and Norrie and Owram, *A History of the Canadian Economy*, chaps 20, 21.
31 Interviews with Kayfetz and Kaplansky; Hayes, "Report on Anti-semitism," JCC, file: Canadian Jewish History – Saul Hayes, JPLA. Kayfetz on Ontario in Rome, *Pathways to the Present*, 35–6.
32 Interview with Kayfetz, 13 November 1995.
33 Tulchinsky, *Branching Out*, 269–74.
34 For antisemitism in British Columbia in the 1950s, see Abraham Arnold Papers, P 5128/20.1, 20.2, PAM. For the British Israelite Association, see ibid., 20.4, and Brown, *Jew or Juif*, 25–8. For a recent example of the British Israel Association's views, see letter to the editor, *Globe and Mail*, 21 November 1995, 7.
35 There is a wealth of information on Gostick, especially in the JCRC Papers in the OJA. On his hate-mongering in western Canada, see chapter 6.
36 Whitaker, *Double Standard*, 63–9.
37 Robert Walker, "How Race-Haters Bait Canada's 230,000 Jews," *New Liberty Magazine*, May, 1957, JLC Papers, 26/8, NA.
38 According to John Porter's study, of the 760 members of Canada's economic elite in 1951, only six were Jews (.78 per cent of the sample, as opposed to 1.4 per cent of the general population), all of whom were associated with either the liquor industry or smaller dominant industries. Despite their over-representation on the highest rung of the occupation and education ladders, Jews were still excluded from the real power structure (Porter, *The Vertical Mosaic*, 286–7).

39 "Saalheimer, Manfred," in Gottesman, *Who's Who in Canadian Jewry*, 423.

40 Finding Aid, URO Papers, CJCA; Report of the National Executive Director to the Plenary Session, 1956, 17–18, Plenary Sessions Files, CJCA; Report of the National Executive Director to the Plenary Session, 1959, 17, ibid.; interview with Sol Kanee, Winnipeg, 20 November 1995.

41 Minutes of the Executive of CJC Central Region, 16 December 1953, 18 May 1955, Central Region Executive Papers, CJCA.

42 Minutes of the Executive of CJC Central Region, 10 June 1953, 25 November 1955; Sixteenth Regional Congress Plenary, 28–29 January 1956, ibid.

43 Clenman, "I Dream in Good English Too," in *I Dream in Good English Too*, 14.

44 Interviews with Kage, Harris, and Kaplansky (Joseph Kage died in 1996).

45 Interview with Givens; interview with Larry Zolf, Toronto, 3 November 1995.

46 Interview with Gutkin.

47 Interview with Kaplansky.

48 Interview with Weiss.

49 For information on the social and demographic composition of interwar Jewry in central and eastern Europe, see Gutman et al., *The Jews of Poland between Two World Wars*; Mendelsohn, *The Jews of East Central Europe between the World Wars*; and Gilbert, *Atlas of the Holocaust*, 32 (adapted).

50 Interview with Gerda Steinitz-Frieberg, chairperson, Canadian Jewish Congress, Central Region, 1992–95, Toronto, 27 May 1996; interview with Krisha Starker, director of the Montreal Holocaust Memorial Centre, 1983–94, Montreal, 30 August 1995; interview with Lou Zablow, CJC National Executive Committee member, 1965–71, Montreal, 29 May 1995.

51 Nathan Leipciger, Survivor Documentation Project: Transcripts of Survivor Testimonies, CJCA.

52 Interview with Nathan Leipciger, chairperson of the Holocaust Remembrance Committee, Toronto Jewish Congress, 1980–88, chairperson of the National Holocaust Remembrance Committee, CJC, since 1988, Toronto, 10 November 1995.

53 Larry Zolf remembers that the immigrants were referred to as *der gerateveter* (the rescued ones); interview with Zolf.

54 Interview with Mendel Good, chairperson of the Holocaust Remembrance Committee of Ottawa in the 1980s, Ottawa, 13 September 1995.

55 See chapter 2; see also Abraham Arnold, "With the War Orphans in Toronto," *Congress Bulletin* (Montreal, April 1948), in the Arnold Papers, P5136/50.1, PAM; Sidney Katz, "The Human Legacies of World War II –

the Redeemed Children," *Maclean's*, 10 February 1962, CJC Papers, P3535/6, PAM, which is largely based on Ben Lappin's book, *The Redeemed Children*. More recently, a touching account has been written by Fraidie Martz, *Open Your Hearts: The Story of the Jewish War Orphans*.

56 Interview with Lappin.

57 Howard Chandler, Survivor Documentation Project: Transcripts of Survivor Testimonies, CJCA.

58 Interview with Musia Schwartz, Montreal, 29 May 1995.

59 Interview with Leo Lowy, Vancouver, 20 November 1995.

60 In the 1949 fiscal year, 69 per cent of the services provided by the Jewish Child and Family Service were to orphans and other immigrants who arrived in the workers' schemes. The increase in the expenditure from 1948 to 1949 "was due entirely to the load that the agency has taken on for the CJC." The achievement by the community was commendable inasmuch as housing was limited and most of the Jewish community was still proletarian and congregated along Selkirk Avenue in the north end. See Jewish Welfare Fund Papers, P3511/13, PAM, on budget; Saul Hayes to Heinz Frank, executive director, CJC Western Region, 13 May 1947, on preparing for 100 to 150 children, P3511/25, ibid., "General Features of Planning Project for Immigration, Reception and Placement of 1000 Orphaned Children," CJC Papers, P3550/5 ibid.;. Frank to Max Solkin, executive director of JIAS, 30 April 1951, on the difficulty in finding housing for immigrants, ibid. On the Hagibor soccer club, see *Jewish Post* (Winnipeg), 16 September 1948, 3, JHS/WC. On the lasting importance of the orphans in the community, see the press release of the twenty-fifth anniversary of the arrival of the first orphans, CJC Western Region, 19 October 1972, CJC Papers, P3535/5, PAM. On the relations between the orphans and young Winnipeg Jews, see Zolf, "The Great Yiddish Mouthpiece."

61 Quotations are taken from John Hirsch, "How I Discovered My Roots," *Jewish Life and Times – A Collection of Essays* (1978), JHS/WC, and a transcript of an interview with Hirsch, 29 June 1972, CJC Papers, P3535/5, PAM. Additional information on John Hirsch was gained in interviews with Larry Zolf and Harry Gutkin; see alsoHarry Gutkin, "John Hirsch: A Humanist in the Theatre," in Gutkin and Gutkin *The Worst of Times, the Best of Times*, 252, 263; Press Release of the CJC Western Region on the twenty-fifth anniversary of the arrival of the orphans to Winnipeg, 19 October 1972, CJC Papers, P3535/5, PAM. John Hirsch died in 1989.

62 Interviews with Lowy, Good, Leipciger, and Schwartz.; interview with Robert Krell, a founding member of the Vancouver Standing Committee on the Holocaust and founder and chairperson of the Vancouver Holocaust Education and Remembrance Centre, Vancouver, 29 November 1993.

63 Granek and Forai testimonies in Survivor Documentation Project: Transcripts of Survivor Testimonies, CJCA; interview with Mike Englishman, an activist in the Toronto Jewish community, Toronto, 8 May 1995.

64 The Kupfer interview is part of the videotape project of the Winnipeg Second Generation Committee and is in the archives of the Jewish Historical Society of Western Canada. The Posner, Chandler, and Kwinta interviews are in the Survivor Documentation Project: Transcripts of Survivor Testimonies, CJCA; see also Kwinta, *I'm Still Living*. Elsa Chandler first spoke publicly about her experiences as the keynote speaker at the Yom Hashoah Commemoration held by the Holocaust Remembrance Committee of the Jewish Federation of Greater Toronto in April 1995. Both Howard and Elsa Chandler also spoke informally with the author.

65 Interview with Steinitz-Frieberg.

66 Interviews with Starker and Schwartz.

67 Interviews with Leipciger and Weiss.

68 Information on Radom during the war is found in *Voice of Radom – Special Edition, 50th. Commemoration of the Destroyed Jewish Community of Radom*. Articles include "The Destruction of Jewish Radom 50 Years Ago" by Henry Rosenbaum; "The Bitter Faith of Radom Jews during World War II" by Jan Franecki; and "The Massacre in Pentz' Park," Henry Zagdanski's personal experiences as told to Adam Fuerstenberg. This book and *Voice of Radom – 50th. Anniversary of Liberation Edition*, edited by Henry Rosenbaum (Toronto: B'nai Radom, 1995), were made available to the author by Professor Adam Fuerstenberg. Additional information on Radom before and during the war was gained in an interview with Henry Rosenbaum, Toronto, 11 July 1996.

69 Lipson, *The Book of Radom*, 99–100, courtesy of Adam Fuerstenberg; interview with Adam Fuerstenberg, Toronto, 3 July 1996.

70 Interview with Rosenbaum. Rosenbaum remembers that B'nai Radom was formed about two years after his arrival in 1952. The Lipson book states that the group was created in 1950, but Rosenbaum disputes that date.

71 Interview with Rosenbaum.

72 Ibid.

73 Ibid; Lipson, *The Book of Radom*, 100.

74 Another example of the split between survivors and Canadian Jews in a post-war *landsmanschaft* has been discussed by Henry Srebrnik, the son of survivors who came from Czestochov, Poland, and joined the Czenstochover Landsmanschaft in Montreal. He notes that the split between the two groups was perpetuated into the second generation, which was somewhat estranged from Canadian Jews geographically and psychologically. He writes that childhood friends "invariably married either the children of other immigrants, or complete outsiders to Montreal ...

but not Canadian Jews." There is only anecdotal information about the degree to which this phenomenon has occurred in Canada, and Srebrnik speculates that second-generation inclusion appears to have been more common in Toronto and the United States. Nevertheless, from other anecdotal information and my own experience, I believe that there has been some common bond between members of the second generation. I am grateful to Professor Srebrnik for sending me his article "Two Solitudes: Immigrant-Native Divisions in Jewish Montreal," Friends of Pioneering Israel, *Eye*, 8:6 (June 1982): 4, 13–14.

75 Hulse, "The Emergence of the Holocaust Survivor in the Canadian Jewish Community," and "Holocaust Survivors in the Canadian Jewish Community"; Gerber, "Immigration and Integration in Post-war Canada." An interesting counter text, although not a scholarly one, is Hoffman, *Lost in Translation*, the personal narrative of a post-war Polish-Jewish girl and her family in Vancouver.

76 Interview with Zolf; interview with Gutkin.

77 Telephone interview with Sam Rothstein, president of the Jewish Community Centre, 1972–74, Vancouver, 29 November 1993. Rothstein's memory clouds the issue, since the Kristallnacht memorial did not begin until the early 1980s.

78 This changed by 1961. In the wake of the Eichmann trial, the Park Movie House was packed with 725 people in attendance (Interview with Steinberg); *Vancouver Sun*, 7 April 1961; *Vancouver Province*, 10 April 1961; Warsaw Ghetto Memorial Committee Report, 21 June 1961, 15/18, JHS/BC.

79 Interview with Waldman.

80 Interview with Levitt.

81 Interview with Lappin.

82 Interview with Ida Lappin, a teacher at Beth Tzedec in the 1950s, Herzliya, Israel, 20 August 1994.

83 Interview with Professor Moe Steinberg, who taught in Jewish schools at the time, Vancouver, 29 November 1993.

84 Linda Wise was a student in the Jewish People's School and provided this insight in a conversation with me. The Borochov School had been founded in 1932 by Moshe Menachovsky, who was its principal until 1955. I attended it from 1950 to 1957. Most of my teachers were survivors.

85 Interview with Kage on the Yiddish press; interview with Lipschitz.

CHAPTER FOUR

1 *The Voice of Survivors* (Montreal: Association of the Survivors of Nazi Oppression, 1966), ZF, Periodicals Collection, CJCA.

2 BB Papers, 36/18, File on JPRC and Constitutional Agreement 1947–65, NA; interviews with Kayfetz. Ben Kayfetz was hired as director of the Committee (Central Region) in April 1947. At that time, there was no national director. Kayfetz eventually became executive director of the National Committee, based in Toronto, and remained so until the end of 1984. He stayed on as an adviser until September 1985.

3 The estimate by the American Jewish Congress is found in JCRC Papers, MG 8s, 1960, 12/32 A, B, C, OJA. The figure cited by the Vancouver Civic Unity Association is found in the Arnold Papers, P5128, File 20.3, PAM.

4 JCRC Papers, 1960, 12/32 A, B, C, OJA; JPRC Report to the CJC Plenary 21–24 June 1962, Toronto, 2, in Plenary Sessions Files, CJCA.

5 Cohen to Arnold, 8 January 1960, Arnold Papers, P5128, file 20.3, PAM.

6 "Recent Swastika Craze in Toronto Abating," *Canadian Jewish News*, January 15, 1960, microfilm, OJA; interview with Kayfetz, 5 November 1995.

7 JCRC Papers, 1960, 12/32A, B, C, OJA.

8 Joan Seager, "The Fatal Disease of Anti-Semitism," *Burlington Gazette*; reprinted in the *Toronto Telegram*, 13 January 1960.

9 *Canadian Jewish News*, 29 January 1960, microfilm, OJA.

10 See the *Canadian Jewish News* for January–May, 1960, microfilm, OJA, for responses to the swastika outbreak.

11 Riegner was the individual most responsible for passing specific information about the extermination camps to the Allies from his base in Switzerland (Yehuda Bauer, "Reigner Cable," in Gutman, *The Encyclopedia of the Holocaust*, 1275–6).

12 Reprinted in A.J. Arnold, "See Another Dimension of Ghetto Memorial," editorial, *Jewish Western Bulletin*, n.d. (April 1960), 15/32, JHS/BC.

13 Professor Morris Steinberg of the Jewish federation spoke at the Vancouver commemoration in 1961. His address was reported in the Vancouver Sun on 16 April 1961. See "Jews Told They Can't Rely on Good Will of Others," CJC Pacific Region Papers, 15/32, JHS/BC; interview with Steinberg.

14 Wistrich, *Who's Who in Nazi Germany*, 62–3; Yahil, "Eichmann, Adolf."

15 *Canadian Jewish News*, 27 May 1960, microfilm, OJA.

16 *Toronto Daily Star*, 6 June 1960; reprinted in the *Canadian Jewish News*, June 17, 1960, 1, microfilm, OJA.

17 *Globe and Mail*, reprinted in the *Canadian Jewish News*, 6 July 1960, microfilm, OJA.

18 Arnold Papers, P5138, file 90.3, PAM.

19 JPRC Report, CJC Plenary, Toronto, 21–24 June 1962, 2–3, Plenary Sessions Files, CJCA.

20 Interviews with Lou Zablow; interview with Aba Beer, first chairperson of the National Holocaust Remembrance Committee, and Isaac Piaset-

ski, past chairperson, Quebec Region Holocaust Remembrance Committee, Montreal, 19 July 1994.

21 Statement by Frank Hall, chairman, Canadian Labour Congress Human Rights Committee, 3 November 1960, JLC Papers, 75, 26/8, NA.

22 Monroe Abbey, chairman, National Executive Committee, CJC, and Sydney M. Harris, chairman, NJPRC, 7 November 1960 in Arnold Papers, P5117, File 241, PAM.

23 JPRC Report, CJC Plenary, 1962, CJCA.

24 Interviews with Piasetski, Beer, and Zablow.

25 *The Voice of Survivors (De Stime Fun Der Sharit Hapleita),* 1963 edition, Association of Survivors of Nazi Oppression Files, JPLA.

26 Interview with Zablow.

27 JCRC Papers, 1961, 12/13B, OJA.

28 Gabriel Bach, "Eichmann Trial," in Gutman, *The Encyclopedia of the Holocaust,* 429–32; Arendt, *Eichmann in Jerusalem.*

29 M.J. Nurenberger, "The Finale of the Affair Eichmann," *Canadian Jewish News,* 17 March 1961, microfilm, OJA. The CJN covered the trial until August.

30 Valerie White, "I Worked for Adolf Eichmann," *Maclean's,* 22 April 1961, 34–6, 72–9. "Trial of the Century," *Star Weekly Magazine,* 11 March 1961. Both articles are found in Holocaust and Canada *Files,* Box 3, JPLA.

31 United Zionist Council and the JPRC, "The Eichmann Trial Statement For the Guidance of Jewish Community Leaders In Canada," 15 March 1961, JCRC Papers, 1961, 12/13A, OJA. Further documents on the Eichmann trial are found in 14/14 and 15/15.

32 David Carmichael, "Mock Hearing – Hamilton Jews Try Eichmann," 12 March 1961, in *Globe and Mail,* 20 March 1961.

33 M.L. (possibly Marvin Needleman of the United Zionist Council), "An Evaluation of Canadian Public Opinion on the Eichmann Trial Based on a Study of Editorial Opinion and Letters-to-Editor," *Globe and Mail* 12 May 1961.

34 "The Eichmann Trial," *Globe and Mail,* 11 April 1961 and 16 August 1961; John Gellner, "Germany and the Eichmann Trial," *Globe and Mail,* 31 August 1961.

35 Interviews with Leipciger, Zablow, and Waldman.

36 Issues of the *Canadian Jewish News,* April and May 1961, microfilm series, OJA.

37 At the CJC plenary, held one week before Eichmann's execution, there was no mention of the trial in the proceedings. This omission did not mean that the trial was not of great interest to Canadian Jews, but rather that the organized community had no input into the proceedings. Canadian Jews, together with the rest of the world outside of Israel, were spectators.

38 *Jewish Standard*, 1 April 1963, Arnold Papers, P5136, file 240, PAM.

39 CJC Plenary, 1962, Plenary Sessions Files, CJCA.

40 *The Voice of Survivors*, 1963 edition, JPLA.

41 Interview with Zablow.

42 This association was founded in Montreal in after a meeting of survivors from Bergen-Belsen in New York in December 1961. At that meeting the World Federation of Bergen-Belsen Survivors was formed. The president of the Montreal association was Paul Trepman. He was a spokesperson for DPs (see chapter 2), and after arriving to Montreal, he became well known as a teacher at the Jewish People's School and director of Unzer Camp. The association's aims were "never to forget," to fight neo-Nazis, to aid former camp inmates, and to hold an annual rally on the anniversary of the liberation of the camp at a monument. The monument was erected in 1964 (Bergen-Belsen Survivors Association Papers, JPLA).

43 One opinion about the gap between the two communities was offered by Lou Zablow when he commented, "They [the establishment] didn't give a damn about us" (interview with Zablow). This was echoed by Gerda Steinitz-Frieberg, who was elected president of her B'nai Brith Women's chapter in 1962. "At my installation," she recalls, "I spoke about the Holocaust and why I wanted to join a service organization, and two women resigned who did not want to belong to a chapter with a survivor" (interview with Steinitz-Frieberg). In contrast, Nathan Leipciger and Mike Englishman remember that some Canadian Jews became more understanding, and a few joined survivors in actively protesting the antisemitic incidents (interviews with Leipciger and Englishman).

44 Cohen et al. *Report of the Special Committee on Hate Propaganda in Canada*, 18–20.

45 CJC Papers, P3535, file 21, PAM.

46 Cohen et al., *Report of the Special Committee on Hate Propaganda in Canada*, 257.

47 Kayfetz interview, 7 November 1995.

48 Ibid.

49 Cohen et al., *Report of the Special Committee on Hate Propaganda in Canada*, 19.

50 Robin, *Shades of Right*, 193–4.

51 Kayfetz interview, 7 November 1995.

52 Cohen et al., *Report of the Special Committee on Hate Propaganda in Canada*, 20–4.

53 *This Hour Has Seven Days*, 25 October 1964, CBC Film Archives, Toronto, courtesy of Larry Zolf.

54 *Association of Former Concentration Camp Inmates/Survivors of Nazi Oppression*, "Text of a Memorandum presented to Board of Broadcast Governors by our Delegation," 17 November 1964, Lou Zablow Papers.

55 Rabbi N. Fredman, vice-principal of the Winnipeg Hebrew School, copy to Heinz Frank, executive director of CJC Western Region, 26 October 1964, CJC Papers, P3532, File 25, PAM.
56 *This Hour Has Seven Days*, 17 January 1965, CBC Film Archives; interview with Kayfetz, 7 November 1995.
57 *This Hour Has Seven Days*, 17 January 1965, CBC Archives.
58 Interview with Zolf; interview with Kayfetz, 7 November 1995.
59 Frank to Kayfetz, 20 January 1965, CJC Papers, P3532, file 25, PAM.
60 Garber to Fraser, 10 February 1965, ibid. Fraser's letter to Garber was dated 29 January, but was not found in the file. Garber's original letter to Fraser is also not in the file.
61 Kaplan, "Maxwell Cohen and the Report of the Special Committee on Hate Propaganda," 245.
62 Interview with Zablow, 29 May 1995. An editorial in the *Montreal Gazette* on 3 February 1964 stated that organizations which distributed hate propaganda "should not be allowed to flourish. For they are not compatible with a democratic society that believes in liberty. Their purpose is to destroy liberty. They have no claim to moderation" ("Support for Genocide Bill," 21 February 1963, in Association of Former Concentration Camp Inmates Survivors of Nazi Oppression, *The Voice*, 1965 edition, JPLA).
63 B.G. Kayfetz, "The Story behind Canada's New Anti-Hate Law," *Patterns of Prejudice*, May–June 1970, 5, JCRC Papers, 1970, 55/79, OJA; interview with Kayfetz, 7 November 1995.
64 *The Voice*, 1965 edition, JPLA.
65 House of Commons Debates, 20 February 1964, ibid.
66 House of Commons Debates, 10 July 1964, 17 July 1964, in Ibid.
67 Cohen et al., *Report of the Special Committee on Hate Propaganda in Canada*, appendix 4, 273.
68 Ibid.
69 "Resolution proposed by the Association of Former Concentration Camp Inmates Survivors of Nazi Oppression, Montreal, Canada," 27 May 1964, ZC 1, Federation of Polish Jews Papers, CJCA; Association of Survivors of Nazi Oppression Papers, JPLA.
70 Cohen et al., *Report of the Special Committee on Hate Propaganda in Canada* 46–51, appendix 6, 319–27; Kaplan, "Maxwell Cohen," 246.
71 Confidential letter from Michael Garber to NJCRC national officers, 24 November 1964, JCRC Papers, 1964, 18/39, OJA.
72 Cohen to Favreau, 9 November 1964, Cohen Papers, MG 31, E 24, reprinted in Kaplan, "Maxwell Cohen," 247.
73 "Favreau Assures Jews of Drive on Hate Mail," *Montreal Star*, 11 November 1964, 30, ibid.
74 Kayfetz, "The Story behind Canada's New Anti-Hate Law," 6, OJA.

75 Interview with Justice Mark MacGuigan, Ottawa, 13 September 1995 (MacGuigan died in 1998).

CHAPTER FIVE

1 *Globe and Mail*, 31 May 1965.
2 "Harris, Sydney," in Gottesman, *Who's Who in Canadian Jewry*, 22; interview with Harris.
3 Sydney Harris, "... And Now for the Facts," 19 April 1964, JCRC Papers, 1964, 18/39, OJA.
4 Ibid.
5 Ibid.
6 Interview with Harris.
7 Ibid.
8 Confidential letter from Michael Garber, president of CJC to NJCRC national officers, 24 November 1964, JCRC Papers, 1964, 18/39, OJA.
9 See chapter 4 on the Rockwell affair and chapter 6 on the Criminal Code amendment.
10 Confidential memo, M.S. (Myer Sharzer) to S.M.H. (Sydney Harris), B.G.K. (Ben Kayfetz), 18 February 1964, JCRC Papers 1965, 3/160, OJA. See also MacGuigan, "Hate Control and Freedom of Assembly."
11 John Garrity and Alan Edmonds, "I Spied on the Nazis," *Maclean's*, 1 October 1966.
12 Interview with Mike Englishman, 8 May 1995, Toronto.
13 Interview with Mike Berwald, 7 May 1995, Toronto.
14 Kayfetz file, 25 January 1965; Kayfetz to Midanik and Harris, 1 February 1965, JCRC Papers, 1965, 3/160, OJA; interview with Berwald.
15 Kayfetz to Midanik and Harris, 5 February 1965, JCRC Papers, 1965, 3/160, OJA; Kayfetz to Midanik and Harris, 9 February 1965, ibid; interview with Berwald.
16 *Notice of a Mass Protest Demonstration*, ibid., 1965, 3/160; *Toronto Daily Star*, 5 June 1965, 8.
17 MacGuigan, "Hate Control and Freedom of Assembly," 233–4. When Beattie bought the house with a down payment of $200, which he had borrowed, a crowd of two hundred in the neighbourhood gathered to jeer, broke windows, and uttered threats. On that occasion, Meyer Gasner remarked: "We are gratified to note that the general population of Toronto, embracing people of all origins, has reacted to this incident with the disgust it warrants ... It is fitting that they have reacted this way, emphasizing as it does that Nazism is the concern of all Canadians, not just a problem affecting the Jews alone" (Garrity and Edmonds, "I Spied on the Nazis," *Maclean's*, 1 October 1966, 38). In May 1965 two thousand people in Ward 8, where Rhodes Avenue was located, pre-

sented a petition to City Council protesting the use of the residence. Beattie was summonsed for breaking city zoning regulations, convicted, and fined $25 (Association of Survivors of Nazi Oppression, *Open Letter to the Jewish Community of Canada*, 17 June 1965, 4, JCC, box: Association of Survivors of Nazi Oppression, file: Open Letters, JPLA).

18 Berwald interview.

19 Garrity and Edmonds, "I Spied on the Nazis," *Maclean's*, 1 October 1966, 38; interview with Berwald.

20 Interview with Englishman.

21 COIN File, JCRC Papers, 1965, 2131, OJA; MacGuigan, "Hate Control and Freedom of Assembly," 235.

22 Interview with Levitt.

23 Ibid.

24 Interview with Harris. Actually, it was Beattie, not Stanley, who was arrested. This occurred one year after the riot in Allan Gardens.

25 MacGuigan, "Hate Control and Freedom of Assembly," 233–4.

26 "Givens, Philip," in Gottesman, *Who's Who in Canadian Jewry*, 309.

27 Interview with Givens.

28 Kayfetz to Harris, 14 May 1965, JCRC Papers, 1965, 22/18, OJA.

29 Association of Survivors of Nazi Oppression, "Open Letter," 4, JPLA.

30 Interview with Harris.

31 MacGuigan, "Hate Control and Freedom of Assembly," 234.

32 JCRC Papers, 1965, 21/5, OJA.

33 Ibid.

34 Special JCRC Meeting, 18 June 1965, at which Sydney Midanik stated: "It was known that Beattie had no permit" (JCRC *Papers*, 1965, 21/36, OJA; see also MacGuigan, "Hate Control and Freedom of Assembly," 235; interview with Harris; Garrity and Edmonds, "I Spied on the Nazis," *Maclean's*, 1 October 1966, 10.

35 Interview with Berwald.

36 CJC estimated the crowd at 1,500, the police at 3,000, and the media between 3,000 and 5,000.

37 *Globe and Mail*, 31 May 1965, 1–2; Arnold Bruner, "Hate in Our City," *Toronto Daily Star*, 5 June 1965, 8; interview with Givens; Minutes of Special Meeting of JCRC (Central Region), 18 June 1965, JCRC Papers, 1965, 24/110B, OJA.

38 MacGuigan, "Hate Control and Freedom of Assembly," 237; Minutes of Meeting of JCRC (Central Region), 26 January 1966, JCRC Papers, 1965, 25/2, OJA.

39 Interview with Berwald.

40 Robert Fulford, "Those Men in Allan Gardens," *Toronto Daily Star*, 1 June 1965.

41 W. Gunther Plaut, "The Riot at Allan Gardens," *Globe and Mail*, 5 June 1965.

42 Bruner, "Hate in Our City," *Toronto Daily Star*, 5 June 1965.

43 Interview with Berwald.

44 Interview with Levitt.

45 Dick Brown, "The Anti-Nazis Planned No Violence," *Toronto Daily Star*, 8 June 1965.

46 Interview with Berwald.

47 Interview with Englishman.

48 Interview with Levitt.

49 Interview with Harris.

50 *Globe and Mail*, 31 May 1965, 2.

51 Canadian Jewish Congress, Central Region, "Report on Neo-Nazism and Hate Literature," 8 June 1965, JCRC Papers, 1965, 21/5, OJA.

52 Interview with Harris.

53 *Globe and Mail*, 9 June 1965; Minutes, Special JCRC Meeting, 18 June 1965, JCRC Papers, 1965, 21/5, OJA.

54 Kayfetz to Midanik, 27 June 1965, JCRC Papers, 1965, 21/5, OJA.

55 Silverberg to Gasner, 9 June 1965, ibid.; Gelbard, chairman of Zaglembier Society, to Canadian Jewish Congress (Central Region), 13 June 1965, ibid.

56 Minutes of Special JCRC Meeting, 18 June 1965, ibid.

57 Association of Survivors of Nazi Oppression, "Open Letter," 2, 9, JLPA.

58 "Yiddisher Kibbutz und di Painleche Nachvaianiishen fun dem Anti-Nazishin Raot in Toronto," 13 Yuni 1965, JCRC Papers, 1965, 35/36, OJA; English-language version, "The Jewish Community and the Painful Aftermath of the Anti-Nazi Riot in Toronto, 13 June 1965," 21/5, ibid.; "Congress and the Riot in Allan Gardens," *Canadian Jewish Chronicle*, 18 June 1965, Lou Zablow Papers, quoted with permission.

59 Entries for the eighteen members are scattered throughout the Gottesman volume. See also Minutes of the JCRC, Central Region meeting, 24 June 1965, JCRC Papers, 1965, 21/35, JCRC Papers, OJA.

60 Minutes, Special JCRC Meeting, 18 June 1965, JCRC Papers, OJA.

61 Interview with Harris.

62 Minutes, meeting of 24 June 1965, JCRC Papers, OJA; emphasis added.

63 Draft Resolution, Community Anti-Nazi Committee, 6 July 1965, JCRC Papers, 1965, 21/35, OJA.

64 Sharzer to Kayfetz, 3 August 1965, ibid.

65 Interview with Berwald.

66 Interview with Levitt.

67 Interviews with Englishman and Harris.

68 Wittenberg to Lipson, 13 December 1965, JCRC Papers, 1965, 26/37, OJA.

69 Minutes, JCRC Central Region Meeting, 26 January 1966, 1966, 25/2; Minutes, CANC Meeting, 2 February 1966, JCRC Papers, 1966, 26/37, OJA.

70 Minutes, JCRC Central Region Meeting, 3 March 1966, 25/2, ibid.

71 Minutes, CANC Meetings, 29 June 1966; 20 July 1966, 26/37, ibid.
72 MacGuigan, "Hate Control and Freedom of Assembly," 233.
73 Ibid., 235–6; interviews with Berwald, Levitt, and Englishman.
74 Minutes, CANC Meeting, 2 February 1966, JCRC Papers, 1966, OJA.
75 Minutes, Meeting, JCRC Central Region, 10 March 1966, 25/2, ibid.
76 Minutes, Meeting of CANC, 10 March 1966, 26/37, ibid.
77 Minutes, CANC Meeting, 2 February 1966, ibid.
78 N3, Fighters against Racial Hatred to Toronto City Council, *A Brief to Safeguard and Preserve the Principle of Freedom of Speech*, 12 March 1966; JCRC Papers, 1966, 26/37, OJA.
79 McGuigan, "Hate Control and Freedom of Assembly," 238.
80 Ibid., 237–9; Minutes of CANC Meetings 9 June; 29 June 1966, JCRC Papers, 1966, 26/37, OJA.
81 Charles Wittenberg, "Nazism Is Not a Jewish Concern Only," *Menorah* (a Jewish weekly printed in Hungarian, article in English), 26/31, ibid. See also "Who Threatens Freedom?" by Max Chikofsky, the editor of the N3 newsletter *Shomrim*, in the same issue of *Menorah*.
82 "1,000 Anti-Nazis Call City Free-Speech Policy Stupid," *Toronto Daily Star*, 6 July 1966, Ibid., 1966.
83 MacGuigan, "Hate Control and Freedom of Assembly," 241–2.
84 Minutes, CANC Meeting, 20 July 1966, JCRC Papers, 1966, 26/37, OJA; Fighters against Racial Hatred, *Newsletter*, 22 August 1966, ibid.
85 Garrity and Edmonds, "I Spied on the Nazis," *Maclean's*, 1 October 1966.
86 Ibid., 9–11, 38–43.
87 "Congress, N-3 in Open Anti-Nazi Competition," *Canadian Jewish News*, 28 September 1966, JCRC Papers, 1966, 26/37, OJA.
88 MacGuigan, "Hate Control and Freedom of Asembly," 244, 249.
89 Ben Kayfetz to CANC and JCRC, "Report on Allan Gardens June 30," 5 July 1968, JCRC Papers, 1968, 37/114, OJA.
90 Interview with Harris.

CHAPTER SIX

1 Interviews with Sol Kanee and Judge Sydney Harris, presidents of CJC, 1971–77.
2 Resolution of the Fourteenth Plenary of CJC, 20–24 May 1965, CA, Numerical Subject Files, box 87/1002–10, CJCA.
3 *The Voice*, 1966 issue, JPLA; interview with Zablow; JCRC Report to the Fifteenth Plenary Session, 16–20 May 1968, Newsletter no. 5, 2, Plenary Sessions File, CJCA.
4 Sabina Citron, "The Anti-Hate Legislation: What It Really Signifies," *The Voice*, 1966 issue, JPLA.
5 Hayes to the National Executive Committee of CJC, 6 April 1965, in Kaplan, "Maxwell Cohen," 265 (emphasis added).

6 "Hate Propaganda Can Be Outlawed," *The Voice*, 1966 edition, JPLA.
7 Interview with MacGuigan.
8 Cohen et al., *Report of the Special Committee on Hate Propaganda in Canada*, 5. The author wishes to thank Judge Cohen for his help in clarifying some of the issues in this section. Cohen spoke to the author by telephone on several occasions in the summer of 1995, recommending articles and books, some of which are cited in these notes. He was unable to be interviewed in person due to poor health. Maxwell Cohen died in 1998.
9 Ibid., 59–67.
10 Ibid., 69–71.
11 Kaplan, "Maxwell Cohen," 254.
12 Interview with MacGuigan.
13 Kaplan, "Maxwell Cohen," 250–1.
14 Pearson to Garber, 13 May 1966, WJCC, P3452, file 28, PAM.
15 Confidential Minutes of NJCRC meeting, Interim Report of Legal Committees, Toronto, 14 May 1966, JCRC Papers, 1966, 25/3, OJA.
16 Kayfetz, "The Story behind Canada's New Anti-Hate Law," 6, OJA; interview with Kayfetz, 13 November 1995.
17 Interview with Kayfetz.
18 Kayfetz, "The Story behind Canada's New Anti-Hate Law," 6, OJA.
19 Orlikow to His Excellency, Dr Kurt Opper, ambassador of the Federal Republic of Germany, 25 March 1964; Opper to Orlikow, 2 April 1964; JLC, "Brief on the Decision of the Federal German Government concerning Nazi Criminals" (n.d., although 1965), JCC Papers, 26/13, JPLA.
20 Montreal Labour Council, JLC, Quebec Federation of Labour, Association of Former Concentration Camp Inmates/Survivors of Nazi Oppression, Fraternal Societies, Memorandum to the Consul General, the Federal Republic of Germany, Montreal (n.d., although 1965), ibid.
21 The figure was reported in the *Montreal Gazette*, 26 February 1965.
22 Resolutions of the Fourteenth Plenary of CJC, 13, CJCA.
23 Hayes and Garber, submission to Pearson, 16 May 1966, in Confidential Internal Letter, 22 May 1966, BB Papers, 36, 1966-67, file 19, NA.
24 Minutes of Meetings of the CJC Central Region Executive Committee, 21 February, 5 May, 13 June 1969, Executive Committee Papers, 1969, OJA; JCRC Papers, War Criminals File, 1969, 41/94, OJA.
25 Harris to Riegner, 16 June 1969, and Riegner to Harris, 20 June 1969, JCRC Papers, ibid.
26 Minutes of NJCRC Meeting, 8 January 1967, JCRC Papers, 1967, 29/3, OJA.
27 Minutes of Central Region Executive Committee Meeting, 13 January 1967, Executive Committee Papers, 1967, OJA.
28 Press release in Ben Kayfetz, "Hate Mongers and the Mass Media," Confidential Report to the NJCRC, 13 November 1968, BB Papers, 1966–67, 36/19, NA.

29 *Sunday*, 22 January 1967, CBC Film Archives.
30 Interviews with Zolf and Kayfetz, 13 November 1995.
31 Minutes of JCRC Central Region Meeting, 1 February 1967, JCRC Papers, 1967, 29/12, OJA; Minutes of Central Region Executive Committee Meeting, 3 February 1967, Executive Committee Papers, 1967, OJA;. NJCRC Report to the CJC Plenary, 1968, 3, Plenary Session Files, CJCA.
32 Interview with Zolf.
33 Resolution of CJC Western Region, 26 January 1967, CJC Papers, P5117/241, PAM. *Winnipeg Free Press*, 27 January 1967.
34 *The Jewish Labour Committee and the Von Thadden Affair* (n.d., 1967), JLC Papers, 26/10; NA. For a selection of press clippings on the affair, see the JCRC Papers, 1967, 33/171, OJA.
35 Interviews with Henry Rosenbaum, Lou Zablow, Sophie Waldman, and Nathan Leipciger. My perspective is also based on witnessing the actions of survivors in Montreal, where I was working at the time, and in Toronto, where my father was organizing fundraising activities.
36 Interviews with Rothstein and Steinberg.
37 Interviews with Cummings and Levitt.
38 Neusner, *Death and Birth of Judaism*, 275–7.
39 Novick, *The Holocaust In American Life*, 149.
40 JCRC Report to the Fifteenth Plenary Session of the CJC, Plenary Session Files, CJCA.
41 Press Release, CJC Western Region, 18 January 1967, WJCC Papers, P3542/26, PAM.
42 Abraham J. Arnold, director of CJC Western Region, "Confidential Report and Evaluation of Recent Visits to Winnipeg by Ron Gostick," 10 February 1967, ibid; interview withArnold.
43 *Winnipeg Free Press*, 1 May 1967; *Winnipeg Tribune*, 6 April 1968.
44 Arnold papers; file 93.1, PS138/93.1, PAM; Report of the JCRC Western Region to the 1968 Plenary, 2–4, CJCA; JCRC Papers, 1968, file 169A, OJA.
45 Report of the Western Region to the NJCRC, 14 November 1969, in CJC Papers, P3527/30, PAM.
46 JCRC Papers, 1970, file 173, OJA.
47 CJC Papers, P3527/16, PAM.
48 Contrary to Hayes's statement, there were virtually no Jewish immigrants in the 1930s.
49 Saul Hayes, "The Changing Nature of the Jewish Community," *Viewpoints* 5:3 (1970): 24–28, in *Viewpoints* File, CJCA.
50 Neusner, *Death and Birth of Judaism*, 254–82.
51 Robert Stall, "'No Thanks' If Anti-hate Law Were Salve – Jewish Leader," *Montreal Star*, 17 October 1966.
52 Minutes of JCRC Central Region meeting, 7 September 1966, JCRC Papers, 1966, 25/2, OJA.

53 File 97, ibid.

54 Minutes of JCRC Central Region meeting, 30 November 1966, 25/2 ibid.; Mark R. MacGuigan, "Free Speech Right Not Absolute," *Toronto Daily Star*, 15 December 1966.

55 Michael Garber, national president, CJC, and Louis Herman, chairman, NJCRC, "Brief of the Canadian Jewish Congress to the Senate Special Committee on the Criminal Code (Hate Propaganda)," Ottawa, 22 February 1968, 14, 19, JLC Papers, 20/21, NA.

56 Kayfetz, "The Story behind Canada's New Anti-Hate Law," 6, OJA.

57 Interview with Zablow.

58 Abe Steinberg, CJC Western Region chairman, "Draft Letter to All Election Candidates in the Western Region," 13 June 1968, JCRC Papers, 1968, 38/169A, OJA; J.A. Geller to Members of the Legislative Planning Committee of NJCRC, 24 October 1968, 35/61, ibid.

59 N3 Public Meeting, 9 June 1968, 36/108, ibid.

60 Kayfetz to Hayes, 6 January 1969, 1969, 38/43, ibid.

61 Kayfetz, "The Story behind Canada's New Anti-Hate Law," 7, OJA; JCRC, Central Region, Minutes of Meetings, 30 April 1969, 26 May 1969, 1969, 38/2, OJA.

62 The JLC brief was submitted on 11 March 1969; the CCLA brief was dated 22 April 1969 (JLC Papers, 26/18, NA).

63 Bill C-3, "An Act to amend the Criminal Code," 2nd. Session, 28th. Parliament, 18–19 Elizabeth II, 1969–70, JCRC Papers, 1969, 55/79, OJA.

64 Trudeau to Orlikow, 22 October 1969, JLC Papers, 26/18, NA.

65 Stephen S. Cohen, "Hate Propaganda – The Amendments to the Criminal Code," extract from *McGill Law Journal*, 17:4 (1979): 741–91, in JCRC Papers, 1971, 55/79, OJA; Kayfetz, "The Story behind Canada's New Anti-Hate Law," 8, OJA.

66 Annual reports of the Shaareth Hapleita Committee of Winnipeg Congress council, 1960–68, CJC Papers, P3535/23, PAM; *Jewish Post*, 4 May 1967, 3 and 23 March 1972, 11, JHS/WC.

67 Minutes of the Shoah Arrangements Committee, 9 May 1971, CJC Central Region, JCRC Papers, 1971, 45/4, OJA.

68 *Report* of the Holocaust Memorial Committee, 123, Seventeenth Plenary Session, 1974, Plenary Sessions File, CJCA; interview with Arnold.

69 Minutes, Executive Committee of CJC Central Region, 25 March; 29 April 1966, Executive Committee Papers, 1966, OJA; *IOI* no. 3144 (10 May 1967), CJC Pacific Region Papers, 15/18, JHS/BC.

70 Minutes, Executive Committee of CJC Central Region, 28 March 1969, Executive Committee Papers, 1969, OJA.

71 Minutes, JCRC Central Region, 21 January; 23 January 1970, JCRC Papers, 1970, 42/2, OJA.

72 Minutes, Shoah Arrangements Committee, 18 March; 9 May 1971, 1971,

45/4, ibid. Minutes, Executive Committee of CJC Central Region, 23 April; 21 May 1971, Executive Committee Papers, 1971, OJA.

73 Minutes, Executive Committee of CJC Central Region, 16 November 1973, ibid.

74 Report, Holocaust Memorial Committee, Central Region, CJC Plenary, 1974, 98–9, Plenary Sessions Files, CJCA.

75 *IOI* no. 3144 (10 May 1967), CJC Pacific Region Papers, 15/18, JHS/BC.

76 Resolutions, CJC Plenary Session, 14–16 November 1971, 3-4, Plenary Sessions Files, CJCA.

77 Notice by the Association of Survivors of Nazi Oppression (n.d., February 1972), Lou Zablow Papers; interviews with Zablow, Piasetski and Beer.

78 Association leaders met with Saul Hayes, who was convinced by them that the CJC should support the protest. Flyer courtesy of Isaac Piasetski.

79 Mark Medicoff, "Play on Nazi Theme at Bronfman Centre Arouses Bitter Controversy," *Canadian Jewish News*, 18 February 1972, Zablow Papers; transcript of a telephone conversation between Lou Zablow, Montreal, and Gideon Hausner, Jerusalem (n.d.); Hausner to Zablow, 5 March 1972; Hausner to the editor of the *CJN*, 5 March 1972; Zablow Papers; interview with Zablow, 29 August 1995.

80 "A Statement from the Director," *The Suburban*, 1 March 1972, Zablow Papers.

81 Michael Ballantyne, "This Is One Show That Won't Go On," *Montreal Star*, 28 February 1972; "Without a Past, There Can Be No Future...," *Suburban*, 1 March 1972, Zablow Papers.

82 Minutes, JCRC Central Region (Core Committee) Meeting, 22 March 1972, JCRC Papers, 1972, 51/2, OJA.

83 Midanek to Kayfetz, 28 March 1972, 51/3, ibid.

84 Minutes, Meeting of the Holocaust Memorial Committee of CJC Eastern Region, 16 October 1972, CJC Pacific Region Papers, file 15, JHS/BC.

85 Invitation to the Holocaust Exhibition, Samuel Bronfman House Museum, Montreal, 18 March-1 April, 1973, BJE Papers, RG 42/B, 2/30, OJA.

86 Minutes, Holocaust Memorial Committee Meeting, 26 April 1973, JCC, *File*: CJC – Holocaust Memorial Committee, JPLA.

87 Beer to CJC Eastern Region, 30 November 1972, CJC Pacific Region Papers, file 15, JHS/BC.

88 *Report* of the first Meeting of the Holocaust Sub-Committee on Education, 18 July 1972, in the Plenary Assembly Report of the Holocaust Memorial Committee, 16 June 1974, D606, 5/10, CJCA.

89 Minutes of the Holocaust Remembrance Committee meeting of Central Region, 30 January 1973, 20 March 1973, JCRC Papers, 1973, 52/3, 53/3, OJA.

90 Report of the National Holocaust Memorial Committee, CJC Plenary, 1974, 47–8, Plenary Sessions Files, CJCA. Regional reports were filed by the Quebec Region (formerly Eastern Region), 79–80; Central Region, 92, 98–9; Western Region, 123; Pacific Region, 129.
91 Resolutions, 22, 31, 33, 34, ibid.
92 Zablow (29 August 1995), Beer and Piasetski interviews.

CHAPTER SEVEN

1 Interview with Steinitz-Frieberg.
2 Interviews with Weiss, Lowy, and Leipciger.
3 Another perspective was presented by Nora Levin in *The Holocaust: The Destruction of European Jewry, 1933–1945*. Other notable early works included Arendt, *Eichmann in Jerusalem: A Report on the Banality of Evil*; Feingold, *The Politics of Rescue: The Roosevelt Administration and the Holocaust, 1938–1945*; and Poliakov, *Harvest of Hate*.
4 Wiesel, *Night*, and *The Town beyond the Wall*. Other important works in this genre in the 1960s included Kosinski, *The Painted Bird*; Levi, *Survival in Auschwitz*; and Schwartz-Bart, *The Last of the Just*.
5 Dawidowicz adopted an extremely internationalist analysis which has been challenged by many scholars. She also did not understand the nuances of jewish complicity and resistance. She maintained her views with steely obstinacy until her death in 1991.
6 Doneson, *The Holocaust in American Film*; Insdorf, *Indelible Shadows*, 267–76. The figure is from Insdorf, who cautions that her list is "by no means complete."
7 See the historiographical articles by Perin, "Writing about Ethnicity," and Palmer, "Canadian Immigration and Ethnic History in the 1970s and 1980s."
8 Dahlia and Fernando, *Ethnicity, Power and Politics in Canada*; Troper, "As Canadian as Multiculturalism."
9 Reed and Lass, "Racism Today – Echoes of the Holocaust"; Short, "Combatting Anti-Semitism"; Novogrodsky, "The Anti-Racist Cast of Mind."
10 Report of the NHRC to the Nineteenth CJC Plenary, 1–4 May 1980, Toronto, 42, Plenary Sessions Files, CJCA.
11 *Zachor* commenced publication in December 1976. Programs sponsored by the twelve local committees, together with national activities and international events, were reported in the first four issues. See also JCC, File: Institutions – CJC – National Holocaust Committee, JPLA; Report of the NHRC, 1 June 1978, unclassified, file: HRC, MHMCA.
12 The NHRC sponsored a resolution that there should be no other community events held on the 27th day of Nisan, so that it should be kept as a

day for the "respect and observance ... for the martyrs of the Holocaust" (Plenary Resolutions of the Twentieth Plenary of CJC, 12–15 May 1983, Montreal, 35, Plenary Sessions Files, CJCA). At the next plenary, a resolution was adopted that the government of Canada should proclaim that date as Holocaust Remembrance Day, "in recognition of Canada's continuing commitment to human rights at home and around the world and in further recognition of the greatest inhumanity man has ever perpetrated against his fellow man" (Plenary Resolutions of the Twenty-first Plenary, 7–11 May 1986, Toronto, 47, ibid). To date, the government has not responded to this appeal.

13 Resolutions of the Eighteenth Plenary of CJC, 12–15 May 1977, Montreal, 7, ibid.

14 Report of the NHRC, ibid; Beer to members of the NHRC, 16 January 1978, 15/32, JHS/BC; *Report* of the NHRC, 1 June 1978, unclassified, MHMCA.

15 Report of the NHRC (n.d., 1976), HRC of TJC Papers, unclassified, OJA; Estie Jedeiken, executive director of NHRC to NHRC chairman and directors, 13 November 1978, JCRC Papers, 1978, 69/43A; "A Programming Kit – Remembrance Day for Jewish Martyrdom and Heroism, 27th. Day of Nisan," March 1982, unclassified, file: HRC, MHMCA.

16 NHRC Report, 1977 Plenary; Plenary Sessions Files, CJCA.

17 *Zachor*, February 1982, Irwin Cotler Papers, J1, 3/2, CJCA.

18 Budget and Priorities Report, NHRC, August 1981, National Holocaust Committee Papers, DA 6, 7/12, CJCA.

19 NHRC Report to the CJC Plenary, 1977, Plenary Sessions Files, CJCA; *Zachor*, May 1977; Beer to NHRC, 16 January 1978, 15/32, JHS/BC.

20 NHRC Report, 1 June 1978, CJCA.

21 *Zachor*, January 1981, DB 07,Quebec Region Papers, 1/1, CJCA.

22 Beer to Dr Robert Krell, Vancouver HRC chair, 9 December 1981, 31/14, JHS/BC.

23 Beer to NHRC Members, 3 November 1981, ibid.

24 Minutes of Meeting of Consultants to the Holocaust Documentation Project, 11 November 1981, Toronto, unclassified:, File: HRC, MHMCA.

25 Holocaust Documentation Report, n.d., DA16, box 1, Holocaust Documentation Papers, CJCA.

26 Holocaust Documentation Status Report, DA 5, Alan Rose Papers, 28/19, CJCA.

27 The author thanks Irving Abella, chairperson of the Archives Committee of CJC in the late 1980s, for providing this information.

28 File: Voices of Survival, Bialystok Papers; Bialystok and Weintraub, *Voices of Survival*.

29 *Report* of the NHRC to the 1977 CJC Plenary, Plenary Sessions Files, CJCA.

30 Beer to NHRC Members, 16 January, 1978; Projection of Activities, NHRC, 1978–79, 15 August 19778, unclassified, MHMCA.

31 Beer to NHRC (n.d., 1978), HRC of TJC Papers, 1978, unclassified, OJA.
32 NHRC Report, 1 June 1978; Report of the NHRC to the 1980 CJC Plenary, 42–3, Plenary Sessions Files, CJCA.
33 *Zachor*, January 1981.
34 Report of the NHRC to the 1983 CJC Plenary, 48–52, Plenary Sessions Files, CJCA.
35 Resolution 47, Twenty-first Plenary of the CJC, 7–11 May 1986, Toronto, ibid.
36 New Brunswick Department of Education, *The Holocaust: A Topic of Study in History 111–112–113*. This course, although optional, was taken by 90 per cent of eleventh-grade students in 1991, according to department officials interviewed by the author.
37 Keith Landy, chair, CJC Central Region to David Johnson, minister of education, Ontario, 3 March 1999, regarding the Draft Document for Grades 9 and 10 for the Canadian and World Studies Curriculum, file: Ministry of Education Curriculum, Bialystok Papers.
38 Rose to Max von Podewils, Ambassador of the Federal Republic of Germany, 6 September 1978; Plaut Papers, vol. 133, file: Statute of Limitations, NA.
39 W. Gunther Plaut, "Shutting the Door of Remembrance Is Risky," *Globe and Mail*, 26 June 1979. For information on Plaut, see his autobiography, *Unfinished Business*. The author thanks Rabbi Plaut for providing information on this topic and others relevant to this paper in informal conversations.
40 CJC Statute of Limitations Interim Report, 6 December 1978, JCRC Papers, 1978, 67/6, OJA; CJC Press Release, 12 December 1978, ibid.
41 Beer to NHRC, 12 October 1978, 71/127, ibid.
42 NHRC Report to the Nineteenth Plenary of CJC, 1–4 May 1980, 45, Plenary Sessions Files, CJCA.
43 Yahil, "Raoul Wallenberg: His Mission and His Activities in Hungary."
44 Quoted in Cotler, *Nuremberg Forty Years Later*, 13; emphasis in the original.
45 File: HRC 1981–85, Bialystok Papers.
46 Adopted Resolutions, Twentieth CJC Plenary, 12–15 May 1983, Montreal, 12, Plenary Sessions Files, CJCA.
47 Alberta Region Report, Twenty-first CJC Plenary, 7–11 May 1986, Toronto, 16, ibid.
48 Interview with Zablow, 28 August 1995.
49 The teach-in was held on 17–19 February 1970 (JCC, File: Institutions – National Holocaust Committee, JPLA).
50 Minutes of the Meeting of the HRC, Eastern Region, 7 October 1975, Quebec Region Papers, DB06, 1/16, CJCA. The CJC Eastern Region then approved a bylaw making the Holocaust Memorial Committee a stand-

ing committee of the region, with subcommittees dealing with education and commemoration (Minutes of the CJC Eastern Region, 21 October 1975, unclassified, file: HRC, MHMCA).

51 *Program on the Seminar on the Holocaust*, Samuel Bronfman House, Montreal, 16 February 1975; Report on the Seminar, 18 March 1975, box 31, unclassified, JHS/BC.

52 "Symposium on The Holocaust – The Jewish Experience in World War II," McGill University, 20–23 October 1975, HRC of TJC Papers, 1976, unclassified, OJA.

53 Gerard H. Hoffman, "Holocaust Teaching in the French Schools of Quebec," *Canadian Zionist*, March–April, 1976, Plaut Papers, file: HRC, 1976–77, NA.

54 Report of the Holocaust Committee, Eastern Region, CJC, 1975–76, Quebec Region Papers, DB04, file 24, CJCA.

55 Interview with Zablow, 28 August 1995.

56 Report of the Holocaust Memorial Project, 20 October 1978, Alan Rose Papers, DA 5, file 28, CJCA; Michael Greenblatt, chair of the AJCS Holocaust Committee, Memorandum to Committee Members, 17 January 1978, unclassified, file: MHMC History, MHMCA; interviews with Isaac Piasetsky, Aba Beer, and Lou Zablow (28 August 1995).

57 Interview with Stephen Cummings, Montreal, 31 August 1995.

58 Greenblatt, Memorandum to Committee Members, 17 January 1978, MHMCA.

59 Interview with Cummings.

60 Interviews with Zablow (August 28, 1995) and Cummings. The importance of the young Montrealers in the establishment of the group is confirmed in interviews with Aba Beer and Isaac Piasetski, members of the committee and influential in their own right since Beer was the chair of the NHRC and Piasetski the chair of the HRC Quebec Region. Confirmation is also provided by Krisha Starker, who, while not in Montreal at the time, was director of the centre from 1983 to 1994 (Starker interview).

61 Budget Memo, 10 September 1979; Report to Officers of the AJCS, 20 October 1978; Proposal, 19 December, 1978, unclassified, file: MHMC History, MHMCA; interview with Cummings.

62 Draft Resolution of Principles, 27 September 1978, unclassified, file: MHMC History, MHMCA.

63 Lawrence Sabbath, "Centre is 'a Warning to the Living,'" *Gazette*, 4 December 1981; information on exhibits, unclassified, box: Exhibit Archives, 1979–83, MHMCA. Other press coverage was given in the *Canadian Jewish News, La Press, Suburban, Monitor*, and the *Westmount Examiner* (Minutes of the Centre Committee, 13 November 1980, file: MHMC History, MHMCA).

64 Report on Status (n.d., February 1980); Minutes, Centre Committee, March 3, ibid.
65 *Memorandum* on the Holocaust Memorial Centre/Jewish Public Library Merger, 15 June 1982, ibid.; interview with Cummings, Starker, and Zablow.
66 JCC, file: Institutions – NHRC, JPLA.
67 Quebec Region Papers, DA 6, 7/16, CJCA.
68 DA 5, 14/31, ibid. The Canadian Centre for Studies in Holocaust and Genocide was an independent organization, based in Toronto, that existed for several years in the 1980s.
69 Interview with Starker, and a follow-up telephone conversation, 8 November 1996. Starker's views about the relationship with the JPL were echoed in the interviews with Zablow.
70 Unclassified, binder: Education – Minutes and Agenda, MHMCA; box: Exhibit Archives, 1979–83, ibid.
71 "Working Agreement between the AJCS and MHMC," 6 June 1985, binder: Board of Management – Agenda and Minutes – Affiliation with AJCS, ibid. This partnership ended in 1989 when the centre became fully independent.
72 "Dear Educator," Letter from Starker to educators about the centre, 19 November 1984; Minutes, Centre Committee, 14 February 1985, binder: Steering Committee – Agenda and Minutes, ibid. In 1993 Yom Hashoah programs were taken over by the centre, effectively ending the HRC Quebec Region's activities.
73 *Montreal Second Generation – Seconde Generation*, December 1984, Quebec Region Officers Papers, K1, 6/9, CJCA.
74 Weinfeld quoted in Janice Arnold, "Survivors' Children Try to Keep Memory of Holocaust alive," *Canadian Jewish News*, 22 April 1982, HRC of TJC Papers, unclassified, OJA.
75 Interview with Cummings.
76 Abella, *A Coat of Many Colours*, 232–5. According to the 1981 census, approximately 95,000 Jews lived in Quebec and 146,000 in Ontario. According to the 1986 mini-census, there were 98,000 in Quebec and 166,000 in Ontario (Statistics Canada, as cited in Robert J. Brym, "The Rise and Decline of Canadian Jewry? A Socio-Demographic Profile," in Brym et al., *The Jews in Canada*, 25). In 1981, approximately 83 per cent of Ontario's Jews lived in Toronto, and 98 per cent of Quebec's Jews lived in Montreal (adapted from Elazar and Waller, *Maintaining Consensus*, 75–6, 167–70. On wealth distribution, synagogue attendance, support for community organizations and for Israel, by Toronto's Jews, see Jay Brodbar-Nemzer et al., "An Overview of the Canadian Jewish Community," in Brym et al., *The Jews in Canada*, 57–66.

77 HRC Report to the Executive Committee of TJC, 24 June 1976; 17 March
    1977, TJC Executive Committee Papers, RG 1/A, OJA; *Canadian Jewish
    News*, 22 April 1977, 1, HRC of TJC Papers, unclassified, OJA.
78 HRC of TJC Files, file: Correspondence, 1978, OJA.
79 Report, 17 March 1977, ibid.
80 Budget, TJC to HRC, Social Planning Papers of TJC, box 5, OJA.
81 BB Papers, vol. 98, file: Edmund Burke Society, NA.
82 JCRC Papers, 1974, 58/43, CJCA.
83 Minutes, JCRC Central Region, 20 January 1978, 22 February 1978, 31
    May 1978, 27 September 1978, JCRC Papers, 1978, 67/2, OJA.
84 Harry Simon, chairman of the Anti-Nazi Committee, letter to the editor,
    Jewish Standard, 27 December 1978, 1978, 67/6, ibid.
85 Report of the Holocaust Remembrance Association to the CJC Plenary,
    1980, Plenary Sessions Files, CJCA; interview with Sabina Citron, 18 Sep-
    tember 1996; interview with Frieberg.
86 Resolution of the HRC, 17 May 1978, JCRC Papers, 69/43A, OJA; Plaut
    Papers, vol. 133, file: HRC Correspondence, 1978, part 1, NA; Simon to the
    Jewish Standard, 27 December 1978, JCRC Papers, 67/6, OJA.
87 Report of the Anti-Nazi Committee to the JCRC Central Region, 31 May
    1978, OJA.
88 Minutes of the JCRC Central Region, 28 June 1978, JCRC Papers, 1978,
    67/2, OJA.
89 Smolack to Milton Harris, president of CJC, Ontario Region, on a resolu-
    tion of the HRC requesting information on the documentation of Nazi
    war criminals, 31 January 1978, HRC of TJC Papers, File: Correspondence,
    1978, unclassified, OJA.
90 Interview with Citron.
91 Minutes of Meeting of TJC Officers, 6 July 1978, TJC Officers Papers, RG
    1/C, OJA.
92 Lipsitz to Gold, Confidential Memo, "Summary and Assessment of the
    Holocaust Remembrance Meeting held on Wednesday, 9 August 1978, at
    the Shararei Shomayim Synagogue," 14 September 1978, ibid.
93 Minutes of JCRC Central Region Meeting, 27 September 1978, JCRC
    Papers, 1978, 67/2, OJA.
94 Minutes of the TJC Executive Committee, 28 September 1978, 16 Novem-
    ber 1978, TJC Executive Papers, OJA.
95 Correspondence, 1978, HRC of TJC Papers, unclassified, OJA; JCRC Papers,
    1978, 67/6, file: Anti-Nazi Committee, OJA; interview with Citron.
96 Interview with Citron; HRA Report to the CJC Plenary, 1980, Plenary Ses-
    sions Files, CJCA; HRA Letter, "Dear Friend" (n.d., 1986), HRC of TJC
    Papers, unclassified, OJA.
97 Interviews with Leipciger, Steinitz-Frieberg, and Citron.
98 "Brief on Recommendations and Comments concerning B'nai Brith Par-
    ticipation in Community Relations Work in Canada – By the ADL Chair

man for District 22," 14 July 1964, BB Papers, 36/18, NA; "Declaration Pursuant to a meeting of officers of CJC and District 22 B'nai Brith," 25 March 1965, ibid.

99 Minutes, ADL Meeting, 4 March 1970, file 1970/6, ibid.; Minutes, JCRC Central Region Meeting, 19 May 1971, 23 June 1971, file 1971/37, ibid.

100 "Congress accuses B'nai Brith of Isolationism," *Canadian Jewish News,* 12 November 1971, ibid.

101 Minutes of Meeting of BB Delegation to Confer with CJC, 20 June 1972, BB Papers, 37/1972, Part 2, ibid.; "Congress, B'nai Brith Study Joint Body on Human Rights," *Canadian Jewish News,* 23 April 1976, 37/1975–78, ibid.

102 Crestohl to Diamant, 18 December 1979, 37/1979, ibid.

103 Alan Rose, executive vice-president, Canadian Jewish Congress to Frank Diamant, executive vice-president, B'nai Brith Canada, 17 September 1981, Morley Wolfe Papers. The author thanks Morley Wolfe for providing this document, and for explaining the controversy during informal conversations in October 1998. For further information on the split, see the following correspondence: Morley Wolfe, chairperson, JCRC Central Region, to Phil Leon, president of B'nai Brith Canada,15 October 1981, BB Papers, 37/1981, NA; Irwin Cotler, president of Canadian Jewish Congress, to Leon, 4 February 1982, Quebec Region Papers, DA 6, 7/15, CJCA; Leon to BB membership, 19 January 1982, BB Papers, 37/1981, NA.

104 Julius Hayman, "Canadian Jewish Congress and B'nai Brith," *Jewish Standard,* 1–14 February 1982, BB Papers, 37/1982, NA.

105 Cruickshank, *The Modern Age,* 468, 470. Professor Cruickshank was my instructor at the Faculty of Education at the University of Toronto in 1971–72 and recommended me for my first teaching position.

106 Haberman, *The Modern Age: Selected Readings,* 417–21, 431–9, 487–8.

107 Minutes of JCRC Central Region Meetings, 23 June 1971, 22 September 1971, 22 December 1971, JCRC Papers, 1971, 45/2.

108 Interview with Kayfetz, 13 November 1995.

109 Minutes, BJE Meeting 30 April 1973, BJE Papers, RG 41/B, 1/50, OJA.

110 Witty to Wolle, 3 June 1976; 2/30, ibid; Report of the HRC, 24 June 1976, TJC Executive Committee Papers, OJA.

111 Harold R. Malitsky, associate director of BJE to all principals, 21 December 1979, HRC of TJC Papers, file: Holocaust Remembrance, 1979, unclassified, OJA.

112 Jacob Egit also served on the JCRC, where he was an outspoken critic of the Jewish establishment in the 1960s. He remained active in community affairs until his death in 1996. ("Egit, Jacob," in Gottesman, *Who's Who in Canadian Jewry,* 409; Egit, *Grand Illusion;* Lipshitz interview).

113 Egit, "Proposal for a Program of Ongoing Activity and Education in Our Community to Further the Knowledge of the Holocaust and Resis-

tance – and Its Meaning for the Present and Future Generations," Egit to the HRC, CJC, Central Region, 25 October 1975, HRC of TJC Papers, file: 1976, unclassified, OJA. Note that there was no such committee; the reference was to the HRC of TJC. See also the *Report* of the HRC to the TJC Executive Committee, 24 June 1976, ibid.

114 Regarding the Bauer lecture and the University of Toronto series, see Report of the HRC to the TJC Executive Committee, 24 June 1976, ibid. Regarding university courses, see HRC of TJC Papers, file: Correspondence, 1978, unclassified, ibid. Regarding the Holocaust Remembrance Week at York University, see HRC Report to the TJC Executive Committee, 17 March 1977; Avraham Weiss, Director of the NHRC to Lydia Toledano and Andrew Kohn, Jewish Student Federation, 26 November 1976, and the program 1976, ibid. Regarding Second Encounter, see 1977, unclassified, ibid.

115 Sheldon Kirshner, "Immigration Policy 'Racially Motivated'," *Canadian Jewish News*, February 3, 1978, unclassified, ibid. Kirshner's full-page article quoted a number of documents given to him by Harold Troper in the early stage of research for *None Is Too Many*.

116 Henry Feingold, "Four Days in April: A Review of NBC's Dramatization of the Holocaust," *Shoah*, 1:1: 15–17, JCRC Papers, 1978, 69/43A, OJA.

117 For the response in the United States, West Germany, and the Netherlands, see the relevant chapters in Wyman, *The World Reacts to the Holocaust*. See also Novick, *The Holocaust in American Life*, especially 209–14.

118 The Fest review is found in the CJC Papers, 31/27, JHS/BC.

119 Plaut to A.W. Johnson, president, Canadian Broadcasting Corporation, 21 February 1978, HRC of TJC Papers, unclassified, OJA.

120 Ruth Resnick, Announcement to Heads of History Departments, Ontario Secondary Schools, 28 February 1978, JCRC Papers, 1978, 69/43A, OJA; Resnick to Heads, 15 March 1978, HRC of TJC Papers, 1978, unclassified, OJA; Minutes of JCRC Central Region meeting, 2 May 1978, JCRC Papers, 1978, 67/2, OJA; interview with Dr Alan Bardikoff, chair of Holocaust Education Subcommittee, 1978–88, 27 September 1996, Toronto.

121 John Baker, teacher of history, Napanee District Secondary School, to Ruth Resnick, 24 April 1978, HRC of TJC Papers, 1978, unclassified, OJA. The course referred to by Baker was the only mandatory history course, as set out by the Ontario Ministry of Education. It was taught in either grade nine or grade ten.

122 Wolfe to Resnick, 12 February 1979, 1979, unclassified, ibid.

123 Frank Diamant, executive vice-president of B'nai Brith Canada, to Glickman, on the agreement on behalf on the League of Human Rights on "The Treatment of the Holocaust in Canadian History Textbooks," 7

March 1980, BB Papers, vol. 79, file: LHR 1980–82; 6 March 1980, file: LHR News Releases, 1980–82; file: Y. Glickman Research Proposal for LHR, 1979–82, NA.

124 Interview with Bardikoff, 27 September 1996; informal conversations with Shefman in the early 1980s.

125 Glickman and Bardikoff, *The Treatment of the Holocaust in Canadian History and Social Science Textbooks*, 12–13, appendix C. B'nai Brith took the responsibility for advertising the book and selling it. Glickman was upset about the apparent lack of commitment to the project. Although the manuscript was ready in late 1981, it was not released until August 1982. Two months later he wrote to Diamant: "[I] express my disappointment, indeed my frustration, concerning the promotion of our monograph." Diamant replied: "Your letter was highly disappointing. You will recall that during the study, which lasted two years longer than initially contracted for." Two years later Shefman wrote to Diamant that between January 1984 and June 1985, eighty-four copies of the book had been sold. This underwhelming statistic indicates that the study was one of the best-kept secrets in the educational network in Canada. See Glickman to Diamant, 18 October 1982; Diamant to Glickman, 28 October 1982; Shefman to Diamant, 10 July 1985, BB Papers, vol. 107, file: Glickman Research Proposal, NA.

126 Alan Shefman, Annual Report, LHR, vol. 76, file: Annual Report 1981–82, ibid.; Shefman, "The League for Human Rights and Holocaust Education," vol. 107, file: LHR Resource Materials Guides on the Holocaust, 1980–84, ibid.

127 B'nai Brith Announcement, Annual Review of Antisemitism (n.d., approximately 12 October 1982), vol. 80, file: LHR Review of Anti-semitism in Canada, 1982, ibid.

128 Files: League for Human Rights Guides; League for Human Rights Correspondence; Holocaust and Hope Tour, 1986, Bialystok Papers.

129 Bar Ilan University Institute of Holocaust Studies International Symposium on "Teaching the Holocaust in High Schools," Toronto, 26–28 August 1980, Cotler Papers, box 3, file: World Gathering of Jewish Holocaust Survivors, CJCA; *Zachor*, January 1981, DB 07, 1/1, ibid.

130 Interview with Bardikoff, 27 September 1996. Bardikoff eventually obtained his doctorate in clinical psychology, and in his practice he counsels survivors and their descendants.

131 "Congress Names New Committee on Holocaust," *Canadian Jewish News*, 8 February 1979, HRC of TJC Papers, 1979, unclassified, OJA; Minutes of HRC Meeting, 24 January 1979, ibid.

132 Memo: To the President's Commission on the Holocaust, 11 July 1979, ibid.; Report of the HRC of TJC to the CJC Plenary Session, 1980, 47–8, Plenary Sessions Files, CJCA; Report of the HRC, 1979–80, to the TJC

Executive Committee, 15 May 1980, TJC Executive Committee Papers, OJA; interview with Bardikoff (2 October 1996) and Leipciger (25 January 1996).

133 Interview with Bardikoff, September 27, 1996.

134 *Zachor*, January 1981.

135 Report of the HRC to the TJC Executive Committee, 18 February 1982, TJC Executive Committee Papers, OJA; HRC, "Student Seminar," file: Yom Hashoah, 1982, ibid.

136 HRC to "Dear Friend," 1 February 1983, HRC of TJC Papers, file: Student Seminar, 1983, unclassified, OJA; file: Student Seminar, 1981–86, Bialystok Papers; Report of the HRC to the CJC Plenary, 1986, 18–19, Plenary Sessions Files, CJCA.

137 File: Educators' Seminar, 1982–86, Bialystok Papers.

138 Task Force, *Multiculturalism, Ethnicity and Race Relations Policy*; Sub-Committee on Race and Ethnic Relations and Multicultural Policy, *Race and Ethnic Relations and Multicultural Policy*; *Final Report of Sub-Committee on Race Relations*; *Race, Religion and Culture in Ontario School Materials*.

139 Griesdorf and Bardikoff, *The Holocaust*; Bialystok and Walther, *The Holocaust and Its Contemporary Implications*; interview with Bardikoff, 27 September 1996.

140 Files: Draft Proposal of TBE Curriculum; TBE Correspondence; In-service, 1982–87, Bialystok Papers.

141 HRC to "Dear Friend," 1 February 1983, HRC of TJC Papers, OJA.

142 File: TBE Holocaust Advisory Committee, Bialystok Papers; Holocaust Studies Advisory Committee, Office Files, Equity Studies Centre, Toronto Board of Education, courtesy of Myra Novogrodsky, director.

143 Bardikoff and Leipciger to "Dear Friend," January 1984, HRC of TJC Papers, file: Bette Stephenson's Reply, unclassified, OJA.

144 Stephenson to Irwin Diamond, principal, Cambridge International College of Canada, 2 April 1984, ibid.

145 Minutes of the ALSBO Curriculum Committee, May 1984; *Report* of the ALSBO Curriculum Committee, 14 September 1985; file: ALSBO, "The League for Human Rights and Holocaust Education, ALSBO," Bialystok Papers; BB Papers, file: LHR Resource Materials, Guides on the Holocaust, 1981–84, NA.

146 *Curriculum Guideline, History and Contemporary Studies, Senior Division*, 49; *Curriculum Guideline, History and Contemporary Studies, Ontario Academic Courses*, 26.

147 Interview with Bardikoff. This view was also expressed by Leipciger and Steinitz-Frieberg.

148 Interview with Bardikoff.

149 W.D. McClelland, superintendent of curriculum and progam development, to Barry Preson, history consultant, Waterloo County Board of
Education, 11 May 1989, file: Waterloo County, Bialystok Papers.

150 HRC Questionnaire on Teaching the Holocaust, 1991, file: Question-
naire, Bialystok Papers. HRC Education members were also active in
pedagogical research. Some of their findings appeared in Alan
Bardikoff, guest editor, "Teaching the Holocaust," *History and Social
Science Teacher* 21 (summer 1986), which includes articles by Bardikoff,
Harold Lass, Frank Bialystok, Jane Griesdorf, and Mary Samulewski.
Nine years later another special issue on the topic, edited by Michael
Charles, appeared in the renamed *Canadian Social Studies* 29 (summer
1995), with articles from members of the HRC and the League's Holo-
caust Committee.

151 Some of the important studies in this genre in the 1970s include Flannery, *The Anguish of the Jews*; Fleishner, *Auschwitz: Beginning of a New
Era?* Littell, *The Crucifixion of the Jews*; and Reuther, *Faith and Fratricide*.

152 On the conference held on 10 March 1980, see HRC of TJC Papers, box 4,
file: Christian-Jewish Dialogue, unclassified, OJA. For the first service,
see Graham Hall, "Christians Remember the Holocaust," *Catholic New
Times*, 10 May 1981, file: Christian Commemoration, 1981, ibid. For
subsequent services, see separate files for each year, ibid.

153 File: Holocaust Education Week, Bialystok Papers.

154 Interview with Leipciger.

155 The projected cost of the memorial was approximately $400,000. TJC
officers informed the design committee that there were no funds available, and that it would have to raise the entire amount (Minutes of TJC
Officers Meeting, 19 August 1982,. TJC Officers Papers, OJA; interview
with Leipciger).

156 Minutes of TJC Executive Committee meeting, 1 January 1982; Leip-
ciger to A.J. Green, of the Lipa Green Building for Community Jewish
Services, 27 January 1982, Office Files of the Jewish Federation of
Greater Toronto, TJC Executive Papers.

157 Interviews with Leipciger (25 January 1996), Steinitz-Frieberg, and
Bardikoff (2 October 1996).

158 Author's correspondence with Pnina Zylberman, director of the Holocaust Education and Memorial Centre, 1996.

159 Interview with Bardikoff, 2 October 1996.

160 Minutes of a meeting to discuss the formation of a Holocaust committee, 9 September 1975, CJC Papers, 31/18, JHS/BC; interviews with Krell
and Waldman.

161 "Symposium on the Holocaust," 27 April 1976, box 31, unclassified,
JHS/BC; interviews with Krell, Steinberg and Waldman; Minutes of
Meeting of Standing Committee, 10 May 1979, CJC Papers, 31/13, JHS/BC.

162 Report of the HRC, Pacific Region, to the CJC Plenary, 1980, 48–9, Plenary Sessions Files, CJCA; Stewart McNeill, "Survivors Tell Tales of Holocaust Horror," *Vancouver Sun*, 11 April, 1980.

163 *Tenth Annual Symposium*, 1985, outreach programs, Mark Silverberg Papers, box 96, unclassified, JHS/BC.

164 "Essay Prizes," 1983, Standing Committee on the Holocaust, CJC Papers, 31/14, JHS/BC.

165 Standing Committee to the Vancouver School Board, 20 September 1983; Jean Gerber for the Standing Committee to J. Wormsbecker, Vancouver School Board, 17 June 1983; Wormsbecker to Gerber, 28 June 1983, 31/13, ibid.

166 Interview with Bardikoff, 2 October 1996.

167 George Major, "The Holocaust Is Totally Ignored," *BCTF Newsletter*, 23 November 1983, CJC Papers, 31/14, JHS/BC.

168 Report of the HRC, Pacific Region, to the CJC Plenary, 1986, 45–6, Plenary Sessions Files, CJCA.

169 Robert Krell, "Proposal for the Vancouver Holocaust Centre for Remembrance and Education," 20 September 1984, Silverberg Papers, unclassified, JHS/BC.

170 File: CJC Pacific Region, Bialystok Papers; interviews with Krell, Waldman, Lowy, and Steinberg.

171 *Jewish Post*, 22 May 1975, 17, JHS/WC.

172 Interviews with Gutkin and Arnold. The brochure and program for the exhibit was graciously provided to the author by Abraham Arnold from his personal papers.

173 Interview with Weiss.

174 For 1972 see the *Jewish Post*, 23 March 1972, 11, JHS/WC. For 1980 see the *Jewish Post*, 27 March 1980, 6, ibid. For 1981, 1982, and 1984 see WJCC Papers, P4641/20, PAM. For 1981 see the *Jewish Post*, 19 November 1981, 6.

175 Proclamation, 8 April 1975, WJCC Papers, P3542/33, PAM.

176 "Seminar on Holocaust Education," 9 November 1975, ibid.

177 Editorial, *Jewish Post*, 22 April 1976, 2, JHS/WC.

178 "Encounter with the Holocaust," *Jewish Post*, 21 February 1980, 3, ibid.

179 Manuel Prutschi, "Monitoring of and Outreach to Educational Institutions" (n.d., approximately January 1984), WJCC Papers, P4641/18, PAM; Prutschi to Israel Ludwig et al., regarding Holocaust Education Kit Outline distributed to ministry and board officials, 20 February 1984, ibid; interview with Manuel Prutschi, 30 August 1996, Toronto.

180 Interview with Weiss; *Jewish Post*, 13 September 1989, A3, 29 August 1990, 3, 19 September 1990, 1, 3, JHS/WC; Author's visit, 20 November 1995.

181 "Edmonton," *Zachor* January 1981; Report of the HRC, Alberta Region, to the CJC Plenary Session, 1980, 4, 388–9, Plenary Sessions Files, CJCA.

182 Mark Silverberg, chairperson, CJC, Jewish Community Council of Edmonton, "Lest We Forget," editorial in *Your Community News*, January 1980, Arnold Papers, file 90.3, PAM.

183 Interview with Good.

184 Interview with Good; Harry Hecht, president of the Va'ad, Report of the Holocaust Committee of the Ottawa Jewish Community Council (n.d.), WJCC Papers, P4641/19, PAM.

185 Hecht, Report, WJCC Papers, P4641/19, PAM; "Ottawa," *Zachor*, January 1981, June 1981.

186 File: Ottawa, HRC, Bialystok Papers.

187 Interview with Good.

188 In this survey of two hundred students in their final year of high school, taken in Metropolitan Toronto in 1993–94, though 89 per cent "knew about the Holocaust and its effect on the Jewish community in Europe," only 20 per cent were aware that Canada had refused entry to Jewish refugees. The survey was conducted by the Canadian Civil Liberties Association. See Michael Grange, "Students Ignorant of Canada's Racist History, Survey Indicates," *Globe and Mail*, 25 September 1995, A3.

189 *Intercom*, 1:2 (1985); Silverberg Papers, box 96, unclassified, JHS/BC.

CHAPTER EIGHT

1 Canadian Broadcasting Corporation, *Magazine* (television program), 19 December 1996. Kenstavicius died two weeks after the broadcast.

2 Kayfetz interview, 7 November 1995.

3 Telegram, British Commonwealth Relations Office to the seven dominions, 13 July 1948. Reprinted in *Commission of Inquiry on War Criminals, Report, Part I, Public*, 26-7. See also Svend Robinson, "Bringing Justice to War Criminals in Our Time," in Cotler, *Nuremberg Forty Years Later*, 46.

4 Harold Troper, Michael Marrus, and John Loftus, cited in Linda Hurst, "When War Is a Crime," *Toronto Star*, 17 December 1995, F 4; telephone conversation with Hurst, 18 December 1995; interview with Kayfetz, 7 November 1995.

5 JCRC Papers, 1962, 14/62, file: The Kirschbaum Case, OJA; interview with Kayfetz.

6 Hayes to Cadieux, 23 November 1965, Cadieux to Hayes, 10 February 1966, JCRC Papers, 1966, 38/168, OJA; "Background Information on Harold Puntulis," Restricted, 10 February 1966, ibid.; Minutes, NJCRC Meeting, 16 January 1966, 25/3, ibid. On 30 June 1966, Kayfetz received information on four suspects, including Puntulis, from Wiesenthal (Samuel Levin to Kayfetz, BB Papers, file 19: JCRC 1966–67, NA).

7 Minutes, CANC Meeting, 29 June 1966, JCRC Papers, 1966, 26/37, OJA; Wiesenthal Visit, Minutes, CJC Central Region Executive Committee Meeting, 17 March 1967, Executive Committee Papers, 1967, OJA; "The Wiesenthal Warning – Killers Among Us," *Canadian Jewish News*, 7 April 1967, 59/103, ibid.

8 Saul Hayes, *IOI*, no. 3144 (10 May 1967), CJC Papers, 15/18, JHS/BC; NJCRC *Report* to the 1968 Plenary Session, 6–7, Plenary Sessions Files, CJCA; Troper and Weinfeld, *Old Wounds*, 106–7.

9 Interviews with Kanee and Harris.

10 Draft Resolution from the Holocaust Remembrance Committee of the Central Region, 1977 Plenary Session, JCRC Papers, 1977, unclassified, file: Plenary Assembly, OJA.

11 "War Criminals Residing in Canada," ibid.

12 Resolutions, 1977, 2–3; Resolution Implementations, 2, Plenary Sessions Files, CJCA.

13 Hayes to Rose, 11 April 1978, JCRC Papers, 1978, 71/127, OJA.

14 M. Jack Silverstone, "War Criminals in Canada," *Viewpoints*, 10:2 (Fall 1979): 26–34, *Viewpoints* File, CJCA.

15 Interview with Givens.

16 Interview with Kanee.

17 "The Nazi-hunter Finds a New Ear," *Maclean's*, 5 May 1980, CJC Pacific Region Papers, 31/27, JHS/BC.

18 Resolutions of the 1980 Plenary, 6–7 Plenary Sessions Files, CJCA.

19 Morris Saltzman, executive director, CJC Pacific Region, to "Dear Friend," 5 August 1980, CJC Pacific Region Office Files; Kaplan to Saltzman, in reply to letter, 26 August 1980, ibid.; Axworthy to Dr Harvey Gerber, in reply to letter of 4 September 1980, 1 December 1980, ibid.

20 Resolution of the Canadian Bar Association Plenary Session, Annual Meeting, Vancouver, 3 September 1981, ibid.; Troper and Weinfeld, *Old Wounds*, 110–11.

21 Pacific Region Report on Action Taken re Nazi War Criminals Resident in Canada, 1980–81, CJC Pacific Region Office Files.

22 Cotler to Kaplan, 30 June 1981, ibid.

23 Cited from Hansard, 15 April 1981, in Kayfetz to Rose, BB Papers, 37/1981, NA.

24 Peter Geigan-Miller, "Citizenship Stalls March on Nazi War Criminals," *London Free Press*, 13 April 1981.

25 Troper and Weinfeld, *Old Wounds*, 124–6. See also Robinson, "Bringing Justice," 47–8.

26 H. Katz, chairman, Community Relations Council, Edmonton Jewish Community Council, to Kaplan, asking why three suspects were not deported to the Soviet Union in line with the decision to extradite Helmut Rauca, 25 June 1982; Cotler to Irving Epstein, chairman, CJC

27 Pacific Region, 31 December 1981, CJC Pacific Region Office Files. On the Rauca case, see Littman, *War Criminal on Trial*.

28 Interview with MacGuigan.

29 Resolution on Nazi War Criminals, 1983 Plenary Session, 27, Plenary Sessions Files, CJCA; Report of the NHRC, 50–1, ibid.; Report of the Legal Committee on Nazi War Criminals Resident in Canada, 65–6, ibid.

30 Troper and Weinfeld, *Old Wounds*, 124–35; Robinson, "Bringing Justice," 47–8.

31 Interview with Citron; HRA Brief to the Federal Minister of Justice and the Attorney General for the Province of Ontario, BB Papers, vol. 107, NA; Gayle Applebaum, "Petition Urges Addressing Issue of Nazi War Crimes," *Canadian Jewish News*, 5 March 1981, HRC of TJC Papers, unclassified, OJA; Rose Ehrenworth of the HRA to Ed L. Greenspan, 5 November 1981, Plaut Papers, vol. 134, NA.

32 HRA to Trudeau, 17 June 1982, Plaut Papers, vol. 134, NA. Regarding the HRA campaign, the *Toronto Star* editorialized that, while some lobby groups, including the Canadian Holocaust Remembrance Association, favour extraditing suspected war criminals, the government was right to prefer to try Canadians in Canadian courts. See "Prosecute Nazi War Criminals," *Toronto Star*, 27 July 1981 Also interviews with Citron and Kayfetz (13 November 1995).

33 Interview with Citron.

34 Interview with Kayfetz, 13 November 1995.

35 Troper and Weinfeld, *Old Wounds*, 139–46; Jeff Sallot, "Ottawa Sets Up Commission to Pursue Nazi War Criminals," *Globe and Mail*, 8 February 1985.

36 Troper and Weinfeld, *Old Wounds*, 146; Irwin Cotler, "Response to the Deschenes Commission of Inquiry on War Criminals: An Emergent Mythology and Its Antidote," in Cotler, *Nuremberg Forty Years Later*, 74.

37 Troper and Weinfeld, *Old Wounds*, 146–8.

38 Ibid., 149–50, 172–217, 344–5; Report on Nazi War Criminals – The Deschenes Commission of Inquiry, CJC Plenary Session, 1986, 74–5, Plenary Sessions Files, CJCA.

39 Rosalie Abella, introduction to "The United Nations and Human Rights Forty Years Later," in Cotler, *Nuremberg Forty Years Later*, 97–8.

40 Kayfetz to Hayes, Confidential, 13 March 1968, BB Papers, vol. 98, file: Ernst Zundel, NA. For biographical information on Zundel, see Manuel Prutschi, "The Zundel Affair," in Davies, *Antisemitism in Canada*, 253–8.

41 Littman to Irwin Snell, ADL in New York, 28 May 1968 BB Papers, vol. 98, NA.

42 Kayfetz to Midanik, 3 May 1968, ibid.

43 R. Ryba, secretary of the JLC to Alan O'Brien, chairman, National Liberal Federation, 16 April 1968, JLC Papers, 26/11, NA.

43 For a comprehensive summary of the movement, see Israel Gutman, "Denial of the Holocaust," in Gutman, *Encyclopedia of the Holocaust*, 2: 681–7. For the movement in France, see Vidal-Naquet, *Assassins of Memory*. For the international movement, with special consideration to North America, see Lipstadt, *Denying the Holocaust*. Zundel's contribution to Holocaust denial is discussed by Prutschi, "The Zundel Affair," 258–65, and in an address by Prutschi given to the Canadian Gathering of Holocaust Survivors and Their Children in Ottawa, 18 April 1985, Prutschi Papers, courtesy of Manuel Prutschi.

44 Manuel Prutschi, "Zundel and the Postal Ban, 1980–1983," a chapter of an unpublished monograph, Prutschi Papers; Prutschi, "The Zundel Affair," 249–50, ibid.

45 Minutes, JCRC Central Region, 27 May 1981, BB Papers, 74/1981, NA; attorney general for Ontario, Resolutions of the CJC Plenary, 1983, 24, Plenary Sessions Files, CJCA.

46 Interviews with Citron, Prutschi, Kayfetz (November 7, 1995), and MacGuigan; Prutschi, "Zundel Trial," "Canadian Jewish Congress Overall Report," Confidential, 8 March 1985, Prutschi Papers.

47 Interview with Prutschi. On the decision by the League to work with the Crown and the JCRC, see Shefman to Conrad Winn, 19 August 1985, BB Papers, 79/1985, NA. Shefman writes: "During approximately the third week of the trial an informal arrangement was made between the League and the Community Relations Committee of Canadian Jewish Congress to work together in providing assistance to the Crown. Following that point, virtually all activity in working with Peter Griffith was a joint operation." Shefman, in numerous conversations with the author between 1985 and 1987, discussed this arrangement.

48 Interview with Citron.

49 For an exposure of Christie, see "Counsel for the Damned," the chapter on Christie in Kinsella, *Web of Hate*, 81–100.

50 Manuel Prutschi, "Antisemitism on Trial: Zundel Convicted, Media Indicted," *Bulletin – The Centre for Investigative Journalism* 27 (spring, 1985), Prutschi Papers; Nicholas Russell, "Handling Hate: Reporting of the Zundel and Keegstra Trials," *Trials and Tribulations – An Examination of News Coverage Given Three Prominent Canadian trials* (University of Regina, 1986), in Memorandum, Prutschi to *Standard* recipients, 25 June 1987, ibid.

51 Interview with Prutschi; Hal Quinn, "The Holocaust Trial," *Maclean's*, 11 March 1985, 42–6; Borovoy quoted in Quinn, 44. On the question over the decision to prosecute, see the coverage of a debate between Prutschi and criminal lawyer Eddie Greenspan in Ron Csillag, "Hatemonger Question Provides Lively Debate," *Canadian Jewish News*, 15 August 1985, in Prutschi Papers.

52 Interview with Citron.

53 Author's conversations with Alan Shefman, 1984–87.

54 See Weimann and Winn, *Hate on Trial*.

55 Interview with Prutschi.

56 Prutschi to members of the National Council of the CJC, Ontario Region, 9 October 1986, Prutschi Papers; Prutschi to Charles Zaionz, chairman of CJC, Ontario Region, and Rose Wolfe, chair, JCRC, Ontario Region, "Summary of Ontario Supreme Court Judgement," 29 January 1987, ibid.; Prutschi to Zaionz and Wolfe, "Media Response," 8 April 1987, ibid.; Joseph Wilder, chairman, NJCRC, to members of National Council, "Zundel Retrial Update," 10 December 1987; ibid.

57 Prutschi to Frieberg, 26 August 1992, ibid. Although the "false news" clause was struck down, section 281 was later invoked, with success, in Ontario. Attorney General Roy McMurtry first charged Donald Andrews and Robert Smith and then John Ross Taylor on separate counts of disseminating hate material. Both trials led to convictions. In appeals that ended in the Supreme Court, the judges ruled 4 to 3 against the appeal. For information on Andrews, see Barrett, *Is God a Racist?* 101–19; Prutschi, Community Relations Report, 3:1 (winter 1986), Prutschi Papers. For the trial, see Prutschi, in Community Relations *Report*. For Supreme Court decisions, see *R. vs Donald Clarke Andrews and Robert Wayne Smith* and *R. vs John Ross Taylor and the Western Guard Party*, in Supreme Court of Canada, *Reports*, 1990, 3: 870–977. I am indebted to Manuel Prutschi for explaining the role of the Jewish community and to the late Federal Court judge Mark MacGuigan for unravelling the legal complexities, in my interviews with them.

58 File: CRC Minutes, 1998–99, Bialystok Papers.

59 An excerpt from the notes and tests of Jim Keegstra's students, Myra Novogrodsky Personal Papers, courtesy of Myra Novogrodsky.

60 For an assessment of Keegstra's world view, see Bercuson and Wertheimer, *A Trust Betrayed*, especially the preface and the introduction; Alan Davies, "The Keegstra Affair," in Davies, *Antisemitism in Canada*, 227–47; Barrett, *Is God a Racist?* 81–100. For reports on the trial, see "The Trial," a chapter in Bercuson and Wertheimer, *A Trust Betrayed*, and reports sent by Manuel Prutschi to David Satok, chair of the JCRC, Ontario Region, and by Alan Shefman to Frank Diamant, executive vice-president, B'nai Brith. The Prutschi reports are found in Satok to members of the National Council, CJC, 2 April, 9 May, 31 May, 21 June, 24 July, 1985, in Prutschi Papers. The Shefman reports are summarized in Shefman to Diamant, 18 June, 31 July 1985, in BB Papers, 79/1985, NA.

61 Bercuson and Wertheimer, *A Trust Betrayed*, 129.

62 Barrett, *Is God a Racist?* 229. Unfortunately, Barrett does not provide a date for this rally.

63 Bercuson and Wertheimer, *A Trust Betrayed*, 126–74.

64 Ibid., 150–1.

65 One such program was held in Montreal on 3 December 1983, under the auspices of the Holocaust Memorial Centre and the Association of Survivors (Box: Program Activities, 1979–86, MHMCA). For others, see Prutschi, "Media Coverage of the Trial is Analyzed in Handling Hate: Reporting of the Zundel and Keegstra trials," Prutschi Papers.

66 Barrett, *Is God a Racist?* 256.

67 David Satok, chair of JCRC Central Region, to members of the National Council of CJC, 2 April 1985, Prutschi Papers.

68 Fraser to Prutschi, 20 August 1985, on thanking him for providing information for Keegstra's cross-examination, in Prutschi Papers.

69 Interview with Prutschi.

70 Davies, "The Keegstra Affair," in Davies, *Antisemitism in Canada*, 227. On the decision to uphold the constitutionality of Section 281, see *R. vs. Keegstra*, Supreme Court of Canada, *Reports*, 1990, 3: 697–869.

71 Interview with Prutschi.

72 Interview with MacGuigan.

73 Interviews with Beer, Leipciger (25 January 1996), Krell, Frieberg, and Good. At the plenary, the adopted resolution read in part: "Be it resolved that Canadian Jewish Congress establish a 'Jewish Holocaust Survivors Gathering Committee' and provide the necessary staff and financial resources required to sponsor a Canadian Gathering" (CJC Plenary, 1983, Resolutions, 47, Plenary Sessions Files, CJCA).

74 Interviews with Beer, Leipciger (25 January 1996), Krell, Frieberg, and Good.

75 Minutes of Gathering Committee Meeting, Kingston, 8 March 1984, Quebec Region Papers, DA 5, box 3, 40th Anniversary of Holocaust Survivors (Gathering), CJCA.

76 Interviews with Krell and Leipciger (25 January 1996).

77 Newsletter of the NHRC, December 1984, HRC of TJC Papers, Holocaust Remembrance Correspondence, 1984, unclassified, OJA; JCC, Jewish Studies – Holocaust and Canada, box 3, file: Canadian Gathering, JPLA; Report of the NHRC, CJC Plenary, 1986, 65, Plenary Sessions Files, CJCA.

78 Interviews with Leipciger (25 January 1996) and Good.

79 Irwin Cotler, "THE GATHERING: From Awareness to Action," *Newsletter* of the NHRC, December 1984, HRC of TJC Papers, unclassified, OJA.

CONCLUSION

1 As of 28 March 2000.

2 *Holocaust and Genocide Studies* 13:1 (Spring 1999): 148–65.

3 Peter Novick has expressed the view that "it's not clear that the Holocaust is an American collective memory in any worthwhile sense" because "it is simply too remote from the experience of Americans for it to perform that function" (*The Holocaust in American Life*, 278). Remoteness does not preclude the recreation of historical events from entering collective memory. If that were the case, then collective memory would not exist. Consider one example, the Battle of Kosovo in 1389, where the Serbs were defeated by the Turks. More than six centuries later that event is being used as justification for the attempted genocide of Muslims in the former Yugoslavia.

4 Jacob Neusner makes much the same point for what he describes as "American Judaism." The historical factors that led to this embracing of the legacy of the Holocaust in the 1960s in the United States were somewhat specific to the events there, namely, the civil rights movement and the reaction against the war in Vietnam. These factors had a marginal impact in Canada. See Neusner, *Death and Birth of Judaism*, 254–92.

5 Harris was referring to the passage in the Bible where, after the death of Joseph in Egypt, his descendants "were fruitful ... and multiplied." After some time, "there arose a new king over Egypt, who did not know Joseph" (Exodus I:7–8).

6 Steven M. Cohen, "Jewish Continuity over Judaic Content: The Commitment of the Moderately Affiliated American Jew" (Paper delivered at the Hebrew University Conference on Changes in Jewish Thought and Society, Jerusalem, 17 June 1992), 16–17, reprinted in Wistrich, "Israel and the Holocaust Trauma," 16. Wistrich does not indicate when the poll was taken.

7 Cited in Novick, *The Holocaust in American Life*, 202.

8 Ibid., 281. Emil Fackenheim has written on many occasions that remembrance of the Holocaust is the 614th commandment in the Jewish faith, and that the failure to keep this commandment would grant Hitler a "posthumous victory."

9 Wistrich, "Israel and the Holocaust Trauma," 7.

Bibliography

ARCHIVAL SOURCES

CANADIAN BROADCASTING CORPORATION (CBC) FILM ARCHIVES

CANADIAN JEWISH CONGRESS NATIONAL ARCHIVES, MONTREAL (CJCA)
Association of Survivors of Nazi Oppression Papers
Bulletin Files
H.M. Caiserman Papers
Irwin Cotler Papers
Raymond Arthur Davies Papers
Documentation Collection: Year Boxes; Periodicals Files
Federation of Polish Jews Papers
Holocaust Committee Files
Holocaust Documentation Project Files
Inter-Office Information File (*IOI* microfilm)
Sam Lipshitz Papers
Numerical Subject Files
Plenary Sessions Files
Quebec Region Papers
Alan Rose Papers
Shtern, Avrum, "Notes on *Landsmanschaften* in Canada"
Survivor Documentation Project: Transcripts of Survivor Testimonies
United Refugee Organization (URO) Papers
Viewpoints File
Workmen's Circle Papers

CANADIAN JEWISH CONGRESS PACIFIC REGION, VANCOUVER
Office Files

EQUITY STUDIES CENTRE, TORONTO BOARD OF EDUCATION
Office Files

JEWISH FEDERATION OF GREATER TORONTO
Toronto Jewish Congress Executive Committee Minutes, 1982–85 (office files)

JEWISH HISTORICAL SOCIETY OF BRITISH COLUMBIA, VANCOUVER (JHS/BC)
Canadian Jewish Congress Papers
Canadian Jewish Congress (Pacific Region) Papers
General Archives
Mark Silverberg Papers

JEWISH HISTORICAL SOCIETY OF WESTERN CANADA, WINNIPEG (JHS/WC)
General Archives
Hirsch, John, "How I Discovered My Roots" (1978)
The Jewish Post (Winnipeg)
National Holocaust Committee Papers
Second Generation Papers
Survivor Videotape Project of the Second Generation

JEWISH PUBLIC LIBRARY ARCHIVES, MONTREAL (JPLA)
Association of Survivors of Nazi Oppression Files
Bergen-Belsen Survivors Association Papers
Bialystoker Center Papers
Canadian Jewish Congress Papers
Canadian Jewish History Files
General Archives
Holocaust Memorial Committee Files
Institution Files
Jewish Canadiana Collection (JCC)
Jewish Studies – Holocaust and Canada Files
Paul Trepman Papers

MONTREAL HOLOCAUST MEMORIAL CENTRE ARCHIVES (MHMCA)

NATIONAL ARCHIVES OF CANADA, OTTAWA (NA)
B'nai Brith (BB) Papers
Canadian Jewish Labour Committee Papers (JLC)
Canadian Jewish Chronicle, 1946–49 (microfilm)
The Canadian Jewish Review, 1947–49
W. Gunther Plaut Papers

ONTARIO JEWISH ARCHIVES, TORONTO (OJA)
Board of Jewish Education (BJE) Papers
Canadian Jewish News 1960–62 (microfilm)
Executive Committee of the Canadian Jewish Congress (Central Region) Papers
Holocaust Remembrance Committee of Toronto Jewish Congress (HRC/TJC) Papers
Joint Community Relations Committee (JCRC) Papers
Toronto Jewish Congress Executive Committee Papers, 1976–82
Toronto Jewish Congress Officers Papers
Toronto Jewish Congress Social Planning Papers

PROVINCIAL ARCHIVES OF MANITOBA, WINNIPEG (PAM)
Abraham Arnold Papers
Canadian Jewish Congress Papers
Winnipeg Jewish Community Centre (WJCC) Papers
Winnipeg Jewish Welfare Fund Papers

ZYDOWSKI INSTITUT HISTORYCZNY, WARSAW
CKZP (Central Committee of Jews in Poland) Papers: Protokols, 1945–46

PRIVATE PAPERS

Abraham Arnold
Franklin Bialystok
Professor Adam Fuerstenberg
Myra Novogrodsky
Manuel Prutschi
Morley Wolfe
Lou Zablow

INTERVIEWS

Abraham Arnold, Montreal, 29 May 1995
Dr Alan Bardikoff, Toronto, 27 September, 2 October 1996
Aba Beer, Montreal, 19 July 1994
Mike Berwald, Toronto, 7 May 1995
Sabina Citron, Toronto, 18 September 1996
Stephen Cummings, Montreal, 31 August 1995
Mike Englishman, Toronto, 8 May 1995
Professor Adam Fuerstenberg, Toronto, 3 July 1996
Judge Philip Givens, Toronto, 10 May 1995
Mendel Good, Ottawa, 13 September 1995
Harry Gutkin, Winnipeg, 20 November 1995

Judge Sydney Harris, Toronto, 13 May 1995
Joseph Kage, Montreal, 17 November 1993 (telephone)
Sol Kanee, Winnipeg, 20 November 1995
Kalmen Kaplansky, Ottawa, 11 September 1995
Ben Kayfetz, Toronto, 7 November, 13 November 1995
Dr Robert Krell, Vancouver, 29 November 1993
Dr Ben Lappin, Herzliya, Israel, 20 August 1994
Ida Lappin, Herzliya, Israel, 20 August 1994
Nathan Leipciger, Toronto, 10 November 1995, 25 January 1996.
Professor Cyril Levitt, Toronto, 9 May 1995
Sam Lipshitz, Toronto, 3 October 1995
Leo Lowy, Vancouver, 24 November 1995
Justice Mark MacGuigan, Ottawa, 13 September 1995
Isaac Piasetski, Montreal, 19 July 1994
Manuel Prutschi, Toronto, 30 August 1996
Henry Rosenbaum, Toronto, 11 July 1996
Sam Rothstein, Vancouver, 29 November 1993 (telephone)
Professor Musia Schwartz, Montreal, 29 May 1995
Krisha Starker, Montreal, 30 August 1995, 8 November 1996 (telephone)
Professor Moe Steinberg, Vancouver: 29 November 1993
Gerda Steinitz-Frieberg, Toronto, 27 May 1996
Sophie Waldman, Vancouver, 26 November 1995
Philip Weiss, Winnipeg, 21 November 1995
Lou Zablow, Montreal, 29 May, 29 August 1995
Larry Zolf, Larry, Toronto, 3 November 1995

SECONDARY SOURCES

Abella, Irving. *A Coat of Many Colours: Two Centuries of Jewish Life in Canada.* Toronto: Lester and Orpen Dennys, 1990.
– and Franklin Bialystok. "Canada". In David Wyman, ed., *The World Reacts to the Holocaust.* Baltimore: John Hopkins University, 1996.
– and Harold Troper. *None Is Too Many: Canada and the Jews of Europe, 1933-1948.* Toronto: Lester and Orpen Dennys, 1982.
Arendt, Hannah. *Eichmann in Jerusalem: A Report on the Banality of Evil.* New York: Penguin, 1963.
Bach, Gabriel. "Eichmann Trial." In Y. Gutman, ed., *The Encyclopedia of the Holocaust.* New York: MacMillan, 1990.
Bardikoff, Alan. ed. "Teaching the Holocaust." *History and Social Science Teacher* 21 (summer 1986).
Barrett, Stanley. *Is God a Racist? The Right Wing in Canada.* Toronto: University of Toronto Press, 1987.
Bartrop, Paul R. *Australia and the Holocaust, 1933-1945.* Melbourne: Australian Scholarly Publishing, 1994.

Bassler, Gerhard P. *Sanctuary Denied: Refugees from the Third Reich and Newfoundland Immigration Policy, 1906–1949.* St John's: Iser, 1992.

Bauer, Yehuda. *American Jewry and the Holocaust: The American Joint Distribution Committee, 1939–1945.* Detroit: Wayne State University Press, 1981.

– *Flight and Rescue:* Brichah - *The Organized Escape of the Jewish survivors of Eastern Europe. 1944–1948.* New York: Random House, 1970.

– *A History of the Holocaust.* New York: Watts, 1982.

– *Jews for Sale? Nazi-Jewish Negotiations, 1933–1945.* New Haven: Yale University Press, 1995.

– "The Reigner Cable." In Y. Gutman, ed., *The Encyclopedia of the Holocaust.* New York: MacMillan, 1990.

Beaglehole, Ann. *A Small Price to Pay: Refugees from Hitler in New Zealand, 1936–1946.* Wellington: Allen and Unwin, 1988.

Bercuson, David J. *Canada and the Birth of Israel: A Study in Canadian Foreign Policy.* Toronto: University of Toronto Press, 1985.

– "The Zionist Lobby and Canada's Palestine Policy, 1941–1948." In David Taras and David H. Goldberg, eds., *The Diplomatic Battleground: Canada and the Arab-Israeli Conflict.* Kingston: McGill-Queen's University Press, 1989.

– and Douglas Wertheimer. *A Trust Betrayed: The Keegstra Affair.* Toronto: Doubleday, 1995.

Bergman, Eleanora. ed. *Jewish Historical Institute: The First Fifty Years: Conference Papers.* Warsaw: Zydowski Institut Historyczny, 1996.

Betcherman, Lita-Rose. *The Swastika and the Maple Leaf: Fascist Movements in Canada in the Thirties.* Toronto: Fitzhenry and Whiteside, 1975.

Bialystok, Frank, and Barbara Walther. *The Holocaust and Its Contemporary Implications.* 3 vols. Toronto: Toronto Board of Education, 1985.

– and Sharon Weintraub. *Voices of Survival – Education Guide.* Montreal: Canadian Jewish Congress, 1990.

Blakeney, Michael. *Australia and the Jewish Refugees, 1933–1948.* Sydney: Croom Helm, 1985.

Bothwell, R., I. Drummond, and J. English. *Canada Since 1945: Power, Politics, and Provincialism.* Toronto: University of Toronto Press, 1981.

Breitman, Richard, and Alan Kraut. *American Refugee Policy and European Jewry, 1933–1945.* Bloomington, Ind.: Indiana University Press, 1987.

Brown, Michael. *Jew or Juif? Jews, French-Canadians and Anglo-Canadians, 1759–1914.* Philadelphia: Jewish Publication Society of America, 1987.

Brym, Robert J., William Shaffir, and Morton Weinfeld, eds. *The Jews in Canada.* Toronto: Oxford University Press, 1993.

Caa, Alina, and Helena Datner-Spiewak. *Dzieje Zydow w Polsce 1944–1968.* Warsaw: Zydowski Institut Historyczny, 1997.

Charles, Michael, ed. "The Holocaust." Special issue of *Canadian Social Studies* 29 (summer 1995).

Chiel, Arthur A. *The Jews of Manitoba.* Toronto: University of Toronto Press, 1961.

Clenman, Donia Blumenfeld. *I Dream in Good English Too*. Toronto: Flowerfield and Littleman,. 1988.

Cohen, Maxwell, et al. *Report of the Special Committee on Hate Propaganda in Canada*. Ottawa: Queen's Printer, 1965.

Commission of Inquiry on War Criminals. *Report*. Part I, Public. Jules Deschenes, commissioner. Ottawa: Queen's Printer, 1986.

Cotler, Irwin, ed. *Nuremberg Forty Years Later – The Struggle against Injustice in Our Time*. Montreal: McGill-Queen's University Press, 1995.

Creighton, Donald. *The Forked Road: Canada, 1939–1957*. McClelland and Stewart, 1976.

Cruickshank, J.E. *The Modern Age*. Toronto: Longmans, 1963.

Curriculum Guideline, History and Contemporary Studies, Ontario Academic Courses. Toronto: Ontario Ministry of Education, 1987.

Curriculum Guideline, History and Contemporary Studies, Senior Division. Toronto: Ontario Ministry of Education, 1987.

Dahlie, J., and T. Fernando, eds. *Ethnicity, Power and Politics in Canada*. Toronto: Methuen, 1981.

Davies, Alan T., ed. *Antisemitism in Canada: History and Interpretation*. Waterloo: Wilfrid Laurier University Press, 1992.

– and Marilyn Nefsky. *How Silent Were the Churches? Canadian Protestantism and the Jewish Plight During the Nazi Era*. Waterloo: Wilfrid Laurier University Press, 1997.

Dawidowicz, Lucy S. *The War against the Jews*. New York: Bantam, 1975.

Delisle, Esther. *The Traitor and the Jew: Anti-Semitism and the Delirium of Extremist Right-Wing Nationalism in French Canada from 1929–1939*. Montreal: Robert Davies, 1993.

Dobroszycki, Lucjan. *Survivors of the Holocaust in Poland: A Portrait Based on Jewish Community Records, 1944–7*. Armonk, NY: M.E. Sharpe, 1994.

Doneson, Judith. *The Holocaust in American Film*. Philadelphia: Jewish Publication Society of America, 1987.

Draper, Paula Jean. "The Accidental Immigrants: Canada and the Interned Refugees." Unpublished PhD dissertation, Department of History, University of Toronto, 1984.

– "The Accidental Immigrants: Canada and the Interned Refugees: Part I." *Canadian Jewish Historical Society Journal* 2:1 (spring 1978): 1–38.

– "The Accidental Immigrants: Canada and the Interned Refugees: Part II." *Canadian Jewish Historical Society Journal* 2:2 (fall 1978): 80–112.

– "The Politics of Refugee Immigration: The Pro-Refugee Lobby and the Interned Refugees 1940–1944." *Canadian Jewish Historical Society Journal* 7:2 (fall 1983): 74–88.

– and Janice B. Karlinsky. "Abraham's Daughters: Women, Charity and Power in the Canadian Jewish Community." In Jean Burnet, ed., *Looking into My Sister's Eyes: An Exploration in Women's History*. Toronto: Multicultural History Society of Ontario, 1986.

Easterbrook, W.T., and Hugh G.J. Aitken. *Canadian Economic History*. Toronto: MacMillan, 1956.

Egit, Jacob. *Grand Illusion*. Toronto: Lugus, 1991.

Elazar, Daniel J., and Harold M. Waller. *Maintaining Consensus: The Canadian Jewish Polity in the Postwar World*. New York: University Press of America, 1990.

Ehrenburg, Ilya, and Vasily Grossman, eds. *The Black Book*. Trans. John Glad and James S. Levine. New York: Holocaust Library, 1980.

Feingold, Henry. *Bearing Witness: How America and Its Jews Responded to the Holocaust*. Syracuse: Syracuse University Press, 1995.

– *The Politics of Rescue: The Roosevelt Administration and the Holocaust, 1938–1945*. New Brunswick, NJ: Rutgers University Press, 1970.

Final Report of the Sub-Committee on Race Relations. Toronto: Toronto Board of Education, 1980.

Flannery, Edward H. *The Anguish of the Jews: Twenty-Three Centuries of Anti-Semitism*. New York: Macmillan, 1976.

Flanzbaum, Hilene, ed. *The Americanization of the Holocaust*. Baltimore: Johns Hopkins University Press, 1999.

Fleischner, Eva, ed. *Auschwitz: Beginning of a New Era?* New York: KTAV, 1977.

Frager, Ruth A. *Sweatshop Strife: Class, Ethnicity, and Gender in the Jewish Labour Movement of Toronto, 1900–1939*. Toronto: University of Toronto Press, 1992.

Friedländer, Saul. "Trauma, Transference and 'Working Through' in Writing the History of the *Shoah*. *Memory and History* 4:1 (spring/summer 1992): 39–59.

Friedman, Saul S. *No Haven for the Oppressed: United States Policy towards Refugees*. Detroit: Wayne State University Press, 1973.

Gedi, Nora, and Yigal Elan. "Collective Memory – What Is It?" *Memory and History* 8:1 (spring/summer 1996): 30–50.

Gerber, Miriam Jean. "Immigration and Integration in Post-War Canada: A Case Study of Holocaust Survivors in Vancouver, 1947–1970." Unpublished MA thesis, Department of History, University of British Columbia, 1989.

Giberovitch, Myra. "The Contributions of Montreal Holocaust Survivors Organizations to Jewish Communal Life." Unpublished MSW thesis, McGill University, 1988.

Gilbert, Martin. *Atlas of the Holocaust*. London: Michael Joseph, 1982.

– *Auschwitz and the Allies*. London: Michael Joseph, 1981.

– *The Holocaust: The Jewish Tragedy*. London: Collins, 1986.

Glickman, Yaacov. "Anti-Semitism and Jewish Social Cohesion in Canada." In Rita Bienvenue and Jay E. Goldstein, eds., *Ethnicity and Ethnic Relations in Canada: A Book of Readings*. Toronto: Butterworth. 1985.

– and Alan Bardikoff. *The Treatment of the Holocaust in Canadian History and Social Science Textbooks*. Toronto: B'nai Brith, 1982.

Goldberg, David Howard. *Foreign Policy and Ethnic Interest Groups: Americans and Canadian Jews Lobby for Israel*. New York: Greenwood, 1990.

Gottesman, Eli, ed. *Who's Who in Canadian Jewry*. Ottawa: Jewish Institute of Higher Research, 1964.

Grafstein, Jerry S., ed. *Beyond Imagination: Canadians Write about the Holocaust*. Toronto: McClelland and Stewart, 1995.

Grange, Michael. "Students Ignorant of Canada's Racist History, Survey Indicates." *Globe and Mail*, 25 September 1995.

Griesdorf, Jane, and Alan Bardikoff. *The Holocaust*, North York: North York Board of Education, 1985.

Gutkin, Harry, and Milly Gutkin. *The Worst of Times, the Best of Times: Growing Up in Winnipeg's North End*. Markham, Ont: Fitzhenry and Whiteside. 1987.

Gutman, I. "Denial of the Holocaust." In Gutman, ed., *Encyclopedia of the Holocaust*. New York: Macmillan, 1990.

– E. Mendelsohn, J. Reinharz, C. Shmeruk, eds. *The Jews of Poland between Two World Wars*. Hanover, NH: University Press of New England, 1989.

Haberman, Arthur. *The Modern Age: Selected Readings*. Toronto: Gage, 1987.

Hawkins, Freda. *Canada and Immigration: Public Policy and Public Concern*. Montreal: McGill-Queen's University Press, 1972.

Helmreich, William. "The Impact of Holocaust Survivors on American Society: A Socio-Cultural Portrait." In Yehuda Bauer, ed., *Remembering for the Future – Jews and Christians during and after the Holocaust*. Oxford: Pergamon, 1988.

Hilberg, Raul. *The Destruction of the European Jews*. Rev. ed. 3 vols. New York: Holmes and Meir, 1985.

Hoffman, Eva. *Lost in Translation: Life in a New Language*. London: Minerva, 1989.

Holocaust and Genocide Studies 13:1 (spring 1999).

Hulse, Leslie Anne. "The Emergence of the Holocaust Survivor in the Canadian Jewish Community." Unpublished MA thesis, Department of Religion, Carleton University, 1979.

– "Holocaust Survivors in the Canadian Jewish Community." *Viewpoints* 2:2 (fall 1980): 34–43.

Hurst, Linda. "When War Is a Crime." *Toronto Star*, 17 December 1995.

Hurwic-Nowakowska, Irena. *A Social Analysis of Postwar Polish Jewry*. 1950; reprinted. Jerusalem: Zalman Shazar Center, 1986.

Insdorf, Annette. *Indelible Shadows*. 2nd ed. Cambridge: Cambridge University Press, 1989.

Kage, Joseph. *With Faith and Thanksgiving: The Story of Two Hundred Years of Jewish Immigration and Immigrant Aid Effort in Canada, 1760–1960*. Montreal: Eagle, 1960.

Kaplan, William. "Maxwell Cohen and the Report of the Special Committee on Hate Propaganda." In William Kaplan and Donald McRae, eds., *Law,*

Policy and International Justice. Montreal: McGill-Queen's University Press, 1993.

Kayfetz, Ben. "The Evolution of the Toronto Jewish Community." In Rose, Albert, ed. *A People and Its Faith.* Toronto: University of TorontoPress, 1959.

Kinsella, Warren. *Web of Hate: Inside Canada's Far Right Network.* Toronto: HarperCollins, 1994.

Kosinski, Jerzy. *The Painted Bird.* New York: Grove, 1965.

Kuper, Jack. *Child of the Holocaust.* London: Routledge and Kegan Paul, 1967.

Kushner, Tony. *The Holocaust and the Liberal Imagination: A Social and Cultural History.* Cambridge, Mass.: Blackwell, 1994.

Kwinta, Chava. *I'm Still Living.* Toronto: Simon and Pierre, 1974.

Langlais, Jacques, and David Rome. *Jews and French Quebeckers: Two Hundred Years of Shared History.* Trans. Barbara Young. Waterloo: Wilfrid Laurier University Press, 1991.

Lappin, Ben. *The Redeemed Children: The Story of the Rescue of War Orphans by the Jewish Community of Canada.* Toronto: University of Toronto Press, 1963.

Levendal, Lewis. *A Century of the Canadian Jewish Press, 1880s–1980s.* Ottawa: Borealis. 1989.

Levi, Primo. *Survival in Auschwitz.* English trans. New York: Collier, 1961.

Levin, Nora. *The Holocaust: The Destruction of European Jewry, 1933–1945.* New York: Schocken, 1968.

Levitt, Cyril H., and William Shaffir. *The Riot at Christie Pits.* Toronto: Lester and Orpen Dennys, 1987.

Lipson, Alfred, ed. *The Book of Radom – The Story of a Jewish Community in Poland Destroyed by the Nazis.* New York: United Radomer Relief of the United States and Canada, 1963.

Lipstadt, Deborah E. *Beyond Belief: The American Press and the Coming of the Holocaust. 1933–1945.* New York: Free Press, 1986.

– *Denying the Holocaust – The Growing Assault on Truth and Memory.* New York: Penguin, 1994.

Littell, Franklin. *The Crucifixion of the Jews.* New York: Harper and Row, 1975.

Littman, Sol. *War Criminals on Trial: The Rauca Case.* Toronto: Key Porter, 1998.

MacGuigan, Mark R. "Hate Control and Freedom of Assembly: The Canadian Nazi Party, 1965–1966." *Saskatchewan Bar Review,* no. 31 (1966): 232–50.

Marrus, Michael R. *Mr. Sam: The Life and Times of Samuel Bronfman.* Toronto: Penguin, 1992.

– *The Unwanted: European Refugees in the Twentieth Century.* New York: Oxford University Press, 1985.

– and Robert O. Paxton. *Vichy France and the Jews.* New York: Basic, 1981.

Marszalek, Josef. *Majdanek: The Concentration Camp in Lublin.* Warsaw: Interpress, 1986.

Martz, Fraidie. *Open Your Hearts: The Story of the Jewish War Orphans*. Montreal: Véhicule, 1996.

Matas, David. "The Jewish Contribution to Human Rights." In *Jewish Life and Times: A Collection of Essays*, vol. 4. Winnipeg: The Jewish Historical Society of Western Canada, 1983.

– and Susan Charendoff. *Justice Delayed: Nazi War Criminals in Canada*. Toronto: Summerhill, 1987.

Medjuck, Sheva. *Jews of Atlantic Canada*. St John's: Breakwater, 1986.

Meducki, Stanislaw. "The Pogrom in Kielce on 4 July, 1946." *Polin* 9 (1996): 158–69.

Mendelsohn, Ezra. *The Jews of East Central Europe between the World Wars*. Bloomington, Ind.: University of Indiana Press, 1987.

Neusner, Jacob. *Death and Birth of Judaism: The Impact of Christianity, Secularism and the Holocaust on Jewish Faith*. New York: Basic, 1987.

New Brunswick Department of Education. Program Development and Implementation Branch. *The Holocaust: A Topic of Study in History 111–112–113*. Fredericton, NB, 1989.

Norrie, Kenneth, and Douglas Owram. *A History of the Canadian Economy*. Toronto: Harcourt, Brace, Jovanovich, 1991.

Novick, Peter. *The Holocaust in American Life*. Boston: Houghton Mifflin, 1999.

Novogrodsky, Charles. "The Anti-Racist Cast of Mind." Keynote address, Conference for Anti-Racist Educators in Ontario, Toronto, 1989. Published in Carl E. James, ed., *Perspectives on Racism and the Human Services Sector: A Case for Change* (Toronto: University of Toronto Press, 1996).

Palmer, Howard. "Canadian Immigration and Ethnic History in the 1970s and 1980s." *Journal of Canadian Studies* 17 (spring 1982): 35–50.

– *Patterns of Prejudice: A History of Nativism in Alberta*. Toronto: McClelland and Stewart, 1982.

– "Reluctant Hosts: Anglo-Canadian Views of Multiculturalism in the Twentieth Century." In Gerald Tulchinsky, ed., *Immigration in Canada: Historical Perspectives*. Mississauga, Ont.: Copp Clark Longman, 1994.

Peck, Abraham J. "Special Lives: Survivors of the Holocaust and the American Dream." In Yehuda Bauer, ed., *Remembering for the Future – Jews and Christians during and after the Holocaust*. Oxford: Pergamon, 1988.

Perin, Roberto. "Writing About Ethnicity." In J. Schultz, ed., *Writing about Canada – A Handbook for Modern History*. Scarborough: Prentice-Hall, 1990.

Plaut, W. Gunther. *Unfinished Business*. Toronto: Lester and Orpen Dennys, 1981.

Poliakov, Leon. *Harvest of Hate*. Syracuse: Syracuse University Press, 1954.

Porter, John. *The Vertical Mosaic*. Toronto: University of Toronto Press, 1965.

Race, Religion and Culture in Ontario School Materials. Toronto: Ontario Ministry of Education, 1980.

Reed, Carole Ann, and Harold Lass. "Racism Today - Echoes of the Holocaust." *Canadian Social Studies*, Special Theme – The Holocaust. 29:4 (summer 1995): 140–2.

Robin, Martin. *Shades of Right: Nativist and Fascist Politics in Canada, 1920–1940*. Toronto: University of Toronto Press, 1992.

Robinson, Ira, Pierre Anctil, and Mervin Butovsky, eds. *An Everyday Miracle: Yiddish Culture in Montreal*. Montreal: Véhicule, 1990.

Rome, David, ed. *Pathways to the Present: Canadian Jewry and the Canadian Jewish Congress*. Toronto: Canadian Jewish Congress, 1986.

– and Bernard Figler. *Hannaniah Meir Caiserman – A Biography*. Montreal: Northern, 1962.

Rosenbaum, Henry, ed. *Voice of Radom – 50th. Anniversary of Liberation Edition*. Toronto: B'nai Radom, 1995.

Rosenberg, Louis. *Canada's Jews: A Social and Economic Study of Jews in Canada in the 1930s*. Ed. Morton Weinfeld. Kingston: McGill-Queen's University Press, 1993. Originally published in 1939.

Ruether, Rosemary Radcliffe. *Faith and Fratricide: The Theological Roots of Anti-Semitism*. New York: Seabury, 1974.

Schwart-Bart, Andre. *The Last of the Just*. New York: Bantam, 1975.

Sefton, Victor W. "The European Holocaust – Who Knew What and When: A Canadian Aspect." *The Canadian Jewish Historical Society Journal* 2:2 (fall 1978): 125–36.

Sherman. A.J. *Island Refuge: Britain and Refugees from the Third Reich. 1933–1939*. London: Elek, 1973.

Sigal, John J., and Morton Weinfeld. *Trauma and Rebirth: Intergenerational Effects of the Holocaust*. New York: Prager, 1989.

Sloan, Jacob, ed. and trans. *Notes from the Warsaw Ghetto: The Journal of Emmanuel Ringelblum*. New York: Schocken, 1974.

Speisman, Stephen A. *The Jews of Toronto: A History to 1937*. Toronto: McClelland and Stewart, 1977.

Srebrnik, Henry. "Two Solitudes: Immigrant-Native Division in Jewish Montreal." *Eye* 8:6 (June 1982) 4, 13–14.

Steinlauf, Michael. *Bondage to the Dead – Poland and the Memory of the Holocaust*. Syracuse: Syracuse University Press, 1997.

Stingel, Janine. "Social Credit, Anti-Semitism, and Alberta's Jews." Unpublished paper, Canadian Jewish Historical Society Annual Conference, Montreal, 1995.

Sub-Committee on Race and Ethnic Relations and Multicultural Policy. *Race and Ethnic Relations and Multicultural Policy*. North York: Metropolitan Separate School Board, 1984, 1986.

Supreme Court of Canada. *Reports/Recueil des arrêts*. 1990. Ottawa: Queen's Printer.

Task Force. *Multiculturalism, Ethnicity and Race Relations Policy*. Toronto: East York Board of Education, 1984.

Troper, Harold. "As Canadian as Multiculturalism: An Historian's Perspective on Multicultural Policy." Keynote address, Canadian Ethnic Studies Association Biennial Conference, Vancouver, 1993.

– and Paula Draper, eds. *Archives of the Holocaust*. Vol. 15, *National Archives of Canada, Ottawa and Canadian Jewish Congress Archives, Montreal*. New York: Garland. 1991.

– and Morton Weinfeld. *Old Wounds: Jews, Ukrainians and the Hunt for Nazi War Criminals in Canada*. Toronto: Viking, 1988.

Tulchinsky, Gerald. *Branching Out: The Transformation of the Canadian Jewish Community*. Toronto: Stoddart, 1998.

– *Taking Root: The Origins of the Canadian Jewish Community*. Toronto: Lester, 1992.

Vidal-Naquet, Pierre. *Assassins of Memory – Essays on the Denial of the Holocaust*. Trans. Jeffrey Mehlman. New York: Columbia University, 1992.

Vigod, Bernard. *The Jews in Canada*. Ottawa: Canadian Historical Association, 1984.

Voice of Radom – Special Edition, 50th. Commemoration of the Destroyed Jewish Community of Radom. Toronto: Radomer Society, 1993.

Wasserstein, Bernard. *Britain and the Jews of Europe, 1933-1945*. New York: Oxford, 1984.

Watkins, M.H., and D.F. Forster, eds. *Economics: Canada – Recent Readings*. Toronto: McGraw-Hill, 1963.

Weimann, Gabriel, and Conrad Winn. *Hate on Trial: The Zundel Affair, The Media and Public Opinion in Canada*. Oakville: Mosaic, 1986.

Whitaker, Reg. *Canadian Immigration Policy Since Confederation*. Ottawa: Canadian Historical Association, 1991.

– *Double Standard – The Secret History of Canadian Immigration*. Toronto: Lester and Orpen Dennys, 1987.

Wiesel, Elie. *Night*. English trans. New York: Avon, 1960.

– *The Town beyond the Wall*. English trans. New York: Schocken, 1982.

Wistrich, Robert. "Israel and the Holocaust Trauma." *Jewish History* 11:2 (fall 1997): 1–20.

– *Who's Who in Nazi Germany*. New York: Bonanza, 1982.

Wyman, David S. *The Abandonment of the Jews: America and the Holocaust, 1941–1945*. New York: Pantheon, 1984.

– ed. *The World Reacts to the Holocaust*. Baltimore: Johns Hopkins University Press, 1995.

Yahil, Leni. "Adolf Eichmann." In Y. Gutman, ed., *The Encyclopedia of the Holocaust*. New York: MacMillan. 1990.

– *The Holocaust: The Fate of European Jewry*. New York: Oxford, 1991.

– "Raoul Wallenberg: His Mission and His Activities in Hungary." *Yad Vashem Studies* 15 (1983): 7–54.

Zolf, Larry. "The Great Yiddish Mouthpiece." in Jerry S. Grafstein, ed.,

Beyond Imagination – Canadians Write about the Holocaust. Toronto: McClelland and Stewart. 1995.

Zucchi, John E. *Italians in Toronto: Development of a National Identity, 1875–1935.* Kingston: McGill-Queen's University Press, 1988.

Index